under the shadow

A TRUE STORY

Pastor Cottingham,

Thank you for your prayers and the loving kindness you have shown to Mark + our family over the years!

Lana Williams

Eph 3:20+21

Lana Yvette Williams

Foreword by
MARK DAVID WILLIAMS

UNDER THE SHADOW

Scriptures, unless otherwise noted, are taken from the
New International Version, copyright 1985 by The Zondervan Corporation.

Cover Design by Timothy Boelter

Published by: LYW Publications
P.O. Box 43667
Minneapolis, Minnesota, 55443
For bookings, information or to order CDs or books:
www.MarkDavidWilliams.com

Dedicated To

My husband and Mark's father, Dave.

His role in this drama was to love, support

and suffer, in loneliness and prayer.

Foreword

My life has proven to be much more interesting than I could have ever dreamed it would be. I have learned that we simply do not know what tomorrow holds. Some people say that the only thing constant in life is change. But I have come to the conclusion that the only thing constant is God. He is there in the good times and the bad. He is the only one who can hear our inner thoughts and prayers. He was my source of strength and hope when all I could do was pray for the next morning to come.

I know that the Lord does not give us more than we can handle. I often say that He thought I was a lot stronger than I did. He knows me better than I know myself. I learned so much in this experience. I learned to be thankful for what I have. We often don't realize all the blessings we have in life until they are taken away from us. I learned that prayer is very powerful. I also learned that suffering produces perseverance and perseverance produces character and character produces hope. These are things that I would not have learned had I not gone through this tragic journey.

I challenge you to find the good in the bad. Look back at a time in your life that was difficult and try to see how your life has changed because of it. Are you a stronger person because of what you went through? What did you learn? Maybe you are having a rough time right now. How is this shaping who you are and who you will become? In times of trial and tribulation I believe that anger and depression are a choice. We must choose to have faith and believe there's a brighter tomorrow. What you are going through or have gone through can truly bring hope and encouragement to someone. I challenge you to let God use you. Fight through the tears and pain and know that God is by your side cheering you on.

I thank you for reading this book and pray that you find hope and encouragement in these pages. I would feel truly blessed to know that what I went through helped and encouraged you in your walk with the Lord.

Mark David Williams

Mark and Lana wish to acknowledge and thank:

Our Father in heaven, whose love is beyond comprehension, Sweet Holy Spirit, our divine comforter and our Lord and Savior, Jesus Christ; by His stripes we are healed and we are forever grateful.

Dave, Mike and Leah Williams, for love, faith, and all of the other beautiful elements that bind us together as a strong and caring family.

Absolutely everyone who prayed, and continues to pray, for us.

The incredible prayer team that emerged to teach us about the power of united and orchestrated prayer. Thank you, Sandy Snider, for your devotion to this precious team!

Our friends; God's precious provision in the midst of our sorrow. We cannot possibly mention them all, but we especially thank Chris and Carole Beatty, Brian and April Neuwirth, Ann-Marie and Pat Edwards, Becki Biermier and the Mickey Robinson family for faithfully staying so close by our side.

The doctors and staff in Trauma ICU at Vanderbilt Hospital, Nashville, TN; without your incredible talent and knowledge, Mark would not be here today.

Therapists everywhere who train devastated bodies to improve their quality of life. May God bless you.

The families we met in The Quiet Room. The lessons we learned from your courage will last a lifetime.

Dave and Lana's employers: Bethany Press International and Furniture Manor, and our co-workers. You generously allowed us the time we needed to be with Mark.

Mark's employer at the time of the crash: The Green Hills Grille. You stayed beside Mark, providing food for his family and encouragement with your upbeat visits.

All of the individuals, churches, schools and businesses that sent notes of love and encouragement...your prayers were the wind beneath our wings. We especially send love to Church of the Resurrection, North Heights Lutheran Church and Celebration Church; you are family, and the divine provision of your love has touched our hearts!

April Neuwirth and Grandma Betty Williams for taking on the task of keeping friends and relatives updated on Mark's condition and progress.

Deb and Phil Rutten for help with final editing and for keeping Lana sane during the writing process by being only a phone call away whenever she had a computer crisis.

Tim Boelter for the cover design. Your talent continues to amaze us.

You, our reader: New friend or old, we pray God will touch your life in a new and precious way as you share our faith journey with us.

Table of Contents

Under the Shadow

START

I was walking through life when shadows appeared. Suddenly and without warning they began to close around me from the North, South, East and West. Oppressive and dark, with slobber at their lips, they moved closer to their prey. Fear, Anxiety, Despair, Anger and Self-Pity I knew by name, but others remained anonymous and that unknown element made them even more terrifying. My world became darker with each progressive movement of the shadow army.

Lord, please chase them away! I prayed as Panic reached me first. Anxiety brushed against my shoulder when Despair slipped his hand in mine; but before another shadow could draw near, the wing of God Almighty stretched as an umbrella above me to put the shadows at bay. Oh, they remained; lurking to make their presence known; eager to pounce at a vulnerable moment, but each time they reached for me there was a heavenly flutter to assure me that protection, peace and rest belonged to me, under the shadow of the Almighty. END

Lana Yvette Williams

Psalm 63:1-8

O God, you are my God, earnestly I seek you; my soul thirsts for you, my body longs for you, in a dry and weary land where there is no water. I have seen you in the sanctuary and beheld your power and your glory. Because your love is better than life, my lips will glorify you. I will praise you as long as I live, and in your name I will lift up my hands. My soul will be satisfied as with the richest of foods; with singing lips my mouth will praise you. On my bed I remember you; I think of you through the watches of the night. Because you are my help, I sing in the shadow of your wings. My soul clings to you; your right hand upholds me."

Introduction

start

Tragedy struck our family; fast and with fury, in the form of a devastating car crash, but even as we reeled from the initial blow, we recognized the hand of God. We knew we would not be alone. Oh, we would hurt; big time. We would struggle with sorrow and heartbreak; anger and frustration would be our relentless foes. It was the familiar touch from the unseen force of the Holy Spirit that assured us that we would, somehow, stretch beyond our own capabilities, to persevere, to overcome and to forgive.

We had been naïve about situations like ours. When we heard about a horrendous car crash on the news we were often led to pray. And later, when we heard that the victim's condition was updated to "stable condition," our prayers relaxed and, eventually, we dismissed that person from our thoughts. We simply did not realize that the declaration of "stable condition" is a wondrous victory but often only the beginning of the struggle.

We had felt some outrage at drunk driving, but were absolutely unaware that the victim of such a crime was seldom singular. The insidious act has tentacles that reach to affect and infect absolutely everyone who cares about the victim. Families are stretched to the limit of endurance, hearts are broken, sorrow and stress wrap themselves around the caregivers and, very often, finances are devastated.

In the earliest hours of our journey I began to journal. I was supplied with strength to make entries nearly every day, no matter how bereft or exhausted I was. I was passionate that the details be chronicled in honesty. The very act of writing down that which was too painful to wrap my brain around was a step toward healing. By entering words to describe the circumstances of the day, I was able to believe that we would read them in a better time, with the nightmare behind us. *STOP*

As Mark gained strength, and participated in the journaling experience, we began to define a goal for the journals. We desperately needed others to understand the day-to-day agony and the joy in the smallest victories that comprise a story like ours.

Why did it become so important for us to communicate? Not only to be understood and to feel less of the frustration that "no one understands," but above all else, to illustrate the all-sufficient grace of a loving God who took us on a spiritual journey that would change our lives. We needed to tell anyone who would listen about the powerful force of prayer. We needed to disclose the "secrets" revealed to us regarding united and orchestrated prayer.

We were impassioned to illustrate the victory available by the blood of Jesus Christ in the life of believers, and to do this in a way that revealed to our precious readers that we were yielded but vulnerable, and imperfect vessels.

What the book cannot reveal is the length of the struggle. Months, even years after the initial crash, we work toward recovery. Mark physically works every day to convince his body to overcome the cruel and harsh trauma inflicted on it. His parents work to try to find peace in frustration or anger that can pop up so unexpectedly. We all strive to return to life as it was, though that can never be. Mostly, we rejoice. We have our family intact. Too many victims of drunk drivers are not given the chance we had to persevere through tragedy. And wonderfully, there is the unexpected blessing of having our eyes opened to many spirit-inspired revelations that make living richer.

How could we not share our journey when every moment of it was saturated with heavenly grace, mercy and provision?

For those of you who take time to read this book, we pray that you will see our purpose in writing is not to invoke compassion for us but to encourage you to vicariously plunge to the depths, feel the shock and then emerge renewed with motivated compassion for someone in a situation similar to this one. We pray that you will taste the injustice of drunk driving enough to resolve to make a difference in lives you may influence.

Ah, and mostly, we pray that you will be awakened to the power and authority available to you in the name of Jesus Christ; power to change the course of tragedy and authority to overcome harsh circumstances.

The names of medical personnel have been changed and a few other names that are relevant to our story have been omitted when necessary, but our story, itself, is factual, raw and real.

We invite you to come on our journey. It is a journey of ordinary people who were never set apart as spiritual giants to trod the hot coals of tragedy without pain, but weak, vulnerable people who felt pain they never dreamed they could endure and…well, who experienced the reality of what happens to victims of a horrendous crash after the words "upgraded to stable condition" have been spoken.

Lana Yvette Williams

"You see lights, feel confusion and know something awful is about to happen, but you cannot know the impact it is going to have until you wake up and your life has been changed forever. Still, a month later, in your dreams you see yourself driving on the same road and the lights come at you again. What is worse this time is that you know what to expect. This time you pray you don't wake up."

Mark Williams, January 8, 2002.

PART I ✦ THE FIRST DAYS
December 7, 2001 – December 9, 2001

Chapter One
A Day Like Any Other

Friday, December 7, 2001

Lana:

"Lana, you have to rest," my husband, Dave, says from the sofa where he sits watching a television special.

In a glance, I catch visions of the pandemonium and horror of Pearl Harbor. Almost too weary to speak, I motion around the kitchen to communicate there is still much to do. I sweep the last of the sawdust on the floor into the dustpan and stare at the wires that hang from outlets.

The new countertops and sink, installed hours earlier, look beautiful. I pick up pieces of the tile that will be installed tomorrow and hold them up to the backsplash, imagining the change that will take place.

We love this home that we have lived in for three years. Situated on the Mississippi River in a quiet neighborhood it delights us daily with sightings of deer, eagle, fox and other wild creatures. In Minnesota we have the added benefit of change of season. We feel as though we live in a secluded Bed and Breakfast setting, yet we can drive a very short distance to see the Minneapolis skyline.

We often wish we had lived in this home when our two sons were growing up because they enjoy this place as much as we do. Our oldest son, Michael, lives in this area and visits for quiet afternoons of fishing. Our other son, Mark, lived here for a brief time before he returned to Nashville, where he had attended college, to work on his music career. We are thrilled that Mark will be home in just a few days and the four of us will have time together.

I put the broom into the closet and look around.

"I really like it." I say.

"So do I," Dave states, "and tomorrow we can see it finished, so you may as well get some sleep."

I know I am not being dismissed, Dave's concern is valid. I have been taking medication for chest pain. The doctor has ruled out immediate heart problems but some type of muscular spasm has been a concern and zapped me of energy. I take Dave's advice and, as I wash for bed, my mind turns to the exciting weeks ahead. When we bring Mark home from the airport in four days we will begin a whirlwind holiday season.

Mark remembers:

It was a typical Friday. I usually worked the lunch shift at the Green Hills Grille. I had been waiting tables there for about ten months and found it to be the most enjoyable of all restaurants in which I had worked. It is a busy place and the clientele and the co-workers are friendly. I would always get a kick out of the amount of talent that you could find amongst a restaurant staff in Nashville. I was never the only "struggling musician." It made for a common bond and I enjoyed the camaraderie.

On Fridays I would often close the lunch shift, which would leave me getting out of the restaurant at about 4:00 p.m. I had plans to go shopping and possibly see a movie with my girlfriend at the time, Ann-Marie, so I hurried home to change and grab a bite to eat. We decided that I would pick her up around 6:30 p.m. so I had time for a quick workout with my weights and weight bench in the living room of my home.

After I picked her up we went to the Cool Springs Galleria to do some shopping. One of my roommates was getting married on December 15th and so I bought him a wedding gift and Ann-Marie shopped for Christmas presents. I planned to do some shopping at the Mall of America when I got back to Minnesota on December 12, so I refrained from buying anything I would have to pack and carry home on the plane.

We were at the mall until about 8:30 p.m. when we decided to go to Logan's Roadhouse for supper. They let you eat peanuts and throw them on the floor, which I think is kind of fun. I had a teriyaki club steak, not thinking to savor each bite as if it would be my last for quite some time. Why would I?

At 9:30 p.m., my friend Matt called to ask us to a movie that started at 10:00 p.m. in the Green Hills area. We chose not to go because we didn't want to rush our dinner or miss out on dessert.

We finally got to Ann-Marie's apartment at about 10:30 p.m. Both of us love to play board games and we chose Scrabble, which was a good challenge for each of us. We finished our game and I left around 12:15 a.m. I had a staff meeting early in the morning and Ann-Marie had grad school classes just as early.

It was raining as I made my way home.

Lana:

I put on my nightclothes and brush my teeth quickly because I remember that I need to confirm a rehearsal date for Mark before I go to work in the morning. Mark has been blessed with incredible vocal talent. No one in our family can take a great deal of credit for it. It seems the Lord simply decided Mark would be responsible for such a talent and gifted him. Mark has cultivated that favor since he was very young. His sweet spirit and devotion to Jesus led him to use his gift in Christian music though he had originally planned a Broadway career.

I have represented him as his Booking Agent and Manager for several years, working alongside him to build his ministry. When word got out that he would be in Minnesota for most of the month of December we began to receive many opportunities for him to minister. He is booked solid for the next few weeks with exciting shows, concerts and appearances penned in many of the squares on our calendar. As I walk to my office to write the confirmation on my to-do list, I remember our phone conversation last night.

"We'll be too busy to enjoy Christmas." Mark voiced concern in that conversation.

"No," I assured him, "you just come home and enjoy singing. I will take care of the rest. It will be wonderful for all of us to be together. Mike is planning to stay overnight for Christmas Eve and Grandma can't wait to see you."

"I can't wait either. Tell Mike I want to get to a Timberwolves game."

Mark always tries to reserve time with his brother when he is home. He gave me a few messages to pass on to friends that he wants to see while he is here and we discussed some rehearsal information he needed regarding a show he will appear in.

"Are you working tomorrow?" I asked him.

"Yes, the dayshift. Then I'm going to go shopping with Ann-Marie. I probably won't buy many Christmas gifts though. Will we be able to get out to the mall?"

"Of course."

Immediately my mind begins to plan what we will do at the Mall of America.

"Okay, well I'll call you before I leave on Wednesday. I get in about 3:00. Is Dad picking me up?"

"He'll be there. Love you son!"

"Love you guys too."

While in my office I quickly jot a couple more additions to my list. Looking at the calendar makes the holiday season seem as though it will fly by. I am especially excited about the New Year's Eve concert with Mary Beth Carlson, a gifted pianist. She is a great friend and it is a joy when Mark and Mary Beth perform together.

I cross Promotional Posters for that concert off my list. I went to see the layout today and they look wonderful. I want to accomplish more but realize how very tired I am and that I do not feel all that well.

Dave pokes his head around the corner. "You don't look like you're resting!"

"Going right now," I say and turn toward the bedroom.

We both know I have a hard time calling it quits at the end of a day.

Try to stay in the moment. I remind myself. I have been reading a book on stress control and the advice has been working for me. Too often I plan hours or days ahead when I should just concentrate on the moment I am in.

In bed I open my Bible and turn to Habakkuk 3:19. "The sovereign Lord is my strength; he makes my feet like the feet of a deer, he enables me to go on the heights." I smile as I read it. *This is an unusual verse you are having me study and memorize, Lord. But I trust you have a good reason for it.* Then I turn to Ephesians 3:20 where I read, "Now to him who is able to do immeasurably more than all we ask or imagine, according to his power that is at work in us, to him be glory in the church and in Christ Jesus throughout all generations for ever and ever." Amen. A pastor at our church spoke on that scripture a couple of Sundays ago and it has stuck like glue.

I whisper prayers for my family as I drift to sleep, including a little prayer I have said nearly every day for many, many years. "Lord, please keep your angels about those I love. Watch over Dave, Mike and Mark, I pray in Your holy name. I love You and trust You, Lord. Amen"

It is nearly midnight when I fall asleep.

Mark remembers:

Ann-Marie's apartment was only ten to fifteen minutes from my house. I had made the drive numerous times as I used to live in a complex on the same road as hers when I went to college at Belmont University.

As I drove down the residential road I saw lights coming straight at me. I was extremely confused and in disbelief. I quickly honked my horn, slammed my brakes and swerved to avoid collision. I was tensed and braced for some kind of impact, but clearly not prepared for what was about to come.

It is nearly impossible to describe the sound, the severity of the jar to your body and the shock of having your car hit head-on by another car. Mix all the fear of knowing what is about to happen with the actual impact and you just pray that it is over quickly.

My car spun and I ended up in the ditch on the other side of the road facing the opposite direction in which I had been heading. The car door, which had been locked, opened on impact. I sat there for seconds taking it all in. I remember thinking, *I can't believe this happened!* I had no idea how badly injured I was. I looked down at my long legs and realized that they were pinned.

I knew my glasses were shattered and I saw blood on the steering wheel. I took a closer look at my legs through my blurred vision and saw that my left kneecap was not on my knee.

I tried to move my seat back to release my legs and realized I could not feel my feet. The seat had fallen off its frame. There was nothing I could do.

I screamed, "Help! Help!"

I knew it was after midnight, but surely someone in one of the nearby homes had heard the impact. I tried to take it all in. I looked at my left arm and was able to move it around. *Okay, it's not all that bad.* For some reason I never tried to move my right arm. The left side of my face was numb. *Oh, God, am I deformed?* I touched my face to see how it felt and it seemed fine on the outside but I could not understand the numbness. It was as if I was shot full of Novocain. I didn't try to look into the rearview mirror, probably because my vision was poor without glasses. Either that or the Lord didn't allow me to think of doing it at that time.

Finally a woman came running to my car. She was out of breath when she asked me if I was okay and told me she had already called an ambulance.

I asked her, "Will you pray for me, please?" There was no response and she turned to check on the other driver. My mind was spinning, *I wont' get to go home to Minnesota next week.* I prayed out loud over and over again, "Jesus, send your angels to help me. Jesus!"

I desperately wanted to do something. I couldn't stand the pain of my legs being pinned and not knowing what was wrong with my face. My nose had to be broken because there was so much blood on the steering wheel. *Oh, God, how did this happen?*

The woman with the phone came back and asked if there was anyone that she should call for me. I told her to call Ann-Marie and told her the phone number. She asked me if Ann-Marie would be okay seeing me in a situation like this and I said "No." I also told her to have Ann-Marie call my parents. Then I heard her talking to Ann-Marie. She told her to come with a friend, if she could, and that I wanted her to call my parents.

When the woman came back to tell me Ann-Marie was on her way I asked her, "Is my face deformed?" That was perhaps the longest silence I had ever felt or heard in my life. I watched as she walked away in silence.

A fire truck finally arrived and then the ambulance. A female paramedic got in the passenger side of my car and began to ask me questions. "What's your name, honey? How old are you? We'll get you out of here soon." She was very conversational as she tried to keep me calm and conscious.

I clearly answered all her questions and kept adamantly saying, "She was in my lane! She was completely in my lane!"

By this time I knew the other driver was a female because I could hear her screaming across the street. I realized that she must be pinned as well when I heard the loud noise of a saw as they began to cut her out of her car. I wondered, *why aren't they cutting me out first? She must be worse than me.* But now I wonder if her screaming got their attention over my "I can't believe this happened" demeanor.

The firefighters came over and analyzed the situation. They asked me what hurt. I said, "I can't feel my feet or my legs and I know for sure that my left knee is broken. That's all I know."

They discussed options for a few moments after trying, unsuccessfully, to move my seat back. Finally they took my seat belt off and had a plan of action. They covered me with plastic sheeting that would protect me from flying debris or broken glass. The female paramedic stayed in the car with me while they cut off my car door. Once that was off they had to cut off the back of my seat. They couldn't saw it off because I was sitting in it, so they literally tried to break it off. It was then I realized my lower back and sitting area were also injured. They could see that I was in pain and stopped to try to come up with another way of getting me out of the car.

I finally said, "Just rip it off, I'll be okay."

They asked me if I was sure and I don't think I had ever been more certain of anything in my life. I was desperate to stretch my legs.

They put a neck brace on me and then continued to twist the seat to try to pull the back off. When they got close to getting it off they told me that they would have to have me move forward as much as I could so they could twist it all the way. When we did this I screamed in pain as it pressed against my tailbone and pushed my legs even tighter against the dash. But the relief that came in the few seconds after that was worth it.

Next, they told me they were going to lift me out and that they thought it would be painful for me, but they had to get me on a board. Two guys lifted me out and it was painful. They laid me on a long board and then almost immediately lifted me onto a gurney.

I saw Ann-Marie for the first time as I was being loaded into the ambulance. One of her friends brought her to the scene and so she was able to ride along in the front seat of the ambulance. She told me she had called my parents and then I asked her to call Matt and his wife, Heather. The paramedic whom I had gotten familiar with began cutting all my clothing off.

I became very cold and so she put a warm blanket on me. She started pressing around my stomach and ribs and asking me if anything hurt. The left side of my ribs hurt but, in that area, that was all. She then asked me my social security number, date of birth, home phone number and if I had any allergies.

I asked her how long it would be before we got to the hospital because the ride was very bumpy, it was still raining and the sirens were deafening. I remember her telling me, "Seven minutes. We'll be there in seven minutes."

That sounded like a very long time.

Isaiah 58:9, "Then you will call, and the Lord will answer; you will cry for help, and he will say: Here I am."

Chapter Two
The Phone Call

Saturday, December 8, 2001

Lana:

When our sons were teenagers or away at college, and the phone rang late at night I would feel the unmistakable grip of panic. Now, when I hear the phone through the daze of early sleep I expect a wrong number. It is 12:35 a.m. Dave and I have been asleep about a half an hour.

"Oh," I moan at the intrusion and roll over as Dave answers it.

Immediately I realize it is not a wrong number, but assume from the tone of Dave's voice, that it is someone from his workplace. He is gathering information. When the conversation continues longer than it usually would, I listen harder and realize this information involves our son, Mark, in Nashville.

When Dave hangs up the phone he says quietly, "Mark has been in a car accident."

I bolt upright, flinging off the bed covers. "Oh, no, no!" In the moments before sleep when I had prayed for Angels to surround my sons, I had felt no strong urgency in that prayer.

"Just wait," my husband says calmly, "we don't know much about anything yet. That was Ann-Marie and she will call us again when they get to the hospital."

"Hospital? How bad is it?"

"She doesn't know yet, they are still at the scene of the accident, but let's pray."

We hold each other and pray and I fight with all my might to push aside the fear that is choking me. I convince myself he has had a fender-bender and will soon call to reassure us, but even with that reasoning, I want to pack and leave immediately for Nashville.

Dave takes his Bible and the cordless phone from his nightstand and bends to kiss my forehead. "I am going to the living room. You get some rest. You may have to fly to Nashville tomorrow."

Somehow I comply and pull the bed covers over me, still in prayer. Of course I cannot sleep and jump up moments later to run to the living room when I hear the phone ring. It is Ann-Marie. She has more information. Mark had to be cut out of his car and has injuries to his feet or at least to one foot.

I am amazed that I am not hysterical. I prepare a mental list of things that need to take place for me to get a flight to Nashville in a few hours. It all seems too complicated for the state I am in and I ask Dave, "Can we get in the car and go?"

"We need a little more information, honey. You don't want to get 500 miles away and find out it was not necessary to go there, or that we should have flown."

If this were a conversation about a fairly urgent trip in another circumstance, I would be annoyed at Dave's procrastination, but I am totally compliant with his leading and feel a hand upon me that I recognize as the Lord's.

"We will most likely be driving down tomorrow. We'll leave early, so try to rest."

Mark remembers:

When we got to Vanderbilt they pulled me out of the ambulance and I could hear them saying, "Vitamin Stat Vitamin", as they wheeled me into a room. Over and over they repeated, "This is Vitamin Stat Vitamin, 27 year old male."

I also heard Matt's voice as they wheeled me in. I was in shock but conscious. In this room there were four to five doctors and nurses. They had to move me from the gurney to an examining bed and when I was on the bed one woman asked me, "Do you have a living will?"

"I suppose I need that, huh?" I actually felt better when there was a chuckle among the doctors. Then they asked me my social security number again and if I had any religious affiliation and church that I attend. I told them, "Christian and I go to Christ Church in Brentwood."

They asked me my height and I told them and when they asked me my weight I replied, "Not enough." This too received chuckles from the staff and I felt pleased to find my sense of humor still working.

Matt came in and I remember him pointing out that my shoulder was huge. He said I looked like I had been working out and that I could play for the Titans. I laughed not knowing that my shoulder had completely collapsed.

I heard someone say, "Okay, I am going to put in a catheter."

"Oh no, do you have to?" I wanted a choice in the matter. But it was already in. I never felt it.

"Can you wiggle your toes for us?"

I tried.

"Good, good."

They asked about my neck and I must have tried to move it.

"No! No, don't move it!" They cautioned. They also checked if I could move my fingers and I could.

I kept asking one question over and over again, "Am I going to lose my feet?"

It seemed a long time before someone answered, "Probably not, but you will be in the hospital for a few days."

I asked Matt or Ann-Marie to go to my house and get some clothes, my contact lenses and my bathroom toiletry bag.

They put IVs in my arm. I don't know how many. Then they told me they were going to take me to the MRI room. I don't remember getting there, but I remember the experience all too well.

The room was extremely bright. They had to move me from my gurney to a hard table. It was horrible! I knew that my tailbone had to be broken. They kept sending me in and out of the tight space of the MRI. They would bring me out and move my arm this way or that way and ask if I could do this or that.

I finally asked, "How long is this going to take?"

"Oh, we'll be here a while."

I was so distraught. I had never been so thirsty in my life. With that thirst and the extreme pain of the hard surface I was lying on, I felt like I was dying.

"Can I have some water?"

"No. Sorry. You'll be going up to surgery soon."

"Can I blow my nose?" I couldn't stand not being able to breathe and being stuck in that tight place. My nose was so clogged I had to concentrate really hard to breathe through my mouth and not panic in the tube. Now and then blood would trickle out of my nose and into my mouth and they would have to come and gently wipe it off with a towel. I had to keep my mouth open to breathe. It was a really awful experience.

"No, you can't blow your nose."

Again I begged for just a sip of water.

"Sorry. I know it's hard, but you can't have anything to drink."

These people were quickly becoming my enemies through no fault of their own. I could hear them in the other room as they would see the results of each MRI.

"Oh, look at that. He's got that too. Wow."

If I had energy I would have yelled, "I can hear you and you are not helping my situation! That's not what I want to hear right now." It was sinking in that I was really messed up.

After what seemed like hours, they took me back up to trauma and someone told me, "We can't send you to the operating room right now because there are a couple of other patients that are more traumatic than you."

"I'm traumatic," I replied.

The man kind of laughed and said, "Yes, you are."

"Can I please have some water?"

"No, you're going to surgery as soon as possible."

That was the last thing I remember.

Psalm 63:1, "O God, you are my God, earnestly I seek you; my soul thirsts for you, my body longs for you, in a dry and weary land where there is no water."

Chapter Three
The Trip to Nashville

Lana:

I am on my knees deeply interceding for Mark in prayer, and I have just called an intercessor from our church to stand in prayer with us, when the phone rings for the third time tonight. I hold my breath and listen to the tone of my husband's voice. The conversation is short and within minutes of picking up the receiver, Dave comes into the bedroom to toss two large suitcases on the floor.

"Pack as though you are going to stay a week or two"

I have mentally packed already so it takes very little time. I toss things into my suitcase: three pair of black pants, about 8 turtlenecks, a belt, comfortable shoes, sleepwear and lingerie. Our toiletry bags are always ready for travel. I am grateful for that as I pull them from the bathroom closet to throw in our suitcases.

It is as if I am standing back and watching myself and I am amazed at my presence of mind as I grab an address book, my briefcase, bills that will soon be due, a warm coat and my boots. I take a car bag, as is my habit when we travel. It contains my Bible and a book I have been reading. My pillow and two blankets also go on the pile Dave is ready to place in the car.

Besides the intercessor, I have also telephoned our pastors. I was disappointed when no one answered until Dave reminded me they were out of town. Though the hour was late, I phoned our friends Mickey and Barbara Robinson who live in Nashville. When their daughter, Elizabeth, answered I apologized for such a late call and she assured me she had been awake. Mickey and Barbara were not home, but she said she would call them and that she, her brother and a friend would leave immediately for the hospital. I know they will be in prayer for Mark and it is important to me that he has someone by his side who knows the art of intercessory prayer.

Now, as we are ready to walk out the door, I call our pastors a second time to leave a message and my friend and co-worker, Giz, to let her know what happened and that we are on our way to Nashville. Giz and I traveled to Nashville only a few months ago for a fun trip. How very different this trip will be!

We have not been able to reach our son, Michael, as he is temporarily using only a cell phone and it is turned off for the evening. Dave called his mother, Betty, to say we will stop by her home with house keys and a list of names for her to call.

From the time the suitcases hit the floor to the time we close our garage door, barely 15 minutes have passed. It is nearly 6:00 a.m. when we pull into Betty's driveway. On the way to Betty's house I prepared a list of names and phone numbers of people to contact here and also Nashville phone numbers she may need. As Dave opens his car door I hand him the list. I wait in the car because I cannot bear to see my sweet mother-in-law right now. I would cry when she hugged me and I have energy for nothing but prayer.

I have never enjoyed the drive to Nashville and I begin to pray we will get there in supernatural time. It usually takes anywhere from 15 to 16 hours if we stop once to eat, and often we split it by stopping for the night. The thought of being so far away from Mark is torment.

About an hour into the drive I tell Dave, "We need to make this trip a sacrifice of praise."

He agrees and we begin to praise God for sparing our son. We praise God that Mark is in a good hospital and that he has such good friends that love him and will stay by his side.

As the calls come in to Dave's cell phone we learn that Mark is in surgery for his left foot, left knee and right arm and hand. We take comfort that we can pray for him in the car as well as if we sat in a waiting room, and the miles begin to disappear behind us in a surreal manner.

We do not talk. Every so often Dave encourages me to sleep. He is concerned for me and I feel concern for him as he drives long hours with little sleep. He insists he is fine and does not want me to relieve him as a driver.

I do not share with him that the chest pains I have had are increasingly worse. It is in my mind often that once we get to Nashville we will be in a hospital if I need one. I am silently begging the Lord to get us there without an added emergency.

We stop along the way to get food and gas. I have no appetite but must eat if I am going to take pain pills so I purchase a bagel and some juice. Dave buys a sandwich and coffee. We take them to the car to eat along the way.

On this long trip, we stop three times for gas using that time for restroom stops and for more coffee for Dave. Dave manages to eat his sandwich one-half at a time over the next twelve hours. I nurse the bagel, eating only when I take a pill.

General conversation is not a possibility. Our words are cryptic. "Do you need some coffee?"

"Can you please try to sleep; you will need the rest when we get there."

"Do you have change for a toll?"

"God, help us."

Occasionally we break into vocal prayer, in honor of our decision to make this trip a sacrifice of praise. We verbalize our trust in God knowing He is aware we are operating on faith-fumes. ⟵ STOP

Every couple of hours the phone rings and we learn more about our son's condition. We find it was merciful to have left with the many hours ahead of us, not knowing the full story.

The information we learn is devastating. The crash had been head-on, and the driver was drunk. We now know that Mark's feet had been pinned and we are told it took about 45 minutes to cut him out of the car. In this latest call we learn that his hip and pelvis have also been fractured.

Our hearts are broken. We cannot allow ourselves to think of Mark in excruciating pain, pinned for 45 minutes in a car. To think of his fear is more than we can bear. It hurts desperately and we hold hands as the tears fall down our faces.

It sounds to me as though his lower body has taken the brunt of the impact and I will not allow my mind to wonder about the fact that he is in surgery for his hand and arm also. Dave and I have no control over a situation that is every parent's nightmare, so it seems important to ease each other's mind in any way we can. When I ask if he is okay to drive, he reassures me he is fine, even though we both know he is too torn up inside to be driving. When he asks how I am feeling I assure him I am fine though the pain in my chest is driving me back against my seat.

Another call reveals that Mark's shoulder may be broken; we pray that this is the end of it. How can he be so broken? I do not allow myself to think he may not make it. He has to. God has a call on his life! He is our beloved son! He has to live!

Our pastor, Jim Rickard, calls when we are about 200 miles from Nashville. He has talked with Mickey and he gives me a clue about what we will face in Nashville. Though he is calling to pray and offer much needed support, he off-handedly mentions, "hard to recognize him". I let it go over my head. I cannot afford to grasp it and I do not mention that comment to Dave.

Please God, I pray in silence, *no more, no more*. As sorrow closes in to nearly rob us of our breath, we offer praise that our son is alive.

We are aware of the exceptional relationship we have with Mark. He is the son everyone dreams of. He is kind and funny and respectful. He knows his mom like no one else. He listens to my dreams and encourages me. He sends us cards that let us know he appreciates things we have done for him. He is deeply spiritual and mature in his relationship with Christ. Though I was privileged to lead him to Christ when he was very young, I often feel he has passed me in his spiritual insight. As parents we are blessed to not only intensely love but also truly respect our son.

Another call from Ann-Marie informs us Mark is out of surgery. It is her understanding that he had two surgeons working on him and she tells us they seem pleased with the results.

Mickey Robinson calls as Dave walks toward the car on our last gas station stop before Nashville. Mickey talks to me as Dave drives. I look at my husband whose face seems set in stone as he stares intently at the road ahead.

Mickey asks when we expect to arrive in Nashville and we are amazed at the time we have made. We report that, if traffic and weather conditions remain the same, we could possibly make Nashville in 13 driving hours! We tell him we may be there in about two hours.

Mickey sounds relieved we will be there soon. His voice is strong and kind. "How are you, honey?"

I try not to cry when I hear concern for us in his voice. "Okay."

"Dave?"

I look at Dave and say "Okay."

Mickey begins to coach me. "God is going to bring Mark through this. You know that."

I know he is waiting for response but I cannot speak.

"You and Dave are in His hands. We are here for you. Lana?"

His words require me to respond with a positive answer.

"Now," he says, and I steel myself, "I want you to be brave when you get here. Mark will need you to react in a positive manner when you see him."

"I know," I say weakly.

"You will not recognize him."

It feels as if my heart flipped upside down and stopped beating.

"We won't? Why?" How easy it would be to throw the phone on the floor and bring my knees to my chest, bury my face and scream!

Beside me, Dave is silent, tears roll down his cheeks as he focuses on driving in the dark early hours of evening. I do not have to repeat any of the conversation. I sense Dave knows some of what I am about to hear and he has not told me, or at least, that he senses it and does not need to know right now.

"He has had some pretty severe facial injuries"

I moan as a wave of nausea washes over me.

"Listen now, honey. He is in stable condition." There is silence as he waits for my response. "Do you understand? That is very…very good."

"Okay," I say grasping at that encouragement.

"He has had a tracheotomy."

"Oh, no, God, no," I turn to Dave to say, "he had a tracheotomy!"

Dave's eyes do not leave the road as tears freely fall down his cheeks. I feel him reach for my hand.

"That is okay, Lana. It saved his life." Mickey continues.

"Okay."

My entire end of the conversation consists of one word replies. I am astounded at the will and energy I expend in that effort.

The admonition of this conversation is summed up as we prepare to say goodbye. "Now, you and Dave get ready for this. We are going to pray and when you get here you will respond with confidence."

We pray, or rather Mickey does and I add my "Um,hm" in agreement. Dave is praying in silence.

I hang on every word this man of God speaks. We love and respect him. I know he is hurting with us and walking in faith, feeding necessary information to us in spoonfuls we can barely swallow, but must get down.

Fear swells up to choke me with questions, "Will he be severely scarred? Will he sing again? Will he walk?" The thoughts are senseless and harshly irrelevant; we must deal with each moment as it comes and I must not think beyond this day.

When Mickey finishes his conversation, he sounds like a cheerleader, "Okay, we will see you soon. When you see Mark how are you going to be?"

"Courageous," I offer.

"No. You will be confident. Everything wrong with him is fixable. It is all fixable!"

I run those words over and over in my mind the rest of the trip knowing I will draw strength from "fixable" for weeks to come.

Dave and I both become flustered as we near Nashville. In general we know where we are going but we have never been to Vanderbilt Hospital before. We follow signs that direct us around the confusion of construction and finally pull into the parking ramp of the building that, thank God, houses one of the premier Trauma Units in the nation.

We have been instructed to go to 10th floor Trauma Center. As we step off the elevator we see into a room across from us through glass walls. Sitting in chairs, facing the elevator so they cannot miss us, are Ann-Marie and her mother, Pat. They immediately stand to embrace us. In their hands are two tiny bundles that look like blankets, which they place on the two chairs they have reserved by hanging their coats on the back.

I know this is very kind but I am desperate to see Mark. It is not necessary for me to voice this; after a quick but warm hug, Pat takes each of us by the hand and walks us to a small desk in a corner of this large room.

"I know this is not the time visitors are allowed in ICU, but these are Mark Williams' parents, they have just arrived from Minnesota."

The woman she speaks to smiles kindly and says, "Come with me."

We pass a doorway just next to the one we have exited and she motions, "Usually, we have people stop in here and visit with a representative before they see their loved one, but I know you have driven a long distance."

Philippians 4:13, "I can do everything through him who gives me strength."

Chapter Four

Trauma

Mark remembers:

When I woke up after surgery I was very confused. My eyes were swollen nearly shut, so I couldn't really see anything clearly. It seemed like I was in the middle of a hallway because I kept seeing people walk past my bed. It was very odd. There was a nurse sitting next to my bed and she told me right away that I would not be able to talk. I had watched enough E.R. on television to know what a tracheotomy was.

I immediately started to breathe funny. I felt like I was not taking in any air. No one told me that a respirator was breathing for me so I should try to relax. That probably would have helped. Instead, I constantly felt like I was about to die.

I believe the nurse left for a moment and the next person I saw was my mom. I was relieved, but confused as to how fast she had gotten there. Was I in surgery that long?

It was so awful to not be able to talk or communicate in any way. There was so much I wanted and needed to say and ask as I was forced to lie there in silence. Questions and unexpressed thoughts swirled through my mind: Do you know I cannot breathe? What exactly is wrong with me? What's broken? How long will I be in the hospital? She was completely in my lane! Was she drunk? Is she alive? Help me. What time is it? Am I in a hallway? I can't see well. Don't leave me!

My energy was so completely gone that all I could do was lie there and look pitiful. I think that even if I could have spoken I wouldn't have had the energy to say anything. But it was comforting to know that my parents were in Nashville.

Two doctors came in to evaluate me and I heard them say something about waiting for the swelling to go down.

Whatever medication they had in my IV caused me to be "out of it" and I was determined to stay out of it so I wouldn't have to concentrate on breathing. When I was awake and alert I did not know how to breathe. At one point I woke up and my nurse was gone. I had no call button and could make no sound or movement of any kind except for my left arm. Since I was convinced I was in a hallway, I kept trying to flag people down with my left arm, which I could not lift very high off the bed. I couldn't breathe and I needed someone to get my nurse!

Help me! I would try to wave as my fingers fluttered inches above the mattress. After about ten people passed without paying any attention to me I assumed that they thought I was crazy.

Finally my nurse came back and I frantically pointed toward my tracheotomy tube with a desperate look on my face and tears welling in my eyes.

She looked up at my screen and said, "Honey, you're getting 100% of your oxygen."

I put my arm down and closed my eyes, which forced a tear to fall down my cheek.

Lana:

The woman from the reception desk opens the first of two large double doors that lead into the Trauma Center. She stops briefly at the nurses' station to explain why she is taking us to see Mark.

My knees are so weak I can barely walk and yet, if I could run I would. I am absolutely desperate for Mark to know we are here.

The woman opens a second set of doors and we enter the Trauma ICU. We have not walked far into the unit when she says, "This is Mark."

We are directly across from the nurse's station and I see several beds, each divided by curtains. We glance at the first bed and then start to walk forward.

The woman stands in front of us so we cannot continue further. "No." She says gently. "This is Mark."

I must look at her strangely because she motions to the first bed.

Oh God! Oh, God! My baby, my son! Jesus! Can that be him? Oh, God, be with us now. Be with us!

I could not recognize my own son!

I sense Dave cannot move so I walk slowly to Mark's bed. It is a long, ago-nizing walk that covers only three feet of space. My legs do not want to move, my eyes do not want to see, my mind does not want to comprehend, but my heart pulls me to his side.

This son we love more than life lies flat on the hospital bed, hooked up to many monitors and machines. His eyes are totally swollen shut and deep red-purple. They protrude from his strangely flat and round face that appears near-ly twice its normal size. The color of his face is a deep, muddy shade of purple.

I set my face in a smile. "Mark?" My voice is a near whisper. "Mark, we're here. Mom and Dad, we're here."

Dave walks up to lightly touch the top of the sheet that covers Mark. "We are here, son. It will be okay."

It is impossible to know if he sees us. His right eye seems to open slight-ly, but his left eye is swollen tightly shut and as round as a golf ball. The nurse that sits at a table beside his bed tells us that Mark is not able to speak because of the tracheotomy tube in his throat.

The only limb that Mark can move is his left hand and we see him lift the fingers of that hand slightly. I take his hand in mine. The squeeze is very weak but Mark knows that his mom and dad are by his side.

We learn quickly that the Trauma Center ICU runs a tight ship. We can go into the unit at any time we want for short periods of time from 9:00 a.m. until 5:30 p.m. and then again from 8:30 p.m. until 5:30 a.m. Two people may go in at the same time and they must wear the badges they give to us. We are allowed two badges with "Williams" printed on them. If we leave the hospital we are told to leave the badges at the desk in the waiting room so that someone else may use them. There is no admittance to the Trauma ICU without a badge.

On this our first night, I go in every fifteen minutes and stay for about five minutes each time. There is no place to sit in the ICU. Perhaps it is because they do not want to trip over or move a chair in an emergency, or perhaps it is to dis-courage people like me from never leaving.

Mark has a one-on-one nurse. This means that someone sits at the narrow mobile desk by his side constantly. These nurses monitor the machines that beep and chart and cause fear to rise in a mother's heart. The nurses are here because the people in these rooms must have a medical person by their side at all times. The serious nature of injuries in this place takes priority over the com-fort of visitors and we realize that, though we are important to Mark, we are something for the ICU team to work around.

Toward morning Mark is awake for longer periods and obviously frus-trated. He cannot talk, he cannot see and he has a fierce need to communicate, which he is unable to do. He tries to mouth words, and to gesture with the left hand that he can barely lift. We struggle to understand and frustration is evi-dent for all of us. The effort exhausts him.

Though his left arm is the only limb without fractures, it has not been spared trauma. We can see ugly and extensive bruising as the arm is slightly moved by his nurse but it does not take us long to grasp the blessing of his ability to use that arm, even minimally. It is our link to sanity.

We take a notebook and pen from the nurse's station and angle the pad flat on Mark's bed and under his left hand. Then I place the pen between his fingers and he attempts to write. The first letters are squiggly, sometimes with one letter printed on top of another. I realize it works best if I move the pad slightly after each letter he writes. It is painstaking and when I read the barely legible words sorrow engulfs me.

"Give me hope."

I recognize the grace of God as I am able to lean in and put my face next to the face I cannot recognize but love so dearly. I search his swollen eyes until I see he is looking at me and focused.

"Mark," I say, never looking away from his eyes, "That I can give you." Somehow I manage a slight smile. I look as intensely as I know how because he knows that our strong history does not include lies.

"I can give you hope, son, because I have been given hope. The doctor's tell us everything wrong is fixable. You will be okay. It will take time, but you will be okay again." I cannot imagine how he feels but, somehow I believe he has received the lifeline I have thrown him.

In this place, Mark is surrounded by people that are in agony or dying. Bright lights assault his swollen eyes, pain shouts and contends for attention in every part of his body. He is unable to mutter a sound, unable to move and he has asked for hope.

Does he believe me? Has he grasped the hand of hope? Though no sound can escape his lips, there is a slight settling to Mark's features and I feel certain that he understands.

Mark's fingers drum the bed. He wants to write again so we begin the slow process.

"Is she alive?"

This tears me apart. He is wondering how he survived such a violent crash, and if the woman who hit him survived. This is Mark. He cares about others.

I struggle to speak. "Mark, she is okay. We have heard that she has already been released from the hospital."

The next time he writes it is to ask, "Was she drunk?"

I wish this could have waited. "Yes, son, she was drunk."

It takes him a very long time to write, "She was in my lane."

I see tears roll out of his eyes.

"I know, Mark. We know."

Dave is biting his lip as he stands beside me fighting tears with every muscle in his tense body.

"We know it was not your fault. We know she was drunk and driving in your lane. You need to rest and to know that everyone knows what happened and we will take care of anything that needs to be taken care of. Try to rest son, try to sleep. Sleep heals."

Will every word I say to him from now on sound so shallow, so empty? How can I communicate with someone whose body has been broken, literally from head to toe because a stranger made the decision to gamble that this possibly would not happen?

What can I say to someone who saw headlights coming at him and felt and heard the violent trauma of the impact as his face smashed against a solid object and his long legs were pushed out of place and up to his chest with his feet pinned and crushed?

What words should be spoken to someone who suffered excruciating pain and unspeakable fear as he was maneuvered and cut from the wreckage, unable to move even enough to wipe away the blood that flowed from his broken nose?

What comfort can I offer to someone who loves to speak and lives to sing and now is mute, unable to voice his horror and fear? Which words would be adequate?

The answers do not come and are magnified because this someone who is suffering so desperately is our precious son who has never caused his parents anguish but has been good and loving his entire life. I know that there are no answers and so I respond as the Bible instructs us to do, I groan in the Spirit, relying on Him to supply the words that need to be spoken.

Dave and I have agreed we cannot become angry at the woman that decided to commit this assault on our son. I clearly see her as no different from someone who took time to load a gun, point it at another person, pull the trigger and hope it happens to miss. There is absolutely no difference in my mind, and yet we must not be consumed with thoughts of her. It will drain our energy and Mark needs every fiber of energy we can pull together.

I call on Philippians, 4:4-7, "Rejoice in the Lord always, I will say it again: Rejoice! Let your gentleness be evident to all. The Lord is near. Do not be anxious about anything, but in everything by prayer and petition, with thanksgiving, present your requests to God. And the peace of God, which transcends all understanding, will guard your hearts and your minds in Christ Jesus."

How I need this promise to be reality! *Father, help me to use this prescription you have given me. Help me to follow Your directions because I know they are best for us. Please give us courage and increase our faith!*

I slide into my creaky chair in the waiting room and pray for protection from anger...for all of us.

> *Psalm 91:1-4, "He who dwells in the shelter of the Most High will rest in the shadow of the Almighty. I will say of the Lord, "He is my refuge and my fortress, my God, in whom I trust. Surely he will save*

you from the fowler's snare and from the deadly pestilence. He will cover you with his feathers, and under his wings you will find refuge; his faithfulness will be your shield and rampart."

Chapter Five
The Quiet Room

Lana:

It is night in the Quiet Room. That is the name posted on a sign as we enter this waiting room outside the Trauma Intensive Care Unit. We do not know how long this room will be our home. We can only experience the moment that now looms before us, new, shocking, and terrifying as we sit in the two chairs that have been saved for us by Ann-Marie and Pat.

I have been in emergency rooms and in ICU's but I have never seen a trauma center before. I am not sure I knew the distinction or if they existed, as I do not watch TV shows of any medical genre.

This room is designated for people whose lives have been turned upside down, for people who walk around in a daze and pray though they cannot think or speak. This room is for people who are wounded and need to be near people who are wounded deeper still.

Worn blue plastic recliner-type chairs line the walls. In Minnesota I work with home furnishings and I would not describe these little torture units as recliners, except that your feet can be raised in most of the chairs. I count 13 of them and each one is occupied. The chairs have unforgiving metal arms and hard plastic seats with backs that do not tilt. We have each been given a pillow, the size of an airplane pillow. Tied with string, it is attached to a lightweight white blanket that leaves lint over every covered part of your body. In normal moments these would not be greatly appreciated, but for those of us in this room, they are welcome treasures.

The leg rest on my "recliner" will not stay up. I have lifted it several times, but each time I move even slightly it collapses. A blond haired woman crosses the room to let us know this will be an on-going battle. She quietly asks if she can place a stationary chair under the footrest for me and kindly does so when

I nod yes. It helps my feet to stay up but makes my chair a bit of a prison when I want to get out of it every fifteen minutes to go down the hall to be with Mark.

The chairs are situated close together and each squeaks and groans, as though complaining whenever someone needs to adjust their body to its unforgiving frame. I am very aware, with each squeak of the chair; the other dozen people in this room are sleeping, or trying to.

I have slept only a half an hour in more than forty hours, and yet I find it impossible to sleep. Next to me Dave is sound asleep and I thank God he has that gift. He can sleep easily in many situations and on many surfaces. Above us a fluorescent light shines directly into our faces. I notice other lights around the room have been turned off but, for some reason, this one has been left on. I constantly move, trying to get the pillow or blanket under either my hip or shoulder or neck so that I am not in pain. I reach into my overnight bag and grab a washcloth to put over my eyes, hoping to hide from the glare of the fluorescent above me.

I notice that Dave is not using his pillow and, when he moves again, it is free from his body. I snatch it with the selfish intention of not returning it unless he asks for it. I also move my chair as close to his as possible. I do not want to wake him, but I need to touch him. I put my arm over and around his. I rest my head against his shoulder though I must strain across the metal arm of my chair to do it. I want to crawl over into his chair, to sit on his lap and say, "Hold me." I need his arms around me. I need the solace, the familiarity. I need to know some things in life are still the same.

As the night progresses I cannot deny that I am in pain. My shoulders and neck ache, my chest hurts and my hip is burning from the awkward chair, but when I think of my son, only steps away down the hall and behind two sets of double doors, I cannot complain. He is not alone in his suffering behind those doors. Neither am I.

I begin to watch the people around me. I can tell who has been here awhile. Of course I do not know if any are as new as we are. The veterans sleep in short shifts, getting up to wander down the hall to see their loved one, then back again to climb into the squeaky, noisy vinyl chairs to sleep once again.

I begin another trip to ICU, but do not make it to the first set of double doors. As I approach I see a deserted corner of the hallway. Quickly I turn into it and collapse to the floor in despair. The tears will not quit. I address them and force them from my eyes. *You will not cry anymore. You will not have a tear-stained face and swollen eyes the next time you go in to see Mark.* I suspect that it is the first of many such willful instructions that will serve me well in the months to come.

I walk back to the Quiet Room to look for Kleenex and find none. How many gallons of tears are shed in this room each day? There must be a box of tissue! I pad in my stocking-feet to the nurses' station and ask for a box of Kleenex. When I return to my bed-chair, two men across the room smile and one whispers, "Are you alright?"

I nod and smile back at them. It's a weak smile, but I sense they know it is the best I can do.

> *Joshua 1:9, "Have I not commanded you? Be strong and coura-*
> *geous. Do not be terrified; do not be discouraged, for the Lord your*
> *God will be with you wherever you go."*

Sunday, December 9, 2001

It is our first morning in the Quiet Room. There is a men's restroom to one side of this room and a women's to the other. This morning as I come out of the restroom, I notice that most people have already left and returned with paper cups of coffee. Nearly all of them are awake at this early hour.

A woman who sits near the telephone smiles and asks, "Did you get any sleep?"

"Not really. I couldn't get used to the chair."

We speak quietly as our environment dictates.

"I felt so bad for you with that light in your eyes. Try to move to different chairs tonight. I'm glad you got here when you did. We were expecting you quite a bit later."

This is a tiny community that bonds quickly. I learn that this woman's twenty-one year old son had a car accident also. His side is badly hurt, the hip and the leg. I feel ashamed to think he is fortunate to have so few injuries. I know that is a lie. If he is in this place, he is in grave danger. I offer my first prayer for someone besides Mark.

Dave woke early and went in to see Mark just before 5:00 a.m. We are not allowed in between 5:00-9:00 a.m. We have been told the doctors will come to talk to those of us waiting in this room at about 7:30 a.m. It is now 7:45 a.m.

I had hoped to drive to Mark's home to drop off our luggage, shower and had even dreamed of a short nap. That was before I spent the night here. It was before I knew how much Mark wants us to be here. Now I cannot think of leaving.

I look into the small brown bag left by a church group that visited the Quiet Room before we arrived yesterday. It contains cookies and apples. I know I should eat, but it is not possible. I found the bagel bag from yesterday in the car when we gathered our things to come into the hospital last night. At least one-half of the bagel purchased more than twenty-four hours ago was still in the bag. Dave manages to eat a piece of fruit along with the coffee he purchased from the McDonald's he discovered located just across the downstairs lobby.

From Ann-Marie, I begin to find out who had been with Mark here in ICU yesterday. They are all people we know well and love as family. Brian and April Neuwirth are a married couple and friends from Mark's college days at Belmont University. Matt Garinger had been a college roommate and he and Mark have been writing songs together. I have not yet met Matt's new wife, Heather, but understand she was here.

Ann-Marie stayed with Mark from the time she was called to the scene of the crash until we arrived. Ann-Marie, also a friend since college days, had just begun dating Mark. He had given her phone number to be called from the site of the crash as she was only moments away from the scene. Her mother, Pat, had rushed to the hospital to wait with Ann-Marie and had been there at our arrival to insist to the nurses that we be immediately allowed to see Mark. I am more than grateful that Mark's college years produced rich friendships not only for him, but for us also.

Mickey Robinson and members of his family had also been at the hospital. We met him years ago in Minneapolis when he visited our church to minister as an Evangelist and Prophet. He is a wonderful man with a dramatic testimony. He was in an airplane crash and severely burned. He was blind in one eye and told he would not walk. Today he can see, can walk and has a thriving ministry. To add to the miracle, he is married to a beautiful woman, Barbara, and is the father of four exceptional children. Mickey's miracle encourages us to believe for a miracle of our own.

It was Mickey's phone call that prepared us for the tragedy we would encounter when we arrived here last night. It had to have been a difficult call to make, but he was the man God chose for that job. We are grateful that he has been updating churches in Minneapolis and Canada on Mark's condition. It is a great comfort to know that prayers are going up on Mark's behalf.

We are blessed and relieved to know Mark had people that love him nearby. At this moment none of our friends are in the Quiet Room and Dave and I are waiting to go to see Mark. My arms ache. It is the way a new mother aches to hold her baby. I physically ache to be with my son. I can think of nothing else but going to his side. I pray he understands we are not allowed into the ICU at certain times and does not wonder where we are.

I look around the Quiet Room and realize that each person in this room is experiencing the same longing. We talk to each other to pass the moments that tick as hours. We offer weak smiles as our eyes meet across the room and I hear professions of faith in every corner.

"The Lord gave us another sunrise."

"Don't worry about tomorrow, today holds enough trouble of its own."

"He never promised it would be easy, only that He'd walk beside us."

These words are all stated by people who need to speak them as much as others need to hear them.

The Quiet Room Dwellers are from Kentucky, South Carolina, Tennessee and now, Minnesota. We learn that Mark is fortunate to be in this premier trauma center.

I find I cannot talk about his injuries yet. I do not want the total reality to grasp hold of me; I fear it will pull me into a black hole I will not be able to climb out of. I urge my mind to repeat Mickey's word over and over again. "Fixable."

There are many phone calls to this room and little privacy. It does not take long to assess the state of each person's loved one. We have entered into an intimacy with people we would not have met under "normal" circumstances and even my shocked mind comprehends the spiritual wonder of it.

"If you are holding your own in this place, you are climbing the hill." I hear a man talk into the phone.

The woman who said she was glad we got here soon knows everyone's name. Her chair is by the phone and when it rings she holds it up and announces a name. It is nearly 8:30 a.m. and the phone rings. She holds it out in my direction and says, "Mrs. Williams."

It is Mickey. We have a brief conversation to update him and he offers encouragement to Dave and me. He will come to the hospital later today.

We are disappointed that our name was not called at the morning "briefing." We had so wanted to talk to the doctor. We need to know if Mark will have more surgery today. Perhaps they do not know we arrived last night.

When Ann-Marie calls she tells me Mark requested in writing yesterday for her to bring his Bible. She will stop by his house today and get it from his roommate. I have my Bible with me, but he wants his own. I understand why when I have his Bible in my hands and see all the highlighted and noted places he has been studying. I will read to him today from areas he has highlighted.

I think to myself, *I need to get him some new glasses, his were shattered. He can't read without them.* I know it is not possible for him to wear glasses right now. His face is swollen to twice its normal size and his eyes are purple slits. It is a prompting though. I want the glasses available before he asks for them.

Ann-Marie arrives early and comes with me to ICU. She asks Mark if there is anyone else he wants to call. Mark is frustrated by his need to communicate and our inability to understand without him speaking. We can see he wants to try a new method and watch as he holds up his left hand to painstakingly move one finger at a time. Fortunately, and perhaps because she is an elementary school teacher, Ann-Marie catches on right away.

"A-B-C-D-E...? E? You want me to call Ed?"

He nods, relieved. Ed lives in Minneapolis and has been one of Mark's closest friends since they were in junior high school.

Ann-Marie shines a bright smile in my direction. "Now let me tell you how smart he is!"

She volunteers to call Ed. Once again, the years of friendship work well. Though Ed is in Minnesota, Ann-Marie has met him on his trips to Nashville to visit Mark. She knows Ed and he will ask her any questions he needs answers to. It is a great relief to me because Ed is nearly part of our family.

———————

In the Quiet Room I watch people read the Sunday paper. I am grateful that this is Sunday; I am expecting a breakthrough of some kind as churches corporately hold Mark up in prayer. I know many people have already been praying and I think of the sorrow and shock that will take place as this is announced to many congregations in Minnesota that love Mark.

Pastor Jim calls to share that at the Christmas party for a church organization yesterday someone had a vision of a fine china cup. It had something poured into it that was "wrong," and it shattered. "The heavenly Father looked down and gently picked up the cup and put it back together again," He told me with confidence.

Let it be, Lord. I pray fervently. *Put my son back together again!*

Brian and April come in to the Quiet Room with hugs and a case of bottled water. Brian asks if he can go to get us food but we still have no appetite. They accept that for awhile but as the day progresses these young friends decide to call the shots.

When Matt arrives he insists on taking Dave and me to Mark's house to shower. He promises we will return in short order. Once we arrive at the house he informs us he is leaving to go to The Green Hills Grille where Mark worked as a waiter and where Matt still works. He knows my favorite meal there and says he will bring it back when he returns to take us to the hospital.

When Matt returns to Mark's house his wife, Heather, is with him. It is the first time we have met. The plan is for Heather to take me to the hospital and Matt will take Dave to the crash site and then to the lot where Mark's car has been towed. He is armed with still and video cameras as well as my favorite Chicken Pasta dish and a chicken and potato dish for Dave.

We sit at the table to eat some of the incredibly delicious food but after only a few bites I feel my stomach churn. It will not accept nourishment. Dave manages enough food to give him some much needed energy and then we place the leftovers in the refrigerator for another time. It is wonderful to be taken care of and we know that though we are far from home, we are with family.

Heather takes me to the Quiet Room, and then leaves to return to work. Matt brings Dave only a short time later. They briefly go to see Mark and then leave again on errands. I am grateful that Matt can keep Dave busy.

I sit visiting with Ann-Marie, Pat and April in the Quiet Room when I look up to see a woman with a bright smile on her face walking towards us.

"Hi!" She hugs me warmly, "I work with Mark." She has kind words to offer and sets a huge and beautiful basket at my feet.

The basket overflows with Banana Bread and Banana Muffins. They are from a cook at The Grille and baked especially for us. Also included in the array are lovely pieces of fruit. I am absolutely overwhelmed at this kindness.

"I want you to call me whenever you are hungry. The Grille is not so far away and I will bring food to you anytime. If I cannot come when you call someone else will." This woman I have never met before smiles as though she loves me.

She is warm and kind and I can see why Mark thinks highly of her. Her eyes mist with tears, "We love Mark so much, you know. We love him. He is a sweetie and I can't believe this happened to someone as good as Mark."

I would like to offer her some wise words but she has expressed my feeling. We hug and wipe away tears as if we have been friends for a very long time.

When she leaves she assures me she will be back and tells us that Mark's friends at The Grille are taking up a "tip" collection for him, which she will bring the next time she visits.

Becki calls to say she is coming over. I need her. She has been a friend of Mark's, and a friend of ours, for many years. Originally from Minnesota, she relocated to Nashville about a year after Mark started college here. She is a spiritual giant though that gifting is housed in the body of a Dwarf. Becki gets around in a customized van and on a three-wheel scooter and nothing gets in her way. She is a capable woman of God and I know she will be a blessing to us throughout this ordeal.

When I see her scooter move out of the elevator I rush for a hug.

Several college friends of Mark's arrive and we decide to take the beautiful basket, along with some water bottles, to the lobby of the hospital. We will be able to visit down there and not crowd the Quiet Room. His friends sit and talk as they eat the wonderful contents of the basket. There are about eight of us but when we return to the Quiet Room more than two-thirds of the contents are still in the generous basket.

I place it in the middle row of chairs and offer Banana Bread to anyone who might enjoy some. I think of taking such a basket to my workplace and how everyone would "pounce" on such a treasure. In this place I receive a polite "Thank you" from several people but only one walks over to take a piece. I decide to leave it there until it is gone. Perhaps it will look good at breakfast tomorrow.

Mickey arrives and immediately goes with me to see Mark. He puts his face close to Mark's so he can be sure Mark can see him and he places his hand, the hand burned so badly years ago, on Mark's left hand. He prays positive words of healing and then he exhorts him, "The songs that you love and cannot sing right now with your mouth, sing in your spirit. *Great Is Thy Faithfulness*, sing it in your mind and spirit."

Mark nods, *yes*.

Great is Thy Faithfulness has long been a favorite song people request Mark to sing. His rich tenor voice wraps itself around that old hymn to inspire praise in anyone who hears it. I can nearly hear him begin to sing it in his spirit. He lies, motionless, hooked up to so many machines and IVs, robbed of his voice, and yet I see the words Mickey speaks to him take root.

I have recognized so many qualities in this young man I am privileged to parent. Now I recognize courage.

I spend my time away from Mark writing in my journal. Entries concern the Quiet Room because it is too painful to write about Mark. I am fascinated with the people who share the room that has become our home.

My mind wanders to our first night in ICU as though it was weeks ago. In fact it was only hours. That night, last night, I noticed a man who sat across from us. He was distinctive because he has a white beard that is slightly longer than average. Each time I looked up, or moved in the awkward chair I saw him. He was staring into space. When his eyes met mine, it was as though he did not see me. I considered that he may be a bit unfriendly. Now I know that I had not yet learned the signals of the Quiet Room. It was he and the man I have learned is his son, who asked me if I was okay when I returned from my time away to cry.

In the light of day, I can see this man's face is speckled with tiny cuts and dry blood. The cuts are from the windshield that shattered in the accident that has left his wife, Cynthia, in a coma behind the two sets of double doors.

His name is Jim Hagewood and Dave and I have already determined that we will pray daily for his beloved Cynthia. Mr. and Mrs. Hagewood do not live in Nashville. They were on their way to visit their son when the accident occurred. Now he spends his time waiting for her to open her eyes.

Our resident receptionist has received the news that her son will go into a "Step-Down" room. This is reason for celebration. It means he is breathing without aid of a respirator and can go to a room where the ratio will be three patients to one nurse instead of one to one. The rooms are still in the Trauma Unit but they are behind the first set of double doors, before the second set and down a hallway. The Step-Down rooms are like a promotion; if you get the next one available you are in the best shape of anyone in the trauma ICU. There may still be more surgeries, and certainly months of rehabilitation ahead of him, but it is a graduation. Each person in this Quiet Room wishes for a Step-Down room for their loved one.

Brian and April arrive with food and the very valuable gift of a calling card. We can now easily make calls to people in Minnesota. What a wonderful idea! As we sit talking between visits to the ICU, Brian suddenly stands to leave for a "few minutes". When he returns, he hands Dave a small bag. Its contents are two toothbrushes, one red and one blue, a tube of toothpaste and some mouthwash. We had been wishing we would have brought our travel bags from Mark's house to the Quiet Room but we can't remember voicing that to Brian. It did not take us long to go to put them to use. We return from the restroom feeling like new people with clean teeth! Once again, we are so blessed by our wonderful friends who anticipate our needs.

It is an excruciatingly long day and when evening comes, I long for the floor. It is more appealing than the "torturecliner", as I have mentally dubbed our chairs, but Quiet Room rules will not allow anyone to sleep on the floor.

It is not important if we sleep or not, we will stay here again tonight. Last night we stayed because Mark wanted us to and he is so precious and in such an awful place that, of course we stayed. I am coming to the realization that we may stay here most nights.

To pass the time when we cannot be by Mark's side or asleep, we listen to each person's story in this Quiet Room. We readily pray for others who are hurting beside us. By God's mercy, the tormenting agony is lifted slightly when we take on another's burden.

James 5:13 and 16, "Is any one of you in trouble? He should pray...The prayer of a righteous man is powerful and effective."

PART II ✦ ICU
December 10, 2001 – December 21, 2001

Monday, December 10, 2001

Mark remembers:

I had no concept of time. There were no windows in the ICU and I never knew if it was day or night. All I knew was that I wanted to be asleep and escape the nightmare. *Let me sleep and wake up when it is all over*, was my prayer.

Somehow morning brought relief. Perhaps it was the concept of "I made it one more day" or "mercies are new every morning." Whatever it was, I longed for morning. If I would ask what time it was by pointing to my wrist and it was not the time I hoped it was I would experience a wave of depression. I plunged deep enough into that depression that I desired to die.

Why did time have to go so slowly? If I could read that would help, or if I could watch television that would help also. But to just stare endlessly at a world I could not see clearly, a world in which I could not breathe freely, a world in which I could not communicate effectively was too much to handle at times. When all you are able to do is lie still and think about all that has happened and not know what the future holds, it really sucks. I could use worse words or I could use sweeter words but let me just honestly state what it was like…it sucked!

Once I pointed to my wrist and mom was tired and did not have her reading glasses on. She said, "I think it is about 1:00."

She could see how upset I became and she said, "Oh, honey, no. Just a minute I could be wrong." She went to see a clock and said, "It is 2:00. I am so sorry, honey."

But it didn't matter. One hour didn't matter when the world stood still.

Lana:

As soon as 10:00 a.m. arrives, I call the store in Minneapolis where Mark got his glasses nearly one year before. I explain the situation and ask if there is an affiliate store in Nashville. The helpful woman tells me that there is and they will fax the prescription. When I call the Nashville store the sales person sympathizes. Her mother was in the trauma center not long ago. She says she will pick out a frame similar to the one Mark had and get the prescription filled. I am relieved I will have glasses for Mark when he is ready for them.

Dave must keep busy. It is his nature. At church he paces at the back of the sanctuary to work as elder, usher, and watchman, seldom sitting through an entire service. He can sit still and relax at home in front of the television set, but even at Mark's concerts it seems he must run the video camera or walk around the back or the balcony of the venue. If he has nervous energy in normal circumstances, it is worse now. He has already made one trip with Matt to the crash site where they took both video and still camera shots. They also went to the impound lot and photographed the car. This morning Matt and Dave have gone to get pictures developed.

When I return from a trip to ICU I see Matt and Dave in the Quiet Room. They have the photographs and several people are looking at them. Everyone is amazed that Mark could survive such a collision.

I will not look at the pictures. I just cannot. I am not in any type of denial. It is far too real that Mark is here, but I cannot bear to think of the impact, I cannot allow myself to think of him pinned in the wreckage, alone and in pain. It is beyond my strength to think of how he felt, what he felt. Photographs would plant even more graphic and unwanted images in my mind.

It is a relief for me that Dave takes care of the things I really do not want to deal with. He takes care of insurance, getting Mark's bills from the house, and copying Mark's driver's license after he retrieves his wallet from the purser at the hospital. He walks to McDonald's and offers me food but I still cannot eat.

Dave continues in the busyness that keeps him sane today as he makes trips to the insurance company and to the police station for a copy of the police report. He makes phone call after phone call, letting people know what happened, filling people in on the changes that take place nearly hourly. While he takes care of the busy work, I stay with Mark. I talk to him, pray with him, read scripture, encourage. Whatever I think he may need, I do. I am limited and he is voiceless. The sadness in his eyes haunts me, breaks my heart and causes wrenching pain in my spirit.

Each day is full of trouble of its own, scripture tells us. We are not to worry about tomorrow. In this situation, we cannot. Each day is overwhelming, each hour and each moment take all our concentration, all our stamina, all our strength.

Dave wants us to stay at Mark's house one night and get some much-needed sleep. I do too. I can barely perceive how tired I am — but I cannot leave Mark. If I leave it could be at that very moment he would want to communicate something. I know he watches for me when we are told to leave the room for the restricted hours. He points to his right wrist with his left hand. It clearly means "What time is it?"

I hate to tell him, because he appears so distressed when I do say the time. It is obvious the hours drag and he feels trapped in a time warp.

Somehow one day turns into the next. In the Quiet Room we are family. People go for coffee and bring back extra cups knowing it will be a welcome gift to someone. Baskets appear from friends and become community property. Today, Ann-Marie's friend brought us a care basket clearly put together by someone who knows what it is like to sit day after day, in a hospital setting. It contains Kleenex, lip balm, fruit, breakfast bars, chocolate, water bottles, and mini packs of cookies. It is well planned and greatly appreciated. The thoughtfulness feels like a warm blanket. Though I cannot eat yet, it warms my heart to see someone else walk over and take an apple or a candy bar to enjoy.

Occasionally when friends stop to see Mark I have to tell them they cannot go in. There are times when it is just too difficult for him to have anyone around and he requests that I let visitors know his wish to be alone. Communication is frustrating for him and for the person who desperately wants to know what he needs. To add to that stress, he is exhausted from dealing with constant pain and the myriad of questions that wear him down.

Even though Mark cannot always have visitors, Dave, Mark and I each cling closely to our friends. We were blessed when we got a call from Chris and Carole Beatty to tell us that they intend to be here for us. Chris is a well-respected vocal coach and has been a part of Mark's life since they met at a Music Conference when Mark was about seventeen. Because both Mark and Chris believe in the discipline and training of a Boy's Choir they had an immediate shared interest. Chris and Mark became friends and as that friendship developed, Chris and Carole and Dave and I became friends. Chris has continued, in varying degrees, to mentor Mark over the years.

After Mark's freshman year at Northwestern University in Evanston, Illinois, where he had been studying Theatre and Classical Music, he was in a dilemma. Should he continue there or try to find a college that would expand his study beyond classical training?

Chris and Carole met us for lunch when they were in Minneapolis to encourage Mark to take a look at Belmont University in Nashville. They enticed us with the fact that they had just moved to Nashville and would love to have him in the area.

The visit Mark and I made to Belmont was one of those strange experiences that convince you that God is involved in all aspects of our lives. Mark was certain that he needed to be at a Big Ten school and had actually ruled Belmont out of his list of considerations on a visit to the campus in his junior year of high school. But things had changed in the way they do when God is leading and directing your life.

Mark did not want to focus solely on Classical training for his voice. He wanted to explore the possibility that the Lord was leading him to Christian Music. And so, on a second visit to Belmont, Mark and I found ourselves in the cafeteria, which was so different from the one at Northwestern where chefs prepared omelets to specific order. I returned to the table after making my own waffle and sat next to Mark in the small and nearly empty cafeteria. He looked up from his food and offered a somewhat sheepish grin. "I'm going to school here. I belong here."

We knew it could only have been the Lord because, though the Belmont campus is beautiful, it cannot visually compare to the majesty or prestige of Northwestern.

There was no looking back and Mark spent the rest of his college career at Belmont University. He absolutely loved being there and formed friendships that remain a blessing to this day for our entire family.

Mark's friends at Belmont held each other accountable in their Christian walk. They talked tough and honest and were more transparent to each other than I have ever observed friendships to be. That intimacy has built a strong level of trust and love between this group and their love for Mark has always been apparent. Dave and I are not the only ones crying for our son.

In a surreal way, we have a network of friends that each play a functional and supportive role in the tragedy we must walk through. I recognize it as divine provision. Pat's knowledge of health insurance is wonderful as she takes care of our insurance questions. Matt's job allows him time during the morning to drive Dave to places he wants or needs to visit. Mickey feeds Mark the hope he needs to receive from someone who suffered and triumphed. Our incredible networks of churches that have come to love Mark through his ministry have rallied prayer support across the nation. Our friends in Canada, India, Israel, England and other nations have sent e-mail alerting international prayer.

Both Becki and April spend time ministering to me. They know me well and they have each brought me beautiful journals and a variety of pens to write with. April has been like a daughter to me nearly from the time I met her. I love her dearly and I appreciate the way she and Brian have always had such an openly honest and caring relationship with Mark. Becki captured my heart years ago and though she is young enough to be my daughter, we have had spiritual discussions in which I felt she imparted the wisdom of a mother to me.

Chris and Carole have stepped in to add support with a friendship that has always been cherished but now carries an intensity of concern. Chris has promised to work with Mark's voice as soon as we know what the prognosis is. He has already been on the internet conferring with other vocal coaches regarding tracheotomy.

Ann-Marie knows a police officer who is studying to be an attorney. He has promised to keep us posted on what happens to the woman who hit Mark. From him and the officers present at the scene, we learn the under-aged woman was charged at the scene and taken to the hospital with minor injuries and released shortly thereafter. A blood alcohol test was taken at the hospital, but it may be several weeks before we learn the results of that test.

Today, when Dave returns with a copy of the police report in hand, we find that there is no question the driver was highly intoxicated. The diagram clearly shows she was in Mark's lane and other information confirms that she is not of a legal age to drink alcohol. I cannot explore the questions that surface. I cannot spend precious moments pondering the ridiculous, senseless, selfish decision that has brought us to this tragedy.

I concentrate on writing about the Quiet Room in my journal as the hours of the day obliviously blur around me. I observe the people that share this room with us and Dave and I become involved in praying for their loved ones. We discover, in a new dimension, that to pray for others eases our own burden.

I want to write in detail about Mark but I cannot. I know he will have questions in the future and that I will not remember all that is happening, but the pain of putting this horror in words is something I am not capable of. It is as if I have a very deep, open wound and I can somehow cope with the pain if I do not move and if I avert my eyes from it. To record details about Mark in ICU is like taking the sharp blade of a knife to twist it in the open wound. I just do not have the courage to do it.

———————

We are wonderfully relieved that Mark is breathing on his own. The trach tube is still in place and will be for quite some time, but the respirator has been removed. We are blessed. While we recognize this as good news, those who have been in this place longer than us seem to grasp the wonder of it more fully and they openly rejoice when we share the news. There are some people in the Quiet Room who are waiting for their loved one to be well enough to have a tracheotomy tube inserted because they are being kept alive by machine.

We are confident that it is because of the power of prayer that Mark may be able to go to a Step-Down room.

As soon as Mark is given that hope, it becomes his entire focus. It is not that he will feel any different in that room, but he will be the only one there and we will be able to stay in the room with him and have some control over things like bright lights and noise. It is difficult to be in this ICU where death seems to lurk in every shadow.

The next surgery scheduled for Mark is to repair his shoulder and to fix his hip and pelvis. I am amazed at how each surgery is so significant in itself and, in fact, can sometimes involve two teams of surgeons working. By themselves each of these surgeries would be more than one person should have to endure, and more than enough for a family to cope with. We have to deal with each one, knowing more lie ahead and yet, we are so ready for each one. Mark especially longs for the time when he will be asleep and not have to face the situation and the pain.

The surgery is long and we wait it out in the Quiet Room with friends by our side. When the surgeon appears he is smiling. He has decided we are an okay family, I think. They generally do not take time to smile much but we have let him know we are praying for him and his team as they work on Mark.

The report is good. The surgery was a success in that Mark now bears even more metal in his body. The first surgery constructed his left foot and knee using metal and also a plate was put into his right arm. The left lower part of his body is cast. He has an immobilizer on the left leg and it is unable to move in any direction. The cast exposes the tip of his toes and then goes well above the knee. His right arm is also cast from the fingertips to the elbow.

Now, as he returns from this latest surgery, his right shoulder is pinned into place by two thick pins. The surgeon tells us that it had collapsed much like ice cream falling down the side of a cone. The pins run from his bicep into the shoulder and they stick out enough that we are cautioned not to catch a blanket or anything else on them. He also has pins and screws in his left hip and pelvis. The pelvis has metal pins or screws both anterior and posterior. We do not understand all of it. We do not know how much we need to know.

Fixable. It may take metal to put him back together and that is not what we would choose, but this is not in our hands. We give it all to God and mouth the word, "Fixable", over and over again.

> *Psalm 61:1-4, "Hear my cry, O God; listen to my prayer. From the ends of the earth I call to you, I call as my heart grows faint; lead me to the rock that is higher than I. For you have been my refuge, a strong tower against the foe. I long to dwell in your tent forever and take refuge in the shelter of your wings."*

Tuesday, December 11, 2001

I return to the QR, as I now refer to the Quiet Room, refreshed. I have wiped my eyes with a paper towel in the public restroom. I combed my hair and brushed my teeth. I put on lipstick because that is what I do when I go to see Mark. That is his mom. His mother wears makeup and fusses with her hair. She loves to shop for clothes and polish her nails. Today the lipstick will have to do and he will not notice that I have slept in my clothes and my black pants are dotted with white lint from the hospital blanket. If he were well he would smile at me and reach over quickly to pull my hair—a lighthearted, affectionate gesture since early childhood—he would look at me with a twinkle in his eye and ask, "Bad hair day?"

Mark has had two incredible and grueling trips to the operating room. We do not know how many actual surgeries have taken place. His body is now housing a lot of metal. He cannot tell us how he is feeling emotionally. To register pain he can hold up fingers to tell us the level, three fingers mean quite a bit of pain, but then he slightly waves his hand to say he is coping. Five fingers mean we should get the morphine. Occasionally a nurse will ask about pain and this son we are so proud of will actually give them thumbs up to say he is okay.

Mark has not been okay today. He is struggling with something horrible and it is too exhausting for him to write it all out for us. Depression has cast a dark shadow.

Dave and I are both in his room, which, we praise God, is now a Step-Down room, when Mark motions that he wants the slate with the dry marker his friends from The Grille have brought him. I hold it as he struggles to get the letters on the board. Slowly I see the letter "I" form, and then a few seconds later "want". He has not asked for anything that way and a sense of dread covers me as he writes the next word, "to". I pull the board away when the letter "d" appears.

"No Mark!" I say, taking the board away and wiping the letters with my sleeve as though they must disappear quickly. "No, son." I say more gently.

Behind me Dave is biting his lip, his hand over his mouth to stifle a sob.

"I will not let you write that, Mark," I say putting my face close to his.

He turns his head toward me slightly and I am amazed I do not see tears. He is determined not to cry because it causes him to cough and the pain in his body is off the charts when he has to cough. He is an incredibly disciplined man. And yet, he wants to die rather than face the enormity of the situation he is in.

Who am I to preach? I had a similar experience years ago as I lie in labor with this precious person. After seventy-four hours of labor, my body had become partially paralyzed. Because I had not dilated, they would not give me as much as an aspirin for the pain and I felt I could no longer cope. I reasoned that if I could die, the baby would have all the help needed to survive. When a pastor I barely knew came to my bedside I tearfully whispered, "I want to die."

He literally yelled at me and disciplined me for the sin of such a thought! It had not been what I needed and now I desperately want to give Mark what he needs.

"We love you so much son; so very much. And we will get through this. It is hard and awful, but you are fixable Mark! You will get better! You must believe us!"

I am amazed I am not crying. I am somehow exhorting with optimism that is not coursing through my body. I am, in myself, drowning in sorrow. I pray against depression as I sit in the chair next to his bed. I pray that for each of us.

When we are asked to leave the room for rounds, we go to the QR. Mark has been resting better and I promise him I will sleep in the chair beside his bed tonight when we are allowed to return.

Dave falls asleep as soon as he sits in his torchercliner. Watching his son suffer has exhausted him.

I watch my husband sleep and realize I have received mercy that, as I started this new day I did not know it would hold one of the deepest valleys I have ever walked through. I did not know that as night closed in I would despair to the point that I would feel, in this one moment, that I would surely lose my physical life. Me. Not the patient, but the mother of the patient. I now know that the torment of seeing someone you love suffer can produce agonizing physical reaction.

I take Mark's cell phone and go into the hall to call Mickey. I am in physical pain but it cannot compare to the mental anguish and the emotional burden that cause me to feel as though I am about to die.

As soon as Mickey answers I know I will not be able to get through the conversation without crying. I have walked to the opposite side of the elevators so no one in the QR can see me.

"Is Mark okay?" Mickey asks immediately.

"Yes, I just wondered if you would pray. He wanted to…" The words are smothered in sobs but somehow we manage to communicate. As we talk I actually slide to the floor doubled over with despair.

"We have our home group here. We are going to pray for you right now. Lana?"

"Yes."

"This is an attack, probably because of the surgery tomorrow. Be strong until we get there. Mark will be okay. God has a plan for him. You and Dave will be okay."

I am only slightly embarrassed that I have fallen apart. It is more important for me to have Mickey come and pray with Mark than to engage in futile pride. Somehow I feel we can handle all the physical challenges that present themselves, but I cannot bear to see Mark struggling to find hope.

I go to the restroom to blow my nose and wash my face, and then I return to the QR to sit beside my sleeping husband. I open my Bible and seek solace.

When Mickey arrives he goes immediately to spend time alone with Mark. I can practically see a battalion of angels follow him as he storms down the hallway, through the open door, ready for battle.

After Mickey leaves, Dave spends time in Mark's room and then I go in to crawl into the plastic chair beside Mark's bed to sleep. I have on my heaviest coat, designed for Minnesota winter, and two fleece sweaters. I pull two light hospital blankets over me and lie shivering. Mark lies on his bed in a hospital gown and no sheet covering him. His dramatic hot flashes, probably caused from the drugs and the fact that he is so heavily cast, cause him to sweat profusely. The only way he can be comfortable is to keep the temperature in his room so cold that it literally feels like walking into a refrigerator.

My peace I give you. Not as the world gives. I manage to doze between beeps from the machines that surround my son's bed.

> John 14:27, "Peace I leave with you; my peace I give you. I do not give to you as the world gives. Do not let your hearts be troubled and do not be afraid."

Wednesday, December 12, 2001

McDonald's coffee cups dot the QR and newspapers are passed around to be read. It is morning with the "family." Some of us still sleep, mouths open, bodies contorted in the torchercliners. Only exhausted people could succumb to sleep in this condition.

I smell fresh oranges and open my eyes to see my torchercliner neighbor, Mr. Lyle, peeling an orange from the basket at his feet. Nearly everyone has baskets of food from caring friends or relatives. The "no food" sign outside the QR has been completely ignored. If there ever was a time to break a rule, it is now.

I rub my eyes lightly. It is hard to wake from my night's sleep of nearly two hours. When I was booted from Mark's room at 5:30 a.m., I came to my torchercliner and finally found sleep. I praise God that I have adapted from my first night in this chair.

I stand to smile at my neighbors and reach for my cosmetic bag. I head to the elevator and press "down." I have discovered the benefit of going down one floor to the restroom in the morning. In the QR we can wait quite some time and then feel the need to hurry because someone else is in line. If I go downstairs, I can use the restroom and still take time to brush my teeth and hair.

I marvel at me. I am so obviously walking in grace. I am a woman who wears makeup for all occasions. Most of my family has not seen me as I look when I awake here in the QR. All of that, vanity, or whatever it may be called, has become so unimportant. To make it through the night, through another day, and to face another unending night…that is the concentration.

I say a prayer that today will be better. Lord, it has to be better. Yesterday was not a valley. It was a deep, deep pit. I sit quietly in my torchercliner to place this day in the hands of Jesus. Dave reaches across to hold my hand and we go before the Lord on behalf of our son.

Today we face the surgery I have so dreaded. At 12:00 p.m. Mark will have surgery to repair the damage done to his face in the impact. It is unthinkable to me that they will be placing metal beside his nose, in his cheek and chin. Unbearable that they will put metal in to support his fractured or collapsed eye socket if the swelling has gone down enough to enable them to work safely in that sensitive area.

Ann-Marie plans to arrive by 9:00 a.m. and we will each go in to see Mark and then Dave and I will leave to go to his house to shower and get something to eat. I did not eat again yesterday until about 9:00 p.m. when we went down to the cafeteria for the first time since we got here. I found soup and jello and

Dave chose a taco. I managed to get about one half a cup of soup down and three or four bites of jello. For me, that was progress. Dave's appetite is poor also, but he manages to eat small amounts at a time during the day.

I look at Dave now as we wait for 9:00 a.m. to come. My precious husband stares into space with his hand over his mouth. He might look as if he is concentrating, but I know him well. He is tormented and suppressing a cry at the least. I can see the sorrow in his eyes and know that he is pressing his hand against his mouth to keep from crying.

I thank God for the light moments that do happen in the midst of tragedy. Mr. Lyle is looking for the front page of the newspaper. Dave has it between him and the man seated next to him because the men pass the newspaper around as any large family would in their living room.

As Mr. Lyle walks around the room to look for the paper, his cell phone rings. He starts searching for it and bends to check a basket of food by his chair. Dave crosses the room and pulls the phone out of Mr. Lyle's back pocket, as he is bent over, to hand it to him. The whole room breaks into laughter. Mr. Lyle's face lights up when he laughs. We have come to love him and his beautiful wife, Marilyn. Each day they faithfully pray for their son, Scott, who is in the trauma ICU.

Yesterday, before we went in to see Mark with a friend, that friend asked, "Where do you put your things when you go in?"

I replied, "I leave them right here"

Carolyn C., who sits near us when she is not visiting her husband, Johnnie, in ICU, smiled at me as I said, "We are all hurting too much to hurt someone else by taking anything."

Carolyn said, "Amen."

Johnnie had an ATV accident. He was working on his land when the vehicle tipped over on top of him and he was unable to free himself. I think they have been here a day or two longer than us.

Across from our chairs, our resident receptionist remains in her role. Her son has been doing quite well, but is now battling nausea. Dave told me he heard that her son was in a truck when it was seared in half by another vehicle and he was unmercifully pulled with the driver's side of the truck as the shift gear imbedded in his thigh.

Life is hard. God is good. This is not a cliché.

"Worry not about tomorrow, for today has enough problems of its own." Mr. Lyle quotes out loud as I sit here, pondering the goodness of a God who would spare our son.

Mr. Lyle often quotes scripture aloud. I believe he draws strength from his confession and he loves to bless anyone who may be listening. I pray that, if anyone is in this place without the Lord by their side, the seed of Mr. Lyle's words will come to rest in their heart. This ordeal would be impossible without the Lord!

I think to myself, *if I have ever thought I was in stress…and I certainly have…I have deceived myself. THIS is stress. THIS is life in the raw. THIS is everyone's coping mechanism grinding its gears.* And my thoughts turn to ministry, and ministering. *THIS is ministry in action as we each reach out to comfort another. This is ministry as Mr. Lyle quotes scripture.*

As each family is called outside the QR to hear the Doctor's report for the day, we observe their reaction to the news through the glass wall. Each person watches the doctor intently. They are looking to see as much as hear what he is telling them. Sometimes they walk through the door with a smile, sometimes in tears and often they simply sink into their chair to gather strength for another day.

Today the Bronson's hope their desperately injured seventeen-year-old son will be strong enough to have a tracheotomy. It is difficult to comprehend that someone can be so weak they cannot have this procedure performed.

Today the Watts' want their son's collapsed lungs to begin to work.

Today the Lyles want their son, Scott, to wake up, and when he does, to have an active and healthy brain.

Today Mr. Hagewood remains in prayer that Cynthia will open her eyes to smile at him.

Today the Williams' pray for Mark as he goes to surgery that will last four to twelve hours and return him with his jaw wired, his nose packed and his cheekbones and chin repaired with metal inserts.

Help us, O Lord, for we cannot do this without You by our side. 2 Cor.12:9 "My grace is sufficient for you, for my power is made perfect in weakness". Lord, we claim your perfect strength in our evident weakness.

———————

On Monday, we met with the maxillofacial surgeon that will operate on Mark today. Two members of his team were in the office with us as he showed us the CT scans along with a model of a jaw. He shared his strategy with us and we tried to follow along. He plans to first wire and stabilize the jaw by inserting bars, pulling to see how the pieces fit and then he will put a plate in Mark's chin. They will then put plates on each side of his nose and insert a screw into his cheekbone, which they will pull to bring the sunken cheekbone back to where it belongs. They are hoping the fracture on the other side of his face will heal on its own when everything else is put back into place. They also hope no plate will be necessary in the right cheekbone.

He asked us to bring a photo of Mark to the meeting, as he needs a picture to reconstruct Mark's face. I handed him the jacket from Mark's *REALITY* CD and he grinned, "We usually don't have such a good picture to work with."

The surgeon regretfully informed us that they will most likely have to wait to do surgery on the right eye. It is too swollen at this time and that affects the ophthalmic nerve. He is not willing to take any risks and we appreciate that.

We like this doctor and his associates and we have total confidence in them. I stifle my fear of Mark waking up with his jaw wired shut, his nose stuffed with packing and his tracheotomy tube gurgling. I try not to think how claustrophobic it could be. Since he has been in ICU he often puts his left hand up when we draw near his bed to say, "Back off!" He gets extremely hot and needs to be fanned as his cheeks turn bright red and sweat beads on his forehead. When that happens he cannot stand to have anyone too near his bed. Will this make it worse?

When we told Mark's friends about the photo there was an animated discussion about giving the doctor pictures of Brad Pitt or George Clooney. It was lighthearted fun, but each of us will be praying that Mark will look like the person we love very soon.

In our briefing this morning we were told that the trauma doctors may cap Mark's trach tube to adjust the size. We understand that would mean Mark will be taking his breaths only through the wired shut mouth. With all my other concerns about this surgery, this news seems more than I can bear for my son.

We pray, selfishly, that his eye will be healed enough for surgery to avoid yet another time in the OR, but we are surrendered to what is best for Mark. The eye looks absolutely awful. Both eyes are huge, swollen purple orbs, but the left one, in question, is a mere slit that opens slightly to reveal blood red where white should be. The iris is a cloudy gray.

I cannot stop tears from sneaking out of my eyes this morning after the briefing though I truly try. Mr. Lyle looks at me and lifts his clenched hand in encouragement, "Come on, and get strong."

I look into his kind smile and weakly say, "If you can be strong, I can be strong."

The people of the QR rise from their chairs and crowd into the hallway to form an orderly line when the hands of the large wall clock reach 8:59 a.m. We are mostly solemn, quiet, and tired. As soon as the red sign outside the first set of double doors changes from "closed" to "open" we file in.

It has been a long time from 5:00 a.m. to 9:00 a.m. Our loved ones have been alone and waiting for us, those who know we are here. Our hearts long for them. Most likely each person in line with us has a prayer on their heart similar to mine, *O, God, help us to give comfort. Help us to be encouraging…hide our sorrow, O, Lord.*

Shortly after we go to see Mark, Dave leaves to make phone calls. I sit beside Mark as two members of the surgeon's team knock on the door and enter the room. I have learned the knock is a courtesy though Mark and I find it quite comical. No patient in these rooms would be capable of answering the door.

One member of this team is a woman. She bends toward Mark and says with a soft voice, laden with accent, "You know me, Mark?"

He nods recognition of an earlier introduction.

"You will now have to do something you will not want to do. This is going to hurt you but we will do it well and only once."

I see the fear well up in his eyes. No, it is not fear, it is terror! But he nods and lifts his hand to motion me out of the room.

He often motions me out when he is about to experience new or deeper pain. I think he does this to protect me as well as himself.

Before I leave the room we are told that they will be taking a mold of Mark's teeth. A substance will be poured that will form in his mouth and then be pulled out in the mold tray. This is a big, big deal when your upper and lower jaws are broken as well as so many other places on your face.

I hurry to the QR and sit by Dave, grateful he is there. We push our chairs tight together and I rest my head against his chest. He holds me as close as he can in that position in that public place. We begin to intercede in prayer and I watch as my sweet husband dissolves in tears.

"How much more can he bear?" He sobs and presses his hand against his mouth to keep the grief from pouring out. He sobs quietly as we hold each other.

It seems quite a long time before the doctors come into the QR to say they have finished the impressions. I hurry to the Step-Down room to see Mark.

He lays there, eyes tightly shut, body tense, but not one remark in writing. When he opens his swollen eyes to look at me it is as if he echoes his father's words, "How much more can I endure?"

I gently wipe the remnants of casting material from his swollen lips and put some Vaseline on them. Then I stand beside his bed without adequate words of comfort.

Ann-Marie arrives with her mother. Pat has taken the day off of work because Ann-Marie's car broke down. There have been difficult obstacles in their way, but they are determined to be with us today.

We have a false start to surgery. As I walk back to Mark's room two smiling black ladies stand outside with a gurney. My heart skips a beat, "Is he going already?" I ask.

They each nod "Yes".

I hurry out to get Dave and Ann-Marie. We give Mark our love and words of encouragement and stand beside his bed to pray for him.

As soon as we do this we hear that he is not going just yet. Here in the Trauma Center, surgeries are often pre-empted by emergency status and, I believe, by the time they will take to complete. We wait, but it is not long before the smiling ladies are back.

"This time we are going," they assure me. "Come with us and wait with him in the holding room."

I am not sure I want to as we have said "see you soon" to Mark a couple of times already today. I don't want to drag it out for him but they are insistent and give me directions, so I head for the elevator when they wheel him off in a different direction.

Dave decides not to come with me as only one person can go in the holding area at a time anyway. The hospital is a maze of hallways and I question if I have chosen the right one until I see the women pushing Mark's gurney ahead of me.

They see me and motion. "Come on, honey, follow us."

I don't know what their title is on a regular day, but today they are angels. They banter and laugh and ease my mind. I am glad for their company and hope the lighthearted conversation they engage in will show Mark this is routine in a place like this.

In the holding room, I want to keep a low profile. I actually just want Mark to know I am there but not to have to see me, but it is not to be with our new friends.

"Here sweetie," one of them says to me and walks over to get a rocking chair. "Sit now."

I pull the chair out of Mark's line of vision and sit to silently pray.

The anesthesiologist comes and talks to Mark and soon he is ready to go to surgery. I cannot stop the rapid beating of my heart. I swallow over and over to keep in the sobs, but I know that I am quite successful in appearing calm. The women have helped in a wonderful way.

When the anesthesiologist leaves, I am ready to exit the opposite direction having already told my son that I love him and will be praying for him. As I stand and turn, hoping to exit quietly, one of the women says, "Come on now, honey, give him some sugar."

I walk to Mark thinking how he would enjoy these women if he were well. I kiss his forehead, say "Love you, son," and walk away.

Mark and I have shared a few goodbyes in our relationship. He travels and has gone to school away from "home." Neither of us likes to say goodbye and neither feels that we are very good at it. Our unspoken understanding as we depart in an airport or a driveway is to give a quick hug, do not speak and turn to walk away. Very simply it is because both of us have tears in our eyes and do not need anything to make the goodbye more difficult. It has been our pattern for years.

In this holding room I turn to walk away quickly and wind my way back to the QR half blinded by tears.

Waiting for loved ones who are in surgery is agony. Mark has had two surgeries, is now in his third and we understand two more await him. We possibly have twelve hours to wait, pray, and try not to wonder how it is going and to push thoughts from our mind of the necessary things that must be done to our son's handsome face. We stay busy but it is a façade. I look at a book or magazine but cannot tell you what I see or read.

I am reading when I see a woman enter the QR. She is alone, in shock with horror written all over her face and I am drawn to her. I watch her for a moment as she paces. It appears she wants to sit but she cannot decide if she should or not. My stomach turns. The look of a new arrival to the QR is heart-rending.

She sits hard in a chair in the center of the crowded room, and in just seconds I am in the chair next to her. Truly it feels as if a magnetic force has pulled me to her. "Are you alone?"

"Yes." She looks at me with tear-filled eyes. I press Kleenex into her hand. "Did you just get here?"

"Yes. With my husband. In the ambulance."

"Is someone coming to be with you?"

"My parents were following us." She looks around as though she expects to see them.

"Mrs. McGregor." A nurse calls her name.

The pretty woman looks up in absolute terror. "Yes?"

The nurse directs her to the little room between the QR and double doors that I call the briefing room.

"May I come with you?" I ask her.

"Would you?"

"Of course."

We follow the nurse into the tiny private room and sit beside each other on the sofa to listen to the nurse explain that this room is for people who are waiting to hear initial news of their loved ones condition.

When the nurse leaves us alone we exchange names and I hold Brenda as she cries. I learn that her husband, Roger, had been robbed and beaten on the head with a hammer.

I tell her my son is in surgery right now and will be for some time, so I am free to wait with her as long as she needs me. It takes only moments before we are each professing our belief in Jesus and praying together. When her parents arrive, I leave the room after giving her a warm hug. I cannot understand why such a precious woman has to suffer so.

Dave and I sit talking with friends when we see Mark's surgeon walk into the QR. It has taken about five hours for the surgery. I look up to see him with a fraction of a second of fear as to why he is here so soon. My fears are allayed by his countenance. He is absolutely beaming. The look on his face is so welcome that I am up and out of my chair and hugging him before he can walk as far as our chairs. He sits in a chair across from us to tell us it has gone very well.

Mark will be quite uncomfortable with the jaw wired, the nose packed and the tracheotomy opening capped off, but it has been successful. This doctor, who seemed reserved at first, as most doctors in these dire conditions are, now seems like a warm friend. We have grown to care very much about him and hold him in our prayers each night along with Mark's orthopedic surgeon.

So many things are hard to express. The way I feel as I approach Mark's room after this surgery is one of them. Gratitude floods my heart that the surgeon is pleased with his work, but fear grips me as I wonder how Mark will look and, mostly, how he will deal with the difficult breathing when his nose is packed, his jaw wired shut and his tracheotomy opening capped.

He is awake when Dave and I enter the room. Relief floods me when I do not see stitches and bandages all over his swollen face. We have been prepared that his face could be as swollen as it had been initially. It certainly is swollen, but not as bad as the first night. Somehow, I sense immediately that he will be okay with this post op.

Mark absolutely thrills me when, in writing, he asks Ann-Marie to go to his house and get him some CDs. She assures him that she will bring in her boom box along with the CDs he requested this afternoon.

We manage to get through the afternoon and Dave walks in the room as I fan Mark. Once again I have on two sweaters and my warmest "Minnesota coat" and I still shiver as I fan my son.

"Mark, do you want mom to stay with you tonight again?" Dave asks.

I know Dave wants to hear a "no", because he is hoping I will sleep one night in a bed and catch up on some rest. I am aware he cares for my health in the midst of all the concern for Mark.

Mark nods; "Yes," he does want me to stay in the room with him. Then he grins in the best fashion possible with a wired jaw in a swollen face and signals to write.

"She snores," he prints on the board Dave holds for him.

That's my boy. Back to teasing as he always has. It is a true moment of happiness.

I ask Mark if he can have visitors as there are people in the QR hoping to see him and others have called to see if they can come to see him. Once again he makes the circular motion in the air with his left hand that means he needs to write something.

"Visitors come now if want." He rests and then lifts his hand from the board to print again, "Few mins no emotion cry laugh."

He wants to see his friends but is fearful they will make him laugh or cry. It is far too painful to laugh or cry and it produces phlegm that needs to be suctioned out of his trach opening. It is an awful process as they stick the long tube down his neck and suction. He coughs hard yet no sound emerges but a pitiful muffled noise. When I see and hear it I feel as if my heart will shatter.

For me, this moment when Mark wants to see his friends is a dream after the despair of yesterday and the dread of today's surgery. God does answer prayer. I know He will restore Mark to accomplish all He has ordained for him to do.

I offer praise that is less sacrificial than it was twenty-four hours ago. *Thank you, Jesus! Praise Your Holy Name! I honor and adore You for this moment of hope and promise!*

> *Psalm 34:17 and 18, "The righteous cry out, and the Lord hears them; he delivers them from all their troubles. The Lord is close to the brokenhearted and saves those who are crushed in spirit."*

Thursday, December 13, 2001

I awake in the QR at 4:00 a.m. I have a dread of sleeping in the step-down room with Mark though I have been staying in there because he has not been sleeping and I think it eases his mind to have someone beside him. There is a chair in there that has a type of extension on it if you break it into two pieces. It is vinyl and the extension moves as I lie in it and I slide down the chair continuously. Because I don't want to disturb Mark, I lie in awkward positions until a nurse comes in to perform some duty and then I feel I can slide my body back into a more normal position.

With Mark's need to have the room air conditioned at all times, even with two blankets, two sweaters and my winter coat I shiver all night. So when he was given sleeping medication last night, and it seemed I could sleep in the QR and wake hourly to check on him, I did just that.

Now as I peek in the slightly opened door, as I have many times during the night, he turns his head toward me. I enter the room and hand him the dry marker board.

"Have not slept." He writes.

"Not at all?"

He shakes his head.

"Oh, Mark, I am so sorry. They gave you the sleeping pill and I hoped you would sleep."

I feel guilty that I have caught short segments of sleep over the last few hours while he was wondering why I was not in the room.

I swallow fear as I look to see they have hooked a bag of blood to his IV. Someone else's blood is dripping into Mark's body. I don't say anything to him but decide to ask a nurse as soon as possible why this is necessary.

I have only begun to read the Christmas Story in Luke to Mark when a nurse comes in to give him insulin. It will counter the high amount of glucose he receives through the IV.

I motion to the bag of blood, knowing Mark cannot see it behind his head. "When did they hook that up?" I ask.

"It is something they do often after facial surgery. Facial surgery involves a lot of bleeding and Mark's blood count determined he needed it."

Mark does not ask what we are talking about and I do not say more.

The male nurse also adjusts the ice bags that surround Mark's face and then turns to close the door behind him.

At the motion of Mark's left hand, I move to adjust the bags further by propping small pillows under them. The swelling looks better today.

"Tell me a story." Mark writes, "Like a little child...so I can sleep."

He is desperate to sleep. His body is full of high doses of medication which I would think would make him sleepy but even the sleeping pill they gave him last night had no effect. I am not sure when he slept last.

It has been a long time since I told a bedtime story. I pick up my Bible and resume reading the Christmas story, speaking in a quiet slow voice that I hope will soothe Mark. It seems to be working when we are interrupted by the respiratory tech who wants to look at Mark's trach opening.

When he leaves, Mark communicates he needs prayer. As I stand beside his bed on the left side, he reaches for my hand and puts it on his left leg, which is covered by a cast and immobilizer. He places his hand on mine. He is asking me to pray for his leg.

I remind him the doctors and nurses refer to him as "miracle man" and then I begin to praise God for all the things we trust Him for. Soon I am interceding with confidence, speaking with authority the promises of God and commanding the broken parts of Mark's body to heal. Suddenly Mark raises his left hand and begins to move it back and forth in emphasis of the words I am praying. It is evident Mark is fervently praying with me.

I move around to the other side of the bed and begin to pray specifically for his knee, then his feet, his other leg, the pelvis, hip, tailbone, bruised groin area, arm, wrist, hand and shoulder. We pray intently and specifically, praising God for the many things that did not happen in the crash and praying for repair and restoration for all that did happen. Mark makes a fist in the air and moves his hand each time I address an area in need of healing. He cannot speak but there is no doubt he is in spiritual warfare.

We have been praying that Mark will be strengthened in his mind and in intimacy with his heavenly Father. Now he wants me to pray for his mind. He has me hold up the dry board and he writes. "Pray for mind Satan playing with images"

I question him and find he is battling hallucination. It seems that earlier today he requested that the nurse ask all the people around his bed leave the room. The nurse assured him that no one was in his room.

We rebuke side effects of the morphine, other potent pain medication and whatever is in the mixture of IVs entering his body. We direct any medication to "Do what you were designed to do and nothing else!" Then we pray for his ears because he feels he is not hearing to full potential. We command the fractures around his ears to heal.

There is a large ice bag that wraps around Mark's head and I cannot touch anywhere on his head, but we pray for his face and his jaw. When we finish addressing the many injured areas, we move into praise. I am blessed by his determination to be part of this prayer time.

I watch Mark's countenance change as he offers praise to God, lifting his left arm. When we finish I stand in awe of the experience I have just shared with my son. I literally witnessed his faith take hold! I literally saw him determine to believe he can be healed and I was privileged to watch as he gave Satan the boot.

I am positive we have just uncovered the key to Mark's recovery. He has used every ounce of strength he has to agree with me in prayer. He is spent but at peace.

"The prayer of a righteous man is powerful and effective"...thank you Lord that we are righteous because of the blood you shed for us.

When a nurse comes in to tend to Mark, I go to the QR and sit with Dave. Only minutes later Becki arrives. She requests time alone with Mark and we know he will welcome that.

Sometime later we see the scooter move down the hall and maneuver with aptness around the crowded room to our chairs. We smile at this friend we love so much. She is smiling also and wants to share with us what she felt led to speak to Mark about. She told him that many people know Christ in His life, in miracles and signs and wonders, but few can relate to Him in his suffering and receive the power of the resurrection. Her words are profound and overflowing with encouragement. She tells us she also got "in his face" about staying tough.

As soon as Becki leaves I return to Mark's room. I sit quietly as Mark dozes, tired from his spiritual adventure. I know the words Becki has spoken are true and I know Mark has embraced them. I sit back and sigh heavily. Kingdom work can be exhausting.

We are allowed two passes that are clipped to our clothing when we go in to see Mark. When only one of us is in the room we try to keep a pass available at the nurse's station so that one of Mark's friends can come back if Mark feels able to have visitors. I am talking to Pastor Jim on the phone in Mark's room when Brian uses one of those passes to poke his head in the door to see if he can enter. I motion him in.

Because one of Mark's greatest fears is that his friends will make him laugh or cry, when I hear laughter I look up from my place in the corner. I smile at the delightful double standard Mark has established. A feeling of joy washes over me to see that Mark has written something on the board that has Brian laughing.

Many of the non-injury issues Mark must deal with are traumatic. For instance, he is wearing a diaper and that is not something a young man his age wants to do. He cannot use a bedpan because of the hip and pelvic injuries and he has a Foley Catheter.

He must deal with excruciating pain because his groin area has not been spared the trauma of the impact. Between Mark and me, these are topics of urgency and he must share his misery because he would rather have me help in an emergency situation than one of the nurses. We deal with these invasions on his privacy and modesty because we must and we are under grace to do whatever must be done to make him comfortable.

These topics are handled differently with Brian. Mark is using the gift of his strong sense of humor to entertain Brian regarding these affronts. I am more than grateful they can be blunt and find humor in what could be humiliation.

The humor was a delight but it is an up and down day. I am very aware if there is an up in a day, it will dip at some point. This is truly not a negative statement as much as a realistic observation.

After being given medication through his mouth syringe, Mark goes into a coughing fit and is racked with pain. To present this picture will explain the nightmare of a simple cough: Mark is in a hospital bed, he is hooked up to numerous monitors that continuously make noise. The lower half of his face is packed in ice. His right foot is so badly damaged it is still too swollen for surgery; the left leg is fully cast from the foot to the thigh and immobilized so he is unable to bend it even slightly. His pelvis and left hip have newly inserted pins and screws in them and his tailbone causes excruciating pain at the slightest jostle. His groin area sustained a violent trauma in the crash and is the cause of debilitating pain with any unexpected movement. His right shoulder, wrist and hand are cast and strapped to his chest so they do not move. The tracheotomy along with the broken and wired upper and lower jaw and broken nose stuffed with packing, will not allow him to feel as though he ever takes a completed breath. While he is highly medicated, any unexpected or sudden pain does not appear to be controlled by the morphine.

With that in mind one can only imagine how a cough will cause jarring to these vulnerable areas bringing pain that contorts his face and causes tears to run down his cheeks. To add to the agony, a nurse will usually appear because his coughing shows up on the monitor. They will see if he coughs in a successful manner and, if not, they will produce an extremely long tube and put it into the hole in his neck and move it around to suction. He will then be forced to cough, jarring the injured areas to a point of unbearable pain.

I can see it begin to happen; the realization that a cough is inevitable. His countenance changes, dissolves. His eyes fill with the fear of a trapped animal. He would cry out if he had a voice. He begins to breathe in a controlled fashion. It is a desperate attempt to ward off the cough that must happen to keep his lungs healthy. I turn to the door and he puts up a hand to warn me to wait.

He is saying, "Do not call a nurse and do not come near."

He takes a breath and coughs hard, really hard and, though there is no noise to the cough itself, I hear something come up in the tube. This time he made the decision not to fight. He intentionally caused himself pain to get a good result and I recognize the bravery of his decision.

He rests back into the bed, his face full of torment. I see his left hand, the only moveable limb reach into the air. He is calling on the Lord. I watch as the Lord moves Mark into a place of tolerable pain and less fear.

What I just witnessed is one of the most courageous things I have ever seen. For two days he has fought with all he has to resist any impulse to cough. It is a process that pulls him into a deep pit of fear each time it happens. As awful as it is, he has been told that it is something the body needs to do to clear the lungs. This time I watched him face it head on and go for the result that would be best in the long run, though causing greater pain for the moment. I watched him put his hand up for strength from The One who truly can give it to him.

I look at him in wonder. From his earliest years I have delighted in him. He has had great accomplishments, but this one I am more proud of than any other. I feel sure I would not have found the courage to do what he just did. I am so encouraged because I know there is a fight ahead and now I am certain that Mark is equal to it.

A nurse comes in and Mark nods that "yes" he will have lunch. Lunch is a can of Ensure and his utensil is a tube connected to a wide syringe. The nurse demonstrates how to fill it and then place the rubber tube alongside his gum line and then release the liquid by pushing on the syringe. I wonder how he will ever do it with one hand, the left one at that. But Mark gives the nurse a "thumbs up" and she leaves.

He lies there, gathering strength, willing courage. He is quiet and I know he is praying to be able to accomplish this new task. I want to scream. I truly do. I certainly want to jump in and do it for him. With just the tiniest bit of liquid released from the syringe I see that he needs to cough.

I move toward him as I see him fumble on the bed for the call button. He puts his hand up. I am not to come over to help him. He rings and the nurse comes in. She inserts the long suction device down the hole in his neck to clean his lungs. I see the blood and sputum come out of it and hear the horrid sound of a cough with no voice behind it.

It is not about me. If it was about what I can endure I would dissolve right now and curl into a fetal position in a warm dark corner and retreat from the world until my insides quit quaking and my stomach stopped churning. It is about my son who has endured great injustice. I remind myself it is about our faith and this opportunity to grow.

After resting, Mark tackles the syringe again with the same determination he has shown in every obstacle of this ordeal.

It is Thursday night or Friday morning when I reach for my journal in the near-dark and write, "I would be certain I was in hell if God did not hold my hand."

I struggle to find a comfortable spot on this vinyl chair. I am dressed in many layers topped off by my furry winter coat and my teeth have literally begun to chatter. If my son was not in such a desperate place I would not be able to physically endure the stress. Quite simply how I feel must not matter. I decide to write about it because it is part of the story but the reality is that it means nothing compared to the place Mark is in.

It is a challenge to not move in the squeaky vinyl chair but I do not want to take a chance that Mark will wake if he has managed to doze. We are struggling. He has not slept in over twenty-four hours. I know that from Friday to Friday I have slept an interrupted and accumulative total of between seventeen to twenty hours. My body aches and I realize that if I were home I would consider myself ill. I have only to lift my eyes to the bed beside me to know we are operating under grace. I cannot imagine what Mark is enduring though I am with him constantly.

I am praying for him absolutely every moment and have new understanding of Paul's exhortation in The Word to pray without ceasing. In the dim light I see him lift his hand to put his trust in God but I hear his breathing become labored and I know he is fighting tears. He refuses to cry; it robs his energy and causes him to cough but I wonder how long he can war against it. He is desperate for sleep. If he were given one wish at this point, aside from total healing, I believe it would be to sleep.

Occasionally he drifts into a light sleep and it seems the moment that happens a bright light covers the room as someone walks in. They stick him in his finger, arm or hip and change his catheter or IV bags. The door is beside the foot of the bed so there is no way to protect him from the light though we have tried by placing washcloths over his eyes. That did not work because Mark was too hot with the cloths over his eyes. We will have to live with the unexpected bursts of light.

Hebrews 13:6, "The Lord is my helper; I will not be afraid."

Friday, December 14, 2001

Today they hooked up another blood transfusion. I hate the look of the bags of red liquid hanging above Mark's head and the tubes that remind me he is receiving blood that is not his own. The liquid is cold and it can make him chilled as it enters his body.

The nurse that has just come into the room takes a few minutes to change his catheter bag and to straighten the part of the trach tube that hangs down beside the bed so it does not make the awful tapping noise I dread hearing. Without a word, she takes care of business and then closes the door to leave us in a dimmer light.

I lay as if I am asleep but I suspect Mark knows I am awake. I am certain he has not slept yet. "How can it be? Why?" My body jerks to attention and I hope I have not spoken aloud, though I would most likely be echoing Mark's own thoughts. I cannot go there. I must not continue on this line of thought.

"Trust." When I hear that word in my spirit, I whisper it into the night. If Mark hears it perhaps he will be comforted as I am. *Help me Lord, so I can encourage! So we can overcome!*

I pick up my journal and pen that are perched on my rib cage and write, "The days are endless; the nights are twice as long." And then, because writing is a coping mechanism for me, I write a poem or possible song lyric and title it, *Endless Night.*

> Midnight moves to touch
> Dawn that can't be found
> I whisper prayers to calm my fear
> Mercy gaining ground
>
> Desperate hours have built
> A fence around my pain
> And silence roars with questions
> No one can explain
>
> When harsh hours don't end, and pain and sorrow blend
> To rob me of my day, you will hear me say
>
> I can't see you, I can't hear you
> In this endless night
> I can't touch you, I can't feel you
> As I struggle toward some light
>
> But I believe in faith that needs no sight
> And I know you're the answer, Jesus, to this endless night

It must be near the time for morning rounds when I notice Mark's eyes are open. It is easy to tell because I can see his long lashes silhouetted in the soft light from the IV unit.

If there has been a question if we are under vicious spiritual attack, I would wonder no more when Mark signals to write "Can't take much more."

I hold his hand and say, "You can, son, because you are on the other side of this." I massage his hand and start to speak peace to his facial features, which are pinched tight in pain and despair. I speak to his feet and work my way up his body, instructing every part to be strong and well made and healed in the name of Jesus. I speak in a relaxing tone; one that I hope will impart sleep to my precious son. I see his countenance relax; the eyebrows unlock their tight knit, the fear-filled eyes close.

Mark chooses to accept the words of peace given to me by the Lord. He is so hot that his hair is wet. I stand beside him fanning and praying in a soothing tone until I think he may be asleep. Finally I tiptoe to my chair to get off my feet and rest, but I barely make it past his bed when another infusion beeper sounds. The buzzers are relentless! The door swings open to the bright hallway and someone comes in to change the bags.

I look at Mark and smile. He is choosing to hold on to the peace we worked so hard to usher in. I see him try to stay where he is at as another beeper sounds loud in his ear. Beep! Beep! Beep!

I long to put my feet up but decide not to lie down in the chair. If I do not angle into it right it will collapse and make noise. My head aches for a pillow and I desire to close my eyes. I slide into the chair sideways and stay in a sitting position. I will not do anything to compromise the peace he has surrendered to. I take my comfort in watching him rest. *Hang in there, Mark. Stay there. Stay in the peace you have finally found!*

Beep! Beep! Beep!

I would scream but someone would probably come and take me away to a padded room on another floor. I feel as if a vegetable grater has been taken to my emotions and scraped them raw, and though it would produce relief, screaming is not an option. Like my beautiful son, I have no voice to express myself right now.

A tech comes in to check Mark's trach. He hates it so! We keep telling him how good it is that he has it; that there are people in ICU that are praying to get strong enough to have one. But it does not change the fact that it is ugly, uncomfortable, awkward, frightening. It is a hole in his throat surrounded by plastic and covered with a wide piece of clear plastic that he continuously fidgets with to get better air intake. It rubs and irritates the tender skin of his throat. The longer piece is connected to a hose that hangs beside his bed and when water becomes trapped in it, it makes the drumming, pounding noise that sounds like a warning signal. "stress, stress, stress, stress". I have grown to deplore that sound.

He coughs and pain racks his body as blood and sputum shove their way out the plastic around the hole in his throat. A nurse enters the room and offers morphine. Mark lays back and gladly accepts the drug that allows him to cope with the horrible, hideous state of his body.

I wait for anger to close in like strangling hands on my throat. Somehow it does not and I recognize mercy. I must be positive at all costs. I must tell Mark that he will survive this and somehow good will come of it. I must believe that myself!

The faceless image of the drunk driver haunts me. She weaves herself into my thoughts to compromise my struggle for sanity in an insane situation. It seems a revelation to me that someone chose a weapon to injure my son. Just as someone would put one bullet after another into a gun and take it with them to a destination where it could cause devastation, a woman put one drink after another into her body and got in her car to drive. We have been told that her blood alcohol content had to be very high as there were no skid marks. She was fully in his lane and never tried to stop.

It is confirmed that she had minor injuries and left the hospital in a short amount of time. I allow myself to realize she was on a mission to destroy, herself or someone innocent. I find myself thinking that she set out to kill, maim and devastate. My instincts tell me that I can't harbor anger, yet it sits at my feet like a pet begging for attention!

Oh, Lord! I force the angry thoughts from my mind and turn to Christ. *Greater is He who is in me than he who is in the world.*

It is an evil place we dwell in, full of people who make wicked and selfish decisions with no thought of the consequences of innocent people. *But You, oh Lord, You are greater. Be my strength and take control of my thoughts!*

I am at war and reliant on the Holy Spirit within me to protect me from dangerous thinking. I draw strength from Mark also. His body is in torment but his mind has escaped the wrath and rampage of anger.

Together we have determined to praise God for what did not happen because it is too painful to think of what actually has happened. We praise God there is no brain, spinal cord or severe internal organ injury. We claim healing in Jesus' name and set our minds on the task ahead.

Mark is brave, so very brave and kind. His smile is frozen by metal wires, but when the doctors come in to talk to him he moves his left hand to shake theirs. When the physical therapist comes to inform him that he will go to live in a rehabilitation hospital where he will learn to clothe himself, to eat, to move and eventually to walk, but that he will be in a wheelchair for quite some time, this man who was totally independent one week ago, puts his thumb up to let her know he understands.

One week ago Mark worked a double shift at a restaurant. He was able to take a shower and go to the bathroom on his own; he worked out on his weight bench, made his own bed, and did his own dishes. On that fateful night he was able to write songs at a keyboard, and pick up a phone and talk with his parents. He was able to walk out the door of his home to get into his car, to go shopping and to dinner with his girlfriend, to make plans for Christmas and to flash a smile that lit up a room.

Now he uses the only limb he can move to lift his left thumb in the air as if to say, "Yes, I will have the surgeries, I will do the rehabilitation and use a wheelchair. Yes, I will fight. Just help me. I want to have more than one limb that moves, to breathe out of my nose and without a tracheotomy tube, to chew food, to sit up, move, walk to the bathroom, to see out of clear, non-swollen eyes, to hug. I want the pain to go away! I want to be whole again!"

We never did leave the hospital yesterday and so today, when Mark has friends to stay with him, Dave and I leave to go to Mark's house to shower and nap for two hours. Becki has spent time with us today and says she will call the house at 8 p.m. to wake us.

In spite of how tired we have been, we are awake and dressing to return to the hospital when Becki phones with our "Wake-up" call. Our place, for now, is at the hospital.

Jim Hagewood greets us with a solemn expression when we walk off the elevator. "I have some bad news. We lost someone here today."

We have only been gone a couple of hours! Our minds run over the list of those we have grown to care about during this intense time. *Who? Who took such a turn today?*

"The Bronson's boy," Jim says with tears in his eyes.

Oh, Lord. Lord this is a hurting world. There is an obscene concentration of pain in this room, on this floor of this hospital. The young man was seventeen years old. His injuries were internal. These are words and information. Just words and information that have now manifested themselves in ultimate pain for his parents.

I sit hard into a chair. His parents are beautiful people, young, attractive and friendly. The mother seems quiet but the father, who looks like a football player, has a ready smile that reveals a bright spirit. We have shared a quiet laugh or two and he is always upbeat as he returns from seeing his son.

Father! In my mind I see Mr. Bronson's smile greet me as we pass in the hall, I hear him ask, "How are you today?"

Now I wonder how he did it. How did he smile? Did he believe for the best? Did he know this was a probability? Are we all living in denial?

I sit with the others in this room in reverent and stunned silence. *This is tough, Lord, I can't bear to watch this kind of pain.* I cling to the hope that we have a future with Mark. We have our son. He is alive. We can touch him and talk to him. With that in mind, I decide that we can endure this trial.

Psalm 48:14, "For this God is our God for ever and ever; he will be our guide even to the end."

Saturday, December 15, 2001

What an unbearable morning! How do people survive without the Lord? Every place on Mark's body is uncomfortable. I pray this will change soon. It is so awful to helplessly observe the state he is in!

His trach opening is still capped and his nose full of packing. He must breathe out of his mouth, through the wires, which involves a sort of sucking in through the teeth. A front tooth is fractured and he wrote that it "hates air." Sometimes the sucking is quick, like a panting dog. His body shakes with it.

Mark may look more frightened than he actually is because his right eye has white around it now and looks wide and full of fear compared to the left eye which is still blood red with the iris an unhealthy opaque gray color. The damaged eye appears small next to the wide frightened eye that can see.

As I write in my journal he is given a stool softener. It seems as if every part of his body that functioned on its own before the crash needs help now. The softener is foul tasting and he has had to take it several times. He takes the plastic cup in his left hand and, with some help, maneuvers the straw to his mouth. He steadies himself in preparation for the taste. It is not the same as taking foul tasting medicine that can be followed by a glass of water. The obnoxious taste will linger until a syringe of water is slowly released into his mouth.

This time as he swallows something goes wrong! It goes down the wrong way and he tries to sit up as any choking person would, but of course he cannot. His eyes grow wide and wild and he coughs releasing the terrible, helpless and breathless trach noise. His nurse sees what is happening and pushes the button to lift his head slightly. She cannot lift him to a sitting position because of his other injuries.

"It's okay, honey," she says gently, "frightening, but you will be okay. You've swallowed wrong. Let's try to cough and then I'll suction. Your lungs don't need stool softener."

She works with him until he can get a breath, and then turns to me. "Scary for mom." She smiles.

"Yes." I say quietly.

Someday I will cry. I will just start and not stop. But not today.

The nurse leaves and Mark takes over. He motions me to the sink for water. He tries to sip a little at a time through the syringe to gain control. He uses controlled breathing exercises learned from years of voice classes. It takes more than half an hour of the breathing, sipping and suctioning before he feels it is under control and he can lie quietly. I am relieved when the horrible, pitiful noise ceases. I think the noise was Mark's effort to clear his throat.

He writes in the air and I bring his tablet. "Morphine sleep."

"She gave you morphine again?" I ask.

He nods.

I am thankful the nurse recognized the pain brought on by coughing.

Because of that episode, Mark's breathing is labored and he is sweaty. I take a towel from beside the sink and, with his permission; I wipe his forehead and arm with it.

He closes his eyes and I stand beside him and pray. "Peace. The peace of Jesus, peace and calm, peace and calm in Jesus' name." I repeat that phrase quietly and slowly for a very long time until I see him become relaxed and finally, mercifully, he sleeps!

Mark has waited four days for sleep to come. I watch him and continue to pray. Soon my eyelids feel very heavy but I continue to stand beside his bed as though I can guard his sleep.

Mark has slept nearly a half an hour! That is the longest time outside of surgery in the past four days. I am so relieved and nearly ready to sit down when his nurse pokes her head in the door with a tray. "They just brought this."

The tray holds a can of Boost and some apple juice. He has been hungry and waiting for it to arrive but now he looks at me and I can see dilemma in his expression.

"Just stay there," I encourage. "Stay in the peace. You can eat later."

He closes his eyes and sleeps a little longer. When he wakes we try to clean his teeth. It is hard to manipulate the foam tipped stick around the narrow area outside the wires. He motions for me to put Vaseline on his lips first. Then I take the sponge and ask him to snare his lips as a dog would so I can begin the slow and painful process.

As I dip the sponge into a medicated mouthwash and prepare to be gentle in manipulating it around the front of Mark's teeth, I have flashbacks to a time when he was capable of almost anything, certainly brushing his teeth. I ache to see his warm, easy smile and feel the precious strength in his hug. I ache to leave the pain of silent greetings behind. For anyone who would watch, I am busy with this preparation, but my thoughts wander as I realize I am consumed by desire to hear his voice.

I lean in with the sponge and his mouth forms the word "No." This time he wants to "brush" himself. I hear the little moans of pain that keep escaping as he carefully and thoroughly works to clean his teeth.

In his "normal" life Mark is a very clean, well-groomed man. It must add to the hell to not be able to brush the backside of your teeth, comb your hair or feel the pleasure of a shower. Once the difficult task is accomplished, Mark decides to try food. I remind him that lunch will arrive soon.

Mark motions to write. "We need to open it." He points to the tray containing Boost and juice that he had requested earlier and then writes again. "Feel bad if haven't tried."

I am a kind person but I have wondered often in the past if I am as fair as Mark is, if I am as considerate. I pull the tray over and discover there is some oatmeal. I take it to the microwave at the nurse's station when we decide Mark will try to eat it. It is watered down and I add still more water mixing it until it is liquid enough to go into the syringe. But it is still too much texture for him.

"Water!" He mouths the word.

It is urgent. I give him the syringe that I have learned to keep ready and full of water. He sips until he feels in control again. We try the Boost drink. That does not go down well either. He falls back and closes his eyes.

I encourage him to draw on the peace he receives when we pray. I remind him it is available whenever he needs it because it is of the Holy Spirit. For now, the food is not as important as the rest. We will rely on the IV that is continuously nourishing his body.

I try to place a small pillow beside his face to prevent his neck from aching, but I hear the sucking sound that means the light weight of the pillow hurts.

Mark manages to drift to sleep again, bless God. I watch the pillow he had folded in two against the side of his head. It moves as he breathes and I pray it will not unfold and startle him awake.

This sleep is good news. Earlier today, in desperation for sleep, I taped a "No Visitors" sign on the door and now I feel some concern about it because friends are planning on driving from Indiana sometime this weekend. I hope by the time they arrive Mark will feel able to see visitors.

I look up from my journal to see the pillow that had been beside Mark's head perched on his legs. His eyes are open and he is practicing breathing techniques. I ask what he needs and he motions for water.

He has to "psych" himself first by controlling his breathing until it is even and he does not feel a need to cough. Then I hand him the prepared syringe and he takes it. It is not easy to control the syringe and push the pump with only one hand but he is determined to master it. He takes a couple of sips and it is okay.

Mark and I take a few minutes to communicate but he is tired and I encourage him to continue to sleep since he is having some success. I am relieved when he closes his eyes. For him, because he needs sleep, for me, because I am always concerned he will see how I truly feel.

Lord, please don't let him see how desperate I am when I see him gasp for air or how helpless I feel when the tiny moans of pain escape him.

I wonder if Mark knows he has become a hero to me. He is brave, strong of spirit and capable. I look at him and feel certain I could never do what he is doing. From my chair I watch him. I must move my neck forward to see past the machines that are between him and the chair that is my bed. He opens his eyes and I see him suck air in and let it out in a cleansing breath. I am so thankful that he understands breathing. I think of having the worst cold imaginable with your nose blocked, throat swollen and sore and then I add having the jaw wired, a broken shoulder, wrist, hand, pelvis, hip, bruised tailbone and groin area, busted kneecap and both feet absolutely smashed...try to breathe, try to take a sip of water from a syringe, try to remain positive.

When a nurse comes in, Mark writes that his head is stuck to the pillow. The nurse lifts his head and says, "Sure enough, it's stuck because you have lots of little cuts on the back of your head."

Mark looks at us as if to ask, "What caused so many cuts on the back of my head?"

"That explains the CDs," Dave says. "Did you have a box in the back seat of the car?"

Mark writes that he did. He had recently sung at a conference and had a partially full box of 100 on the back seat.

"When I took pictures of the car I noticed several of your *REALITY* CDs on the front seat and floor; all broken. They must have hit you on the back of your head."

Mark motions to write, "Save those CDs, Dad. I want them."

Dave and I leave Mark's room to confer with the trauma surgeon. While we are in the hallway for our morning briefing, Dave asks the surgeon if he can see Mark's x-rays.

"Do you think you really want to?" The doctor asks.

When he asks that question I remember how Dave had to fight for control when we saw the CT scan of Mark's head with all the cracks and fractures, etc. I silently agree with the doctor that he should not see them, but Dave insists. The doctor shrugs and turns with a motion for Dave to follow him.

I am very appreciative of all the doctors here and have a great respect for this trauma surgeon who performed the emergency tracheotomy on Mark. Occasionally, after a briefing, Dave has expressed concern that I may have been offended by the curt report we received and the matter-of-fact communication of this man. But I find those very things comforting. I see, by the kindness in his eyes, that he cares but that he is in a mode of urgency all the time. People are dying and he cannot stop it from happening. I recognize that we are on the good news end of things when we receive a quick report.

After what I refer to as our "yucky" morning, the afternoon seems smoother. Mark has managed to get some Ensure liquid down and has rested.

He asked me for the Fantasy Football sheets that Matt brought to the hospital a couple of days ago. Fantasy Football…I never thought I would be so grateful for this game I do not understand. Both of our sons enjoy this game where they can choose their own team of players and exercise their competitive spirits.

The distraction is a blessing but not entirely effective because as Mark attempts to watch TV, it is hard for him to see the game and the light from the television set bothers his eyes. He drifts in and out of sleep and struggles to listen, if not watch. There is frustration in the attempt to watch this sport he enjoys so much, but I am encouraged that he knows the game is on and wants to attempt to watch.

Dave has convinced me to make a quick McDonald's run to get out of the room. It is right across the hospital lobby so we will not be gone long. I am pleasantly surprised that the hamburger I order tastes good and I am able to eat almost half of it with some fries.

I admit to my husband and to myself that it was good to get away but as I walk in the door to Mark's room I am astonished to see, of all things, the telephone receiver on his bed!

My immediate reaction is, what fool did this? I guess the phone rang and they gave the receiver to him.

Mark can "talk" today because of a new cap on his trach, but he can manage only a few words and they come out as a hoarse whisper. He wants to conserve his voice for when it is needed. It seems that no one thought ahead to the end of the conversation when Mark would be alone in the room. How was he supposed to hang up the receiver?

It is obvious the experience frustrated Mark when he motions to write. "You need to be here one of you all the time."

It is true! Someone must always be with Mark.

Mark has requested that I restrict visitors for awhile but when our good friend, Greg Long, stops by with his wife, Janna, I walk to Mark's room with Greg, confident that Mark will want to see him.

The QR news of the day reveals that the Watts' son got his tracheotomy yesterday and they report to our group that they saw immediate improvement. Their son recognized his wife and blew her a kiss. The family has been here from South Carolina for about twenty-six days and we rejoice with them that today their son was able to sit up. We understand that it was a frightening moment for all of them but they report that it went well.

Mr. and Mrs. Lyle went home for the night and a friend stayed in their place. They looked so refreshed when they came back and greeted everyone with hugs as though they had been gone more than a few hours. They only live 60 miles from here, and yet they stay every night in the torchercliners. *Lord heal their son, Scott!*

Tonight we were blessed with visitors once again. Chris, Carole, Becki and some of Mark's Grille friends came to spend time with Mark. The staff comments often that Mark has more visitors than any patient they have seen before. Our friends in the Quiet Room make similar comments. Mark has always been blessed with good friends and we have never been more grateful for that than we are now.

Lord, I am beginning to see the process of "sowing and reaping" in your kingdom in a new light. For years I have prayed for peace and comfort for the people involved whenever I see or hear an ambulance. And when my son needed peace and comfort in that horrible situation, You were there. For years we have made relationships our priority and now You give us great comfort through relationships. Open my eyes, Lord, to see how I can sow into others lives that they may experience this incredible overflow of love that You lavish on us.

> Isaiah 49:13, "Shout for joy, O heavens; rejoice, O earth; burst into song, O mountains! For the Lord comforts his people and will have compassion on his afflicted ones."

Sunday, December 16, 2001

Ann-Marie arrives early to stay with Mark and Dave and I leave to go to Mark's house for a couple of hours. Our plan has been to each take a quick shower and change our clothing, but my husband looks exhausted so we probably will sleep for awhile.

It is hard to leave Mark when I know he would prefer we stay with him all the time, but I am trying to listen to advice from Becki's mom. She has been through much with her children and she sent word to establish some boundaries and find time to rest when we need to.

As difficult as it is for us to leave the hospital, once I am at Mark's house the warm water in the shower feels so good I can hardly tear myself away from it. Dave sat on the sofa as soon as we got in the house and he has fallen asleep in front of the television. I head for the bed. I am not worried about sleeping more than an hour or two. It has not happened for a long time. I do not remember putting my head on the pillow but I wake in the same position I laid down in an hour and a half later. I pull clothes from the washing machine that I had put in before our nap and throw them in the dryer while Dave showers. As soon as we pull the dry clothes from the dryer we leave for the hospital.

We look forward to a visit from our Pastor later today. Last week when I spoke to him at his home in Minneapolis I voiced concern that Mark and I share about Dave driving back to Minnesota alone. We know he is exhausted and it will be emotional for him to leave us to drive that long distance back to an empty house.

Pastor Jim told me there were several people in the congregation who had already expressed willingness to fly down and drive back with Dave. He said he would check into it. Praise God, Pastor is flying in today. He will stay a few days and then drive back with Dave. *Bless his flight, Lord!*

On our ride back to the hospital, I entertain curiosity about the woman who hit Mark. Everyone around us has been either asking questions or supplying information. We have been told that she could go to jail for vehicular assault. I know she is not in jail at this time and I wonder where she is. What is she thinking? Has she been social this week as we approach the holidays? Has she gone Christmas shopping? Baked cookies? Has she taken a walk? Has she brushed her own teeth, chewed on a piece of meat, showered and washed her own hair? Has she had a conversation? Stepped down hard and confident on her feet? Has she been able to breathe out of her nose? Open her mouth?

Enough! I can feel myself move toward anger and I dare not flirt with it. The woman in question has moved us from a family dreaming of Christmas together, watching Mark perform concerts, and spending time with friends, to a broken hearted family, torn apart by 1000 miles and writhing in pain. Dave shares that he struggles with the same torment and we pray that, by God's grace, we will move past these thoughts.

Dave and Ann-Marie go to Mark's room and I clean up the area around our torchercliners. Bits and pieces of food are everywhere and I realize that I have wasted a lot of food this week. People often ask, "Have you eaten today?" I know I am thin. I lose weight easily and I see in my face and the way my clothing fits that I have already lost several pounds.

Last night I answered, "Oh yes, I had a muffin for breakfast." But now, as I clean, I find that muffin with two small bites out of it. That was my food for the day. I ask God to bless this time as a type of fast on behalf of our son.

I take time to eat a banana out of a basket before I join Dave. I return to Mark's room at the same time that a nurse comes in to take an A-line out of Mark's leg. What follows is a most horrendous experience!

The nurse asks us to leave the room. Dave and I stand in the hallway growing more concerned as time passes. What could be taking so long? Finally Dave pokes his head in the door and it proves to be a life-saving act.

The nurse, with wide-eyed expression, says to Dave, "Get a nurse right away please!"

Dave calls to a nurse who rushes into the room and when she leaves we find out just what happened. After the first nurse pulled out the line, the area began to bleed profusely. She began to apply pressure. Neither she nor Mark could reach the call button because she did not dare to let up on the pressure. Mark could feel and see the bright red blood trickling down his leg and onto the sheet. He watched the white wash cloth the nurse grabbed turn bright red as it soaked up the blood, then several pads were soaked and the bright red continued to spread over the sheet. It was an answer to prayer when Dave poked his head in the door.

Once again, I cannot imagine the horror of what Mark endures on an hourly basis. Any one of the nightmares that assault him would be difficult to deal with, yet they continue to multiply.

Brian and April stop by but Mark is not up to visitors so we visit in the QR for awhile. Everyone understands I cannot stay away from Mark and they give me much grace when I excuse myself to go to his room continuously. When Dave leaves for the airport I encourage Mark that his Pastor will soon be here. Pastor Jim has been our pastor since Mark was eleven or twelve years old. He is a man of prayer who believes in the healing power of our Lord. I am expecting an increase in healing while he is here. Both Mark and I are so grateful that Pastor will drive back with Dave though we cannot bear to think of Dave leaving.

As we wait for Dave and Pastor to walk in the door, Mark and I discuss our disappointment that the maxillofacial surgeon will not be able to operate on Mark's eye tomorrow when he goes in for surgery on his right foot, ankle and toes. The surgeon was very clear that he cannot operate at this time because there is still too much swelling. They are quite certain that the eye will droop without surgery, but that in itself, amazingly, is not the reason for surgery. If that were all, it could actually be optional and Mark has decided he would opt for the surgery if that were the case. He does not want one eye smaller and, or, lower than the other for the rest of his life. The main reason for the surgery is to correct the double vision that occurs when the eye is out of place, and in Mark's case the doctor tells us the surgery is necessary, but it will have to take place at a later date.

One of the reasons for disappointment in the delay of the eye surgery is the tracheotomy. Mark is frantic to get rid of that! I do not have the heart to tell him that it will be in until all surgeries have been accomplished. We just help him get by one day at a time. He understands it is best to leave it in for the surgeries but we do not talk about how long it could actually be. They have started making the throat opening smaller, as I understand it, by using gradually smaller inserts.

Mark asks for the board and writes that he has had it with the pain in his groin area. Whenever he coughs he is in excruciating, unbearable pain. Of all the suffering, this pain has been the most difficult to deal with. We have devised a plan that provides some relief. When Mark signals that he needs to cough, I grab a bed pillow and place it across his midsection. I then lean over the pillow and press my body into it. Though it does not stop the pain, it seems to stabilize the traumatized area.

When the nurse comes in he asks to try an icepack.

The nurse smiles kindly, "You can try it but most men do not like that!"

"Anything," he says.

She brings a couple of bags of ice and shows me how to refill them if they bring relief. After only a short time Mark reports this is a successful effort.

Mark has a visitor and so I wait in the QR for Dave and Pastor to arrive. I feel such relief when I see Pastor Jim walk into the QR. We have been through many life-changes with him and that has fostered a loving and trusting relationship. Mark is also very happy to see his Pastor, but he is exhausted and in pain, so their initial visit is short.

As Dave and I sit visiting with Pastor Jim in the QR, he reminds us of a prophecy over our church of unprecedented favor. I become aware of how it has already been shown to us by much mercy and many acts of kindness.

I am standing beside Mark's bed when a nurse comes in to give him pain medication. She smiles at him and then hesitates before telling him, "You can have the yellow stuff that you swallow and it will last three to four hours, or you can have a quick shot in the IV which will last about one hour."

Mark asks for a drink of water from his syringe while he thinks about it.

I look at the nurse. "It must really taste awful for him to have to consider this so seriously."

She smiles, "I wouldn't want to drink it!" She looks at Mark, "but it will give you the best sleep for the longest time."

Mark looks at her and mouths the silent word, "liquid."

To be sure, it is the more difficult choice to swallow the vile liquid when there is no water chaser with the syringe. But it is the right choice for more rest.

The nurse fills the syringe. It probably takes a full minute to get it all down because Mark has to swallow carefully to avoid coughing.

By the time all of this has taken place it is 11:00 p.m. and I have not been able to lie down on my chair for more than two to three minutes before Mark needs something. I am beginning to feel it close in on me. I am beginning to feel the anger. None of it is directed toward Mark, he is so precious and in such pain. But

I am allowing myself to wonder how someone could have made a choice to hurt him! It is unfathomable! Unreal!

This entire ordeal is a surreal yet living, pulsating, neon nightmare! *Help me! More than that, oh Lord, help our son! Jesus! Protect our minds for we could lose them in the middle of this unspeakable anguish!*

> Psalm 32:7, "You are my hiding place; you will protect me from trouble and surround me with songs of deliverance."

Monday, December 17, 2001

During the night I intermittently doze and wake to look at Mark over the top of the stand between us. I position myself so I can see the top of his head. I look for his long lashes to see if his eyes are open.

After I stare in the dim light to focus on his face and content myself that he is asleep, I crane my neck to check to see that all the familiar numbers are registered on the monitor above my head. I do not know what each number means but I know the range they must stay in. If they look okay, I doze and wake a short time later to check again.

I am asleep this morning when someone comes in to say, "Ma'm, y'all have to go now."

As I get up to leave, Mark motions that he wants his teeth cleaned, so I grab the sponge on a stick and dip it in the mouthwash solution and put it in his left hand. On my way out I tell the nurse at the desk that he wants his teeth cleaned. She starts to get up but I let her know, "He's doing it."

"By himself?" She asks surprised.

I smile at her, feeling such pride in my son. "Yes, just remember to get it away from him before he falls asleep with it in his mouth."

She laughs lightly and it is evident she is pleased at his determination. We had a conversation about Mark's need for sleep last night and now I thank her for helping him by restricting activity in and out of his room during the night.

She shares with me that people are being admitted into the trauma unit too fast. There is a concern that Mark could get moved to another room and we desperately hope that does not happen. He is doing well here.

I swing the double doors open to find that the QR is full of new faces and it is an awful thing to witness the sorrow. Fear and pain are evident as tear-stained and shaking people find a chair to sit in. The weekend seems to accelerate traffic in this place.

Because I sleep in the step-down room, I have taken the broken chair in our row as mine. It seems only fair that someone who must sleep in a torcher-cliner all night should be able to put their feet up. I pull up a stationary chair and prop my feet on it in preparation for sleep and look around to take an inventory of QR friends before I close my eyes.

Carolyn sits up and smiles at me before she leaves with the friend who stayed by her side last night. She asks if we want coffee. Dave's asleep but I know he will want some, so I raise my forefinger and mouth, "one." We do not speak out loud because the occasional sleep sounds we hear around the room are precious to us.

Dave is just completing his wake-up stretch in the torchercliner when Carolyn returns to hand him a cup of steaming coffee. He is so pleased to have it. After a couple of sips from the Styrofoam cup, Dave stands and walks to the elevator. I suspect he now goes to ninth floor to the bathroom also.

Mr. Lyle has his McDonald's bag in hand as he enters the room. He goes for a walk very early each day and returns with food for his beloved wife. A woman I have not yet met, is asleep in the torchercliner beside Mrs. Lyle. They have befriended her and, no doubt, brought her some comfort her first night here. Now as she wakes, he offers her some breakfast. I smile to see how he balances the McDonald's bag on top of a lampshade to keep it warm until his wife awakes.

I would like to eat but do not want to leave in case the trauma doctor comes out to say when Mark's surgery will be today. A shower sounds really good too, and I smile to think that just wanting those things is progress.

Dave returns and we talk about the past night. I tell him about the nurse Mark had and how she pushed him. At first I wished she would just let him rest, but she "made" him breathe into his Breathalyzer. It is a plastic device that has a tube attached. He breathes into the tube and his breath pushes a bead in the plastic container upward. Last night she exhorted him to get it higher with each effort and he seemed to take a degree of delight in impressing her with his ability to expand a little more nearly every time. It was a very tiring task, and all of his training in breath support worked in his favor.

More great news to report to Dave, when he asks this morning, is that we slept! Mark actually slept from 11:45 p.m. to 3:45 a.m. and then from 5:00 a.m. to 6:15 a.m.! It was so awesome! He was so restful, so at peace! I believe Pastor being here is a comfort to him.

Brian, April and Courtney stop by early this morning with their good friend, Andrea, who is staying at their home for a few days. She drove from Kentucky to see Mark.

Their visit is welcome but, true to the roller coaster theme, Mark is having difficult time breathing. His nose packing has dried up. The nurse says that they will probably remove it today while he is in surgery. What a relief it will be for him to be able to breathe from his nose.

While they visit with Mark, Dave informs me that he has plans to get a car in working order for me to use after he returns to Minnesota. Last October when Mark was in Minnesota we had him drive our Nissan back to Nashville because his car was not working well. Though the car had never previously needed repair, it was in need of work at the time of the crash. Mark had been driving his older but larger car on that fateful night. We have debated which car would have fared best in the crash and have decided God was in control. It does no good to question something like that.

Dave stands up to give me a quick hug and then leaves to get Pastor at his hotel. They will go to Mark's house to get the Nissan and take it to the dealership for repair before returning to the hospital. I feel very blessed that I will have a car to drive and that it is a car I am familiar with. It is another of those touches that let me know God is watching over us. Once again we recognize unprecedented favor and provision.

While I recognize we are in God's care, I am not ready to be left alone here with Mark. I am so not ready! I know Dave must return to Minnesota and I already miss my husband when I think of it. I do not want to experience leaving Mark's room early in the morning to walk into the QR and not find Dave asleep in the chair next to the one I climb into.

It is just one more thought to force from my mind as I go to ninth floor to brush my teeth and change my sweater. I let the Lyles know that I will be back in five minutes. I do not want to be away if someone comes to notify me Mark is going to surgery.

Dave and Pastor walk off the elevator just before 9:00 a.m. when we are allowed to go in to see Mark. Mickey arrives only moments later. As we get up from our chairs to go and see Mark, a nurse calls the QR desk to say Mark is being taken to surgery. We all hurry to his room ignoring the rule for only two people to enter. After all, two of us are Pastors who are allowed to go in with family members.

The gurney is outside Mark's room and they are preparing to move him to it as we get to the door. We enter anyway and pray for Mark. He is ready. In the desperate circumstances that have trapped him, he sees surgery as an escape. The estimated time in the OR today is four to five hours. They will repair his right foot, put pins in four toes and basically reconstruct the heel with metal.

We begin the long and far too familiar wait. This involves conversation and prayer with other QR family and our own friends and family. It also involves reading the Bible or picking up a magazine with the intent to read it.

Unfortunately the written word does not translate to my grief-shocked brain.

It is calming to have Pastor here. He programs Mark's cell phone for me so I can reach Dave in Minneapolis by pressing just one number.

About 11:00 a.m., April calls to say she will pick up sandwiches and meet us in the dining area in a half hour. She asks who is with us and I let her know Pastor and Mickey are here. Andrea will be with April and another friend, Andy, is planning to meet us for lunch. We will have a full table in the cafeteria, but April will bring enough for everyone.

———————

Immediately before we leave for the cafeteria I walk to the nurses' station to give them the cell phone number and notify them where we will be if we are needed. I turn back toward the QR to see a horrific sight!

A person on a gurney is being rushed down the hallway to surgery. Somehow I know it is a woman though her head is bald and an awful shade of green. I only catch a flash as the gurney moves past me. Then, immediately, I see her mother, supported by another woman come far enough into the hall for her to collapse in despair. I signal Dave to come and pray. Pastor and Mickey follow.

The mother tells us the story. Her daughter's car radiator overheated and she pulled to the side of the road. She called her mom to ask what to do and while she was on the phone a car ran into hers. The mother had heard the explosion as her daughter became trapped in a burning car! I see it as divine provision that someone traveling on that road had a fire extinguisher and broke the window of her car to use it.

Mickey kneels on the floor beside her and says. "Look at me. Come on, look at me." She opens her eyes and looks into Mickey's kind face as he says, "I was burned that badly."

She stares at him and says in wonder, "And look at you!" as though he were an angel.

Mickey says, "I was blind. I was told I would never walk but I am married with four beautiful children."

We all prayed for the woman and her daughter and then Mickey asked if she knew the Lord.

"I know my higher being."

He inquired further about Jesus.

"I know Jesus walked this earth." She was unyielding in her recognition of the Lord.

I told her that if she would follow Mickey's prayer the Holy Spirit would comfort her through this ordeal.

Mickey told her about Mark, "He is a beautiful man of God with an incredible voice. He was hit one week ago by a drunk driver and he is being healed by the Grace of God."

I am amazed at a heavenly father that loves this woman so much He would orchestrate that Mickey be in this place at this time for her comfort.

The men continue to pray and I leave to meet April, Andrea and Andy. There is an inviting variety of deli sandwiches in the collection of paper bags April places on the largest table we can find.

Mickey tells us stories of his horrendous airplane crash, and God's amazing love, while we eat in the cafeteria. Mickey shakes his head when he mentions Mark and I know he relates to the suffering in a way no one else at the table can.

The sandwich is delicious and I see Dave smile approvingly as I eat it.

As the men engage in conversation at one end of the table, Andrea and April share with Andy and me what Mark said to them last night.

"Take off my sheets." Mark had instructed Andrea. "Go ahead, I want you to see everything they have done to me and check to see how it looks."

Andrea, who is in medical school, finds this fascinating and painful at the same time. Once again this friendship was born in college. Mark trusts Andrea and knows she will be interested in his new scars and casts because of her desire to be a physician. She commented on the fractures and gave him some insight into the medical terms he was hearing.

April tells me that they looked at a picture taken in the autumn at a football game. It was Mark and four friends smiling as they shared a fun evening. The girls had commented to Mark, "How cute."

"Sad" Mark wrote on his board.

"Why?" they asked and handed him the board again.

"Never look that way again." He had written.

They quickly assured him that his face is not scarred or deformed. Mark has not looked in a mirror yet and does not want to. They frankly told him he is black, blue, purple, green and swollen, but not scarred. Because of the years of trust and sharing in their history, they know he expects them to tell him the truth.

Andrea smiles, "I told him, 'Pumpkin, you look good.'"

We all grin at the nickname. For years she has called Mark "Pumpkin" even addressing mail she sends him to "Pumpkin Williams." Just as faithfully, he calls her "Princess."

We return to the QR and on this, the longest morning yet (some contest), we hear Mark is out of surgery and on his way up to the tenth floor.

I sit down to talk with the Watt's son's wife. She says her husband can sit up occasionally now. After twenty-eight days they are beginning to see improvement. She shows us how she is putting together a scrapbook of his cards. I decide to use her idea to enable us to organize the many greeting cards that arrive each day for Mark.

As we talk she suddenly looks intently at me and when she speaks I get goose bumps. She is talking about Mark's CD, *REALITY*.

"The words…the words." The pretty young woman touches her chest and rests back in her chair. The emotion she struggles with is visible. "It is as though he knew about this place when he wrote them."

"Prophetic?" I ask.

"Yes. Definitely."

As we finish our conversation, Brenda walks into the room. She has come to visit us and has brought two pastors from her church. She sits beside me to hold my hand as she does when we see each other.

Our conversations are always intense. We sit with our heads close together looking into each other's eyes and pouring out our concern for each other. She tells me Roger is remembering now. He knows the race of the man that attacked him, and that he had a white beard. Each time someone even slightly resembling the attacker walks by his room he becomes very upset and says "I know you."

Brenda tells me Roger's watch is dented where he held up his hand to fend off the blows from the hammer-wielding thief. He will soon be transferred to a rehabilitation hospital. The doctors have decided they will not operate on his brain, but will do some facial repair. Before she leaves, Brenda writes down her home address and tells me she purchased a portable CD player today and has listened to Mark's CD. The young minister of music who sits beside her says that he listened also and they tell me that they can't wait until Mark is well enough to visit their church to do a concert.

We stand in a circle holding hands to pray when we get the news that Mark is back in his room. Dave and Pastor Jim go in so I can continue to pray with Brenda.

When we have finished our prayers Brenda hugs me and says, "Lana, I have to tell you, when we put on Mark's CD, it was the first time since I have been here that I was able to lift my hands to the Lord."

She cannot know how that will bless Mark when I tell him.

Pastor Jim returns to say, "Mark wants you. It's the worst pain of his life."

Now that is an awful statement to hear. As I hurry down the hall I have visions of him being pried from his car, lying on a cold, hard x-ray table with multiple broken bones and yet, he is now in the worst pain he has ever faced? I rush through the double doors.

When he sees me he lifts up his left hand. I grab it and, though he is not at full strength, he squeezes my hand so tight I feel my bones could turn to dust.

Mark remembers:

I remember the surgery on my right foot very well. Of the five trips to the OR, it is the only one that I can remember being awake immediately before. They took me down in an elevator and pushed my gurney into a room that had other pre or post-surgery patients in it.

A young woman came to my side accompanied by a young man who appeared to be an intern. The woman informed me that she was going to change my trach to a smaller one before surgery. They had already experimented with a smaller one that would supposedly let me talk a bit, but it didn't work and was very uncomfortable.

She asked the young man if he would like to do the change. My first reaction was, "Oh, great, I am a speechless guinea pig for this kid!"

He took my trach out and inserted a smaller one. I immediately noticed a difference in my breathing. I could get absolutely no air! All I was able to do was to wave my arm and gasp for air while they watched my blood pressure rise. This became a concern for them.

The woman told me to relax, but I simply couldn't. I felt like I was being suffocated and could not communicate that feeling. After a good minute or two of gasping for air they decided they needed to put me out. That is all I wanted! Why couldn't they have changed the trach after I was out instead of putting me through that experience? I had tears running down my cheeks and my heart was racing rapidly. I felt the horror could have been avoided.

When I woke from surgery, I knew something was wrong. *Why can I feel my foot? What is that throbbing pain?*

I was in the post-surgery room and I tried to mumble the word "pain." Once again the frustration of not being able to communicate my pain or discomfort overwhelmed me. It must have been the movement of my mouth and my expression that caused a nurse to ask, "Are you in pain?"

I nodded violently and she told me they had given me something and it was all they could give me.

When I arrived upstairs my family could see my misery. They went for help and asked a nurse if I had received my morphine post-surgery. No one could find it on my chart. They could not give me any morphine in case some had been given to me already. They were concerned about an overdose.

All the while the nurses were making calls and trying to figure things out, I was squeezing the living daylights out of any hand I could get a hold of.

My mom, dad and pastor all took turns letting me crush their hand. I was really feeling an incredible throbbing and constant dull, heavy pain in my foot and it seemed to be getting worse. It did not help me to know that, once I finally got the morphine, it would take awhile for it to take care of the pain.

A nurse came in to admit a terrible mistake had been made and she gave me the highest dose of morphine allowed. It did very little and for a couple of days I lived for the next dose of morphine, praying it would catch the pain.

My only desire was to be knocked out so I could sleep through the nightmare that haunted me day and night.

Lana:

In a state of helplessness I watch my son as a constant parade of nurses brings a variety of pain medication. They know they have dropped the ball and they are so very sorry. As Mark came out of the anesthesia, he was to receive a hearty dose of something. Because of poor communication, he did not receive it, and when they realized it, they had to get permission to give him such a dose. That caused too much time to pass. As it is explained to us, now the brain knows there is pain in the body, and foot surgery is always extremely painful even when it is not of the great magnitude Mark has just endured.

The nurses struggle to break the transmission of pain to the brain, but nothing will work. It is not hard to imagine the pain of this latest surgery. Mark's foot is elevated on a box-type apparatus that sits on his bed. There is a tube sticking out of his heel that is a drain. It makes me queasy to see blood moving from that tube into a pan, but that is nothing compared to the absolute gut-wrench that takes place each time I see the discolored toes sticking out of the cast. Protruding from each toe is a piece of metal that is turned at the tip like a cup hook. We are told the toes were crushed so badly that these pins were the only way to repair them. Anyone who sees them looks away. It is too much to take in.

After a few hours of the intense struggle with pain, two techs come in to say that they want to bathe Mark. He looks at me in horror! Move him? The pain of a bed bath is intense and it takes several people to move his broken body to cleanse it a section at a time. It is unthinkable to add to his pain.

We manage to stall until we see who is on the next shift. We are pleased with the name we see. It is a male nurse with a kind and bright smile and he is capable. For now, we deal with the pain; we will face a bed bath later if we must.

A nurse we have not seen before comes in to say Mark is now going to receive a liquid narcotic on top of the morphine IV.

In his raspy whisper he says "No."

I feel sure he is wondering if she knows he has already taken the maximum dose they can give him for pain.

A familiar nurse comes in and explains that, yes, he is at the maximum dose on the morphine IV but he can still get the maximum dose on this pain reliever also because of the extreme circumstances.

I understand his concern. After all, he has been struggling with hallucination from the dose already administered.

"Do you mean," I say slowly because we really do need to understand, "that it is as though he has had the maximum amount of Tylenol but he can still have some Advil?"

"Exactly!" She looks relieved.

Now that we understand Mark takes the gross tasting liquid immediately. Then he motions to write.

"Sorry." He pens on the board with his left hand.

The nurse softens for the first time today, "Oh, honey," she says, "I didn't mean to be lecturing you. I just wanted you to understand it was okay to take all of this medication. I am so sorry you have to go through all of this."

For Mark, pain ebbs and flows but never disappears. I decide I am not leaving when they come by to tell me to leave at 6:00 p.m., so when the kind but strict woman from the QR walks by Mark's room and says "It's the bewitching hour, you have to leave!"

I simply say, "He just got back from surgery so I'll be here for awhile."

I am determined to run the show from this point on. The nurses will not dictate to me when Mark does or does not need me. He alone can do that.

At 7:30 p.m. I go downstairs to eat. Dave has left to take Pastor Jim to his hotel and Pat and Ann-Marie accompany me to the cafeteria. I confide in them that I have just had an angry moment and want to know more about the woman who hit Mark.

They tell me that their friend in the police department has told them she will be charged with either DUI or vehicular assault and she may go to jail. I am feeling as though she planned the entire event. She prepared her body just as someone prepares a weapon and I am tormented by the thought. It is good to talk to them and get it off my mind.

April calls to say she wants to stay with Mark tonight so we can get some rest. I look at my husband who has bags under his eyes, shows apparent weight loss and can barely keep his eyes open and feel so very tempted but I think of the intense pain Mark is in and kindly refuse. April is just as kind but stubborn in her insistence. She leaves the option open.

As soon as we are allowed, I go into Mark's room with Dave and Dave leaves soon after so Ann-Marie can use his badge to come in. She is prepared to watch Monday night football with Mark and to read him the sports page.

When I return to the QR, Pat is waiting. "Go to sleep," she says.

Like a child obeying a loving mother, I sit in the torchercliner and doze. When I open my eyes fifteen minutes later, Pat informs me April will be here at 11:00. The decision has been made. Dave has accepted her offer to stay the night. He is asleep in the chair next to me. I am too exhausted to protest. I know that they are taking care of me with the same love and concern that I take care of Mark.

I feel guilty as I go to tell Mark but I know the relationship he has with April. They are like brother and sister. I am totally confident in her staying with him. He will tell her anything he needs without hesitation and they will call us if they must. We will only be a few minutes away.

Mark says he is fine with April staying. Even in his misery he seems to recognize that his dad and mom need to rest.

As I return to the QR I feel near-panic wash over me. I am desperate to get to Mark's house to sleep. Each moment seems a frivolous waste of time. I have allowed myself to think of sleep and my body is now screaming for it!

When we get on the elevator to leave, Dave staggers and nearly falls. I question if he is even strong enough to get to the house. We are putting our bodies to the test. When we walk in the door of the house we do not even speak. We do not undress but fall into bed fully clothed at 11:00 p.m.

> Psalm 119:40, "Remember your word to your servant, for you have given me hope. My comfort in my suffering is this: Your promise preserves my life."

Tuesday, December 18, 2001

When I wake it is because of a 6:30 a.m. wake-up call we requested from Ann-Marie. We have slept from 11:00 p.m. to 6:30 a.m.! That is our longest amount of sleep yet. Still we can barely move. We shower and organize a few things so there is walking space in the bedroom and then we leave for the hospital.

As we get off the elevator I see April asleep in a torchercliner. No doubt she was asked to leave Mark's room and came to the QR to finally sleep. I tiptoe to the table next to her and grab the disposable camera we have been using. She does not wake when I snap a shot of her. I want as many pictures of things like this as possible. Someday this will be a memory and it will be important for Mark to see the faithfulness of those who love him.

I sit beside April and she smiles as she wakens. She tells me that the night went better than expected but that Mark could not sleep because of the pain. "I don't see how you do it," she says, "I didn't sleep at all and his room is freezing!"

We laugh at that which is not funny and hug before she leaves. I pray she will be able to get some sleep before she has to go to work later today.

When I do not see the doctor for early rounds I tell the nurse that I wish to speak with him at some convenient point in this day.

We are blessed that people that work here are playing Mark's CD at the nurses' station, in their cars and homes. It started with us giving one of the CDs to a nurse. Dave and I heard it playing at the station as we walked past early the next morning. Since then we have been asked about the CD several times and have decided that we will give free CDs to anyone interested who has given care to Mark in this place.

Shortly after I get to Mark's room a nurse enters to change one of the IV bags and she tells him that her friend's husband plays for a well-known band and asks Mark if he knows them.

Mark nods. Yes, he is acquainted with that band.

The nurse smiles and says, "She wanted to know who my patient is, but I told her I cannot say."

Mark signals to write, "Not known."

I tell the nurse "He wants you to know that he is not a well-known artist, but he really is well-known, because people in many countries are praying for him. He just wants you to know he is not famous."

Mark smiles.

We have been in prayer for some time this morning when Mark motions for me to hand him his writing board. It has been a struggle for him to breathe today. The tracheotomy cap change before his last surgery has made it even more difficult. If we understand right, they need to keep putting smaller pieces into the tracheotomy opening so it can begin to close and they can finally remove it all together.

He wants to communicate how he felt when the tracheotomy cap was changed to a smaller size. "She told me it would be uncomfortable," he writes. "I could not breathe."

He writes in segments and interjects in the raspy whisper he is now allowed to use.

"I was convulsing for air and had horrendous coughs. My heart rate was going up, up, up. They were going to give me something for it."

He closes his eyes to rest before continuing, "I thought I would have a heart attack."

I am with him nearly around the clock and yet it seems that nearly every time he is away from our sight something traumatic happens to cause new suffering.

Mark is able to eat some breakfast. Well, he has squirted some breakfast into his mouth through the syringe. He had a small amount of juice and a touch of yogurt totaling about one-half ounce each.

I request some strawberry Ensure but there is none available. The nurse decides to mix some strawberry ice cream into vanilla Ensure. We stir it until it is total liquid and insert it into his syringe. I am grateful when he is able to swallow some of it. He even smiles at the taste. Each time he eats we record the amount on a chart outside his door.

The trauma doctor stops in as we requested and we tell him about the extreme foot pain.

In his matter of fact manner he states, "Everything else is old. This is new. You are broken. Sorry to say it like that, but that's what is going on. I'll order you some new pain medication. I can't heal you, but I can help control your pain."

Mark gives him a "thumbs up" and though his words are somewhat tough, they are honest and I can see Mark appreciates his time. I would nominate this doctor for "Man of the Year" if Mark was not on my ballot.

When the new pain medication arrives, the nurse tells him it needs to be squirted into his mouth rather than through an IV. He hesitates, but, in his staunch fashion, begins to give it to himself. The nurse beams back at him, so proud. Then we load a second syringe with water to chase the taste. Maybe now he will be able to rest.

Dave and Pastor Jim are at the car dealership. They will pick up the car and drive it to Mark's house. After they leave for Minneapolis tomorrow, someone will take me to Mark's house and I will then drive back to the hospital.

I try not to think that Dave and Pastor Jim will leave tomorrow. I have to recognize that they would have left by now if not for the surgery scheduled tomorrow. It is to be the last one, God willing. Pastor was sensitive that Dave would want to be here for that surgery so they have decided to stay and leave immediately after Mark is out of surgery.

We decide that, because of the long trip ahead, Dave needs to go to Mark's house to sleep tonight. The men have talked it over and have decided they will try to drive straight through to Minnesota, but they have assured me that if weather is bad, or they are too tired, they will stop at a motel.

For now we are together and at 8:30 p.m., we go in to see Mark. It comforts us to know that his favorite nurse is on this shift. It helps us that she will be with Mark tonight and that Ann-Marie will stay at the hospital.

> Isaiah 26:3, "You will keep in perfect peace him whose mind is steadfast, because he trusts in you."

Wednesday, December 19, 2001

Dave and I slept a few hours then woke to throw his clothing into a suitcase and hurry back to the hospital. Mark is scheduled for surgery at 1:00 p.m. today. The length of this surgery is undetermined because it is "tedious." To avoid double vision and drooping, they must create a shelf on the floor of the eye socket using titanium mesh. They need to be especially careful of the ophthalmic nerve and sensitive surrounding tissue.

We arrive in the QR shortly before Pastor Jim arrives with Mickey and Barbara. Ann-Marie is sleeping soundly in the torchercliner and wakes to fill us in. She says Mark slept quite well last night and so did she. I envy her ability to sleep with all the distractions. I thank her with a hug and she leaves to go home to eat and shower.

Mickey seems impatient to see Mark and decides to go in though it is not yet 9:00 a.m. His title of "Pastor" can get him in early and he intends to use it, but as soon as that decision is made, we get the word that Mark's surgery will take place earlier than scheduled and we all hurry in to see him. Mark looks dazed. His life is full of rearranged priorities and each carries urgency. His head must be spinning.

When Barbara walks to his bed and bends to put her face near his, he lights up with recognition. She gives him a tender kiss and we gather, many more than are ever allowed into this room, around Mark's bed to pray. Then Pastor Jim, Mickey and Barbara leave and Dave and I stay with Mark.

Soon they wheel Mark away on the gurney and tell us that he will be in a holding room downstairs for quite some time. They encourage us to go and wait with him.

I tell Dave I am quite certain I can find the area for the holding rooms and we gather our reading material from the QR and tell Pastor Jim where we are going. We find the area but Mark is not in the same room as before, but rather in a private room. We walk in and I catch my breath as I see a bag of blood hanging from the metal unit above his bed. The nurse assigned to Mark explains that the doctor ordered a transfusion because Mark was facing a lengthy facial surgery and some count they had taken showed a need for blood.

I say a prayer that the blood of Jesus will cover this blood that is now mingling with my son's. How many transfusions has he had? How many people gave their blood to help him? Though I have never weighed enough to give, I am thankful that Dave is a regular donor. It feels as though we have given that we may receive. Even so, the bag is an unwelcome sight to me. It makes my stomach turn. I try to look at it as one more obstacle to hurdle.

I pray as I pray each day, for everything they put into my son's body. I instruct the IV contents to perform the function they are designed for and nothing else. I pray against any side effects.

A nurse comes in to manipulate the bag and get the blood to flow freely. We are told it is cold and sometimes moves too slowly and has to be helped along. I know that once before, Mark became very cold during a transfusion.

Fear hangs in the air like a stagnant cloud. None of us voice it. Each of us struggles to resist the oppression, but it is thick. A holding room is a place to wait and anticipate. It is a fertile playground for imagination.

This may be the last surgery and yet, personally, I find it the most frightening. It involves his eye. Will he have his sight? Will his eye look normal? He has been through so many surgeries in such a short time, will he be weak? Will he get sick from the anesthesia when he has had so much in so short a time and has been on such high concentrations of pain medication?

All of the questions are nearly tangible weapons that assault me. I speak the name of Jesus and we pray for protection for Mark and for the surgeon and his team. I use the power of the name of Jesus to sweep the dusty coating of fear from my heart and mind and begin to concentrate on encouraging Mark. We spend our time praying for the surgery and the surgeons. My underlying prayer is that my son will not sense the fear that is gripping me.

When one of my very favorite doctors from this team comes in, I tell him about the last surgery and the lapse in medication. We want assurance Mark will have adequate medication to overcome the post-surgical pain. He makes a note to be certain adequate pain medication is prescribed. We sense he has taken care of this detail already, but he writes these instructions in our presence for our peace of mind.

This kind man took time only a few days ago to put his hand on Mark's shoulder and look him in the eye when he said, "Hang in there. You will be well again. You have a good family and that means everything."

When they finally come to take Mark to surgery, Dave and I are instructed to wait in this room as it is near the OR and we can receive updates. We brush away concern as to why we cannot go to the QR as we have for all other surgeries.

How the enemy loves to divide in order to conquer. Ten floors up our friends and Pastor are waiting and praying. Here we are alone and we feel the assault. Not one time before or during the surgeries have I felt such desperate fear! I am walking the room and praying in the Spirit. Dave is alternately praying and reading the paper.

I hate the feeling of this room. Mark's room upstairs holds peace in the midst of turmoil. During one of his early surgeries Becki and I went into the room that seemed considerably larger with the bed missing. We prayed over the room and banished any negative spirits and welcomed healing and peace. We prayed the blood of Jesus would cover every person who entered that room. I offer prayer now for the room we wait in, which surely has been a hot-house for fear in the past. I wish I had prayed this much earlier because we are reeling from the intensity of the morning.

"Why can't we go upstairs?" I ask.

"I don't know. We just have to wait." Dave manages to be more complacent of things in general than I am. While that can agitate me in "normal" circumstances it is what I need now.

One of the members of the surgical team opens the door after nearly ninety minutes. "We want you to know we are only now beginning surgery. It took a very long time to position him."

Only now starting! We begin to realize how difficult it is for the team to get Mark into a position that will work for surgery because of his many injuries and movement restrictions.

The next report comes after nearly three hours of our pacing, praying and struggling desperately against the worry that seems to entrap me like a tight, wet sweater I cannot remove. The same member of the team pokes his head in the door again. He is a man who does not smile often. He has a mask over his mouth now, but his eyes avoid contact with ours. I am hoping it is because he is shy.

Usually they say, "Mark's doing great, it will be awhile," or something to that effect. This doctor says very slowly. "He's.....okay."

My heart is thumping wildly.

He walks over to the window. "It is going to be at least two to three more hours. This is very tedious." He looks out the window as he speaks and not at us. Without another word he turns on his heel to head out the door.

I jump at the chance to tell the doctor, "We will be upstairs in the Quiet Room." Then add quickly, "Is that okay?"

"I'll let the doctor know you went up there."

He probably is not back in the OR room as fast as we are at the elevator down the hall. We punch "10" and run into the QR.

The feelings linger but are immediately lighter as we settle into our chairs. We talk and pray and Dave has a cup of coffee. Soon we feel we are on even ground again. I vow that if there have to be any more surgeries, I will not spend the time away from the QR. Even though Dave and I were united in prayer, we were in a cold and sterile atmosphere away from support and it proved to be extremely difficult. It's a valuable lesson. Isolation is not the choice in a situation like this.

Barbara returns with a gift and a card. She has brought me a beautiful angel and even more than the gift, I welcome her company. Ann-Marie comes in and then another friend of Mark's arrives shortly before the surgeon walks into the QR. He is wearing a wonderful, welcome grin as he crosses the room to sit by us.

The surgery went well. They have placed a piece of titanium mesh under Mark's eye to hold it in place where the eye socket had collapsed. An incision has been made by the lower lashes. The surgeon believes the scar will diminish and become difficult to see as Mark heals. We are more than grateful for the talent of this man.

Chris and Carole come into the room in time to hear the good news. Carole has been led to pray specifically for Mark's eye since the first time she saw him after the crash.

At about 5:00 p.m. Dave and Pastor Jim prepare to return to Minneapolis. I know they cannot stay any longer. Pastor has already prolonged his visit to accommodate this surgery and Dave needs to return to work after nearly two weeks here in Nashville. I have been dreading the moment when the elevator doors would close on them but I remind myself that I am surrounded with friends and good doctors committed to helping Mark.

When the elevator doors close behind my pastor and my husband I hold out my hands, palms upward. *Here Lord. Take all my fear and apprehension. I am too weary to hold it.*

I pick up my Bible and turn to Matthew 11:28-30. "Come to me all you who are weary and burdened, and I will give you rest. Take my yoke upon you and learn from me, for I am gentle and humble in heart, and you will find rest for your souls. For my yoke is easy and my burden is light."

This moment is a revelation of that familiar scripture. I exchange my heavy burden with my savior, not because it is an easy thing for me to do, but because I am in a place where I can do nothing else.

Psalm 57:1, "Have mercy on me, O God, have mercy on me, for in you my soul takes refuge. I will take refuge in the shadow of your wings until the disaster has passed."

Thursday, December 20, 2001

Yesterday I visited the hospital gift shop. I wanted to find a soft stuffed dog. Mark loves dogs and appreciates stuffed animals. I decided it is something he can put by his left hand to stroke to get the fingers moving and perhaps it may bring some solace. I found the perfect floppy dog. He is black with a face that makes me smile.

I know Mark cannot see it very well but he did pay some attention to it. I placed it under the fingers of his left hand and I saw his fingers move slightly. It is soft to the touch and yet it can be squeezed to strengthen his hand. It was sweet to see him "pet" it now and then in its position under his left hand.

Today as he recovers from the latest surgery, I see the floppy dog has been elevated to a higher status. It lies on Mark's stomach, his hand on top of it. As he feels stronger, he lifts the dog up toward his face to see it better. His left eye is covered with a cool, wet cloth but he manipulates it toward the right eye so he can see it.

Ann-Marie asks, "Are you going to name it?"

He signals to write. "Hope."

Mark is lying in bed with towels around his head, one draping down to hold the eye patch in place when a nurse comes to change his eye patch. She lets us know that they will be in and out often tonight as they must change the pads every two hours.

While the night starts out fairly serene it is soon interrupted with extreme coughing. This continues and Mark needs to be suctioned.

I will never get used to the sound, or lack of sound, of the trach-cough. I remember the first time we heard it I thought Dave would fall onto the floor from the sorrow that visibly hit him. It is the combination of the laryngitis type sound and the look of sheer horror that covers Mark's countenance that rips at my heart. When we see the long suction tube that needs to be inserted down the opening in his throat it seems more than we can bear.

Painful, indeed, are those long seconds when the suction instrument is deep in his throat and he has no way to breathe; when he struggles and anticipates the certain pain that will come when he coughs.

I watch, lost in the nightmare of a parent who must observe their child plunged into fear, pain and helplessness.

Mark is tired when that episode is over and he drifts to sleep. I manage to sleep a little though Mark's room is still a refrigeration chamber. I have learned how to stop myself from sliding down in the vinyl chair every few minutes by bracing my arm underneath my body as a brake.

Each time I wake from a "catnap" I check Mark to be sure his eye patch has not fallen away. This time I see that it has slipped down to his pillow and I wonder if I should put it back and wake him, or just let him get the rest he so desperately needs. I struggle with the dilemma for a few minutes and then the nurse comes in to change his catheter bag and eye patch.

I smile when she looks toward my dark corner and exaggerates a shiver and I am relieved when she turns and adjusts the room temperature on her way out the door.

> I Peter 4:12 and 13, "Dear friends, do not be surprised at the painful trial you are suffering, as though something strange were happening to you. But rejoice that you participate in the sufferings of Christ, so that you may be overjoyed when his glory is revealed."

Friday, December 21, 2001

There are some things about mornings that have become warmly familiar and I embrace them. For instance, this morning Mr. Lyle walks into the QR, hat atop his head, a pleasant grin on his face and his hand clutching the McDonald's bag that will be his wife's breakfast. I have returned from the night in Mark's room and am in my torcher-cliner, blanket pulled up to my chin in an effort to be warm. He walks over to me to tap the soles of my feet with his newspaper in greeting.

I have come to love Mr. and Mrs. Lyle. I know that Dave feels the same because before he left for Minneapolis yesterday he hugged Mr. Lyle really tight. They are precious to us and their attitude is an example for anyone in this room.

Through half-closed eyes I watch Carolyn walk off the elevator with her daughters. They all have McDonald's coffee cups in hand. They smile and lift their hands in greeting. We have learned to communicate without speaking out of respect for those who are able to sleep.

I turn my head on the small pillow to doze a while longer but someone is talking out loud. I look up and catch Caroline's eyes. She moves her eyes past me and raises her eyebrows. New arrivals are conversing in a regular tone of voice and they seem to go on and on. Someone near them awakes from much needed sleep to turn side to side in their chair in a silent plea for mercy but the newcomers continue their conversation.

In the chair next to mine, Dave's chair for nearly two weeks, a stranger snores loudly. I miss my husband and offer a prayer for him. I hope he is near Minneapolis by now and that he will soon arrive home to crawl into our queen size bed with the plush pillow-top mattress, covered by our soft down comforter. He will look out the window when he awakes to see the snow covered river that, in warmer weather, flows past our home and the deer that will carefully make their way, single file, across the ice to our yard.

He can hug Michael, which I long to do. He will read our mail and see how our newly remodeled kitchen looks. I know that it will be many weeks, perhaps months before I can do those things and I push aside my desire to be with him.

I have given up on sleep and sit with my blanket up to my chin facing the elevator. I decide that I have come to recognize far too many doctors. The elevator unloads them and they walk to the trauma center for their rounds. I see one team and know the business they are about, another steps off and he is going to check something of another specific. It is a steady stream.

I desperately miss my good solid hour of sleep between 5:30 a.m. and 6:30 a.m. that I lack today, but it is now 6:30 a.m. and I decide I will go down to ninth floor to see Brenda. She left a note for me last night that Roger will check out of the hospital today at 9:00 a.m. I attempted to find her when I went downstairs at 6:00 a.m. to brush my teeth and comb my hair but the woman at the nurse's desk told me Brenda needed forty-five minutes to finish getting Roger ready for the day.

I find myself thinking that one week ago he could have gotten himself ready and walked out the door to get in his car and go to work. I know that it is not such a victory as it sounds that Roger will be transferred today. There is much hard work ahead.

As the doctor-parade from the elevator continues, I see one of my favorites. He is from the facial surgery team. He turns and looks my way and mouths the words, "Good Morning."

I hear Mr. and Mrs. Lyle laugh and tease each other. They have spent another night in the torchercliners and still maintain sunny dispositions. I wonder if Scott is as dear as his father and I offer a prayer for his recovery.

I decide to go down to the cafeteria at 7:00 a.m. I hurry because I do not want to miss the doctors if they stop to talk to me. I return with a bowl of oatmeal and a slice of raisin toast and the food tastes wonderful.

I smile at an optimistic rumor in the QR that the Caroline C. may move her husband to a rehabilitation hospital today.

Phone calls trickle in with consistency. A friend from Minnesota calls to say "The old gang is praying." The "old gang" is in reference to a group who spent much time together in our early twenties, much like Mark's friends who are with him now. Another friend from Minnesota calls to say she is "so proud" of Mark and is sending us phone cards to help with long distance calls. She is a friend we met many years ago when Mark was at his first audition for a talent show. She was moved to tears by his singing and has been a good friend and supporter of his ministry since that time.

We hear of entire churches that are holding us up in prayer. We are humbled and pleased to hear of bodies of believers from all over the US and in many countries. Our home church is very international in its networking, so many people outside the US have heard Mark's CD, and Dave's sister is a missionary who has lived out of the states most of her adult life. Those factors, plus e-mail, have alerted a strong community of prayer. The international community of believers becomes a pretty tight knit group when one of them is suffering.

2 Corinthians, 4:17 and 18, "For our light and momentary troubles are achieving for us an eternal glory that far outweighs them all. So we fix our eyes not on what is seen, but on what is unseen. For what is seen is temporary, but what is unseen is eternal."

PART III ✦ REHABILITATION HOSPITAL
December 21, 2001 – January 11, 2002

Lana:

Well, we had quite a surprise today! It is evening as I write and we are in a wonderful, *private* room at a rehabilitation hospital.

This day has been full of events. We understand that Caroline's husband moved to another rehab hospital and I heard Watts' may also go there.

It seemed they decided to move Mark very suddenly. We have been praying to move and that we will have a private room because of Christmas in a few days. We want to decorate it for Christmas and to feel free to have more than two friends visit at a time.

Dave and Mike will be coming to Nashville and we want to have space to be together. We were, however, prepared to be in a non-private room because we thought anything would be better than to spend Christmas on the floor of the trauma unit.

We think Mark merited a private room because of the extent of his injuries. He cannot move on his own and he certainly cannot get up to go to the bathroom. Right now they have him in a diaper. This is something I think would devastate him, but he has been so focused on getting out of the trauma unit that he will comply with anything.

The ICU nurse on duty today advised that Mark not ask to have the catheter out. She said it would be a smoother transition if he would handle that a day or two after his move. We appreciate that she took time to advise him and that she recognizes how dramatic this change will be.

He certainly had drastic preparation to prepare him for the move! One moment he had a tracheotomy tube and the next he had an empty hole in his throat. We have been assured that they have respiratory technicians at the rehabilitation hospital that can give Mark excellent care.

The ICU physical therapist came in to assign Mark another dramatic challenge. In the few times she has seen Mark she has expressed her pleasure that he is gaining strength. This is not something that is visually noticeable to any of us, but they measure things in different degrees than we do. Today, with help of a few people, she moved him into a throne type chair to see if he would be able to sit up. They hoped he could sit a few minutes and wait in the chair until the ambulance arrived to transport him to the rehabilitation hospital.

The chair was highly padded, but within moments Mark was in excruciating pain because of his hip, tailbone and pelvis and we could not find anyone to transfer him back to his bed. It takes several people, each strategically placed, and with knowledge of how to move a severely injured person, and then all moving at the same time, to get him from the bed to the wheelchair, or even from one side of the bed to the other. Great care must be taken for smooth movement.

We could not find even one person with time to move him! My son was crying in pain with sweat running down his flushed face. I was not going to stand for it. When no nurse would respond quickly I walked to the desk and told his therapist what was happening. She immediately went to his room and took control, instructing me and a nurse she had called to in the hallway, "Take off those restraining belts!"

We did so quickly and she lowered the back of the chair only slightly. With that small amount of relief, Mark was finally able to take a breath. The nurse who had witnessed his pain and helped us with the restraint left the room and returned immediately with pain medication.

It was a horrendous experience, which only served to make us apprehensive about the challenges ahead. I cannot help but wonder if the move to a wheelchair was a necessary prerequisite before releasing Mark to the rehabilitation hospital. It seems strange that Mark needed to be in a chair immediately after we heard he was moving and only minutes before he was transferred. I may be thinking too much about this last minute experiment. Besides, despite how miserable Mark was, he must have passed the test.

I thank God Ann-Marie and April were available to help me move Mark's things from his room. We had accumulated many items. The three of us scampered to get his CDs and CD player along with a few decorations, etc. out of Mark's room and then we tackled the QR. It had been home and we had baskets of food and coats and blankets to gather. We put all of it into Ann-Marie's and April's cars and returned to the ICU eager for our move.

Dave and I had visited the rehabilitation hospital before he left for Minnesota because we were told it was where Mark would move, if a room became available, when he was to be discharged from the trauma center. We were impressed with the facility and that is good because it is our understanding that Mark will live at this place for about two months.

When the ambulance arrived they transferred Mark to the gurney and wheeled him out. I rode with April in her car. We found the hospital easily and learned that visitor parking is located in a garage that is about a two-block walk by the time you drive into the ramp to park, cross the street and walk to the hospital entrance. Once inside we went down a long hallway and then an elevator took us to second floor. We found Mark's room down the hall from the therapy "gym" that we noticed as we exited the elevator.

When we first arrived, we parked under the canopy outside the entrance so we could unload our belongings. We have become accomplished at this type of move and knew we needed a cart from inside to move everything. The pleasant woman at the desk found a cart for us and instructed us that we need to wear neon stickers with our name on them each time we come into the hospital. April and I commented to each other about the levels of security we have experienced. We suspect it is because of the degree of celebrity in this city.

We were so happy to find Mark has been assigned to a private room and that I will have a cot to sleep on. This is a wonderful answer to prayer!

We are fully aware of God's hand in each detail of this ordeal. He has given such grace and mercy and shown His care in many tender ways. Today He lavished us with the knowledge of His care when we first arrived in this new place. As Mark's gurney was pushed off the elevator, he heard, "The dog parade will begin at 1:00 p.m."

He told me he was not certain if he really heard that or if the morphine he received just before the trip had kicked in. I left the room to find out and as I rounded the nurses' station outside Mark's new room I saw several dogs. A sweet looking yellow Labrador paraded past me with antler ears on. Assorted dogs in costume reminded me that Christmas is drawing near.

I sucked in my breath...*could there be,* I wondered, *do you suppose there might be a Dachshund?* We have owned two Dachshunds and have dearly loved them both. I speak for both Mark and me to say that Dachshunds are one of our favorite things on this earth! I walked past the nurses' station and nearly cried when I saw a little Dachshund in her owner's arms. I quickly approached her. *How loving you are, Lord!*

"So sweet." I crooned. "Oh, your dog is so sweet and my son loves Dachshunds! He was just admitted, is there any way you could take her to see him?" I pointed behind me to Mark's room.

Strangely, from the second I saw the little Lab, I had no doubt that Mark was about to see one of his favorite things on this earth. I knew it was "a Godthing."

How delighted Mark was that, in the first fifteen-minutes in this strange place, where he knew he must stay for a very long time, a Dachshund was being held beside his face to give him a friendly lick on the cheek.

When the young woman with the Dachshund left I looked at Mark and smiled, "We will be just fine here, Son, I know we will."

It seemed a foretaste (literally), of things to come when April, Ann-Marie and I went for lunch at a restaurant next door to the hospital. The food was good and it was a relief for each of us to experience a change in the environment where we share food.

Before April left for work, she drove me to Mark's house so I could get the Nissan, pick up a change of clothes for myself and gather a few things that Mark requested. I worked quickly to throw a load of clothes in the washer and dryer and take a shower. I wanted my first solo drive to the hospital to take place in daylight.

I was amazed at how quickly things get done if you do not fuss about them. I was ready to return in no time at all and found the ramp easily. I felt safe walking the two block distance to the hospital in dusk.

When I got to Mark's room I was blessed to see how he looked. He just seemed calmer and I sensed that he will rest better in this place. I told him that the swelling on his face is noticeably better today, and he informed me that they weighed him with a hammock like contraption that lifted his body off the bed. He was unhappy to report that his tall frame of more than 6'1" now weighs less than 125 pounds! His weight is a huge concern for everyone.

As darkness signals the end of this busy day, Mark writes that he is having a "mad day." Ann-Marie and I agree with him that he deserves one.

Earlier today, before we left Vanderbilt, Mark broke down. Once he gave into the tears they were relentless. He has struggled against that emotion for so many reasons. I asked him why he was crying so I could try to help and he pointed to the CD player, which was playing Michael W. Smith's new worship CD. "Let it Rain" was the title of the song playing. Mark was not weeping because of his physical condition alone, but because his heart had been touched by the worship he had entered into.

In my new "tough" mode I pushed aside the desire to cry with him and entreated him to stop crying. I honestly told him that I was fearful that he would start to cough but more than that, if the staff saw how upset he was they might end up keeping him another day. Mark accepted that logic immediately and exercised amazing control to ensure he would be released from the trauma unit as planned.

Now, hours later, in a new and strange environment, I watch as he exercises the same control over his anger and decides to watch television as a distraction.

I know that Brenda and Roger are in this facility so, when Mark is ready to rest awhile, I decide to leave him with Ann-Marie and go to find Roger's room. I let Mark know I will be back shortly, and he says in the quiet voice he is using now and then, "Jonathan is coming to play violin for me tonight. Let's make him very welcome."

I smile at my son who always cares so much for others and look forward to meeting Mark's friend, Jonathan.

When I find Brenda, I meet Roger for the first time. It is emotional to meet this man I have prayed for. He wastes no time to tell me how much Mark's music has meant to him. Brenda told me he broke down weeping when he heard Mark's CD and that he plays it over and over and takes it out to show his visitors. I understand he wants to meet Mark as soon as possible.

As I leave their room I see a handsome young man that is obviously a Christian by his countenance standing beside the nurses' station. I smile at him and turn the corner toward Mark's room and then realize this must be Jonathan. I turn back to introduce myself and lead him to see Mark.

We visit briefly before I decide to hurry down the hall to get Brenda to hear Jonathan play. I am blessed that Roger feels up to walking down the hall also. He moves slowly but with determination. It is obvious Roger is a tender-hearted man and I am so pleased they will share this moment with us.

What I write about now is one of the most spiritually saturated nights of my life: Roger sits on a chair beside and near the top of Mark's bed. Only brief introductions have been necessary as each person has heard of and prayed for the other. In an emotion-laden voice, Roger expresses his appreciation of Mark's music and as Brenda meets Mark for the first time, she tells him that she calls me her "Angel."

Ann-Marie and I sit on my cot on the opposite side of Mark's bed from Roger, and Brenda stands beside her husband holding his hand. Jonathan stands at the foot of the bed to offer prayer and then he lifts his bow to poise it over the violin. His eyes close and we enter into holy anticipation. The Spirit of the Lord is evident as the familiar melody of Amazing Grace fills the room.

After the first line, "That saved a wretch like me," Mark begins to cry. I touch his head to pray sensing that these are healing tears. I see Roger move in his chair to tilt his body toward Mark. He holds his hand over Mark's head and begins to pray silently as the incredible music floats around us. It sounds as though three violins are playing. I have never heard such a heavenly sound before. We are motionless as the room becomes saturated with the presence of the Holy Spirit, sweet and thick.

When the ethereal sound ends, Roger stands beside Mark's bed and prophesies over him. He assures Mark that God is taking care of him and that Mark will do greater things than he had ever thought possible.

I am undone. The tenderness of the Holy Spirit and the kindness of this man whose face harbors fresh wounds from an attack by a hammer-wielding thief have reached deep. I silently praise God as this man who cannot receive surgery for his brain injury stands to prophesy and sow love into Mark's heart.

When Roger finishes, Brenda prays for Mark in her quiet voice with its thick Southern accent. Mark receives each word, crying quietly. I then ask Jonathan to join me as I pray for Brenda and Roger, I watch Mark silently join in. By this time the room is brooding with the Spirit. We know all we pray is already in the throne room of heaven; we feel we are at the very feet of the living God. As we close our prayers, Jonathan begins to sing, "Our God is an awesome God." It is slow and reverent rather than the rousing hymn it can be.

We quietly sing along with him. Mark, still waiting for a singing voice, closes his eyes and joins in with his spirit. Then Jonathon brings the song to an end with a sweet solo.

When Brenda and Roger leave, Jonathan prays for Mark. We know it is past time for visitors, and on our first night here we are not sure how strict the rules are enforced, but we can sense Jonathan does not wish to leave. He pulls a book from his backpack, *Experiencing God.* It is one he has been reading and he wants to share it with Mark.

With his left hand, Mark reaches to shake Jonathan's hand. He hangs on to it for a moment and looks up into the eyes of his friend and says in a weak voice, "This will forever be an important part of my testimony."

The healing taking place is nearly tangible. When Jonathan closes the door Mark and I sit and breathe in the Holy Spirit. Mark whispers, "I smell incense burning."

We hear the sweet sound of Jonathan's violin and realize he has received permission to play near the nurses' station so others can be blessed. I sneak out and take a picture of him. I doubt he even saw the flash. He is in his own world as he plays; the world of his Heavenly Father. We are blessed to hear the quiet strains of Christmas music as Jonathan strolls through the halls for quite some time.

This room has been anointed with peace; a baptism that will last well beyond our first day in this place.

I crawl under three blankets; one belonging to the hospital and two familiar ones brought from Minnesota. I move to attempt to conform to the dips in the well-used plastic mattress and smile at the love we have been shown this day.

My cot is so close to Mark's bed it barely allows a person to walk sideways to reach the IV or change his catheter bag. I am able to lie on the cot under blankets as we pray, which is a blessing for me. Mark and I pray together until he drifts to sleep. Then I look up to the dark ceiling and pray for Mr. and Mrs. Lyle and Mr. Hagewood.

I am sure that Caroline left the QR today, quite sure that the Watts' left, and we are blessed to be in a new place which signifies a victory. Mr. and Mrs. Lyle and Mr. Hagewood are the last of "our group" to stay behind; though I am sure they have many new people to minister to in the QR this night. *Lord God, please heal Scott, please heal Cynthia.* I pray as I drift to sleep.

Mark remembers:

The first time I laughed my mom thought I was having a reaction to the drugs. It had been a long time since I laughed, in fact, I avoided it because it was so hard with my jaw wired.

A nurse I had not seen before came in to check on my IV and give me my medications and my shot in the stomach. I had been getting a shot in the stomach each morning. It was a blood thinner to prevent clotting. Each time they gave me the shot they would comment on the fact that it is to be put into the fatty or subcutaneous tissue…and it appears I have none.

I have always been a thin person, but with the wired jaws it got out of control. My nurse got her needle ready and came over to give me the shot. She pinched the little fat she could find, took the needle and held it perpendicular above my stomach, looked at the needle, shrugged her shoulders and jabbed it straight down. I was in shock. The procedure, as I have experienced it, is to insert the needle gently at a 45-degree angle. After a few seconds of utter disbelief and time to let the pain subside, I began to laugh uncontrollably. Because my jaws were wired I couldn't really let the sound out that I would usually let out and it caused my whole body to shake.

I was relieved when the laughter didn't cause pain. The nurse was still in the room so I couldn't explain to Mom why I was hysterical. I saw her look at the television set to see if something was funny, but a commercial was playing. She then looked at me with amusement and concern. I tried to motion to her that I would tell her later but saw her struggle against laughter too. We find laughter contagious and knew we shouldn't get started with someone in the room, but it was too late.

Lana:

I usually turn away when Mark gets his stomach shot because it is a painful experience that I feel he would want to deal with sans an audience. But today a strange noise made me turn around and I saw an unusual expression on his face. His eyes were open wide, then they closed suddenly and his body began to shake. I experienced a feeling of alarm before I realized he was laughing.

One aspect of the wonderful relationship Mark and I share is that when we laugh together we give ourselves to it and usually end up with tears streaming down our faces and holding our stomachs, and so I have a dilemma, because I don't want to do that to him. If laugher produces tears, he will have to cough, and that will hurt. Despite this realization, I can feel myself giving in to the welcome experience of sharing laughter with my son.

"What happened?" I manage to say as soon as the nurse leaves the room. "Is it the medication?"

He shakes his head, still laughing, his lips pulled across the mouth that cannot open. It sounds as though he is sobbing as he tries to restrain himself and he appears to be deep in a mixture of pleasure and pain.

"She stabbed me," he gasps between laughter, "she …harpooned me. It was like she was popping a balloon!"

We give in and laugh. For the first time since the crash we feel the joy of laughter. It washes over us and then we cry, as frustration melts the release.

It must be hard on a freshly harpooned stomach and, once again, I am amazed at the beautiful and complex personality of my son. His first laughter in weeks was born out of pain.

Proverbs 17:22, "A cheerful heart is good medicine."

Saturday, December 22, 2001

Mark looks good today. He received such a healing last night followed by the laughter early this morning.

Mark asks for scripture many times during a day. I pick up his Bible and read from places he has underlined or highlighted. This morning when he requests scripture I read 1 Peter 5:10, "And the God of all grace, who called you to his eternal glory in Christ, after you have suffered a little while, will himself restore you and make you strong, firm and steadfast. To him be the power forever and ever. Amen." We add our own "Amen" to this living word.

I am grateful Mark is doing well because I need to leave for a good part of the day. April and I are going to shop for clothes for Mark. He needs some pants to wear to therapy. They will need to zip or button up the side of the leg to fit over the large casts on his legs. It will be interesting to see how we get the pants on when he cannot lift his hips but we trust the therapists have a plan. Mark is excited to think of wearing something other than the hospital gown. We are once again blessed that Mark will not be alone when I am gone. Ann-Marie will stay with him.

I have found a restroom down the hall that is large enough to change my clothing in. I hurry there to brush my teeth and change out of my sleep clothing. When I get back to the room Mark tells me he would like to try a milk-shake. That is encouraging and a great idea so I call Ann-Marie to see if she can pick one up for him on her way here.

But when she arrives with the shake, we start to question if Mark can have it before we meet with the dietician. Proving he is on the road to recovery, Mark smiles wryly in our direction and says, "So what will they do to me…kick me out?"

Ann-Marie holds the milkshake and directs the straw to Mark's mouth. He sips with pleasure. We need not have worried about introducing something new to his diet because he can only take a couple of sips. I show Ann-Marie the little kitchen that is only steps from our door. We can keep the rest of the milk-shake in the freezer after we label it with Mark's name.

I load up my travel bag with anything we do not want in the room and leave for Mark's house where I will meet April. April, her daughter, Courtney, and I, drive to a local discount store and are successful to find extra large size clothing that meets the criteria given us by Mark's therapists.

I am blessed when Courtney wants me to sit in the back seat with her. She is nearly two years old, cute as she can be, and a delight to me. While at the store we develop pictures through the one-hour photo option and I pick up a few gifts for Christmas. I choose things that will make it feel like Christmas without spending much money. Then we drive to Mark's house to clean.

The house was clean when we arrived two weeks ago but we have done nothing but fall into bed and use the shower and clothes washer when we have been here. April decided we should give it a cleaning and put fresh bedding on the bed Mike will sleep in. She wants everything to be nice when Dave and Mike arrive to spend Christmas with us. Strange as it sounds, I probably would not have thought of it.

It is later in the day than we expected it to be when we arrive at the house. April suggests that I go back to the hospital to observe Mark's therapy and she and Courtney will stay to clean Mark's house.

She does far more than needed by washing our bedding also as well as shower curtains and any wash in the laundry room. She calls me to say it looks really good. I can't thank her enough. I know the cleanliness of the house has been abused in our quick trips in and out.

I am glad to be back at the hospital in time for Mark's therapy. It involves getting him into a wheelchair. This is a major undertaking and takes several people to make it happen. He is not able to sit for more than a few minutes before a team must be gathered again to move him back to bed, but it is progress and we thrive on progress.

Psalm 68:19, "Praise be to the Lord, to God our Savior, who daily bears our burdens."

Sunday, December 23, 2001

In spite of our excitement to be in this place, we had a terrible night's sleep, or lack of sleep. People were partying at the nurses' station. I got up about 2:00 and wanted to open the door to ask them to be quiet but I thought Mark was asleep at the time and I didn't want to wake him.. It kept up until morning rounds. There was a lot of loud talking and laugher very much like a party. If it happens again we will need to say something.

Breakfast went well. Mark drank some grape juice and watered down oatmeal and I watered down some applesauce for him. Later he drank all of his Boost drink. We are amazed that they bring him pureed everything for meals. Even fish. That was the worst, I believe. Just taking the cover off the bowl was nauseating. Whatever they serve in the cafeteria he gets, pureed, and on Friday they served Mark fish through a straw.

At 10:30 a.m. Mike and Dave knock on the door. They have driven through the night in an effort to stay ahead of a snowstorm.

It is so good to be together. I have been concerned about the first time Mike and Mark would see each other but Dave has prepared Mike well and Mark is just simply grateful to see his brother.

My "boys" begin to talk about football as they would at any time. Mark had me contact his fantasy football rep to find out who he has starting and he welcomes this banter. I am proud of Mike and the way he reacts to see his brother in this condition. It is obvious and understandable that he is deeply touched by this tragedy but he immediately responds to help Mark in any way he can. Mike's degree in Sports Medicine gives him confidence to help Mark move around when needed.

Later Ann-Marie arrives to stay with Mark, and Dave, Mike and I go to

Mark's house to unpack the car. The vehicle is loaded with gifts and cards from family and friends. There are cookies and candies in bright boxes and tins. I really need to see these things to remind me it is Christmas.

As we unpack the wonderful display of love and concern, I wonder how I will keep up with the thank you notes. I do not want to forget to thank anyone who has shown us kindness.

I am thrilled to have an entire suitcase of fresh clothing, complete with accessories, from home. I made a list of things I wanted to have and my beloved mother-in-law, Betty, went to our house to pull them together with great efficiency.

We take as little time as possible to unload and for Dave and Mike to shower before we return to the hospital. In the car we discuss that this is Mike's first trip to Nashville. Would he like to see the lights at the Opryland Hotel? He has driven a long distance and we encourage him to see a little of Nashville while he is here.

"No," he replies quietly, "let's just spend time with Mark."

Chris arrives shortly after we return to the hospital. He has an acquaintance of Mark's with him. They visit with Mark and then Mickey and Barbara come into the room. As has happened before in this experience, friends of Mark's talk to each other and begin to realize that they have other friends in common. It is interesting to watch the divine appointments that are taking place.

I have always believed that Mark is one of the wealthiest people I know in regard to friends. No doubt it is because he is such a great friend himself. This is evident as his room begins to fill with people.

A manager from the Green Hills Grille enters with a small Christmas tree. It fits nicely on the shelf by the closet and it is complete with lights. Beside the funky little tree, she places a wonderful plant on a sleigh with a snowman ornament. It's beginning to look a lot like Christmas!

When Ann-Marie returns at 7:00 p.m., Dave and Mike and I walk to the restaurant next door for supper. Dave is so very tired from the long trip on the back of his return trip only a few days ago, complicated by the stress of being in this situation, that he can barely eat. When we return to Mark's room, Dave falls asleep sitting in a chair. I want to take him to Mark's house to rest but Mark has been looking forward to Mike being there to watch football with him.

Mary Beth Carlson calls and it brings me a good measure of joy to hear her voice. She is a gifted pianist and composer and Mark has been blessed to minister with her at many events. I am blessed to call her friend; in fact we are so alike that we have often called each other sister. Mary Beth has information about the Benefit concert they will hold for Mark on New Year's Eve.

One of the events I had been organizing before the crash was a New

Year's Eve concert with Mark and Mary Beth. It was supposed to have been a wonderful concert in a party atmosphere. I am more than grateful that Mary Beth has taken the initiative to make it a benefit concert and that other wonderful artists have agreed to perform.

As I hang up the phone, I realize how much I miss Mary Beth and other friends. How much I miss the way things were. There is no doubt this holiday will be different from any we have known before but I trust God that it will hold its share of blessings. I look at my sons as they spend time together and praise God for the good things in life.

It is amazing to me that tomorrow is Christmas Eve. Usually I would be busy with all the touches that make it special. We were to have both my family and Dave's in our home this year. I had looked forward to it. With this dramatic turn of events, I will not bake one cookie but Mark has asked me to plan to make rice pudding as soon as he can eat it.

It has been another roller coaster day. Mark is battling constipation. He received a liquid stool softener with all his morning meds, but it has not been enough. The nurse told him the pain relievers he is taking basically "turn to cement" in his system.

Early this morning he was in absolute agony from about 2:00 a.m. until 5:00 a.m. They had to give him laxatives. When the first plan failed, they gave him a suppository. Because he is not mobile and the laxatives and suppository could work at a time when they may not be able to assemble a team to move him to a commode, he must continue to wear a diaper. We are concerned as another night draws near that he will suffer again. Merry Christmas, Mark.

Despite the circumstances, Mike has decided he wants to stay the night with Mark. This is great because they can have time together and Dave and I can go to Mark's house to sleep. We are very aware that one of us must be in the room with Mark at all times as he cannot move any body part by himself except for his left arm and to move his head side to side. If he has a leg cramp, we must move the leg for him. If he needs a sip of water, we must reach it, hold it and return it. Mike is more than capable and I welcome the thought of a night's sleep.

Dave and I are touched by Mike's readiness to be by his brother's side. Instead of giving in to fear or timidity, it seems each person who loves Mark and sees him in this condition desires to bring comfort. We are all very sad that Mark is a prisoner in his own body. None of us want to imagine the horror he is living with and we want, no we need, to help in any possible way.

Hebrews 11:1, "Now faith is being sure of what we hope for and certain of what we do not see."

Monday, December 24, 2001 Christmas Eve

The roller coaster continues on track and we are becoming nauseated from the ride. Each day is packed full of struggle, yet each day we claim victory in the name of Jesus. It has become infinitely important to us to find good in bad.

Today they brought in a motorized wheelchair, with controls on the left, of course. It takes three people to get him into the chair and it is hard work for everyone including Mark. He managed to sit in that padded chair for nearly thirty minutes but was in such excruciating pain from his hip, pelvis and tailbone, even in the reclining position, that they thought he would pass out by the time they got three people together to get him back into bed.

I have been the third person needed to move Mark, and so have other friends and family members when needed. We hold the two heavy casts on his feet and move with the techs. The left knee is still immobilized, so we need to be very careful it is kept perfectly straight during any transfers. The right leg is cast and there are those pins that stick, like cup hooks, out of Mark's toes. We must be very cautious that those pins do not catch on his bed sheets or the pillowcases propped on the floor. It is a challenging job but we are more than willing to be the needed pair of hands that aid Mark.

Now, as he is "deposited" into his bed I sit and look out the narrow opening in the draperies. We need to keep them drawn, because Mark's eyes are sensitive to light. I stare at, the parking lot across the street and struggle with tears. It is absolutely unbearable to see him in such pain!

The nurses already love Mark, "Bless his heart," they say often. Sympathy is available but no one can stop the pain or the necessary manipulations that will spike it. It is something Mark must "walk" through. No matter how we desire to ease his burden, he must endure this, to some degree, alone.

The therapists report to Mark each day and they state that they are very encouraged and feel he is doing amazingly well. I watch as two of them come into the room. One is here for occupational therapy and one for physical therapy. They talk to Mark for a moment and then one of them lifts his legs while the other slides a board under them. I am amazed when they Velcro a skateboard type of apparatus to his left foot. At their instruction, Mark tries to slide his right leg back and forth across the board. The goal is only to move an inch or two, but it is a struggle.

He is definitely up for the challenge and works the right leg by himself and then the therapist helps him to pull the knee slightly upward. The left leg, with the broken kneecap must have the skate apparatus on the foot to move side to side. It is slow and painstaking, but it is progress.

I sit on my cot writing while the therapists work with Mark. Suddenly we hear running in the hall. Someone has fallen by the staircase and everyone available is needed.

When the physical therapist returns she instructs me on the motorized chair. It is quite amazing. There are levels of speed and bars to show how much "juice" is left in the battery. We will plug it in at night. It is equipped with a large pillow on the seat, but even that does not make it comfortable for Mark. It is an interesting concept but the therapist admits that he may not be ready for it yet. We decide to park the chair in the hallway for the night.

It is apparent that Mark is a challenge for everyone. He has more broken bones than usually are seen on one person. If the right side can do something then the left hip and knee will stop it from happening and if the left side can do something the broken shoulder on the right side, with pins protruding from it, will stop that from happening. Each phase of therapy planned needs to be adjusted.

Today we noticed an incredible bruise on Mark's left arm. It has been two weeks but today he was able to lift his entire arm and we were appalled at the size of the large purple mark. Closer inspection revealed an imprint of the steering wheel. We take a picture of it for our file and one of Mark's friend's jokes that it should have been an imprint of the car manufacturer's logo. He thinks Mark could have had some endorsements.

The bruise is another revelation of the violent impact. We need to joke about it because the truth is every other injury is so horrible that a bruise of this nature was not even noticed for nearly two weeks!

God surely is Mark's strength and He is the strength of our family. We know God spared Mark's life for a good purpose. We praise Him continuously for helping Mark to cope with the trauma of such an impact. It was violent beyond words, something I cannot allow myself to even think about and yet Mark must deal with it every second of every moment of every hour of every long day. If the truth be told, to a different degree, so must we.

Our Christmas Eve tradition is to have a Williams' family gathering in the late afternoon and then we go to church at 10:00 p.m. Mark sings on the worship team and usually has a solo. Dave and I read narration or scripture. After church, we go home and everyone puts on his or her pajamas. We each get whatever we may want to eat from the kitchen and then gather around the tree to open gifts. It gets very late…and we love it.

On Christmas Day, we sleep late, have breakfast and then enjoy a family get together with my side of the family in the afternoon. I guess I would be at the last minute food preparation stage if we were home. But we are not home.

My mind wanders because I am concerned about finances. The bills will not stop coming just because Mark and I are not working. I look at the funky

Christmas tree and dwell on the "reason for the season." *I trust you, Lord. You loved us enough to come to earth and dwell among us. You loved us enough to die for our sins that we might have eternal life. I trust you that the bills will be taken care of.* I force myself to think only of our loving God, to take my thoughts captive and to stay in this moment of time with my family.

While Mark and I deal with the therapy and daily care, Dave and Mike leave to go to Mark's house where they will nap and shower and then run some Christmas errands. When they return they are hungry and we take turns to eat a late lunch. Yesterday I stopped at the grocery store to get sandwich makings and I brought a small cooler from Mark's house, which I have placed near the door in his room. I have stocked paper plates, cups and napkins and bottles of water. Pop is available in the cafeteria vending machines. We take turns walking, cooler in hand, to the empty cafeteria to eat. Though it is not ideal to eat alone, it would not be right to eat in Mark's room when he is not able to have food. I have heard that hunger makes a good cook and the deli meat and cheese on fresh bakery bread taste like fine Christmas fare.

At 3:00 p.m. Dave and I gather up the two large shopping bags that I have prepared and walk over to the Vanderbilt Trauma Center. We take the elevator to the 10th floor and step off to see a much too crowded Quiet Room.

We walk over to Mr. and Mrs. Lyle who seem very happy to see us. We share warm hugs and then we give them a large tray of sausage, cheeses and crackers along with paper Christmas plates to share with everyone in the QR.

I have stuffed the shopping bags with a collection of smaller gift bags, each containing a gift. For Mr. Lyle there is a book and some stationery for Mrs. Lyle. When Mr. Hagewood comes into the room we greet each other warmly and we give him a gift bag that contains a book.

I put out paper plates and napkins so that everyone will feel welcome to eat if they are able. Dave and I enjoy conversation with Mr. and Mrs. Lyle and Mr. Hagewood for a while and then we each pick up one large shopping bag and walk around the room to stop beside each person sitting in a torchercliner and we give them a gift.

They are small gifts of chocolates, tins of cookies, tablets, note cards and pens. As we hand each person or couple a bag, we introduce ourselves and tell them that we have been where they are and we let them know that we are praying for them.

I can almost smell the fear in the people who have just arrived in the ICU Quiet Room. I can see it in their eyes. Sadness grips my heart as they accept the gifts with questioning smiles.

As we walk back to the Rehabilitation Hospital, Dave hands me a tissue, but I see that his eyes are moist also. We hold hands and walk silently. I feel him squeeze my hand tightly and know he is feeling the same emotions I am feeling. Somehow we know the gifts have made a difference. Simple gifts from a couple of strangers that we hope have expressed what we were too emotional to speak: "We are so sorry you are in this place for Christmas, but please know someone is praying for you."

We walk back, holding hands and praying for those who are spending Christmas in a place we are so blessed to be released from. We vow to each other that this visit to a trauma center on Christmas will become tradition. We snuggle a little closer as we walk back to spend Christmas with our sons. When I look at Dave, we smile at each other through tear-filled eyes.

At 7:00 p.m. April stops by to bring us homemade chili and rice. We heat it in the cafeteria microwave and eat it out of Styrofoam cups. Again, we eat in shifts so Mark is not alone in his room on this Christmas Eve. The chili is delicious. The tradition of eating it with rice is new to us, but we really like it. We are so appreciative of April. She is singing with her church choir and celebrating with her family and yet she found time to make us chili and deliver it to the hospital. We pray God's blessing on April, Brian and Courtney.

Even with this kindness, it is impossible to feel like Christmas. Impossible. But we put on a good show. Mark's nurse stops in to tell us we get the non-existent prize for the most Christmas spirit. The lights on the funky little Christmas tree shine brightly and Christmas music plays softly on the CD player. The bathroom, which Mark cannot use, and everyone else is restricted from using, is packed full of wrapped gifts and we begin to open them, taking our time to enjoy each gift.

Mark is a talented giver of gifts. He delights in giving thoughtful gifts for any occasion and loves to shop with a surprise in mind. Now, as Ann-Marie opens his gift to her, Mark begins to cry. Several days ago, Mark talked to Matt to describe to a "t" the type of sweater he wanted Ann-Marie to have. Matt and Heather went shopping for it and brought back the perfect sweater, beautifully wrapped. But it is evident the helplessness of this situation has just manifest itself in Mark's emotions.

We try to assure him that this Christmas is different for each of us and that gifts are not the important part. Ann-Marie tries on the beautiful sweater and expresses her gratitude that he is there at all to give it to her.

We each struggle to get past the emotions that assault us; we smile at each other, share lots of hugs and keep moving on with our Christmas celebration, knowing that it is by God's marvelous grace we are all getting through the pain and confusion.

I am thrilled to open Dave's gift to me; a cell phone. It is absolutely perfect!

When the gift giving has ended Mike and Mark decide to watch the video *Christmas Vacation*. It has been tradition to squeeze that movie in our family time at Christmas. They are tired, but determined to watch it. I try to join them but fall asleep sitting up in a desk chair. I wake intermittently to see Dave asleep in a chair also and soon Mark surrenders to sleep. Through a sleepy haze I watch Mike turn off the television and gather their coats. I hug them and lay down on my cot before they have left the room.

> *I John 4:10, "This is love: not that we loved God, but that he loved us and sent his Son as an atoning sacrifice for our sins."*

Tuesday, December 25, 2001 Christmas Day

Mark slept pretty well. I had to get up three times to move his leg for him and he had a sip of water twice, but he did sleep in between. As I sit on my cot this Christmas morning I hear him snore.

His breakfast arrived about 7:15 a.m., and I asked if he wanted to eat or sleep and he opted for sleep. I'll microwave the oatmeal in the little room off the nurses' station when he wakes up. They have brought pureed eggs and sausage but it has slight chunks in it so he will not be able to sip it. Chunks of any size do not work as they stick on the wires that hold his mouth shut.

Ann-Marie arrives at 9:00 a.m. and I am just now feeding Mark his breakfast. When I took the pureed oatmeal and cup of coffee to the microwave I overcooked them. The littlest things seem so big. I quickly ordered more oatmeal, hoping they still had some. When that oatmeal came it was too hot, so I added ice. These things would all be small if we were not here in this place, exhausted. I feel I have run a marathon.

When I arrive at Mark's house, where Mike and Dave are dressing for the day, I begin to cry. In my exhaustion I had actually driven past the house and had to circle back. I know I need to rest for one hour but as I undress to lie down I break into deep sobs. Dave comes to the door as I stand halfway between the bed and the closet, unable to move. I motion to all the photos that decorate Mark's bedroom. They are such happy pictures of friends and family documenting special memories. The smiles of friends, family, Mark and myself stare back at me. They seem to mock me and say, "This was the past…very long ago."

I ache to see the captivating smile that draws me out of a somber place and into the joy of life. I long to hear my son's contagious laughter. I want to join him and laugh with abandon. I long to feel his strong arms give me a hug. I NEED to see him cross the room in his long and easy stride, to watch him run down the stairs to quickly retrieve something and run right back up. I want to see him sit at a table with friends and eat a big meal topped off with dessert; to smell the fresh scent as I walk past his room after he has had a long hot shower before a night out with his friends. I want him healthy! God I want life with our son back!

Dave crosses the room to hold me in his arms. I can feel him laugh slightly at the funny sounds that escape from me. If I were not in his arms I would collapse. When I emerge from the depths of despair and Dave knows I can hear it, he talks about being positive, being brave. I want to give in to the hands of hopelessness that pull me down. It would be so easy because this façade of bravery and courage is exhausting. It is a façade. I am relying totally on the grace of God. I have nothing left of my own reserve.

Dave is encouraging me but I know this is my time to crash and be honest. "It is so unfair...so unfair!" I sob.

I allow myself the cry. Somehow I know I will be stronger when it is out of me. Like poison from a wound, it must be released.

In just a short time I am back. I cannot afford to stay in despair. Mark needs me and his need is greater than mine. I crawl under the covers of the bed and Dave tucks me in with instructions to sleep. He is leaving for the hospital with Mike.

Aware that I should take advantage of their being here for Mark, I fall asleep for two hours. I had planned one hour, but slept solidly. I drag myself from the bed to organize things in boxes that should go back to Minnesota with them. I keep in mind that Mark's lease will be up soon and we do not need anything extra to contend with. I may live from a suitcase very soon so I pack with diligence.

In the shower I realize how achy I am. My lower back, neck and shoulders hurt from the torque of my body as I reach to feed Mark and hold his cup in position so he can sip slowly from the straw. I am willing to do it as long as necessary; I just need strength to continue. I pray, as I love to do, in the shower. This day I ask for physical and mental strength for myself that I may be all I need to be for others.

I arrive back at the hospital at 1:30 p.m. It was a long time for me to be away but the guys were fine. They have been watching movies on the little television with a VCR we brought from Mark's house. One movie they watched was *Rain Man* and Mike entertains us with his impressions. He is uncanny to sound like anyone he determines to imitate and we welcome the laughter.

It is an immeasurable blessing to have Mike here. He is helpful and his warm smile, that always touches my heart, now helps it to heal. He keeps us laughing. It is a visible relief for Mark to have his brother here. Family, life's greatest blessing.

The entire Robinson family, minus Jacob who is out of the state, arrives for a visit around 7:00 p.m. Mickey, Barbara, Michael, Matthew and Elizabeth crowd into the room with another friend, David, who brings his guitar along. Michael Robinson, who has cerebral palsy and uses a wheelchair, has a gift for Mark and he is excited to give it to him. He tries to wait patiently until the time is right but his enthusiasm is contagious and we are all looking forward to seeing what it is.

Elizabeth gives Mark a CD signed by Michael W. Smith. And Mark is touched by the sentiment written on the CD. Then Matthew brings in Michael's Christmas gift from his parents, a Karaoke machine with microphone, and he tells Mark that Michael is going to sing for him.

Michael informs Mark that he can choose one of two songs from Mark's *REALITY* CD. "You can choose number two or number seven."

Mark chooses selection number two on the CD, "You Are Loved."

Everyone in the room is touched by this gesture. We have heard, from the family, that Michael often sings along with Mark's CD and that he is not shy about doing it!

Matthew starts the CD and Michael sings along with the words. He has obviously worked at learning it and is not intimidated at the challenging vocal range. I watch the handsome young man and listen to his offering for only a second or two when the tears begin. I am not alone. Everyone is crying softly. The blessing is enormous and the gift is one of the best that could have ever been given.

The room has begun to fill with the presence of the Lord and people are enjoying sharing and singing. The Robinsons have brought us a feast and now encourage us to enjoy the food. Dave and Mike and I take turns going to the cafeteria to eat ham, mashed potatoes, vegetables and salad. It is incredibly tasty and we eat heartily. But we eat quickly because our hearts are calling us back to Mark's room.

While I am in the cafeteria eating, Ann-Marie and Pat come in with more food from the family dinner they have just attended. They offer delicious turkey and incredible lemon cake among other things. I wish my appetite were in full swing because the food is wonderful. Ann-Marie and Pat opt to stay in the cafeteria rather than return to the room. I finish eating and hurry back to the room where I find church in progress.

The moment I walk into the room I am hit with the evident power of the presence of the Holy Spirit. Each person in this room, and that now includes Brian and April, is in an attitude of reverent prayer. Mark's friend, David, is quietly playing his guitar and everyone is interceding for Mark.

When it becomes very quiet Mark begins to speak. The hush in the room allows us to hear his quiet, emotion-laden voice. "There was a time when I did not sleep for four days and four nights." Anticipation is heavy in the room as Mark says, "God gave me a vision."

He relates this very personal vision to the people in this room because he trusts them with his heart. Tears flow as we feel the presence of the Lord surround us as though we are wrapped in a warm blanket. We all sit in silent reverence, contemplating the Love of God to give such a vision to Mark.

I sit down beside the desk and quietly try to write each word Mark speaks. When I look up, I see that Brian is video recording this holy event. April sits on my cot, close to Mark, tears running down her face.

If there was one without tears in the room after Mark shared that which the Lord had revealed to him in the midst of suffering, it was quickly remedied when Michael Robinson offered his prayer. "Lord, I want to publicly thank you for what Mark has meant to my life."

He continued praising God for Mark's CD that has "gotten me through tough times." Everyone in the room knows how acquainted Michael is with tough times. His sweet innocence and sincerity soaks and saturates our hearts.

Michael Robinson and Mark had a bond of friendship before, but now they are joined together in a way the rest of us cannot relate to. We would, truthfully, not want to be able to relate to the common ground of pain, dependency, and frustration they share, but we are blessed to relate to them in their faith. This potent combination has inspired us all to touch the Holy of Holies on this most blessed day.

Mark's friend, David, begins to prophesy by singing and praying over Mark. "You have been given the harp of David," he says before playing his guitar and singing a prophetic word over Mark.

The evening is winding down; we can all feel it. I am as blessed as everyone by the holy atmosphere we are in, but it is in the back of my mind that Dave and Mike will soon leave for Minneapolis. Dave stands in the semi-circle we have formed around Mark's bed and offers thanks to our precious Father in Heaven for the friendships in this room and for their support. His voice is heavy with emotion and he wipes away tears. As Dave finishes his prayer, the people in the room surround him to pray for the trip home that he and Mike will take tonight. Mike has gone down the hall to visit with Pat and Ann-Marie in the cafeteria and I am sad he is missing this moment.

Hugs are prevalent as we all say goodnight. Barbara hugs Mark and then me and she says there is no place else she would have wanted to be on Christmas. Somehow, we all feel that way. God has taken an unhappy circumstance and given us an intimate evening of His holy presence that we will never forget.

Dave and Mike leave at 9:30 p.m. They are going to drive through the night to avoid traffic and to stay ahead of bad weather. It is so hard for me to see them leave. I push away feelings that I am left alone to cope with this horrible situation and embrace the remnant of peace left from this beautiful evening. I will not be alone. God has provided good friends. Mark has excellent care. We will be fine.

I go down the hall to change my clothes and brush my teeth. I have already turned off the lights in Mark's room and when I return I can find my way to the cot by the light in his bathroom. We leave that on and close the door. The sliver of light that filters out the bottom of the door aids me in finding my way around when I need to be up during the night. I am ready for sleep and I try to be quiet as I crawl under the covers of my cot.

The plastic mattress makes a rustling noise and I hear Mark say, "Where is Dad?"

"Honey," I say, trying not to feel concern, "Mike and Dad left for Minneapolis."

"Why didn't he say goodbye?"

"You are tired because of the sleeping medication, Mark. Dad placed his hand on your head and prayed for you before they left. Mike said goodbye too."

Instinctively I reach out and touch his forehead. It feels clammy and I swallow my concern. I tell myself that the sleeping pills erased his memory of Dave praying for him and I offer prayers on his behalf. I also pray for Dave and Mike throughout the night.

Luke 2:10, "Do not be afraid, I bring you good news of great joy that will be for all the people."

Wednesday, December 26, 2001

I am pleased when Mark sleeps most of the night. I am in a sleep mode similar to one a mother has the first nights she returns home with a new baby which means that I am awake to a degree at all times. I wake to look at him, listen for his breathing, and pray for him continuously. Somehow my mind and body are fooled into thinking they have rested by the little "catnaps" I take throughout the night.

We are grateful when Mark has his last IV removed! The nurses have grown increasingly concerned as he has only one arm to put them into and it has been grossly overworked. Each time a new IV has to be administered they struggle to find a spot to put it in. The latest one was quite traumatic with blood all over the place. The nurse that removes it this morning expresses her relief.

Ann-Marie arrives at 9:00 a.m. It is wonderful she is on Christmas break from her teaching position; it helps me so much. As soon as she enters the room and exchanges information with me, I leave to go to Mark's house to shower and gather bills and a few other essentials Mark needs.

I put money together for a deposit. We are blessed that people have sent money to help us out. It is going to be awhile before either Mark or I will generate any income and this money will take the crunch off of our credit cards when I must buy food, pay Mark's weekly bills and purchase things he needs. I make a quick stop at the bank and hurry to Mark's house where there is nothing relaxing about the shower I take in record time. I need to return to the hospital before the paramedics come to take Mark to see his maxillofacial surgeon.

I am back in time to take the short trip by ambulance with Mark but before we can do that, the paramedics must come up with a game plan to get Mark on to the gurney. They are greatly relieved when three staff members come in the room to assist them with the transfer. I watch as five people work to get Mark off his bed and on to the gurney.

Mark stays on the gurney for the entire appointment and it goes well. We really have no words to show our appreciation for this gifted surgeon who has helped Mark in such a monumental way but we offer him our thanks before we leave the room to schedule a future appointment.

We have two victories to rejoice in today. The IV that came out of Mark's arm earlier in the day, and now, at this appointment, the wires holding Mark's jaw shut have been cut. The bars the wires were secured to remain in his mouth and will need to be removed in the future.

For now, we are instructed that rubber bands will go over the bars on two teeth at the top and two teeth at the bottom on each side. They will need to be removed to eat, but the good news is that Mark can start to have some soft food such as mashed potatoes or jello. He has been waiting a long time for this. We praise God for this wonderful encouragement.

As soon as we arrive back at the hospital, I let the dietician know that Mark can have some "semi-real" food tonight. They are thrilled for him. When the tray arrives we know we have a new obstacle to conquer because the bands holding his mouth closed are very small. They are the type used in orthodontia resembling macaroni rings. To stretch them across two teeth at the top and two at the bottom in a mouth that is not opening wide and is quite sore, proves to be a challenge and both of us fight frustration.

I am working the little pick-apparatus to do this for Mark because it takes two hands and he only has the use of one, the left one at that. It is awkward and uncomfortable and we do not look forward to this struggle each time he wants to eat. We decide he will brush his teeth immediately after eating each time to save on this frustration.

We never realized what an endeavor it would be to brush his teeth for the first time after the wires were cut. He brushes his teeth with the tiny brush I have purchased. It is not a problem to this point, but then he tackles his tongue. All the liquid medication and food that have gone into his mouth for these weeks have left accumulation. It is unpleasant but he brushes and then I rinse and wash the toothbrush and he brushes again, I rinse the brush again and he continues until his mouth feels and looks clean. There is a suction unit on the wall behind his bed. I turn it on and he rinses with water and then suctions his mouth.

I can see the relief when he is done. He is tired but sinks back into the pillow and rests with a smile. *Lord! How I take it for granted that I can have a fresh taste in my mouth anytime I desire to! Thank you for all the luxuries in life that we pay no heed to.*

Tonight we have rich prayer time again. When we finish, we talk about the vision Mark had in ICU. I take more notes as he talks about it. It is a deep faith builder but we are not certain if he will share it with anyone in the future or if it is an intimate and personal revelation for his life and ministry.

We find that the prayer time we experience in the evening is a forerunner for the day to come. It is sustenance and we face a new day with more confidence because of time spent with our Heavenly Father.

> Jeremiah 29:11, "For I know the plans I have for you, declares the Lord, plans to prosper you and not to harm you, plans to give you hope and a future."

Thursday, December 27, 2001

I have been too exhausted to journal in detail each day. It is amazing the energy it takes to get from morning to night in this intense atmosphere.

Mark slept well last night but woke about 4:00 a.m. because his leg was in intense pain, the heel in particular again. That heel has been a problem each day since the surgery. We called for some pain medication and then he slept until breakfast came at 7:00 a.m. The food was too thick again. They want him to talk with a speech therapist before eating food that is more than liquid and we have not seen the therapist yet. I watered the food down and went to request a meeting with the speech therapist today.

Therapy sessions can start early here. Usually by 8:00 a.m. both the physical and occupational therapists have arrived in his room. It takes between 5-10 minutes just to get him to sit on the edge of the bed. We have learned how to move his legs together without bending the left one in the immobilizer. The therapists readily admit that Mark is a physical challenge but they cannot say enough about his great attitude.

He is extremely weak but does his part to put on an extra large zipper front work-out jacket. The first step is to put the jacket on his cast arm and then flip it across his back by using his left arm. It is a huge struggle but he manages to pull the sleeve on the other arm and, to the delight of the therapist, he even zipped it up using the tips of the fingers available outside the cast. He readily accepts each new challenge and if he did not have the deterrents of weakness and pain, he would accomplish every task on the first try.

The morning routine is concentrated. Mark eats and that is nothing like just sitting down to eat. It is a project to get the food to the right consistency and feed him. Then, most of the time the next step in our day is therapy and at some point before, after or in between, a nurse comes in to give him his stomach shot for blood thinner and the "cocktail."

Medications must be liquid and he is taking pain medications along with a multi-vitamin, Colace and Pepcid to counteract the other drugs. It is a nasty tasting combination that they usually mix in juice that he can sip through a straw. He takes it without complaint…well, disregarding the face he often makes.

It is a marathon and I look forward to a moment when I can sit on my cot and put my feet up. I have just done that when a man comes in to put a trapeze on Mark's bed. This must be attached to the foot of the bed and that is a slight problem because Mark's legs are longer than the end of the mattress to begin with. Now a metal piece will cut into that space so that when he needs to move a leg, we must carefully lift the leg around the metal. But this apparatus will enable him to pull himself up when he has shifted down in bed and will enable him to sit from time to time.

The bar goes above his head and attaches at the footboard and headboard. The triangle that dangles from a chain is adjusted so he can reach up with his left hand and move his body. It is another step toward independence and Mark jokes that his left arm will be "pumped" up from the exercise.

As I sit on my cot I ponder Philippians, 4: 8. "Dwell on those things, Lana," I can hear the Lord encourage me. "Dwell on whatever is true, whatever is noble, whatever is right, whatever is pure, whatever is lovely, whatever is admirable. If anything is excellent or praiseworthy, think about such things. Do not think on that which is before your eyes. It is temporary and my promises are eternal."

Sweet Savior, we could not do this without you by our side. I feel like we are on a never-ending track with hurdle after hurdle lined up. We must jump one after another day after day, hour after hour and we cannot see anything ahead except more hurdles.

How awesome you are to have created the relationship Mark and I share. We are so united in this; so confident in each other's role. It has always been that way for us. You have gifted us with a unique partnership, an incredible bond. It is so natural that I would not have known how unusual it is if people had not openly commented on it so often. When the comments came, we chose not to question, only to accept the blessing with the confidence that You have ordained such a wonderful relationship.

Not for one minute do I believe this nightmare was the total purpose behind your plan, but here we are, mother and son, together twenty-four hours a day, seven days a week. We must share intense, painful decisions and lay our hopes and fears on the line. We must address these things in no uncertain terms, to You, our heavenly Father, and declare the power of Your name over this situation. How much easier You have made it because we do not have garbage between us. How much easier it is because our respect level for each other is so high. You have blessed us and we respond with a full measure of praise.

I look at my son as he closes his eyes to rest and all the expected emotions rush over me. *How precious he is Lord, in Your sight and mine. Please allow me to remain strong for him.*

Mark and I have decided that as soon as Ann-Marie arrives I will go and take care of Mark's house payment and car insurance and find him a large t-shirt he can get on with some ease. I will miss Ann-Marie when she goes back to her teaching position next week. It has been helpful for me to leave for part of the day. I can get a bagel or something quick to eat about 11 a.m. or I can eat something about 3:30 p.m. each day, depending on when she is available to be with Mark.

I am averaging one meal a day and though I do not like it, it seems to be working fine. Today I will bring the small cooler from Mark's house and stop at the store to fill it with bagels, bananas and crackers or cookies. When hunger strikes, I will be prepared and not so dependent on others to bring food when they come.

Deuteronomy 33:27, "The eternal God is your refuge, and underneath are the everlasting arms."

Friday, December 28, 2001

I dream of a day when things will simply go well. Today Mark feels comparatively good, but he is not able to eat because of the bands on his teeth that are frustrating to remove and replace, complicated by the necessity to see the speech therapist before he begins a new diet. The communication has not been perfect and the dietician has already changed his menu from liquid to soft food so he has nothing to eat. We have been promised a visit from the speech therapist sometime today.

We were also told there was a therapists meeting today and they reported that Mark was the most motivated patient they have ever worked with. I wonder why, if that is the case, he has had little or no care today. The eye ointment did not get put into his eye; he put in his own nasal spray and there has been no bed bath. One reason may be that the staff here has begun to rely on me to see to Mark's needs. I recognize how busy they are and try to take care of as much as possible on my own.

A couple of techs did come to put him in his wheelchair and he was able to sit for nearly two hours. He was, however, more than ready to go to bed after one and one-half hours, it simply took me another half hour to round up enough help to transfer him from the chair back to the bed.

Shortly after that the resident doctor made his rounds and came to see Mark. He read some of Mark's chart to us and told Mark, "This is not a record you would want to go for, Mark, but they (the trauma orthopedic team) say here that you had the most fractures they have ever seen come through!"

As I listen to this report I think, "Wow! This is a huge trauma center! No wonder one of the trauma unit doctors confided in Mickey, "He had me scared. I didn't know how we would put him back together again." We can only look at it as another opportunity to praise God!

With the cornucopia of frustration handed to us, Mark and I both are struggling with our attitude. I suspect I have a form of cabin-fever. The room is crowded and easily cluttered with simple necessities. We keep the drapes drawn because bright light of any degree bothers Mark's sensitive eyes and this probably contributes to our claustrophobic condition. I am dreaming of the good old days when we could go out to a movie or at least watch one on television without multiple interruptions.

We do have videos available to watch because Chris and Carole brought us some last night when they visited with their stuffed floppy dog, HB. We were amazed to find that HB is an identical twin to the dog that I gave Mark when he was at Vanderbilt. Out of all the stuffed dogs in the world, this really is a wonder. Not only that, but Mark had decided that the name he chose for his dog, "Hope", was not masculine enough and he dubbed his dog, "Hope Bocelli", after Andrea Bocelli. Chris and Carole's dog's name is HB so they share the same initials. What an amazing coincidence. Not! We are in continuous wonder at the little things God does to let us know He is with us.

Because it is not possible to watch a video without constant interruption, Mark and I deal with our frustration by focusing on lighter subjects. We talk about my dream to have a laptop computer so I can write while I am here because I would like our journey to be more permanently chronicled than in my paper journals. We welcome the ability dreams have to pull us away from circumstances and who knows, perhaps we really will get a laptop.

Mark wants to nap so I take this opportunity to run my errands. I drive to his insurance agency to pay his insurance and then I drop off film. While at the photo store I have an extra copy made of a picture I found at Mark's house.

I smile to remember the story behind it. A couple of months ago my friend, Giz, and I flew to Nashville to visit Mark and see some sights. While we were here the three of us took a day trip to Memphis because we wanted to see Graceland. We had a wonderful time and bought two souvenir photos of the three of us outside the gates of Graceland. Giz enjoyed the photo so much that she hand carried hers on the plane, unwilling to pack it. After we arrived home she discovered she had left her photo on the plane. She was not content to write it off and called the airline. They searched the plane but it could not be found. So, today I took Mark's copy and had it duplicated. I will send it to Minneapolis as soon as possible and hope it gives her a smile. I allow myself one moment to miss Giz, and to think of how different life was when we spent time together in Nashville such a short time ago.

While on my errand run, I find the books I want to use to keepsake the greeting cards Mark continues to receive and then I drive to another area to a Target store to find a large zip front top for Mark. It is the second zip top I have purchased but I imagine this will be his wardrobe for awhile so he will need a couple of them for me to alternate and take home to wash.

When I get back to the hospital I find Mark in a wheelchair. He is supposed to try to sit in it as long as possible. He tells me the case-worker stopped in and that we have a new concern. She told Mark that if the healing in his legs does not catch up to his upper body he will need to leave this hospital until the legs become able to bear his weight. When I go to her office to ask her more about it she explains that it is a matter of insurance. Insurance companies only allow so many days in the intensive therapy setting of this hospital. We will waste them staying here when the therapists cannot help Mark to learn to walk again.

Mark and I feel overwhelmed. It seems impossible for me to take him to his house for two or three weeks. How would I even move him to a commode? I am troubled. We want to think this weight bearing could happen soon but we are realistic. His left foot is healing quite well, but the broken kneecap stops that leg from being weight-bearing. The right foot is still in a great deal of pain and is a good week behind the left foot as the surgery was one week later.

I am desperately frustrated and admittedly frightened. I sometimes wonder if it would help to confront the drunk driver. I know that is not a possible scenario but I want to yell at her, "Do you see what you have done to our lives?"

Though that cannot happen, I do express some honest concern to Mark so that we can discuss our options. He is in agreement that we cannot cope at home alone. There is just no way that I could lift him from bed to commode and back when it takes several trained people to do it here. I am sure I could be taught to give him his stomach shot each day though it would be well out of my comfort zone. I wonder how I would ever change bedding or move him to bathe him?

Mark and I are honest with each other about our concerns and yet we keep our vow to stay positive. We look each other in the eye and agree, "Somehow it will work out." We are constantly professing faith in a way far bolder than we actually feel. It is our belief God will honor that confession of faith. Faith is more than what we feel.

Discussion and profession finished, Mark decides to sleep; his stint in the wheelchair has tired him and required him to ask for pain medication. I am flirting with the idea of a nap myself but the phone rings.

I answer the phone as quickly as possible to allow Mark to sleep. Dave tells me he is just calling to say he loves us and that he hates to wake up in the morning to see I am not there. I feel the same. I miss my husband, my friends, my work, getting a paycheck, going to social events, talking on the phone with no restrictions and lighthearted conversation. I miss the joy of this time of year when I would be attending many of Mark's concerts and social events with family and friends.

I could easily have a real pity party; my son is wearing a diaper for heaven's sake! But I am blessed to know that strength is in praise and I begin to praise God for all He is doing for us. He has spared our son. He allowed the passenger door to open, though Mark is certain it had been locked, to allow someone to hear his screams for help and for someone to sit beside him as they worked to extract him from the car. God is taking care of details, protecting us and continuing to provide for Mark's care. *I trust you Oh, Lord! I love you and I trust You!*

I hang up the telephone and scrap the idea of a nap thinking that a psychologist would have something to say about my decisions, but I have no energy to be creative. To avoid the torment of a wandering mind, I keep busy. Instead of a nap I decide to continue my quest to de-clutter our small living space. The busier I am the less time my mind has to consider that which is unthinkable.

As I rearrange the room I see the last thing Mark wrote on the dry marker board before he was able to begin to speak again. "Is there a verse…that which does not destroy us makes us stronger…find. I did look for the verse and decided it was more of a proverb than an actual biblical quote but that request shows where Mark is in his walk with the Lord. Even in ICU he had confidence that God will bring good from this tragedy.

I walk down the hall to brush my teeth before Mark's dinner tray is wheeled into the room and then I help Mark to freshen up before Pat and Ann-Marie arrive. They have promised they will bring me a sandwich and I look forward to it.

I had a piece of toast when I went to Mark's house this morning. I also ate a small bag of popcorn when I ran to Target. In the store I realized I was feeling quite weak. I need to be smarter. I am not eating either because it is not convenient or because I forget. I did not get the cooler filled with food today because I ran out of time. Perhaps tomorrow.

My hunger has not made me covet Mark's supper. When his dinner tray is brought to him he accepts the challenge of tasting pureed veal and vegetables. I know I am grinning widely as I watch him place the spoon carefully in his mouth. I expect a nasty reaction to the food that looks like "someone already ate it," but he seems to enjoy it. I know he will gain strength quicker now that he can have nourishment in more than liquid form.

We know we need to discuss the immediate future. How we would love to avoid the subject! On January eighth Mark has an orthopedic appointment and so much hinges on the outcome of that visit. The date that seems so very far away taunts us. Will the doctor pronounce Mark able to bear weight and solve many of our problems, or will he sentence us to an unknown move for a few weeks while we wait for the day when Mark will be able to stand up?

I hesitate to remind Mark that the lease on his house is up the end of January and both of his roommates are planning to move out. That would leave us with the full burden of rent. Mark has obviously already given this some thought and he wants to talk to Jason to see if he might consider staying one more month. That would help, but the main burden would remain…how will I take care of Mark outside of a hospital setting?

We have been told that there is another alternative to going to Mark's home. It is a nursing facility. We can barely bring ourselves to talk about it. I have talked with the caseworker enough to realize that we have very little to do with any decision that will be made. We are not able to stay here if Mark is not weight bearing after the January eighth appointment. No argument, no application for pity or mercy.

Mark and I assure each other that perhaps the probable move is not as devastating as we think. We repeat our hope that somehow, God will allow us to jump this hurdle as He has all the others.

We discuss this but Mark nods off as we talk. I have noticed that he sleeps very often now. As soon as he finishes his therapy he goes to sleep. His day consists of eating, therapy and sleeping. He manages to watch a few favorite television shows in the evening but often falls asleep as soon as they are finished. I believe this is part of the healing process but I continue to watch him for signs of depression.

Having visitors is an incredible energy booster. When our guests arrive I eagerly go to the cafeteria to eat my sandwich and then return to enjoy a pleasant visit. When Pat and Ann-Marie leave, Mark and I immediately get ready for bed. The highlight of our day is this time when we can go before the Lord without interruption.

As I return from "my" bathroom down the hall I see the respiratory tech talking with Mark. He has just finished cleaning the wound from the tracheotomy, which he calls a "stoma." Before he replaces the gauze bandage, he shows us that it is nearly closed. Now that amazes me! The hole in Mark's throat is covered by gauze and cleaned twice daily but it has not been sutured. It closes on its own. Imagine a hole in the throat that closes on its own! Lord you have made our bodies in wondrous ways!

Tonight we read *My Utmost for His Highest* again before we pray and Mark asks me to read 1 Thessalonians 5:16-24. He knows the word and which passages he wants read at certain times. I am so proud of the way he has sown into his Christianity. It is proving to be a great comfort for both of us in his time of need.

> *1 Thessalonians 5:16-24, "Be joyful always; pray continually; give thanks in all circumstances, for this is God's will for you in Christ Jesus. Do not put out the Spirit's fire; do not treat prophecies with contempt. Test everything. Hold on to the good. Avoid every kind of evil. May God himself, the God of peace, sanctify you through and through. May your whole spirit, soul and body be kept blameless at the coming of our Lord Jesus Christ. The one who calls you is faithful and he will do it."*

Saturday, December 29, 2001

Mark slept well until about 4:30 or 5:00 a.m. when he woke to say he was having difficulty breathing. The left side of his upper back was in pain. I felt such fear knowing they are constantly concerned about blood clots.

We raised the head portion of his bed and he began to implement deep breathing exercises. I massaged his back for about a half hour and I informed the nurse, who brought him pain medication.

Mark has barely dozed off again when a tech comes in to check his vitals and to let him know he will have therapy at 8:00 a.m. We are supposed to receive a schedule in advance to inform us when therapy will take place, but they do not always have them prepared.

Mark is obviously not happy about the early session. I have to go to the station to ask for his breakfast tray so he will have time to eat. It arrives fifteen minutes before the therapy session, which, with all the particulars that must be taken care of in the feeding process, is not enough time. Mark has never enjoyed breakfast and now he must spoon down unrecognizable pureed sausage and eggs when his eyes are barely open, and do it quickly so that it can settle before his session.

To top off his morning, they have just come in to remove the catheter. I stand in the hall praying for the pain that will most likely accompany this procedure. I return to his room to find out that the catheter has been taken out, and definitely caused him pain. The people working here have most often been honest about the amount of pain Mark can expect from a procedure.

Mark says that the nurse told him "This won't hurt very much." He looks at me with wounded eyes. "It was a woman who said that."

I can tell he is trying to exercise his sense of humor and see the smirk that works at his lips in spite of the pain.

Mark tells me that when she pulled it out she instructed him to "take a deep breath," and then in his words, she "yanked it out."

The catheter had been in since December 8, and so Mark has been instructed to drink a lot of water and told that he will need to retrain himself to "void." That moment of instruction signals the beginning of a difficult day. Mark keeps drinking water and trying to void on his own but he cannot.

He is being carefully monitored and soon a tech enters with a small machine to perform an ultrasound of his bladder. When she lifts his gown she tells him the ultrasound is not necessary. The area is very swollen and she must insert a catheter.

This cute little redhead is one of Mark's favorite nurses and he trusts her completely but the thought of inserting another catheter...and removing it again, is a real test of courage.

I go into the hallway to pray and, when I return, Mark tells me what happened: The nurse explained she would use a plastic catheter. She opened one and tried to insert it but could not. By this time Mark was in a great deal of pain from the swollen bladder. The nurse took a different catheter and inserted it. She continued to insert it until it reached a certain point and the fluid was able to leave his body.

Mark said that, though the insertion was awful, at the point of intense relief he told the nurse, "I love you."

To throw complication into the mix, Mark is constipated from his medication and has to swallow warm milk of magnesia mixed with prune juice as well as other laxatives three times today. He will probably, and hopefully, need to be transferred to the commode frequently over the next few hours.

When Ann-Marie comes to the room I walk down the hall to the cafeteria to eat the sandwich she has brought for me, still exercising my strict rule about no eating in Mark's room. When I get back I see her standing in the hallway outside his room. That means Mark is on the commode. We stand near the door even though Mark told Ann-Marie he would use the call button when he was ready to go back to the bed.

We are enjoying our conversation when we hear Mark's voice over the intercom. "I am ready to be transferred." which is his tactful way of saying, "Please get me off the commode!"

We expect someone to hurry toward his room to help him because of his condition. Everyone on this shift knows that he is sitting on a commode with one fully cast leg propped on a chair because it is immobilized; the other, also fully cast, is resting on pillows because the heel must be guarded from any hard surface. His arm in the cast is on a pillow propped on the arm of the commode and he is helpless to move in any direction without assistance.

To our amazement, no one responds. I look at Ann-Marie and say, "I know there are several people at the desk." I also know they have just had pizza delivered.

"I hope I am wrong." I say to her as I move to walk around the other side of the nurses' station. When I round the corner I see five or six people sitting, talking and eating pizza. The nurse assigned to Mark has her back to me as I approach. *I sure hope she is busy charting something.*

I walk by casually but purposefully. I want them to know I have seen what they are doing. A tech sees me and gets up from her chair. She reaches for a breath mint and as I circle around she picks up rubber gloves. I suspect she has suddenly decided to go to Mark's room to help him!

I come alongside the nurse and two techs sitting beside her. They are eating pizza! Mark called for help nearly five minutes ago and they are eating pizza! I look directly at the nurse to let her know I have seen what she is doing and keep walking in the circle around the desk.

As soon as I get to Mark's door Ann-Marie walks in the opposite direction past the station. I doubt that two minutes pass before three people go in to assist Mark back to bed. Ann-Marie and I look at each other and shake our heads.

Shortly after we are welcome back in the room, Ann-Marie leaves. It is finally "bedtime" in the hospital and we can be alone with the Lord to bring our many concerns before Him. We are led to read Psalm twelve and Philippians, the third and fourth chapters. It is a little later than usual but nothing will keep us from our prayer time. It is our lifeline.

Prompted by the Lord, I pull the manila envelope that holds the greeting cards from the desk and begin to read individual cards, agreeing with the sentiments and the wishes of the sender. I remind God of the prayers of the saints and His promise that He will be present where two or more agree. Spurred on by the sentiment printed on each card, I send up prayer related to the verse and ask the Lord for help with the physical struggles Mark is facing today.

We are very intent when one of the techs comes in the room. When she asks about his day I mention it was difficult and that we are just now praying and agreeing with the messages on cards that have been sent.

I tell her, "I know you are a Christian, and will understand if I keep on praying."

She smiles, "I will join you." She prays in agreement with our prayers for Mark for a few moments and then accomplishes that which she came to do.

When she finishes her task, she looks at Mark and then at me, "Do y'all believe in the laying on of hands?"

We both say, "We certainly do."

"Then, I want to pray for Mark."

She places one hand on Mark's chest and takes my hand with the other. She mentions the sweet presence of God in the room and prays for healing.

We all say "Amen" and then she says sweetly, "I could just stay in this room all night."

We are blessed. We know the presence of the Lord is evident in this room. Those who do not know the sweetness of the Lord do not rest the way we are able to.

Mark has been in that relaxed state for the past hour and I dread the opening of the door that will announce they are coming in to insert the catheter again. *Please answer our prayers Lord! Allow Mark to do this by himself!*

I pray for the Lord to bless the dear tech who prayed with us. I know we are not alone. God takes such care to manifest His presence in many ways.

It is nearly 9:30 p.m. and they will soon come to give Mark his evening medications. We have requested they wait until 9:30 p.m. instead of 8:30 p.m. We need the evening time and have discovered that Mark sleeps better if he can watch television for awhile before the lights go out and we begin our prayer time.

Lord! I plead in silence as I look at the clock on the wall. *I know how hard it will be if they must do the catheter again!*

We know you are here, Lord. Thank you for moments of peace. The storm clouds gathered today and it was one assault after another. But in this moment we feel your hand stretched out to calm the waves. Please! Please let all these functions take place for Mark so he can sleep this night! Show your mighty hand and the power of prayer and accomplish this for my son, in the name of Jesus who is able to accomplish over and above anything we can ask or imagine.

Mark decides to confront the situation and three people have worked to move him to the commode. He knows he cannot stay there for a long time because pain will not allow it, but he does not want to be awake all night with the misery of constipation. The long process is extremely uncomfortable and not successful. The night nurse tells him he can choose to stay on the commode or get back into bed and have a suppository. He knows he needs to get some rest and his hip will not allow him to sit any longer, so opts for the suppository.

While the nurse is in the room she checks his bladder and informs him it is getting full but she does not want to "cath" him because of trauma to the area. She wants him to get on the commode for a third try. It is no easy thing to transfer him, but three of us work to get him back on the commode. By this time Mark is shaking.

I take my place in the hallway to wait and pray. It is torture for me to know he is in such distress. As I stand and wait, I listen for the bell to ring at the nurses station, hoping it will be Mark using his call button to signal success. Most often I stand near his door so I can hear him call, "Mom!" but if I do not hear him for some reason, he will use the call button.

I listen as the bell rings. The voice of the one calling comes loud and clear over a loud speaker. I hear an elderly woman. "I need a pain pill."

"No, Ma'am", the nurse says, "You just had one."

Finally it is Mark's voice. "I need a nurse please." I pay attention to how his voice sounds. I think it sounds good and hope he has had some success.

"Are you done?" the nurse asks. Nothing much is private around here.

"I think so." We can tell he is afraid of being too certain.

The nurse smiles at me across the hallway. Our smiles echo our relief. The nurse and a tech go in and I hear the toilet flush. "Yes!"

The nurse comes out to say, "He did both and we won't have to use the catheter!"

My arms fly into the air. "Praise God!" I say.

Things are in a different stratosphere here. Very little makes sense. There is such joy…real joy, in knowing one more hurdle has been jumped.

Mark is so exhausted that moving back and forth from the commode is no longer an option, so he concedes to a diaper in case all the medication works at once and they cannot get three people together in a hurry to move him.

Once he is back in bed I clean his hands for him as he cannot wash them in the sink He also has me hand him wipes to clean himself. Sometimes I wonder what the nurses and techs do. They do not clean him up after he has used the commode, and he is so limited to do anything for himself. I tell myself the care is mostly good. It has been Mark's observation that some people are nurses and techs because it is a job and others are called to it.

After he cleans up, we work to put his bands in his mouth for the night. I put Vaseline on his sore lips and the nurse comes in to put in his eye cream. He uses the nose spray on his nose. Whenever Mark blows his nose horrible chunks of something come out. We thought it was leftover packing but we are assured it is not. Of course, that only makes us wonder what it actually is!

We prop the pillows under his right foot and straighten his left leg onto a pillow. I tuck a folded sheet under his side to protect his hip and we put another pillow under the cast arm. It is a new form of tucking in my son for the night.

We say a prayer of thanksgiving that God has helped us through yet another horrendous experience. On a scale of one to ten we are at least at twenty in the tired department, but we are more than grateful as we prepare to go to sleep. I walk across the room to turn out the lights and before I turn back I hear Mark snore.

> Hebrews 10:23, "Let us hold unswervingly to the hope we profess, for he who promised is faithful."

Sunday, December 30, 2001

I am so thankful they have cleaned "my" bathroom. It is a public restroom down the hall from Mark's room. I go there each morning to use the toilet, brush my teeth and generally freshen up. I have started to keep an overnight bag in Mark's room to hold my night clothes, which consist of a fleece top and stretch type pants and slippers. I wear these to sleep in to stay warm and because sometimes I need to quickly go into the hall in the middle of the night. I feel better walking around in comfort clothes than I would in pajamas. Changing saves on the clothing I have along, because my usual style of dress happens to include clothing that needs to be dry-cleaned.

I do not wash up at night. I have cleansed my face every night for more than thirty years, faithfully applying moisturizer but now I have not washed it at night for nearly a month. I examine my eyes in the mirror and see dry stress lines. I feel I am losing ground in the battle I have been so diligent in to take care of my skin. My skin is not the only place I notice dryness, I have been experiencing nose bleeds.

In the morning in "my" bathroom, I change quickly and put on lipstick. Sometimes I use a paper towel to wash my eyes. This is a rule broken by someone who has taught skincare. Paper products have never before touched my face for cleansing. I brush my hair, giving it a squirt of hairspray and return to Mark's room. My total time away is about ten minutes. I time it so that I leave his room by 7:00 a.m. to return before his breakfast arrives at 7:15 a.m.

Today we have more "rest" time because it is Sunday. There is no therapy. After Mark eats his breakfast I go to the cafeteria with the donuts and juice I have in the small cooler under his shelf.

When I get back I see Mark has been moved to the commode and a tech he appreciates so much for her thorough bed baths is on her way in to help him move back to bed. Mark's eyes light up when he sees her. "Is there any chance you could give me a bath?"

As soon as he asks we realize the other person helping him is probably the one who should be in charge of that task. But his assigned tech is okay with it, as is this tech that Mark feels so comfortable with. She knows she is very good at what she does and she seems to enjoy the fact that Mark appreciates her.

Earlier this morning I talked with her in the small kitchen off the nurses' station. "The Bible says we are to do all things the best we can so God can be glorified," she told me in her engaging African accent.

Now she tells Mark she will be back about 6:00 p.m. to give him a bath. We decide he should lose the hospital gown today and try the zip jacket we have been waiting to try. He has a baseball hat that he wants to wear. We know our visitors today will be so happy to see this new look.

Chris and Carole are expected to come over to give us communion later. I have thought about communion from time to time but had never mentioned it to anyone. Chris, who seems to anticipate our needs, called to offer it and we gladly accepted.

I feel today will be better than the difficult trial we call yesterday. Mark ate well for breakfast and was able to void on his own. He is still battling constipation but feeling a little less nervous about it.

Our door is open as we anticipate our guests and Mark and I hear a bit of the conversation from the room next door. A tech is having trouble convincing someone to cough. Mark can sympathize. However, this tech is not mincing words about what will happen to the man if he does not accomplish this. Sometimes the language and humor in this place are very foreign to us. There is harshness about the people who see so much every day. Evidently the tech next door has decided the kind approach will not work for that patient and has decided on a scare tactic.

We laugh as we remember the first time in this place that a tech came to clean Mark's stoma, or trach wound. At Vanderbilt everyone had been careful to encourage him by letting him know the wound looked good. The tech here took the bandage off and said, "I could drive a truck through that, buddy."

We have learned to let some of the comments fall on deaf ears. It is just a particular kind of humor that we are not privy to.

It is 11:30 a.m. and Mark is getting his bed bath. I stand in the hall and smile. The tech who gives such good bed baths knows Mark will have company today and has arranged her schedule to accommodate his bath. Her heart is one of a true servant. She takes a full half-hour to be sure he gets moved and his back gets washed. She washes his hair by placing a tub under his head. This is something the other techs pretty much avoid so he relishes having his hair wet down and lathered up.

As I sit outside the door waiting for Mark's bath to be finished, a nurse walks by and hands me a package of clean chubs and fresh towels. There has been a shortage today and she is making certain we have fresh linens. This, again, is unprecedented favor and I am grateful for the fresh linens. The linen closet is just outside Mark's door and I change his linens every day. I cannot do the sheets unless he is in therapy so I let the nurses do them unless he has been sweaty during the night. But I change the cases on each of the seven pillows in the room. We use that many to prop around him, rest his foot on when he is on the commode, etc. I feel it is important to change the linens so that Mark can feel fresh. It is not possible for him to have a real shower or bath and this is just one little thing I can do for him.

I thank the nurse for setting apart a supply just for us. We feel this wonderful favor many times during the day. I am sure it has a lot to do with Mark's great attitude, and I know the nurses and techs appreciate all I do that saves them time and effort. But it is more than that, this favor, it is fulfillment of that which The Lord has promised to us.

When I get the okay to go into Mark's room I see our kind tech has dressed him in his zip jacket and is combing his hair. He grins. Mark has always been a well-groomed man. He always has quality haircuts, wears nice clothes and cologne. To lie with continuous bed-head that actually feels sticky has been hard for him.

The phone rings immediately and when I finish the phone conversation I have to laugh quietly to myself. What has not changed? Pre-hospital, I seldom if ever discussed bodily functions even with my closest friends. Now I am having discussions with our distinguished male friends about constipation and swollen testicles. It seems perfectly natural. These men care and pray for Mark and they ask about these things so I tell them. I am greatly relieved that no one glazes over or takes these torments lightly. They have been some of the most difficult frustrations Mark has had to face.

In spite of the problems, we feel it will be a good day. Mark is freshly bathed and looking good in real clothes. We have great friends coming to spend time with us and fresh linens on the bed. We cannot spend time thinking of the place we are in, but rather focus on the grace that surrounds us.

If we had been home in Minneapolis this week, Ann-Marie would have been visiting. We had pre-purchased tickets to a wonderful comedy show in a small theatre in the city. Today we would have had friends over to watch the football game and I would have made home made chili or beef au jus with all kinds of side snacks and crème de menthe cake. Yesterday we would have spent the day at the Mall of America. Tonight and tomorrow Mark would have been at rehearsal for the big New Year's Eve concert tomorrow night.

We are so grateful the concert planned for New Year's Eve will now be a benefit concert. We have the poster Dave brought for us taped on the closet door. It has a wonderful picture of Mark, pre-crash, and each time I look at it I pray he will look so handsome again. Now and then a nurse will comment, "That's you?" It shows us Mark still has a way to go to look healthy again.

I like to dangle the carrot of "someday" in front of myself. Someday we will be free again. Someday we will sample life again. Mark will be well and laugh and walk and sing. Someday. For now we are here and we will deal with it and we will have thankful hearts because we are together and alive.

This afternoon I got away to shower at Mark's house. He always is anxious to see the mail I bring. He is blessed to receive cards nearly each day. We open the cards and talk about the kindness of whoever sent them. It is a highlight in our day.

Today there is a piece of mail from the hospital and I set it aside to look at it after I show Mark his cards. After I open it I tell Mark I am going down the hall for a minute. I make a phone call from the phone in the deserted cafeteria.

When Dave answers I try hard not to cry. The piece of mail is a bill, with a dollar amount due that many people would expect to pay for an entire house, and it has arrived so soon.

I have a problem with bills and debt. I just always have. I do not deal with them very well. They can overwhelm me and I know the bills we are about to experience are going to come often and will be for very large amounts of money. Dave encourages me not to dwell on it. "What can we do?" he says. We will get an attorney very soon to help us know how to deal with this aspect of the trauma.

Lord, the obstacles are so high! But, You, Oh, Lord, are mighty and able to provide. I praise Your holy name!

When I return to Mark's room, more mail arrives from the reception desk downstairs. Each day cards come that have notes that say, "You don't know me but…" We are deeply grateful for people who take time to encourage Mark and me as we walk through this valley. I pray I will be kind enough to encourage others more often when we are on the other side of this.

It is just a pleasure to look at Mark and see him in his bright windbreaker and shorts with his hair clean and combed. Such joy. April and I have tried to wash Mark's hair before, but it just never looked as good as today after this professional touch.

Brian, April and Courtney come into the room and say they want to take me to lunch. How wonderful. I am amazed when people think of my needs. Mark's are so overwhelming that I really do not expect any attention. I am honored.

We decide to go down the street to a favorite pancake place. Brian leaves before us to secure a place in line. We have a good lunch and a great conversation. April and I have always been able to talk easily and now we share things that give us both a better understanding of relationships between friends of Mark. Dynamics are complicated when someone has such extensive injuries. Quite simply, some people are up to the challenge of a friend in the hospital for a long time…and others are not. We discuss all the people who have been in "the circle," as it is called, of Mark's friends. It is good for us to talk about it. We need to give as much grace as possible to each person that is in Mark's life and it helps to try to understand each reaction.

After lunch we wait for Chris and Carole. When they arrive Chris gives us communion. The communion is administered in the tradition of the Episcopal Church Chris and Carole love. The wafer is broken and dipped into wine, in this case, grape juice, and given to us. Chris then prays a beautiful prayer from his Book of Common Prayer. We have been ministered to in such a sweet way. Once again we sense the presence of the Lord in Mark's room.

Carole and I leave to take a walk so Chris and Mark can have some "guy-time." Chris had called me earlier to ask if this might be possible. Of course it is. I trust Chris to be Mark's confidant in ways I, as a woman and mother, cannot, and I value the time he spends with Mark.

Chris uses some of their time to take Mark through vocal evaluation. I know he has been most anxious to see what is going on with Mark's singing voice. I am optimistic because his speaking voice sounds normal to me. The initial report is good. Mark's range is intact and pitch is still good. It will take time and exercise to get things back, but the prognosis is hopeful. We are excited.

Not only has Chris ministered to us in a spiritual context but he also has motivated Mark in their time together. As soon as they leave, Mark asks to have the large piece of particleboard we keep propped beside his closet. I put it at the foot of the bed and lift one foot at a time on top of it. I then strap the skateboard on his foot. Still lying in bed, he begins sliding his foot back and forth doing two sets of thirty on the left foot and nearly the same on the right. The right heel causes pain but he does well and pushes to finish.

Feeling quite satisfied that he completed therapy on his own, he requests that we watch a movie. We pull out his movie selection and decide to watch Toy Story II. Of course we expect the movie will have interruptions. The first one is the respiratory tech, who comes in to dress the trach wound. He tells us the wound is healing well and now needs to have a scab form on it. Once the scab forms, they will not have to dress it any more. We know this will have to take place before we are dismissed unless the next hospital he goes to will have respiratory techs. Our understanding is that is not likely to happen. We begin our prayer time thanking the Lord for the tender care of so many people. On this day we mention Chris, Carole and our special tech.

Matthew 25:40, "I tell you the truth, whatever you did for one of the least of these brothers of mine, you did for me."

Monday, December 31, 2001

The day started out well. Mark's therapists that had been gone for the Christmas holiday were so pleased with his progress.

Mark now has a pain patch on his chest and it seems to work well to keep the pain at a more even level. He has struggled desperately today with constipation. The nurse told him simply that it is a common effect of the various medications in his system. However, nothing they have given him has taken care of the problem. It is important he does not strain because when he does he hears air escape through his trach wound. Absolutely every part of his body has been affected by this trauma. And each, on its own, is difficult to deal with. I pray a covering of grace on Mark. It is all so overwhelming!

It is now 9:30 p.m. and this trying day is drawing to an end. My son, who uses any excuse to have a party when life is as it should be, is ready for bed on this New Year's Eve. His mother, who shares his love of social get togethers is every bit as ready to close her eyes on this day. It is hard to imagine the celebration going on across the nation. We are blessed that, in Minnesota, there is a party given in Mark's honor to raise money to help us through this difficult time.

Mark and I share a time of prayer and I intercede heartily on behalf of Mark that he may have success on the commode and that he will void so it will not be necessary for them to insert another catheter.

Before we sleep Mark asks to try the urinal. As I stand outside the door, listening for his call, I pray, nearly begging the Lord. Someday this may seem a small thing, but in this moment it is monumental.

In a fairly short time I hear, "Mom!" and I go into the room.

Mark proudly holds up the urinal and its contents.

Unexpectedly I fall to my knees with my arms in the air. I am praising God and half sobbing, half laughing. We both begin to laugh, knowing we are near hysteria and desperately grateful for this victory.

After I alert the nurse to measure the contents of the urinal, I walk down the hall to change and when I return to the room I go to Mark's bed and gently lay my head on his chest. I cannot hug him without the possibility of hurting him and he cannot hug me. I just rest my head on his chest and in one second we are both quietly sobbing.

Philippians 4:6, "Do not be anxious about anything, but in everything, by prayer and petition, with thanksgiving, present your requests to God."

Tuesday, January 1, 2002

Mark opted to sleep when they brought his breakfast at 7:15 a.m. We were able to stay quiet until about 8:00 a.m. because there will be no therapy on this holiday. At 8:00 a.m. I went to the little kitchen off the nurses' station to microwave his pureed eggs and sausage. He spooned them down quite well.

For lunch he had pureed chicken with mustard sauce and something else. We had to consult the menu to name it as it was not recognizable even by scent.

We laughed at the menu that announced "Bow Tie Pasta." It was not possible to recognize the creamy liquid as pasta, much less Bow Tie.

We have decided the tea Mark enjoys may be a contributor in the constipation so he opts for cranberry juice today. It is a good choice for his urinary tract. We are trying to be smart with what he eats aside from what comes on his tray. He is managing to drink prune juice a couple of times a day also, though he insists it is an acquired taste, especially when it is warmed in the microwave. Each meal takes a good amount of preparation as his jaw is still held in alignment by the tiny elastics.

When he is finished eating, Mark brushes his teeth and swishes with a prescription mouthwash. This is not an easy process either. I hand him a loaded toothbrush and stand ready with a water bottle and straw. He must use a suction tube to get the liquid out of his mouth as he is in bed for all his grooming, so I turn on a suction device mounted on the wall behind his bed and hand him the long tube attached. He closes his mouth as you would in the dentist office and the liquid goes up the tube and into a container behind his bed.

Once Mark's mouth is clean, he performs his jaw exercises and puts the bands back on. I hold a mirror in front of him and watch him struggle to manipulate the bands onto the bars above and below his teeth. I continue to be amazed that absolutely everything he has to do for "routine" is hard work.

Dave calls to tell us the benefit concert was awesome. Approximately 500 people attended and it continued into the morning hours because no one wanted to leave. We are blessed. He will dub the tape he videoed and send it soon.

Mark and I decide to try to squeeze in a half-hour nap before Ann-Marie comes at 1:30 p.m. By the time she arrives I have helped Mark to take a bed bath and dress for the day. He looks and feels fresh on this first day of the New Year.

At 2:30 there is another knock on the door and we are blessed to see Chris and Carole. At nearly the same time, Brian and April call to say they will stop over tonight. We are praying Mark will feel well enough to spend time with all these people we love so dearly.

Chris pulls his Bible out of his leather backpack and begins to read scripture and soon we join him in prayer. As the prayer time draws to a close, Chris looks at Mark and says, "What would you like to verbalize in prayer, Mark? Would you pray and verbalize your requests for what you want out of this time?"

Mark thanks God for many things and prays for continued healing. I sit back and breathe a relaxing sigh. Chris is so good for Mark. He anticipates his needs and seeks response from Mark that I can see is therapeutic.

Chris always has wonderful "toys." Today he takes out his digital camera and photographs Mark's feet, in particular the toes with pins in them. They are both horrifying and fascinating to all of us. He also takes pictures of the pins in Mark's shoulder.

Carole and I enjoy making faces at each other and smiling as he takes the photos but we are both delighted at his insight. Someday we will be very glad to have pictures of this time, not because we will need help remembering, but because it will help others to see, and better grasp, the intensity.

We share some good laughter as we always do when we are together, and then Chris takes out the gift of the day. I say "gift of the day" because Chris usually comes with something for Mark. In the past it has been a baseball hat to hide bed-head or movies to borrow. Today it is his personal CD player. Mark has one but the one that Chris offers for use has large earphones. The idea is to shut out all the background noise that is part of the hospital setting.

Chris inserts a CD. It is a Boys Choir. Mark and Chris share respect for boys choirs. This one features adult singers and a full orchestra. Chris instructs Mark to conduct, as best he can with his left hand, and encourages him to move the fingers of the right hand that protrude from the cast also. He tells Mark this will also have cardiovascular benefits.

Chris puts the earphones on Mark and tunes in the CD and we continue in conversation. Soon we see Mark's left arm rise up; his eyes are closed and a smile crosses his face. With just a hint of self-consciousness, he begins to conduct the music he is hearing.

We respect his privacy and look away as we carry on our conversation. Occasionally, when we look Mark's way, we see that he has entered into peace. Our visit is highly blessed and I marvel at the creativity of this dear friend who is so obviously thinking of Mark's benefit both when he is with us and when they are away.

When it was time for Chris and Carole to leave, Chris walks over and touches Mark's forehead to pray for him. "Love you more than we can say, brother. It's good to spend time with you any place, any time."

Mark is visibly touched by the gift of friendship which has been shared for years, but that now has added dimension. I have known for many years that Mark touches people because of the person he is in Christ. I have always been blessed by that gift. Now I am grateful for it. We praise God often for the blessing of friends He has rallied on our behalf. We are very aware that the love we are shown affects the way we are able to deal with this difficult time.

Alone again, we watch television and discuss if we have time to watch a movie. Friends from The Grille are expected soon. It is Tuesday and they want to bring Mark the Tuesday Tomato Herb Soup Special which is a favorite of his. They have promised to take all the chunks out of it. They will also bring my favorite meal from that restaurant; there will be two servings for Ann-Marie and me.

My mouth waters to think of the food. I have not eaten three meals in one day since before the crash. Today may be the first time. I had a blueberry muffin this morning and at lunch I walked to the cafeteria. I ate a few bites of cafeteria chicken and had my first taste of black-eyed peas.

The kind man in the cafeteria told me it is Southern tradition to eat Black-eyed peas on New Year's Day. It is good luck. I took them out of respect for his kindness and was surprised to find I liked them. I ate very little but found room for the wonderful Chocolate Fudge pie that was left from yesterday's trip to the restaurant next door. My appetite is improving.

All day we have promised ourselves we would watch a movie, but when the time comes when we could do that, we are too tired and decide to go to bed early as usual.

We spend our time before sleep in prayer for healing as we do each night. Tonight our conversation continues after prayer when Mark says he wants to discuss the book we hope to write about this experience. As we talk in the dark, I mention the room Dave and I stayed in at the Trauma Unit was called The Quiet Room. He remarks about how strange it is that he had a vision of a very different room with the same name.

He wants to talk about that vision to be sure I have it chronicled in my journal in entirety. He talks and I write. He has talked well beyond the time we usually allow for conversation after he takes his sleeping pill when I notice his speech is slurring.

"We can talk more about this vision tomorrow son, get some sleep." I say gently.

"Mmm," he agrees.

Before I even settle in to the noisy mattress I hear a sound from Mark.

"Oh!" It is an exclamation.

I listen to see if he will say anything. When he does not, I start to drift to sleep. When I hear it again, it is a combination of sigh and moan.

"Are you okay, son? Do you need something?"

"Something strange just happened."

"What? Healing?" We pray intensely for healing every night and we are in a constant state of expectation.

"I think so. There was this chill all the way down my left leg and knee and then down my right leg. My entire body was vibrating…then earlier, when we talked about the room, a tear came out of my eye, which I didn't cry, and then my right eye too….ooh," he moans again, "I can feel my leg, my left leg. I can feel the foot pretty good. Ooh." Mark's words are interrupted by moans. "I have huge chills."

"Spiritual?"

"Yes."

It is nearly dark in the room and I do not get out of bed as we talk. I am thankful Mark knows the difference between spiritual and physical manifestations. He is definitely receiving healing. He has not been able to feel his leg or feet in the casts. We think this is because of swelling. We believe the swelling has just gone down in a miraculous way.

Words of praise pour out of us. "Thank you Sweet Lord! How wonderful You are, Name above all Names…we magnify Your Holy Name."

As I continue in praise I realize Mark has fallen asleep. He is resting in his healing.

A new year has begun.

> Psalm 46:7, "The Lord Almighty is with us; the God of Jacob is our fortress."

Wednesday, January 2, 2002

Each day presents its challenge and today is no different. Breakfast was delivered at 7:15 a.m. and Mark and I tried to determine a time in the day when I could go "home" to wash the shorts he wears for therapy and take a shower and answer e-mail. We decided I should leave at 8:00 a.m. and hurry back to watch him in therapy.

It is now 9:30 a.m. By the time I help him with the breakfast tray, help transfer him to the commode and back, put his clothes out in case they dress him in therapy…well it all takes time. Mark is wearing a diaper to cover him during the many transfers from his bed and to prevent bedsores. He cannot put on regular under shorts and he wants to be sure he can wear elastic waist shorts for therapy. I cannot blame him and want to get home to wash a pair as he only has two.

It is so late already that I decide to wait until after the 9:30 a.m. therapy session to go to his house. The scheduled therapy is a group session but they come too late to get him there in time. The people who scheduled him obviously did not know just how immobile he is. When they arrived in the room they could see it would take fifteen minutes to get him to a chair and down the hall to the session. Too bad we did not know what the plans were or I could have gone to Mark's house.

The morning medications did not get mixed well and so when Mark drank them by straw they stuck in his throat and he was miserable for quite a while. They brought the shot for his blood thinner in but forgot to give it to him. I am sure Mark would prefer that I not remind them, but when I decide to go "home" at 12:40 p.m. I go past the nurses' station to let them know the syringe is still sitting on the counter.

I am on a mission. I need to get the clothes into the washer and dryer, take a shower, check and answer e-mail and eat a bowl of cereal all within one and a half to two hours. The adrenaline is pumping.

I turn into the driveway just past the row of trees a little quicker than usual and see a strange car by the garage. I know Jason is out of town but remember him saying a friend may be staying here overnight. I hope he is not in the shower or my time goals will be unattainable.

I grab the heavy bag of dirty clothing and turn the key in the lock only to find the door is dead-bolted on the inside. I knock heartily several times and then walk around to the front of the house to ring the doorbell.

There is no response and I am not feeling patient. My heart is beating a bit rapidly as I hurry around to the back of the house to pound on the window of the bedroom this guest is sleeping in. I know I am not being very hospitable as I hurry to the front door to ring the bell again. As I walk around the corner, I see the side door open and a sleepy young man says "hello."

He will always remember me as the rude lady who woke him from deep slumber so she could wash clothes and take a shower and generally blow through the house like a tornado.

I decide to take a chance and wash the clothes and take a shower at the same time. It works. The shower is not perfectly comfortable but it is a quick one anyway. I grab the hair dryer and hit "high." Just as I finish drying my hair the phone rings. I do not check caller ID when I am here. I always answer it quickly.

"Mark?" I am so surprised he was able to reach a phone to call me. I am more than glad the nurse put his cell phone beside him when I hear his story. They put him into a wheelchair so he could sit for awhile and the pain hit immediately. His hip and pelvis have become unbearable and he has called for the nurse. That was several minutes ago and no one has responded.

"Can you buzz again, honey? I want to bring your clean clothes and they need another 15 minutes in the dryer."

"Okay."

I am confident they will be there immediately to help him. After all, his voice comes across the loud speaker and he can be quite specific that he is in pain.

I thought I was moving at full speed before, but I step on the gas now. I throw clean clothes into the duffle bag I carry back and forth. I pull on my clothing and pluck clothes from the dryer. I grab the movies he has requested from his collection and toss in fresh underwear for myself in case I cannot get "home" tomorrow.

I muscle the bags through the house and down the steps to the car, then go back for my purse when I hear the phone ring again.

"Mark!"

"No one is coming!"

"You are still in the chair?"

"Yes."

I can hear the pain in his voice and know he is crying.

"Buzz. Don't be afraid of annoying them. Just keep buzzing until they respond! I am on my way!"

I drive as quickly as possible to the hospital, pull into the area of the parking garage I always use and grab all the things I must take with me. I walk out the garage, around the corner and down the block as fast as my cargo will allow me to move. I am out of breath before I open the lobby door. I hurry down the hall with two duffle bags banging against my legs and their straps pulling hard at my shoulders.

I hit the elevator call button and climb on board. I am tempted to leave the heavy, awkward bags by the elevator door until I check on Mark, but manage to get them down the hall and around the corner to his room. I throw the door open and drop the bags, fully expecting to see him in bed.

"Unbelievable" is all I can say when I see him in the wheelchair.

"The speech therapist came in and was able to tilt the chair to take some pressure off my tailbone and pelvis," he tells me in a weak voice. He is pale and cringing in pain.

I walk into the hall with all the demeanor of a very small drill sergeant. The first tech I see gets the story. "I need your help right away. Did you know Mark has been in the wheelchair since 11:30 a.m.? He has called to be transferred several times and called me at home. Twice."

I like this tech and I can see by the look on his face that he did not know. He hurries into the room with me, calling someone else's name on the way. The three of us transfer Mark to his bed and prop pillows around him to ease his pain. The helpful tech apologizes for the lack of communication.

I am so frustrated I put my head into the pillow on my cot and bite my lip so I will not cry! I am here twenty-one to twenty-two hours, two or three days a week and twenty-four hours all other days. I NEED time to get away and take a shower, wash clothes and take care of e-mail. I am not asking for time to go to a movie, have lunch or go on a shopping spree. The professionals here have to be able to see to his needs for the two to three hours I occasionally need to be gone!

Once my heart stops pounding against my throat and I can take a normal breath again, I realize the blessing of my being here with Mark. I know he is getting better faster because I am here for his every need. He does not have to cope with the frustration of no response or slow response very often because I am able to be his advocate. We are blessed. Blessed. I know it. I do. I know it. I nurture the thought until I am assured of its truth and the frustration subsides.

Two college friends of Mark's stop by and stay for a long visit. What a darling couple. They are so in tune with each other and so full of the Lord. They speak perfect words to their friend who needs to hear what they have to say. The balloon bouquet they bring with them barely fits through the door. Their laughter is medicine. They are a gift to us on this tiring day. They are as wind in our sails.

This night our Bible study before bed is wonderful. 1 Peter 4: 12-13, "Dear Friends, do not be surprised at the painful trial you are suffering as though something strange were happening to you. But rejoice that you participate in the sufferings of Christ so that you may be overjoyed when his glory is revealed."

Romans 15:13, "May the God of hope fill you with all joy and peace as you trust in him so that you might overflow with hope by the power of the Holy Spirit." The Holy Spirit breathes life into the words and we absorb them. The Word truly is our daily bread.

I can barely walk back to bed after checking the room temperature and turning off the lights. How tired will I be allowed to get without getting ill? *Allow me the fullest measure of grace, dear Lord. I need to be able to keep on keeping on.*

Unfortunately, the early morning medication problem has lingering results and Mark is still coughing from the discomfort in his throat. He is extremely restless. When the nurse comes to check Mark's temperature, he listens to his chest. We are relieved it is clear. The nurse makes a note that the morning "cocktail" should be mixed with Boost instead of juice. Hopefully it will work better.

Our beds are so close that a person can barely stand sideways between them. I am a good foot lower on the cot. This proximity means that I will awaken at every sound or movement from Mark's bed. I thank God he takes sleeping pills so he does not hear me if I must move to adjust my body on the plastic mattress with the contoured lumps.

Maybe tomorrow I will get a nap. I have said that each night for weeks now with it never happening, but it is a possibility I like to hold out to myself in the middle of a sleepless night.

Psalm 18:2, "The Lord is my rock, my fortress and my deliverer; my God is my rock, in whom I take refuge. He is my shield and the horn of my salvation, my stronghold."

Thursday, January 3, 2002

It was a long night again last night. Mark often wakes with hot flashes and I wipe his head and change the pillowcase, and often the pillow, so he can go to sleep again. Last night it was especially bad and I pulled the covers down for him. As I did we discovered that he had fallen asleep with the nylon work-out pants that we put on him for therapy for the first time yesterday.

I had to pull them off and it was quite the undertaking. The pants have elastic at the waist but he cannot lift his hips to pull them down and once they get to the knee we have the immobilizer, the big fat casts and the toe pins to work around. I did not want to turn on a light or call for help because we both hoped to go back to sleep.

I managed, with some difficulty, to get the pants down and realized they were literally soaked. I felt the cotton sticking out of the casts and realized they, too, were damp. We decided to leave the sheet off for a while so it all could dry.

Mark was so relieved. We would have laughed to think of how absurd it was that we had missed something as obvious as nylon pants...but it was not really all that funny.

For breakfast Mark eats some watered down oatmeal and some yogurt. I have purchased some containers of his favorite yogurt and put them in the refrigerator by the nurses' station with his name on them. He loves to be able to ask for some any time it appeals to him and that I can get it quickly. He follows the yogurt with vanilla pudding, which they regularly stock in the same refrigerator.

I make frequent trips back and forth. The kitchen is only a few feet from his room and I take pleasure in being able to offer him some foods he can finally enjoy. On this last trip to the kitchen I decide that I want breakfast also. It is a meal I always eat under "normal" circumstances, so I pull an individual helping of Raisin Bran off the shelf. Back in the room I pour some of the milk that Mark will not drink anyway onto the cereal and grab a plastic spoon from the stash I keep in the room. Ah. From now on I will do this each morning.

With breakfast under both our belts we are on our way to speech therapy. It is quite the endeavor. Mark is tall with very long legs. His left leg is still in a cast with an immobilizer. It is probably quite comedic to see me try to maneuver his wheelchair with that leg so far ahead of us. When we reach a corner I must stop the wheelchair and walk ahead to peek around the corner to be sure no one is coming in our direction, then I push the chair and angle around the corner with Mark's leg leading the way.

I am a bit apprehensive as to what Mark's reaction will be to this class. He is the only male besides the therapist and approximately 40 years younger than anyone else. I imagine most of these people have suffered strokes. The instructions are to stick out your tongue, pucker your lips in a kiss-gesture and then to blow through a straw. Praise God Mark can do all of that with no effort. But I recognize there will be much for the jaw to learn after it has been wired shut for so long. Just as he has had to retrain his bladder and bowel, and we praise God they are working normally now, he must train every other traumatized part of his body. It is an overwhelming thought.

He makes it through the class but is very quiet on the way back. "I don't think I need that." he says in a near whisper when we are back in his room.

"Let's try it one more time to see if there are other activities of benefit." I say. "If not, we will request you skip it."

He agrees with that.

Mark falls asleep immediately after he is transferred to bed and I decide to go to the cafeteria for lunch. My appetite is back and Mark is able to be alone long enough for me to go down the hall for 20 minutes.

When I return I find one of the nurses visiting with Mark. She comes in from time to time to "counsel" with him. She is young, but not as young as he is. Somehow she has sensed he is wise beyond his years and spiritually strong. She shares her heart about some family problems she is facing and asks him to pray for her. I offer praise to God that people see that in Mark. They know he belongs to God and they trust him with their heart's cry.

After Mark finishes lunch we go to therapy. Today they work on extended reach for his arm and they have him place cylinders on round pegs. So very basic, but needed to get his fingers to work once again. Then they help Mark to sit on the edge of the raised mat and they toss a large beach ball to him. This is done to see if he can keep his balance sitting up. He is able to catch it but not throw it back.

Just before we left for therapy, Chris called to say he had contacted a friend who, in Chris' words, is a "Spirit-filled believer and an acquaintance who has been an attorney and now is a successful businessman." He has invited this man to stop and meet Mark and consider becoming our attorney or refer us to an associate. We do not know where we will stand in a civil suit because we do not know much about the financial state of the person who did this to Mark.

This gentleman stopped by this afternoon. He was on a fact-finding mission. His visit was short, as he needed to return to work. He is a kind man and Mark, Dave and I would love to have an attorney who is Christian.

He called this evening and offered his home phone number and he invited Dave to call him from Minneapolis. He understands that Dave needs to be involved in any decisions also. We so appreciated his prompt call and his interest in Mark.

Tonight we are tired as usual and Mark's request is to read all of James 1, so we begin our process of getting him ready for bed at 7:30 p.m. Before we can begin to pray and relax for bed, we need to get his teeth cleaned, eye cream in, bathroom time taken care of, day clothing off, pillows propped and my quick trip down the hall to change my own clothing finished. It takes us about an hour and a half to take care of it all.

Once Mark's bedtime medications are given, we close the door, turn off the main lights and get to work. Mark's eyes are still sensitive, so I read from *My Utmost for His Highest*, and then the scriptures we have chosen for the evening, by the light from the crack in the bathroom door. Then we pray.

We do not waste time on any wimpy prayer. We go boldly before the throne of heaven knowing we are covered by the blood of Jesus. We address each injured area and speak healing in the name of Jesus. Mark usually falls to sleep before I can make my way through all of the injuries from head to foot. Then I crawl into bed and silently speak my personal prayers as I drift into sleep, knowing that soon I will awake to a nurse coming into the room, or to Mark speaking my name.

James 1:2-4, "Consider it pure joy, my brothers whenever you face trials of many kinds, because you know that the testing of your faith develops perseverance. Perseverance must finish its work so that you may be mature and complete, not lacking anything."

Friday, January 4, 2002

"If you plant an Oak tree someplace really nice and it doesn't go through any stress, it'll be the spindliest little thing."

I listen as Mark's tech, offers his take on Mark's suffering. His heavy southern drawl accents his philosophy.

As Bill speaks I watch him efficiently set up Mark's breakfast tray so that Mark can access the food himself! I am amazed. I have been opening all the trays and packets and then feeding Mark. This is the first time I ever saw a tech ready the tray in such a way. I will never do it differently than what I just saw.

He takes the covers off the pureed egg and oatmeal bowls and quickly rips the tops off four sugar packets at one time to line upright between the server plate and the bowl. He opens the milk, Boost and jelly, pulls the paper covers off two straws and pops one into the milk and one into the juice. It takes him about one minute and Mark is set.

Ah, but then he moves to snap the lower part of the tray out so all the food is the right height for Mark to reach it and there is more room for everything. I am impressed. We have been here two weeks and every day before this the tray was left on the sliding cart for us to deal with. This is so much easier and it allows Mark to do some of the prep and feeding himself.

This tech tells us he was trained in the "old school." Well, that's the school to go to! He is capable when it comes to transferring Mark from bed to wheelchair or commode. He just takes charge, plunges ahead with whatever is needed and gets things taken care of. For him to throw in his own type of backwoods philosophy, flavored with a deep southern drawl, is just icing on the cake.

A nurse interrupts Mark's breakfast to give him his "stomach shot." He manages to smile at her as she inserts the needle, "Ow. I hate the way that burns." He laughs lightly and rubs the area gently.

When she leaves we look at each other and grin. He is absolutely full to the gills of the phrase, "This will just be a little prick." Each time he gets a shot he waits for the words and rolls his eyes at me.

I tidy the room and watch Mark eat his breakfast. He absolutely hates to eat in the morning and to eat pure mush is not altogether appealing. He tackles it much like our tech today tackles the difficult tasks in his day.

One segment of this day proves pretty miserable for Mark when a respiratory tech comes in to clean his stoma, which is what they call the tracheotomy wound. It is miserable for him, but the rest of the day turns out to be better than what we have come to accept as "usual."

We are more than ready at the end of each day to begin what has become the ritual of getting ready for sleep. We have it pretty organized and both look forward to the scripture and prayer part as a reward after all the preparation. We have come to see this as an adventure in which God reveals Himself a little more each evening. Tonight we offer praise that today was "better than usual." *Ah, thank You, Lord. Better. That's a good place to be.*

Deuteronomy 33:12, "Let the beloved of the Lord rest secure in him, for he shields him all day long, and the one the Lord loves rests between his shoulders."

Saturday, January 5, 2002

This morning has been absolutely horrendous! It has seemed endless and it is only 8:05 a.m.!

Mark woke a little before 6:00 a.m. to relieve himself. He had to drink liters of water before bed because the pain medications got stuck in his throat again, so we, not the nurses, have decided that they need to be given a half hour before bedtime and the sleeping pill set aside until he is ready to go to sleep. The way they have been doing it defeats the purpose of the sleeping pill.

Since Mark was awake I ran down the hall to "my" bathroom. It was a good thing I took the opportunity while I had it because I had just fallen back to sleep when our efficient southern tech, Bill, came in at 7:15 a.m. to check Mark's vital signs. It all started hard and heavy right then. Suddenly, Mark was in excruciating pain. I worked to move his right leg up and down to stretch it out but nothing worked. At first he could not even bear to have me touch it. He requested pain medication.

The medication has just been delivered now at 8:20 a.m. As I write about these things I know they would not loom as such large obstacles if we were not exhausted. But, in fact, we are exhausted and our emotional sails are threadbare. Any bout of pain takes the wind out of both of us.

Peg is our morning nurse. She comes in as Mark and I are discussing if I can get away to go "home" and shower today. Peg assures me they will not let Mark sit without help available to move him and she looks me in the eye when she says it.

"You need to go, and you look like you really need to rest." Peg is much taller than I am. She smiles down at me and places her hand on my shoulder. "Go," she says softly as a mother would. "Go and get some rest."

I turn away toward the sink where I can busy myself. There are tears in my eyes that I do not want anyone to see. I just can't bear to hear sympathetic, kind words spoken directly to me. Kind words can all go to Mark and I receive from that, but one act of kindness toward me and I dissolve. I am so vulnerable and so very, very tired.

After Peg's kind admonition I decide that I will go home to shower but then Bill comes in the room with a very interesting idea that will take a great deal of time. He is determined to give Mark a bath.

Bill disappears after his announcement regarding the bath but soon he is back with a gurney type bed covered in bright blue plastic with holes on each end. The intent is to transfer Mark to this padded plastic gurney, and wheel him to the assisted bath down the hall.

As Mark and I stare at the apparatus, Bill busies himself wrapping Mark from shoulder to toe in plastic. Each cast is wrapped and tape bound tightly around it. With me out of the room, Bill adds a diaper for modesty. After much wrapping to cover all Mark's casts and scars, they head down the hall. I am instructed to follow.

The assisted bath is a large tiled room where a gurney can be moved around. Bill wheels the gurney right into the open shower. The lower half of Mark's body is totally in the shower area so the bed can drain from the openings at that end. Then Bill takes a hand held shower and wets Mark down. In his no-nonsense manner, he begins to lather soap and apply it briskly to Mark's body. Mark is lying on his back on the gurney and because he cannot roll over on his own even slightly, Bill works hard to include Mark's back in this effort.

Mark smiles. This is his first backwash since the crash. I can see there is pain involved when body parts are moved, but, despite that, Mark appreciates this kind effort greatly. When Bill lathers Mark's scalp and scrubs, I hear a deep sigh from my son. There is no decorum in the rinsing. He just puts the shower head over all the soapy places and lets the water run out the holes at the end of the bed. It takes many, many towels to dry Mark and the process is painstaking. Bill lifts an area or limb of Mark's body to dry it and then he must dry the bed beneath. Because this process takes a long time I begin to feel concerned the relaxing effects of the shower are being countered by the pain and strain on Mark's body.

He sends me a look to confirm that, yes; he is uncomfortable and very, very tired. But only a second later, he offers a weak smile to show that he is relieved to finally feel clean.

After Mark is back in bed, I begin to prop pillows around him and I feel concern when I lift one of his legs to put a pillow beneath it. "Your cast is wet."

The cast on his left leg feels damp, but the right cast is actually wet. I walk into the hall to tell Peg and she shares my concern. She comes into the room and puts a new Ace bandage around the outside of the cast. Almost immediately the bandage absorbs water from the cotton and cast material. I remind Peg of the important doctor's appointment coming up and that we want Mark to be looking good. She promises to keep changing the bandage and I decide it is okay to go home while Mark naps.

It does not take a full two hours to wash clothes, check e-mail and shower. When I return I immediately check the cast and find it is still wet. I tell the nurse and she removes the ace bandage to let the cast air-dry. We put a towel between his leg and the pillow it is propped on and I am diligent to change the towel often. When I check the cast at 4:30 p.m., I notice that it seems to be leaving less residue on the towel.

I want some "real" food and so I go to the nurses' station where I know they keep phone numbers of local restaurants in a desk drawer. I call and order a club sandwich from next door and decide to splurge on a piece of their fudge pie knowing I will eat half of what I order today and enjoy some tomorrow.

Mark tunes in "Little Shop of Horrors" on cable while I go to get my sandwich. I know he would love to play one of the parts in that play and I hope he will start to dream of the day when he can do that rather than to suffer from uncertainty as he lies in this hospital, trapped in casts.

I make sure there is another movie for Mark to watch and that someone will spend the evening with him because our attorney and his wife have invited me to go to church with them. I really want to go, but I struggle with leaving the hospital for any length of time.

In the public restroom that I think of as my bathroom, I put on some nicer clothing and makeup and find myself looking forward to going out for the evening. Mark has told me that it is a wonderful church and I will enjoy it.

Our attorney's wife comes up to the room to meet Mark and they visit for a few minutes before we leave.

We drive up to a very large church, which my companions have expressed a great enthusiasm towards. I am ready for this!

Worship is wonderful. It is much like our home church with a lot of energy and talented leaders. I find it interesting that in this huge congregation I happen to sit beside someone who is from Minnesota. God is continuously letting me know He is in this experience.

Suddenly, during the worship, I have an overwhelming feeling that I am going to dissolve into sobs. I cannot. I will not. *What Lord? What is it?* I do not recognize the emotion as a nudging of the spirit. It is something else. The source of emotion becomes apparent as I look around the crowded sanctuary to see people raising their hands, clapping and singing with gusto. There is movement everywhere and I nearly say it aloud. *These people are healthy! This is what life is supposed to be like!*

I have been around ill and disabled people on an hourly basis for weeks and to be thrust into a room of healthy people overwhelms me. I gain control and appreciate my new friend beside me as she offers friendly snippets of conversation between worship and the speaker.

After the service I am introduced to several people and one man tells me that he will stop by to see Mark sometime soon. His name is Gary and he is friendly and kind but I do not expect he will really take time to come and see Mark.

It is after hours, meaning after 9:00 p.m., when we arrive back at the rehabilitation hospital. That means I must call Ann-Marie on her cell phone to ask her to come to the front door to let me in. She meets me at the door and then leaves from the lobby after telling me Mark is sleeping. I find my duffle bag in the dark of Mark's room and pad down the hallway to change. I go to sleep with a grateful heart that I have spent time in the house of the Lord.

Psalm 122:1, "I rejoiced with those who said to me, 'Let us go to the house of the Lord.'"

Sunday, January 6, 2002

We take Sunday mornings slow. There is no therapy and so I usually keep Mark's breakfast aside and heat it when he awakes about 9:00 a.m. He is just finishing his breakfast at 10:15 a.m. when Gary knocks on the door.

Wow. Last night he said he would visit and he did not delay. He knows Chris and Carole and so there is immediate common ground for conversation. We enjoy his visit and when he leaves he says he will stop by with his son sometime. I know he is a man of his word and we look forward to that visit.

Yesterday the buzz was all about the snowfall that was to take place during the night. At church it was even expressed that there may not be a service in the morning. I am very curious but when I walk to the window to look out I ask Mark, "So where is it?"

He wrinkles his nose, "They really do not know what snow is here. Is it even wet?"

"Yes, I think it rained, or perhaps it snowed and has already melted." Two Minnesotans smile at each other.

The tech for today pokes her head in the door to say that she will be busy. She has nine patients and that is ridiculous. Because Mark had a bath yesterday I tell her I will clean him up. It is quite a physical undertaking. The therapists like to think he is learning to dress himself, but even they must admit that he is a challenge to dress because of all the immobile limbs and casts.

If Mark is allowed a good half-hour, he can pull the large nylon pants on using all the contraptions they give him to assist. The reality behind the dressing process is that the pants must go on over the large casts on his feet, not to mention the pins protruding from his toes, before he can use the "Reacher" to begin to pull them up. Mark's legs are very long to begin with and he cannot reach forward very far because of the hip and pelvis injuries…it is simply not possible for Mark to pull on a pair of pants.

Then there is the shirt. It would be hard for someone to imagine pulling on a shirt when pins stick out about two inches from his shoulder and that shoulder has absolutely no mobility. It is a joke. A cruel one to be sure, but we can laugh in a frustrated way at the challenge of getting clothing on my son.

Today when we choose his clothing, we opt for some flannel lounging pants. I fill a little plastic tub with warm water and soap. Mark cannot move to wash under his arms so I do it for him. Then I give him the soapy cloth and a second cloth soaked with clear water. I leave the room for a few minutes while he finishes washing.

When I think he has had sufficient time I crack the door and say, "Ready?"

"Yes."

We manage to get on a pair of boxers and the lounge pants without compromising his modesty. We start with the left leg which is in the immobilizer and slide the waist elastic up as far as possible and then slide the right foot on the mattress as far as possible and pull the waist of the pants over that leg. The casts are heavy and it's not easy to lift and pull at the same time, but I must do it.

Mark cannot reach down to help, but tries to use the "Reacher" contraption they have given him, which reminds me of tongs with an extended handle. The problem with that is the fabric can get caught in several places so we decide that I will work with one leg a few inches at a time and go around the bed to do the other and back again until we have completed the task.

Once I have the pants near his hip, he reaches up to the trapeze above the bed and says, "Ready?"

I nod and he pulls with his left hand on the trapeze to lift his hips from the bed. I reach behind him on both sides, keeping his modesty sheet in place, and give a quick tug. He falls back onto the bed and I straighten to rub my lower back.

We would congratulate ourselves but we are not done yet. I take a wet cloth and wipe his head massaging it slightly and then I brush his hair. He puts the stick with foam on the end of it into the mouthwash on his tray and I turn on the suction tube. Mark takes his time to clean his teeth and I actually delight in how thorough he is. I can only imagine the "yuck" of weeks of not being able to clean his teeth.

The linen closet outside our door is a blessing and I open the door, make my selection and change each pillowcase before I prop them in strategic places around Mark's body. We have six or more pillows in use on the bed at any given time, each at work to add comfort.

When the last pillow is in place, I flop onto my cot with a sigh and we laugh. I rarely have had to perform such physical work in my lifetime and Mark finds it very amusing to witness.

"Ridiculous," I murmur. I find it absolutely ludicrous that they are toying with the idea of sending us home alone until Mark can be weight bearing.

We cannot rest in our accomplishment because Mark has therapy at 1:00 p.m. and he has not received a lunch tray at 12:35 p.m. Not only does he have to eat but also we have been told it is our responsibility to get him into his wheelchair. Of course we cannot accomplish that without a couple more people to help us. I find this interesting and wonder just what people do when there is no friend or family member able to be with them every moment of the day to coordinate these things and help to make the transfers.

I walk to the nurses' station to inform the nurse that lunch has not arrived, and it is only a short time until a food tray is placed on Mark's bed tray. There is no menu on the tray and so we play our new game, and do our best to guess what he is about to eat. Pureed food is not very distinctive. Our newly acquired educated guess is broccoli with rice or broccoli with eggs and some kind of meat. It may be pureed sloppy joe. A recognizable bowl of tomato soup seems safe and Mark tackles that first. We shake our heads at the packets of crackers that come with soup. When you drink your meal through a straw chances are pretty good the crackers will be returned.

As soon as Mark begins to eat, the phone rings. Becki's call is welcome. She plans to come to visit and if she stops for lunch for herself on the way, she will bring some for me.

One of Mark's friends from The Grille called earlier. A manager gave her some money to buy Mark some shorts for therapy and some Boost or something he can eat. Her phone call was to ask what Mark needed. We told her we had plenty of Boost…and we do. If you were to open the top cupboard door you would see we are collecting quite a supply. Mark cannot drink it each time it comes on the tray because it is too filling and we save it in case he wants it later, but that seldom happens. Our supply reminds me of the commercial with the little boy who hides his pop tarts in his school locker; we open the door carefully. We suggest to this kind friend that some pudding would be a welcome treat.

Becki brings me a salad and one for herself. We go to the cafeteria to enjoy the food and conversation. I always have looked forward to seeing Bec, even more so now.

Shortly after Becki leaves, the friends from The Grille arrive. They bring two pair of large shorts that will slip on over Mark's casts and a huge variety of individual pudding cups. They are a delightful couple and the time they spend with us is enjoyable. We are more than grateful for their kindness and I pray a blessing on them when they leave.

Philippians 1:6, "…being confident of this, that he who began a good work in you will carry it on to completion until the day of Christ Jesus."

Monday, January 7, 2002

I need to begin to research facilities today. To be more specific, I need to find a nursing home in case we are forced to leave the rehabilitation hospital to go to such a place until Mark is weight bearing. I have sent out requests for information and we want to spend a good deal of time in prayer for Mark's appointment tomorrow.

I stop at the nurse's desk to request a list of Mark's medications to take to the doctor's appointment. We are praying the orthopedic surgeon will say that he is able to put weight on at least one foot. If that is the case, we will be able to stay here. We have been told that it is not likely to happen, but we continue to believe in miracles.

The appointment tomorrow is a true event. No one is taking it lightly. The prayer team in Minneapolis has been praying in earnest and our friends here intercede at every opportunity for this crucial appointment. Chris, Carole and Mickey all come to pray with us and, at the conclusion of our time of prayer, the word of assurance is that no matter what the doctor decides tomorrow we will be where God wants us to be, and more important still, God will be with us.

After another long day, it is time for bed and we find that our private prayer time tonight is absolutely phenomenal. It is a true adventure with the Lord. We read *My Utmost for His Highest* as we do each night. Tonight I follow that by reading Psalm 1 and Psalm 100 and then we go to Psalm 99.

Mark is breathing as though he is asleep and I am anxious to climb onto my lumpy cot. I move as quietly as possible to pull off my slippers, dreaming of sleep. I cock my head when I hear, "Philippians."

I am always blessed by Mark's scripture requests. Often he has memorized them as if in preparation for this time. Other times, as this time, he does not know the scripture. It is a prompting from the Holy Spirit.

"Where in Phillipians?" I ask and begin to turn the pages of his Bible.

"4:12."

I smile; it's a favorite of mine. "4:12, okay. So, the Lord just told you to go there?"

"Yes." His voice is sleepy, almost as if it carries weight.

We are in awe of the application for our lives when I read Phillipians 4:12 and 13. When I finish reading, Mark says, "My left leg is moving up and down, up and down."

We begin to praise God rejoicing in the manifestations that occur in our prayer time to encourage us. We are full of joy. Suddenly I am less tired and fired up to pray. I turn to Habakkuk, repeating the passage I had been directed to memorize for a full month before this happened. I had questioned the Lord just slightly, as to why I was memorizing that verse. I could not attach a specific meaning to it, but I was convinced I was to spend time on that verse. Today I am so grateful I obeyed.

"The Sovereign Lord is your strength, Mark. He makes your feet like the feet of a deer, He enables you to go on the heights." Something in my spirit soars as I claim this promise for my son.

I have a wonderful time praying in the spirit and addressing each of Mark's injuries. I know he is mostly asleep, but feel certain he is listening and agreeing as much as possible as I pray over the parts of his body.

I have really been at it. After thirty minutes or so of energetic intercession, I feel very prayed-out and am satisfied with the thorough job I have done, directed by the Holy Spirit. I am so tired I can barely stand up. I pull off my slippers and begin to settle in to my creaky plastic mattress.

"Are you done?" The words carry disappointment.

"Well," I say feeling a bit defensive and more than a little tired. "We did pray a long time. You were asleep for some, but I have read scriptures and prayed in the spirit and prayed over your body. What would you like to pray for?"

"Pray that I can have children."

How many pieces of my heart can be chipped away without it disintegrating? He has always longed for a family and now he is worried because of the trauma to his reproductive organs.

"Of course; I did pray for your urinary tract and reproductive organs, but let's be more specific."

We pray for everything that will be necessary for him to father children. We cover all we can think of and then we claim the last scripture I had read before getting in to bed. Psalm 100:5. "For the Lord is good and his love endures forever, his faithfulness continues through all generations."

"That means, Mark, through me to you and to the generations that will come from you." I lie back in my bed and pull the covers up. "I love you so very much, son."

"You too." I hear the quiet reply that seems to carry relief.

My bed is on his left side, and I see his left hand reach up to the bed guard and extend beyond it, searching for mine. I reach up to hold his hand. I stroke it gently and place it back on his bed.

"Sleep good, precious boy."

A few deep breaths later I hear him question, "Did you say something?"

I didn't realize I had whispered aloud. "Yes. I am praying for your brother right now. I'm praying God will comfort his heart and draw him near."

"Good," Mark says and falls to sleep.

Philippians 4:12 and 13, "I know what it is to be in need, and I know what it is to have plenty. I have learned the secret of being content in any and every situation, whether living in plenty or in want. I can do everything through him who gives me strength."

Tuesday, January 8, 2002

This is a big day for us. I read from Isaiah 46:4, 41: 9, 10 and 13 and 58:8 and 9 as I wait in the cafeteria while Mark has his bed bath. I am led from scripture to scripture as I continue in John 4: 13 and 14, John 14:13 and 14, John 15:7 and John 16:23. Wow! I am confident to move into this day. We will concentrate on these scriptures in our prayer time tonight and by then we will know if we can stay here or if we must move. I return to Mark's room knowing I can be there for him whatever decision is made today.

We are learning that, when you travel by ambulance, you play a waiting game. We are usually told to be ready by a certain time, and we have a doctor's appointment at a specific time, but it does not always coordinate as expected. Today we have two pleasant paramedics. A man named Jim and a woman named Sue. They transfer Mark from the bed to the gurney and we all get into the ambulance. It is a short trip to the medical center.

Mark must wait in the hallway on the gurney and Jim waits beside him, but Sue is quick to go with me to register Mark because it is evident that he is uncomfortable. He does not vocalize any complaint but now and then pain registers itself in his facial expression.

Soon he is moved to another area where the leg casts will be removed. This is a room similar to an emergency room setting where there are four beds divided by curtains. The first cast to come off is on the left leg and it goes nearly to the thigh. I turn away when I see the saw, but look back as soon as the noise stops.

Mark is in a sitting position on the gurney and watches as the cast is cut but when the white material is pulled apart to reveal his knee I see him literally turn as white as the sheets beneath him.

"Should I take your glasses, Mark?" I ask, knowing he will not see well without them and hoping to distract him by my voice.

He pulls them from his head. "Yes."

The sight that caused Mark to blanch is exposed to me when I reach for his glasses. His knee is stapled shut and looks absolutely terrible. I can only imagine how I would feel if I looked at my body and saw such a horrendous sight.

We have little time to think about it because Mark's gurney is immediately pushed down a hallway to the x-ray area. Mark confides in me that he is very nervous about the x-rays they are about to take. He cannot help but remember the night of the accident and the excruciating pain of the cold and unyielding x-ray table beneath the broken places on his body. It is one of the most vivid and worst of his memories.

Sue and Jim wait with us in a long hallway and the conversation flows as they learn of Mark's injuries. Each time someone starts to come down the hallway, one of us jumps up from the bench we are sitting on to go to the foot of the gurney. Once again, Mark's height is a factor; his feet protrude just beyond the foot of the gurney and the right foot with the pins sticking out of the toes is a concern. None of us could stand to see someone bump into it, or get something caught on the pins. Especially Mark.

The x-rays are a challenge. It takes several people to move him from the gurney to the table and then pillows must be placed by his hip and one under the right foot because the pain would be unbearable without them. Moving him into position also proves a challenge for the technician who must have several people help in any change in position that is necessary. There are many, many fractures to x-ray.

All in all, the x-rays have taken longer than Jim and Sue had planned for the entire trip to take. And once we are finished in this area, we still have two doctors to see. The paramedics express concern about getting the ambulance back into circulation. They explain to me that they cannot leave and come back because Mark and the gurney are as one person. He needs the gurney and they are responsible for the gurney and whoever is on it.

They check in with their dispatcher and get the okay to be where they need to be for now and we sit back and talk and wait. I am praying the entire time; even as I talk my spirit is in the room with Mark, pleading for mercy.

The same procedure, involving five people, is used to transfer Mark from the x-ray table back to the gurney and we proceed to the waiting room again, only this time a nurse sidesteps our wait and directs us down the hall to the same room where Mark had his casts removed.

In this room, Mark will be examined and possibly have stitches removed. As we wait we begin to see that Mark has created quite a bit of interest for the medical personnel. He has such extensive breaks and fractures that personnel stop by to see the x-rays and to meet him. One intern comes in and says, "So, you are the broken one. I have heard about you."

Mark's surgeon's assistant jokes, "I will go and get your thousand x-rays."

We are pleased that the orthopedic surgeon who performed most of the surgeries will see Mark himself today. We know it is unusual and we are grateful.

As the x-rays are placed on the light box on the wall beside Mark's gurney, we are both overwhelmed to see them. There is metal everywhere! It is really too much for us to take in. The most difficult to see is the right foot. The heel looks as if it is totally comprised of little macaroni rings and the pins that protrude from the tips of his toes extend through his foot nearly to the heel. It is a metal foot and I know both of us are wondering how they are going to get those long pins out of the toes.

The surgeon tells us that he is very pleased with the way things are healing. There is no infection anywhere. He orders stitches to be removed and tells us that he will see us back here in three weeks. With those words, our hopes of Mark being weight bearing are dashed. He is very clear that he expects Mark will be weight bearing in three weeks…but not before.

Though we are disappointed that Mark is not yet strong enough to stand, we are not surprised and we are grateful that his surgeon is so impressed with his progress. When he shakes my hand I say to him, "Thank you for putting Mark back together."

He shakes his head and grins at me. "It was definitely a challenge."

It is evident he is proud of the work he has done and that is a great relief for us.

The next surgeon comes in to look at Mark's arm and hand and we learn for the first time that a couple of Mark's fingers have been held together with pins. When the cast is cut away we see objects that resemble pushpins sticking out of his little finger through to the ring finger. These are unceremoniously pulled out with no warning and without help of anesthetic of any kind. They are about two and one-half to three inches in length. It took Mark by surprise that they just pulled them out, but he weathered it well.

The person working on Mark sets about the task of removing the staples. It is an unpleasant process but Mark tells me it is not so much pain as dealing with the snapping noise as the metal is cut and the tugging as each is pulled from the tender skin.

Next are the feet and I am relieved Mark is not looking. The stitches in the feet are a grotesque network resembling a puzzle or patchwork quilt. On the left foot several lines of stitches go across the entire length of the top of the foot and on the right they go across the top also but behind the ankle we see a nasty L-shaped cut that goes from the bottom of the foot to above the ankle. The stitches are covered with caked on blood and my heart flip-flops at the atrocity that has been forced on my son.

Once the many stitches have been pulled, we are told that new casts are going to be put on. Mark is told he can pick a color for these fiberglass casts. Both will go from just below the knee and over the feet to the toes. He will not have an immobilizer on his left knee anymore. That should help so much when he needs to be transferred to the commode or wheelchair.

We smile when the tech brings him a color chart to choose from. He picks royal blue. That is no surprise because it is his favorite color.

Jim and Sue and I wait outside the door while the casts are put on. They have been in touch with their superiors again and explained the dilemma they are in with waiting for Mark. They seem more relaxed now and tell me that they want to be with Mark for the rest of this experience. Bonds form quickly when people see such need.

With the bright casts in place, Mark is done at the hospital for the day. The doctor has prescribed in-patient therapy again in three weeks. That means we must move out of the rehabilitation hospital for that period of time and then return. As much as we have dreaded such a prescription, somehow there will be grace to deal with it.

Jim and Sue put Mark back in the ambulance and deliver him safely to his room at the rehabilitation hospital where, with the help of me and a tech, they transfer their tired patient to his bed.

Mark nods toward the nightstand where we keep a supply of *REALITY* CDs. I tell them that Mark wants each of them to have one. They are very happy to receive the CDs and tell Mark that they want to get to a concert of his one day. They also promise that they will check on Mark when they are back in this facility. I am glad for the time we have had to witness to them and we pray for them after they leave the room.

Mark and I are both spent but we force ourselves to talk about the day because I want to journal his feelings.

"I couldn't believe it," he tells me, "when I saw the pins and screws in the x-rays! And when I saw those staples in my knee...how many were there?"

I had counted the double puncture holes as I propped pillows around his knee only moments ago. "29."

"I freaked out. If I had been standing I would probably have fainted."

I smile at him. "I could tell."

"Those pins in my hand! Mom, did you see how long they were? That was weird. It was like a really long needle being pulled out backwards. They had to twist and then they pulled them right out."

We talk in an effort to digest all that has happened and is about to happen, but soon Mark needs to ask for pain medication. His hand is hurting where the pins were pulled out and his entire body aches from being manipulated on the x-ray table.

"Did you see the pins and screws in my hip and pelvis?" He asks with a yawn. "And the wires in my knee?"

I nod and yawn in return.

"Do you know how they are going to pull the big pins in my shoulder out? How about the long pins in my toes? Will they put me to sleep? I hope so."

"We will have to wait to find out." I say, unable to voice my suspicion that they will pull them as they did the pins in the hand.

"Let's rest for twenty minutes before your caseworker comes." I yawn again. But Mark is ahead of me and sound asleep.

I lie down and contemplate the conversation we will have with the caseworker. She will advise us about what we need to do over the next few weeks. It seems there is no time to rest from one emotional onslaught to the next. I manage to fall asleep for ten minutes before the therapist comes into the room.

"Whoa." She says as she pulls the sheet from Mark's legs.

"Like them?" Mark grins looking at the royal blue casts that cover both legs from toes to knees.

"I bet they feel good...compared to the others." She says.

"They do."

"Itch?"

"Not bad so far."

"Good. Well, let's see what that knee can do."

Already? I want to ask, but I know that they can't waste time.

I hold Mark's left leg straight out as we have for weeks now, with much care that the knee does not move. The therapist puts a huge stack of pillows on the floor beside the bed until they are nearly level with the top of the mattress, and then she places his leg on the top pillow. It is at a very slight angle from the bed and even that slight change causes a good deal of pain for Mark.

"Okay," she says. "It's going to hurt, but I want you to try to tell the difference between good pain and bad pain. We don't want any bad pain."

Mark nods and raises his eyebrows to me as if to say, "I don't particularly want any good pain either."

The plan is to use gravity. The therapist lets Mark and his knee get used to resting on the top pillow, and then she has me hold and support the leg as she removes one pillow and gently places the leg on that next lower place. It hurts big-time, but Mark moves ahead with it. The same resting time is taken and then she removes one more pillow and they are done. That is all he can tolerate for today.

The therapist smiles at Mark, giving him thumbs up to show she is pleased with his progress and cautions him to take pain medication before the next few sessions. When she leaves, the caseworker comes into the room. The news is good. Mark's insurance should work for us. We all keep forgetting that the drunk driver should be responsible for all of this, but that is still in question and far in the future. For now we must bear all the responsibility for these mounting bills.

We discuss facilities and I give her my input because Pat has forwarded a list of "ratings" for local nursing homes. Convenience is also important, as I do not know if I will be able to stay in Mark's room the way that I can here. Mark is especially concerned that we are close to his house because he does not want me driving a long distance at night when I am tired. We narrow our choices to three that suit the criteria. I will try to visit one or two at least, and as soon as possible.

Our caseworker smiles and assures us we will not be "kicked out" until we have a place to go. We do feel like we are being kicked out and she knows that, because we have had good and open communication and we understand each other. She told me she spent her weekend away thinking of our predicament and I can see in her eyes she shares our frustration.

Mark reminds me that the Robinsons host a prayer meeting in their home tonight and asks me to call and update Mickey.

"Will you ask them to pray for my hand?" Mark asks. We have learned to be specific and, in spite of pain medication, Mark's hand is still aching from the pin removal. "Also for my knee, it is not happy."

I smile at the understatement.

When I talk to Mickey, I add my own request: a place to stay for three weeks. It is frightening to leave here. We know the nurses, we know the routine, and we feel safe and cared for. Any unknown thing is stress because of the overwhelming things we do know.

Chris calls to see how things went at the doctor, as does another friend who goes to Mickey's church. Friends from The Grille stop by bringing the Tuesday night special that has been specially strained for Mark. It is so kind of them to do this each week.

Unfortunately Mark does not feel well enough to have company. Everyone understands this and respects it. The cute couple place the soup on the tray and stay only long enough to offer some words of encouragement and update him on who is dating who at The Grille.

Mark's stomach hurts. He tells the nurse and soon she enters the room with warm prune juice mixed with Milk of Magnesia and he drinks it down. This poor tasting combination works the best for him.

As the shift change takes place, one of our favorite male nurses comes into the room. He will be gone a few days and we may have moved by then, so this may be our last time to see him. He smiles, "I want you to know I have enjoyed helping and working with you. I wish you well."

It touches my heart to see that he is emotional.

"I hope you come back here in three weeks."

We do too.

We begin our prayer time early because we are extra tired from the day. We exercise praying in tongues and concentrate our requests on a good night's sleep for both of us as well as more healing for Mark.

Mark has been contemplating the act of suffering. During prayer time he says, "There are too many people who talk about or dwell on the suffering of Christ when in reality, there are a lot of people who have suffered physically even worse than he did. You can read about it in books about martyrs. Some people have suffered longer. People forget that it is WHY he suffered that is so important. He did it willingly and unselfishly. He chose to suffer on our behalf and that produced salvation."

Oh, God, you are doing a mighty work in my son!

1 Peter 4:1 and 2, "Therefore, since Christ suffered in his body, arm yourselves also with the same attitude, because he who has suffered in his body is done with sin. As a result, he does not live the rest of his earthly life for evil human desires, but rather for the will of God."

Wednesday, January 9, 2002

When we get to Wednesday each week I receive an assurance in my spirit that spurs me on. The prayer team in Minnesota unites to fast for Mark each Wednesday. It is an amazing gift, as we have not personally met some of these prayer warriors. Their connection to Mark is that they own a *REALITY* CD or he has sung at their church. A couple of them are friends. It is humbling and exhilarating at the same time to know that, for a very special group of people, Wednesdays have become "Marky days,"

It also helps that last night Mark slept well. What a blessing! I was led to pray 1 Peter 4: 1 and 2 and we read from Revelation before going to sleep. This morning we have been playing CDs. Mark has requested to hear praise and worship music as constantly as possible. His choice right now is Michael W. Smith's "Worship." He has a couple of favorite selections on that album and has me play them over and over again. They bring him peace and seem to encourage him.

Yesterday and today Mark has had to ask for higher doses of pain medication. His shoulder in particular is causing a great deal of pain. Still, he is looking forward to Elizabeth and Natasha coming to visit today. They will come about 10:00 a.m. and I will take home a load of clothing to wash and also some things we have accumulated in the room that could be taken out of here ahead of our move. We have been told that the move could happen quickly.

As soon as the young women arrive, I leave. I am beginning to know my way around many areas of Nashville quite well. I pull out of the parking lot and turn the corner toward Mark's house making a change in my usual route to stop at the Post Office and to go to Target. I make quick work of the Target trip, not allowing myself any distractions and soon I am back at Mark's house. I put a load in the washing machine and then check our e-mail. This systematic effort works well. When I am done on the computer, I put the wet clothing into the dryer and hop in the shower.

"Mom," Mark says almost as soon as I have walked into the room, "where is that verse you read last night; the one about the author and perfecter of our peace?"

I look it up in Hebrews and read it aloud.

"Elizabeth prayed that same verse today, which is interesting because once before at a prayer meeting we all opened our Bibles to what we had been reading that day and both of us were reading the same place in Micah."

God is amazing with spiritual connections.

I am reminded that, a couple of days ago, we were reading in Isaiah and the next day, when I checked e-mail, the same verses had been sent our way by friends at about the same time we had been reading them the night before. The Spirit is hard at work to encourage us.

The day has gone fairly well; we have had our time of prayer and I am crawling under the covers of my cot expecting that Mark is nearly asleep.

"I want to talk." His voice is serious.

"Okay, should I get my journal?" So often we want to record things he remembers.

"No. I know you are prophetic, I think you know what I need to talk about."

"Yes. I know."

I say a prayer that the Lord will bless and protect our conversation because it is very personal to Mark. The Spirit has spoken to me about this already and I am ready to hear what Mark has to say because he needs someone to say it to. I am honored my son trusts me with his thoughts.

I can feel the relief in the air as he voices his confusion about the way he feels about his life and the direction it was taking before the crash. We decide that his life has been turned upside down and that God will sort out all the questions once he is well and can think clearly once again. For now, he must give all his energy to his healing.

We talk for quite a while and then, he falls asleep...I think. Or does he lie awake as I do for quite some time, praying for protection over his life and all the decisions to come?

> Hebrews: 12:2, "Let us fix our eyes on Jesus, the author and perfecter of our faith, who for the joy set before him endured the cross, scorning its shame, and sat down at the right hand of the throne of God. Consider him who endured such opposition from sinful men, so that you will not grow weary and lose heart."

Thursday, January 10, 2002

Mark slept through the night! Wow. I remember many years ago when I awoke to realize that, as an infant, he had slept the entire night. The joy is no less now. It is 8:30 a.m. and he has received pain meds that he requested when his tray came at 7:30 a.m. He did not really touch his breakfast and fell asleep almost immediately after taking the medication.

We got the most amazing mail yesterday! Celebration Church in Minnesota sent a huge bright yellow poster. It was covered with individual greetings penned in bright colors. We rejoiced in each one, reading the note and talking about the blessing of each person. Pastor Lowell Lundstrom, who has become so precious in our lives, wrote these words to Mark:

"Mark,

✦ You are going through the University of Adversity

✦ The school colors are black and blue

✦ The school cheer is "Ahhhhhhh!"

You will graduate with a PhD—Powerful, Holy and Dedicated.

Best wishes, Lowell

Mark is blessed to have several holy men as mentors. Pastor Lowell holds a special place in our hearts along with his wonderful family and the precious people in their congregation.

We also got a great card from an intercessor at our church. The card stated that Mark is under the care of the Great Physician and that she consults with Him every day. We believe she does and we're thankful. Besides the card there was a box in which something was carefully wrapped. It was a musical angel! It had a "Lennox" look, white porcelain with gold trim. The note enclosed said that this dear woman had given this angel to her niece when she had been in a car accident. She had wanted to send it to Mark but it did not belong to her anymore. When she told her niece about the situation, she said to send the angel to Mark. We are putting it in a place of honor where it will not be vulnerable.

God's people are so precious. His love flows from one to another when people are surrendered to Him. We certainly are benefiting from God's love manifested in His precious servants.

I need to make a few phone calls and then I want to leave about 10:00 to go to the house to shower. I would like to take extra time to put on some make-up and wear something nice because I am invited to lunch.

I will meet our attorney's wife and her friend at The Green Hills Grille. We have chosen that location because we are all familiar with it. Mark has instructed me to ask for a server that knows him. I am to say who I am at the front desk, if they do not recognize me. He knows that will insure quick and good seating in a very busy atmosphere.

I wait until they are ready to give Mark a bed bath and it is 10:30 when I finally leave for Mark's house. I need to be at the Grille at noon. The Grille is not far from Mark's house and I am ready for a fun lunch. Parking is congested as it always is. This is a place that really cannot contain its popularity. I am grateful for valet parking. The guys in charge get cars into ridiculous parking places and then...wonder of wonders...get them out again.

The valet knows me and so does the young woman at the desk. We are seated almost immediately even though there is a line of people waiting. Mark is highly respected here and I am always treated as royalty.

This new acquaintance is an attractive woman with a story to tell. She has had cancer several times and believes in healing. She is full of great advice and encouragement. We order wonderful cuisine and talk as though we have known each other for ages. Then the great treat of the day...they say they are coming back to the hospital with me to pray for Mark.

The valet jumps to get my car. Once again, I am queen because I am the mother of the beloved prince.

When I get to the hospital, Elizabeth is visiting with Mark and I am happy that he is seldom alone. She leaves just as my luncheon companions arrive. The first thing our new friend says after introductions is how good Mark looks. He cannot hear it enough and neither can I. We are dreaming that Mark will look like Mark one day again. We are blessed he looks so good under the circumstances; we just remember how he looked before.

I know this woman of God is sincere. Mark does look remarkable for all he has endured. A great deal of that is his countenance. He is always pleasant, smiles a lot and his eyes exude light from the Father.

She shares her testimony of healing with Mark. He is glued to her words and nods as she speaks. After they talk for a few minutes, she pulls a vial of oil from her purse along with a stack of recipe cards and a Sharpee pen. She carefully instructs Mark to get The Word in him until The Word comes out of him. We are not to speak any negatives, which we have been bound to from the beginning. We also are not to rehash his injuries, but to claim they are healed. The pen and cards are to write scripture on and to post them all over his room.

Just before she leaves, she hands us a list of scriptures that contain promises of healing. We feel we have been given the keys to unlock the last door in a mystery we had only partially solved.

April calls as she prepares to go to work and Dave calls to see if we have heard anything from our attorney. The attorney has sent letters to both insurance companies regarding his representation. It is a first step in a long process.

I heard that Caroline and Johnnie C., from the Quiet Room, are here now so I tell Mark I am going to look for them. I find them in the cafeteria. It is wonderful to see Johnnie sitting in a wheelchair and eating. His eyes are bright and he has a wonderful smile, just like his wife. We were told that he had been "written off" at the other hospital he had been sent to. We understand that they told Carolyn that he was shutting down. But God intervened and he is doing quite well. I could not tell how well, and I am sure they wish for more than they have, but he is a miracle.

Some friends from The Grille are in the room with Mark when I get back. They stay a short time and then we decide to have a nap. I sleep so hard that when the phone rings I sit up and bump into the wall.

Mark's supper tonight is pureed turkey tetrazzini It looks exactly like when a dog vomits. I give him so much credit because he really tries to get most of it down. He also ate some pureed peas and peaches. Now he is enjoying some ice cream I brought him from my lunch at The Grille.

It has been one of the better days so far.

> Psalm 25: 4-6, "Show me your ways, O Lord, teach me your paths; guide me in your truth and teach me, for you are God my Savior, and my hope is in you all day long. Remember O Lord, your great mercy and love."

Friday, January 11, 2002

Yesterday, I heard a patient mention the name of a nursing home. I thought it might be more than coincidence to hear the name of a facility when we are in need of one. It looked good on our printed sheet that ranked facilities and it is close to Mark's home. I let our caseworker know we may be interested in that one.

Very early this morning I notice a woman dressed in a suit at the nurses' station. Shortly after, we learn she is here from that nursing facility to interview Mark. Wouldn't you know she wants to interview him right when he has been transferred to the commode? Mark and I try to keep his room clean and fresh smelling. I am constantly cleaning and spraying disinfectant, but it is hard when a small room is your living room, dining room, bedroom and bathroom all in one.

That doesn't seem to daunt the woman. She does ask if Mark is incontinent and I tell her that he is, in fact, on the commode at this very moment. The interview does not take long but we can't know if we are found "acceptable" or not.

I have made it quite clear to our caseworker and anyone who will listen that I want Mark to have a private room while he is in a nursing facility. They look at me and smile as though I can ask for the moon but probably will not get it. I smile back, knowing my God is in control.

When Barbara and Mickey arrive, Barbara kindly insists on going with me to visit the facility. It is wonderful to have her company but we made a quick trip of it. Neither of us is impressed with the facility, though I certainly do not know what I am looking for.

We discuss it in the car as we drive back to the hospital. It seemed clean and convenient but somehow we both feel we can do better for Mark. I hate the thought of him having a very elderly roommate that would perhaps be incontinent or have a disease like emphysema where they would cough all the time. I don't mean to be unkind or lacking in sympathy, but it is depressing enough for a young man in his twenties to contemplate a stay in a nursing home. Barbara agrees with me.

We would love to have lunch or take a little shopping trip, but we drive right back to the hospital so she can spend some time with Mark. I am very grateful she went with me and it helps to talk about the place with someone who has seen it and especially because she has experience with such facilities because of Michael.

The day moves forward and it is soon time for Mark's therapy session. As he is wheeled away I hear that another nursing home is being considered for him. I leave immediately to drive over to look at it.

My heart leaps a little as I drive onto the grounds. This facility is in a very beautiful neighborhood and it is aesthetically impressive as you drive in. I was told it is the Opryland hotel of nursing homes…that may have been a stretch, but it certainly is more elegant than the first one Barbara and I visited. The residents appear to be wealthy and there is a ballroom area where a clothing sale is being conducted. I see several elderly women exit a bus that has obviously taken them on a shopping spree.

Our caseworker called ahead and as soon as I arrive I am greeted by a well dressed, professional looking young man. He introduces me to a woman who takes me on a tour, but when I see the room that is available for Mark I know immediately that we do not want to be here. It has a strong smell of urine and is very small. In the lobby I happen to meet the man who is Mark's potential roommate. He is in a wheelchair, being pushed by his daughter, who is considerably older than me. The kind woman who has been giving me a tour introduces us.

Then she says to me, "He would be the roommate."

Immediately the situation becomes comical because the man's eyebrows shoot up and he leans as far forward as possible without falling from his chair, never taking his eyes off of me.

"This is my roommate?" He asks with a good deal of excitement in his voice.

My tour guide and his daughter laugh heartily.

"No." The guide says. "Not her, her son."

It was a light spot in the day, but once back in my guide's office we review some paperwork and it looks like Mark's insurance may not cover this place. I imagine it is quite expensive. I do not have a good feeling about the facility and am relieved when she voices her concern that it probably will not work out for Mark to stay here. I drive away in peace that we are not to spend time here.

When I get back, our friendly caseworker calls to say she has been in touch with the first facility we went to today. She tells me it is possible we will go there. Mark has expressed he wants to go to that facility because it is close to his house. I know he is being considerate of me in case I cannot stay in the room with him.

We so dread this move that we have decided if it is too horrible we can always go to his home and hire a nurse and get a hospital bed and all the other paraphernalia needed to function. We know the move has to take place and so, we surrender and give our fear to the Lord.

I do not take time for lunch in this busy day and at three o'clock our caseworker calls the room. "Get ready my friend. The ambulance will be here at four o'clock to take Mark to the nursing facility."

While we know that in the real world an ambulance arriving for transfer at four o'clock may translate to six o'clock, I move like a crazed woman to get everything packed. I am aware of the size of my small car and wonder if I can pack a cart and take it downstairs, get the car from the ramp, load it and get to the house, unpack and return to repeat the process two times in the next hour.

Though adrenaline has kicked in and I am in a panic mode, I am intent on hiding my frustration from Mark because there is absolutely nothing he can do to help me. I keep my back to him as I pack because I am near to tears. It would be wonderful if the "powers that be" in this setting could understand how emotional the uncertainty of a move like this is, and if they could give us more than a one-hour notice. I instruct myself to be fair in my thoughts. The decision makers are governed by rules that cannot be broken.

Just as I empty the last contents from the closet, Chris and Carole call to see if we have heard anything and I tell them the news. They say they will be right over with some suitcases and boxes and offer the use of their Suburban to move everything. Gratitude is too weak a word for how I feel.

In the midst of my spinning mind I think of Dave. I know it is hard for him to be so far away and I know he must struggle to pay the bills when both Mark and I are out of work, but I selfishly miss having him close by to help me.

There are moments when I feel absolutely isolated and challenged beyond my physical and mental abilities. This is one of them. I remind myself that I am not alone. Chris and Carole, AKA "Angels By Our Side," are on the way.

I voice my gratitude as I continue to pack. "God is in control and He loves us so much!"

Sometimes I feel ashamed that I can be frustrated when I know God supplies our every need. I can get bogged down in the moment and there are so many intense situations that confront us. I chastise myself for allowing despair and then again I know that, if anyone knows my heart, it is my father in heaven. He does not condemn me and I must not put condemnation on myself.

This situation is hard. It is unthinkable. It is horrible. If I give myself permission to accept that truth and the weakness in myself, I gain some relief. God is sufficient for all my needs and I will be strong in Him!

———————

The packing is done. Chris has taken everything to the Suburban and I have packed the Nissan with anything that can go to the house. We sit in the room and talk and wait. Chris and Carole have been waiting with us for two hours. It is 6:00 p.m. and the 4:00 p.m. ambulance that we rushed to be ready for has not yet arrived.

I had hoped to get to the new facility early in the evening so we could settle in, and so we would know what kind of room Mark has. We do not know if I will be able to stay with him in his room tonight or if I will have to go home after we get him settled. I know it is stress for Mark to wonder about his roommate and, in general, about going to live in a nursing home. Neither of us wants me to have to leave him alone tonight.

We have tried to prepare ourselves and both of us believe that God has it all orchestrated. We keep telling ourselves that it is temporary. There is no question that the unknown can be stress.

"Did you have supper?" I ask Chris and Carole.

"Not even lunch."

They were on their way to get something to eat when I told them about the move and they packed their Suburban with suitcases and boxes and left immediately for the hospital.

Mark is the only one who has had some food in the last seven hours.

"I will go and get us supper." I say lightly. Everyone knows I am headed to the nurse's kitchen and that we could end up with Cheerios.

I open the familiar drawers and cupboard doors and forage. I return with Fig Newtons, applesauce and fruit drinks. We all agree they taste really good.

The nurse on duty tonight is upset with the ambulance company. She calls them often and the reply is the same each time, "They are on their way." She is so sympathetic to our plight. Finally, I ask her, "Can we call the nursing facility and ask what kind of room he has? It is going to be "bedtime" when he arrives."

She calls and comes in with the good news that it is a room designed for two people but there is no roommate for now.

We should have made the call hours ago. It is such a relief. I will be staying in Mark's room tonight! It is all easier knowing that I won't have to leave him in a strange place when he cannot make any moves by himself. The four of us take time to praise God!

The nurse brings Mark all of his pain medication except for the sleeping pill. That means we do not have to worry about anything like that when we get to the "new" facility.

Once the ambulance arrives the move only takes about a half-hour to transfer Mark to the gurney, to the ambulance, drive to the facility and move him into his bed. The room seems nice enough. It is at the end of a long hallway. We have had nurses right outside our door since the first night and this seems strange, but we are hoping we will get more rest in this room.

Ann-Marie meets us at the new facility and we know Mark will not be alone so Chris and Carole insist, enforced by Mark, that I go to The Grille with them for some food.

We are waited on quickly by Mark's friends. The food tastes great and I enjoy my time with Chris and Carole, but we do not linger because we are all tired and nothing has been unpacked. Chris and Carole deliver me safely to our new temporary home and say goodnight.

There is no question that we are up later than the other residents in this building. Of course, I am a child compared to them. I wonder how Mark feels about that, but the truth is he may never see the other residents. He will be in his room all the time except when he goes for therapy.

It is not our choice to be here, but we will trust God and His love for us.

Luke 11:11, "Which of you fathers, if your son asks for a fish will give him a snake instead? Or if he asks for an egg, will give him a scorpion? If you then, though you are evil, know how to give good gifts to your children, how much more will your Father in heaven give the Holy Spirit to those who ask him!"

PART IV ✦ THE NURSING FACILITY
January 11, 2002 – January 29, 2002

Lana:

As we prepare for bed I can't help but feel this is a cruel, nasty joke. Mark's legs are longer than the mattress on the bed by six or more inches. I requested a bed extension almost immediately but it won't be here for days. Now that he is totally reclined it is obvious this will not work. His feet are hanging off the bed and we are both concerned about one of them dropping from the weight of the casts or him bumping a foot or catching the pins on his toes. There is no cross bar above the bed for him to lift himself if he slides down in the bed. How will we transfer him from the bed to the commode or wheel chair without a trapeze?

The second problem is also pretty frustrating. They do not have a commode for him. Our late arrival on a Friday night leaves us with little option. We must use one that is way too short for him. I am frustrated that Mark may have to go back to using a diaper when a sympathetic and creative tech rigs up a wastebasket and places the commode on top. It is obvious they have not had a person of Mark's height here before. I assure Mark that I will call the rehabilitation hospital in the morning and get the commode he needs.

I finally have a bed, but when I try to sleep, I literally keep one eye open. I am constantly going to Mark's bed to move his feet from the edge. At one point I sit in the uncomfortable wing back chair that is halfway between our beds. I cannot sleep any better there and return to the bed.

It is four o'clock a.m. and I have not slept yet. I am under spiritual attack. I have been crying hard and cannot stop. In the dark, I reach for a t-shirt I have not put into a drawer yet and make an effort to blow my nose quietly. This is a nightmare! The bed feels as though it does not welcome me and I am in incredible pain! I cannot find a comfortable place even though I have longed to sleep in a bed rather than a cot for so many weeks!

I miss Dave. I miss Mike. I miss my home. And Lord, I must admit I am feeling a bit envious of my husband who is able to sleep in our comfortable bed and look out the window to see the beauty of the river flowing past our backyard. He can snuggle into our down comforter...Oh, Lord, forgive me! I know better. Dave misses us as much as we miss him! He is miserable also!

I feel myself sinking into despair and I know it is a bottomless pit. I cannot go there! *Oh, Jesus! Jesus help me!* I begin to pray in the spirit battling this oppression that is nearly tangible. Suddenly I know the problem. It is as though words are spoken to me, "Someone recently died in this bed."

To this point the night has been agonizing. The physical pain and mental struggle have exhausted me and yet I am wide-awake. The revelation of what has been going on brings peace. I address the issue in prayer and soon fall asleep.

> I Peter 5:8, "Be self-controlled and alert. Your enemy the devil prowls around like a roaring lion looking for someone to devour. Resist him, standing firm in the faith..."

Saturday, January 12, 2002

I wake at 6:45 a.m. grateful that I managed to get nearly two hours of sleep. I actually miss my public restroom as I try to dress and wash up in the tiny bathroom in our room. It is a half bath with no shower, as Mark could not use one anyway; it also houses the unusable portable commode. I literally cannot turn around. But I manage to wash up and finish helping Mark with his first breakfast in this place. The food is not acceptable. They have him recorded as eating soft food. Not yet. I have to go and find some juice and we dilute the oatmeal with water until he can sip some through a straw. The techs have brought me breakfast too. Some scrambled eggs, oatmeal and toast. I really try to eat, but cannot.

It is 9:30 a.m. and we hear a knock on the door. Mark and I smile at each other. It is amusing to hear knocks when Mark cannot move from his bed at all. Perhaps the nurse that is knocking knows I am here.

I turn toward the door as it opens. It is Dave! I could not be more amazed. All through the night as I pictured him in our cozy bed at home he was driving to be with us.

I just stare at him until he finally speaks, "How are you?"

I walk across the room and break into sobs as he pulls me into his arms. We hug for a long time and then I kiss him and caress his beard. He knows I don't like him to have a beard but he has kept it for these weeks because, after all, he is living alone and he is enjoying the beard! Now I just want to caress his beard and let the tears fall.

"Are these happy tears?"

Mark speaks behind me. "She didn't sleep last night." I had shared my revelation with him earlier this morning. And as a testimony to the bizarre circumstances we are in, he agreed it made perfect sense.

Dave walked to Mark's bed and was overjoyed to find he can hug his son better than at the time of his last visit. But as soon as we are alone on a walk down the hall he expresses concern that Mark looks "emaciated." It is true, Mark's more than 6'1" frame now weighs about 110 pounds. As I washed his back earlier today I noticed he would measure only a few inches from front to back as you view him from the side.

We discuss what to do. Mark hates the liquid supplements but we have already discussed that he must keep forcing them down. He cannot digest a lot of ice cream because he has some lactose intolerance. Dave and I talk about this dilemma and try to find a solution.

As the day progresses I become aware that Dave is frustrated. He drove a long distance to see us and he expected a certain amount of freedom in my time. It is hard for him to see I am needed nearly every minute. He had hoped to go to The Grille for lunch or see a movie so we could have time together. He is disappointed that, though Mark has made a great deal of progress, he has such a long way to go. I can see he is concerned for both Mark and me that the situation remains so intense.

"No wonder you are exhausted," he says as we stand in the hallway outside Mark's room. We have just helped him on the commode and Dave has seen how physical it is to do that and once accomplished, he had expected we would go into the hall to give Mark his privacy and return to the room in a few minutes. After we stand in the hall for ten minutes and he expresses his impatience, I shock him to say that, depending on what is going on with Mark, I have stood in the hallway for longer periods of time than this.

I think it is good for Dave to see how this all works. I cannot just take off and go anywhere, ever. Not even down the street to grab a sandwich. Mark is absolutely dependent on someone and the techs cannot, or do not, respond soon enough if he is in great pain or dizzy from sitting on the commode. It is obvious he could not do what I am doing hour after hour. I know that I am covered by grace.

Though Dave is frustrated that we are not going to supper, he realizes what needs to be done and knows that, had we known he was coming, I would have asked someone to stay with Mark. We order a pizza and eat it in the employee lounge. There is no cafeteria here.

Though I did not have much notice I call Ann-Marie and tell her Dave is in town. She readily offers to spend the night at the facility so that I can go to Mark's house with Dave. We have another friend lined up for tomorrow night. I look forward to cuddling next to my husband and getting a good night's sleep.

At 9:00 p.m. Dave leaves for Mark's house because he has been awake for more than 48 hours. I help get Mark ready for bed and order his sleeping pill. We pray together as it has become so important for us to do each night and, when Ann-Marie arrives, I give her the devotional and a list of scriptures and ask if she will read them to Mark until he falls asleep.

Dave is in bed already when I arrive about 10:00 p.m. I had hoped to toss a load of clothes in the washing machine but instead I crawl into bed next to him grateful for his warmth and fall to sleep.

> Proverbs 3:24, "When you lie down, you will not be afraid, when you lie down your sleep will be sweet."

Sunday, January 13, 2002

It is 7:15 a.m. when I open my eyes. "Breakfast time at the rehab hospital...habit." I say. "Want to wake up?"

"No."

I snuggle in and we sleep awhile longer.

On the way to the hospital we stop for Krispy Kreme donuts. Ann-Marie stays long enough to pass along information from the "night shift" and to have a donut and then leaves for the day. She is going to get the pillows I saw advertised in the Sunday paper. Mark needs more pillows to prop around him and the ones they have here are slippery as they are plastic and they also are too soft to be effective for propping.

Dave is going to take care of the commode problem today. I have called the rehab hospital and they said they will get a commode for Mark. Two of the nurses we have a good relationship with have it all figured out. Dave will go up to the floor Mark had been on by a back stairway and they will "slip" him a commode. We will return it when Mark goes back there. We thought we had purchased the commode he had in his room, but apparently not. It is absolutely essential. We can't have him on a wobbly chair over a bucket and take a chance he could lose his balance. I am amazed that the people here even think it could work.

Dave returns with the sturdy and clean looking commode. He has quite a story to tell and we all laugh as he shares the trouble they had sneaking the commode from the building only to find it would not fit in his trunk. One of the nurses gave him the keys to her car and he brought it over and then returned her car and drove back here. We are amazed at the kindness of the nurses at the hospital and know that Mark has found a place in their hearts.

Dave decides to go to the mall we can see from Mark's window and so I use the time to give Mark a sponge bath. I make an attempt to shampoo his hair. It's not easy to put towels under his head and use a scrub bucket, paper cup and more towels so it doesn't drip all over. Of course, when I am done I need to change his pillowcase. At the rehabilitation hospital the linen closet was right outside our door. I could change pillowcases whenever we felt the need. Here I have to track some down and the supply is definitely low.

Dave has brought the video from the benefit concert and we are excited to see it but find that we have to watch it in segments as we have so many interruptions or we get tired. It is really wonderful to see about 500 people enjoying a wonderful New Year's Eve concert and to know that we benefited from it in such a wonderful way!

We are impressed with the concert. Such wonderful friends and musicians performed. The talent was incredible and we are very blessed that people gave of their time and talent to encourage and aid Mark.

When we hear scripture quoted on the video, we jot it down until we can take time to look it up and dwell on it. We know it is going to be a very relevant part of our journey.

We are about halfway through the video when Dave returns with two terry cloth wraps for Mark. They close with Velcro and he thinks they should work well when Mark is having a bed bath or transferring to the commode. But the gift that most excites Mark is a small personal fan. It is quiet and efficient and will be a great comfort when he has one of the "hot flashes" that nearly drive him wild. They continue to begin suddenly and take over his body as he breaks into a sweat. The fan will be used often!

The third gift is a stress ball. Mark can use it to start to build up strength in his hands. I marvel because Dave was only gone about an hour but he also managed to pick up three golf shirts for himself. He explains the sale was too good to pass up! I love it!

We have just turned the video back on when Ann-Marie walks into the room with the pillows and pillowcases we saw advertised. She also brings him a clock for the room with large digital numbers so he can see it during the night when he does not have his glasses on. This is very thoughtful as Mark is often awake in the middle of the night wondering how long it is until daybreak.

Andy is going to spend the night with Mark. He wants to spend time with Mark and readily agreed to stay the night. I really appreciate the easy way Andy responds to our needs. I am so comfortable with him.

Andy arrives about 9:30 p.m. and we quickly show him a few things including the way we have Mark's feet propped up by pulling the mattress high at the head and putting pillows in the bottom between the mattress and footboard. Half of the length of the pillow is tucked into the footboard and half extends to support Mark's feet. At least his feet don't fall off of the bed any more.

We advise Andy that he will need to call for additional help when Mark needs to get on and off the commode and I ask him to stay near the door in case Mark needs help before a tech can respond. Andy tells us, "Go home and sleep." He is here for Mark.

The night passes far more quickly when we go to Mark's house to sleep than it does in the hospital though I have a hard time getting to sleep initially because all I can think of is that Dave leaves again in the morning. He will drive 15 hours alone and probably in bad weather to return to Minnesota. He has already weathered blizzard type conditions on two previous trips. I feel as though part of my heart is being torn out. I know what a sacrifice he makes to be here for us. *He's a good man, Lord. My Dave is a good dad and good husband and he is lonely. Give him traveling mercies, I pray, and help his days to be full of good and busy things so that he does not get too lonely.*

> *Ephesians 5: 1 and 2, "Be imitators of God, therefore, as dearly loved children and live a life of love, just as Christ loved us and gave himself up for us as a fragrant offering and sacrifice to God."*

Monday, January 14, 2002

We arrive at the nursing facility about 8:00 a.m. and thank a sleepy-eyed Andy before we send him home to get some rest. We love him even more when Mark shares that Andy slept with his head at the foot of the bed and probably with one eye open so Mark's feet did not slip from the bed. It is not an easy thing to feel such responsibility for someone who can do little for himself I have a new respect for caregivers. I believe Andy does also.

Somehow, at 10:00 a. m. Mark, Dave and I manage to say goodbye…again. I react as I usually do in situations I don't want to be in. I get busy. In the hallway I meet our caseworker and she tells me she will stop by later with more paperwork. It's Monday and our first workday here at the nursing facility and I imagine we will find plenty to do. I then head to the desk to find out the name of the woman who has the hair salon here. I want to make an appointment for Mark to have a nice haircut and a good shampoo. I am sure it will perk up his spirits to be well groomed.

I call our maxillofacial surgeon's office to confirm for tomorrow. I have learned that we are often late when we travel by ambulance and want them to know that is still our mode of transportation.

As the morning progresses I realize that, though people here seem nice, I have to say the descriptive word for my feeling about this place is "hate." I literally abhor it. I am sure this is a decent nursing facility, but it is hard to be here. Mark's room is second from the end of the hall so I have quite a walk whenever I go anywhere, whether to the nurses' station, the therapy room or the elevator.

As I walk by rooms with open doors, I hear "Help. Help me." Or they call out, "Come in. Come in." It is heartrending. I have already learned not to stop because there is nothing I can do. I have tried it and felt incredibly sad. I smile or nod or, on more recent walks, just keep walking. If I feel guilty I reason that I have more responsibility of my own than I am capable of taking care of.

Today a strange thing happens as I get on the elevator. I jump and look around as I hear a cry.

"Help!"

The elevator door closes and I expect the cry to be shut out, but I hear it again.

"Help!"

I hear it over and over again and look in every corner of the elevator for a speaker. There is absolutely no way I could be hearing someone cry out. The elevator moves far too slowly because I need to escape the voice. When the door opens, I walk off quickly and feel relief when the door closes behind me. The voice that followed me for two floors is silenced. *Lord, this place is not very fun when you are sensitive to things of the spirit.*

As I walk down the hallway, I ask the Lord what I can learn from all of this. How can I help? What can I do? Why am I allowed to feel such agony in regard to the residents of this place? I realize I can pray, and though it does not seem enough, I resolve to do that often.

We prayed over Mark's room to clean it out from anything that is not of the Lord after our first night of torment. Now, as I walk the hallways I pray for the entire building and its residents.

I am looking forward to the afternoon because our Angels By Our side, Chris and Carole, are going to meet me in Cool Springs to look for a laptop. Mark and I have decided to use my credit card to purchase one. We will be able to write e-mails and I can type journal entries. At the same time, Mark can begin to use it and it will be good therapy for his fingers. We were really excited yesterday when Chris informed us we will probably be able to play DVD's on it also.

I am on the phone with Chris, getting directions to where I am to meet them, when two therapists literally storm the room. Before we have a chance to protest, they move Mark to a wheelchair in a way very different from that which we have been taught to carefully use for transfer.

"Don't use your left arm," one of them coaches as Mark tries to place some weight on his only good limb so that all of his weight will not be on his injured hip.

"It is weightbearing," he says, knowing the lingo needed to communicate.

"It says here it is not." The woman refers to the paper in her hand.

Mark shoots me a look and immediately I see shock cover his face.

His left leg has been dropped to a bent position before I can get around one of the women to brace it. Mark lets out a loud gasp of agony and I grab the leg while still holding the phone receiver in my other hand.

"That leg can't be bent!" I shout and then apologize to Chris whose ear is on the other end of my voice.

I hurry out the door, canceling my meeting with Chris and Carole as I run after the wheelchair that has been whipped around the corner and is quickly headed for the therapy room. I hang up the phone knowing Chris understands that, once again, a priority has been exempted.

I feel a bit foolish. I want to be here for Mark but in no way want to be an over-protective mother. I take great care to not react in any way that could slow him down. I try not to show all the sympathy I feel and to encourage him to push himself toward more victory. But I saw the expression on his face as they whisked him out the door and know my place for this first therapy session here is with him.

Once we arrive in the therapy gym, the therapist seems quite nice and takes time to find out about Mark's injuries. It turns out the people who moved Mark are not therapists but techs. I am upset that they strong-armed him when they did not have complete knowledge of his injuries. As I explain to Chris and Carole over the phone, once Mark and I are back in his room, they did it backwards. They should have come in and introduced themselves to Mark and interviewed him regarding his injuries and then moved him after they knew how to do it. It was a frightening experience for me and a painful one for Mark. It did nothing to enhance our confidence in this facility.

Mark is glad when Matt stops by to visit and I am glad when he offers to go and get me a sandwich. He is also going to get smoothies for both Mark and me. I can't wait.

When Matt arrives with the food, I chew heartily on the sandwich and nearly inhale the smoothie. Mark drinks only a little of his because his stomach is upset. I can't imagine why.

Mark takes a nap and wakes shortly before Jason arrives with a treat in his hand. A smoothie! I love to see this roommate of Mark's. He is often out of town, but he makes an effort to stop when he is home and it means a lot to both Mark and me.

As the guys visit, I sit on my bed to write in my journal and ponder how each day has an element of unpredictability. Tomorrow we have an early doctor appointment and I did not get a chance to go home today to shower and get a change of clothes. Mark does not like me to leave at night, partly because nights are so long for him, and partly because he worries about me driving at night. Everything has changed so drastically. I guess I will bluff my way to being clean in the morning. I'll wash up in the tiny bathroom and wear the same clothes I wore today. Fortunately, I always keep a supply of fresh underwear in my overnight bag.

Another observation becomes apparent as the guys enjoy their conversation. Something new is happening to me. As evening approaches I need to keep intensely occupied because a sense of dread descends on me. I do not want to sleep in this place. I am so grateful Mark and I spend such rich time in prayer before bed. It helps to chase away the heavy feeling.

I Peter 5:7, "Cast all your anxiety on him because he cares for you."

Tuesday, January 15, 2002

Mark awakes to grits for breakfast again. Each time the nutritionist stops to ask us what he wants for breakfast he says, "Not grits!" And then the next morning we see grits on his tray.

The ambulance is scheduled to come at 10:00 a.m. and we are grateful when they are only about 20 minutes late. We have an appreciation for the paramedics, and they are always kind to us.

This appointment is to check how Mark's eye looks since the eye surgery. I voice my concern to the surgeon that the eye is not moving right. When Mark looks up I can see all the white under his iris. The result is a frightened expression. The doctor instructs us to massage the scar and assures us that should help. I am greatly relieved it can be fixed.

At the end of another long day, we read 1 Thessalonians 5:16-24 after our devotional reading and Mark has a vision as we pray.

"There was a large hotel." He tells me, "It was elegant and there was an elevator on each end of the hallway and even a few in the middle of the hallway. People kept going up and down in the elevators. A shepherd stood in the hallway and he kept trying to gather people together but they just kept riding up and down in the elevators and ignoring him. I had a sense he could have gone to the lobby, but that he was assigned a certain floor."

We prayed for revelation and soon Mark said. "It shows that shepherds need to be on each level that people live at. The sheep have become too independent and analytical. They do not trust anyone or anything, especially if they seem different from themselves. People do not recognize the value of the shepherd's simple message and what he can offer them, and the higher they go intellectually, or the more they achieve, the harder it is for them to recognize he is worth listening to. As Christians, we need to be able to relate to all levels of interest in Christianity. Even as we grow spiritually, we cannot forget where we were, or put ourselves above someone else on a spiritual level."

It was our night to see visions in the spirit realm. As I prayed for Mark I saw a bright gold then white light move across his body. I recognized it as healing light. I was sitting on a chair with my eyes closed as I saw this and I became aware of oil on my hands, legs and feet. In the Spirit, I saw the oil flowing and rising. It began to move as waves on a lake on a day with mild breezes. It became deeper and deeper and moved up over Mark's bed to cover his feet first and then moved to his head. It ebbed as a tide would.

We felt so grateful for the visions that we determined anew to be of good cheer and try to rise above our circumstances.

> *Joel 2:28 and 29, "I will pour out my Spirit on all people. Your sons and daughters will prophesy, your old men will dream dreams, your young men will see visions. Even on my servants, both men and women, I will pour out my Spirit in those days."*

Wednesday, January 16, 2002

I do not drink coffee. I have not for more than eight years. I was told by my doctor that it is not good for me, but it is in my diet now. I just cannot get away for food and there is not a cafeteria here. I could request a tray like the patients receive, but, well, once you have one you would rather never see another one.

This morning my breakfast is a muffin saved from yesterday and coffee. I can walk down the hall and get a free cup of the hot beverage and it tastes good. But I already notice the symptoms that made me give it up years ago.

I am ready to leave to meet Chris and Carole to get the laptop today. Mark and I are excited to begin the process of writing about our experience to this date. Mark has his remote and nurse call button as well as the telephone all propped beside his left arm, and I have put a video in the little television set we brought from home. He is ready for me to leave for a few hours.

I meet Chris and Carole in the Cool Springs area and we look at several laptops, carefully comparing their features. We confidently decide which one is best only to find they do not have it in stock. Another store has it, but it is located on another side of the city. I am relieved when Carole gets into my car with me and we follow Chris to the other store where I purchase the laptop.

It has taken quite awhile and involved driving a long distance. I find myself concerned that Chris and Carole may feel frustrated but that is not the case for our Angels By Our Side. In fact they decide we should go and get some food. I call Mark to be certain April is there with him and then the three of us go to a Mexican restaurant where I eat the best burrito I have ever tasted.

Of course Mark is always on my mind and I wish I could take him a burrito. I know that is not possible, but I see that the place next door seems to specialize in muffins. I make a quick trip in to purchase a muffin and a more exotic fruit juice than would be served at the nursing facility. I am really blessed when Chris and Carole come back to the hospital with me so they can visit with Mark.

Once more, Mark's room is filled with visitors. April has spent the afternoon with Mark and needs to leave for choir practice as soon as we get there. She and Mark have been visiting with Becki, who stopped by to show us her new scooter and Becki has brought along a friend of hers.

April hurries off to practice as soon as we arrive, so we are very surprised when she returns about a half-hour later. Instead of getting to her choir practice on time, she went to The Grille and had them puree one of Mark's favorite dishes. Once again, I am so grateful for her friendship to Mark and to me. He is too tired to eat more than a taste tonight so I carefully mark the box and place it in the refrigerator down the hall.

Chris easily steps from his role of computer consultant to therapist and begins to help Mark bend his knee. We have a fun time visiting with everyone but I sense that Mark is not feeling very well as his end of conversation becomes quiet.

When everyone leaves, I go to the nurses' station to get Mark some Mylanta because his stomach is upset. We note that he has had an upset stomach every night he has been here. Tomorrow I will get food at the grocery store that he can eat as we are certain the food he has been served here is causing this distress. As soon as he takes his Mylanta, I take a couple Advil and rub a soothing ointment on my complaining shoulder and then we begin our evening prayer.

> Proverbs 3:3-16, "Let love and faithfulness never leave you; bind them around your neck, write them on the tablet of your heart. Then you will win favor and a good name in the sight of God and man. Trust in the Lord with all your heart and lean not on your own understanding; in all your ways acknowledge him, and he will make your paths straight."

Thursday, January 17, 2002

Immediately this morning we are greeted by the bright smile of one of our regular techs. "I listened to your CD last night and it's all that! I really like it!"

Mark's face lights up. It has been a bright spot in this ordeal for us to give CDs to those who help Mark and we are often prompted to do that. The response is always wonderful and it provides us with a sense of ministry while we are in a place where we cannot actively minister to people because of Mark's physical limitations and my depletion.

The resident doctor comes to talk to Mark for the first time. He assures Mark about his urinary tract concerns and explains that what he is experiencing is normal with a severe pelvic injury. It will resolve itself in time.

I had an opportunity to discuss Mark's ongoing battle with diarrhea with the head of nursing today when she stood in the hallway with me as we waited for the doctor to leave Mark's room. We specifically addressed the weight concern because Mark continues to lose weight and it is critical that he begins to gain ground in this area. It is a huge concern and yet I cannot discuss it with Mark because he avoids the subject. It has always been a struggle for him to gain weight and he has lost a lot of ground. Though this nurse expresses shared concern, she is not able to offer any new advice and it really does not matter because I have already made the decision that I will take charge of this situation. I will get Mark the kind of food I think will stay in his body and help him gain his weight back. I try not to think of the grand amount of money we are charged for food each day whether he can eat it or not.

When April and Brian come for a visit, Brian hooks our laptop to the phone on my side of the room. We can now e-mail. It is wonderful! As soon as our guests leave for the evening, we go on-line, but only for a short time as sleep beckons us.

We have decided that tonight we will try a new technique to prop Mark's feet up because of the too short mattress. We have been told that an extension will not work on his bed so we have been relying on pillows at the foot of the bed after we pull the mattress up beyond the headboard. We tried something similar last night but it caused a lot of foot pain during the night.

Along with the bed adjustments, we are concerned about Mark's stoma, or tracheotomy wound. At the rehabilitation hospital the wound was carefully cared for. Here no one even looks at it. I called the rehab hospital yesterday to talk with a respiratory tech. He told us that we should still be taking care of it. It has developed a cone-shaped scab and we don't know what to think of it. The therapist told me to take care of the scab by dabbing hydrogen peroxide on it, followed by sterile water. He said the scab will eventually fall off and another may appear. This will continue until it is completely healed. I immediately went to the nurses' station and requested peroxide and sterile water.

There have been alerts on the television today that snow is expected. Mark and I find this so amusing. We now hear that a grand total of 1/200th of an inch fell! In Minnesota, we don't even notice that amount of snowfall.

We have a new neighbor next door in the last room in the hall. They moved him in yesterday and he made his presence known last night. I was sleeping very well, thank you, when I heard a loud noise. Always in a mode of expectation my body was instantly alert. I listened in the dark to be sure Mark did not need me.

I heard it again, "Hey!" and again a moment later, "Hey! Hey!" The man was yelling at the top of his lungs apparently not able to use his call button. I put my slippers on and padded down the hallway to the nurses station to let them know he had a need.

Today I heard a nurse trying to convince his wife to stay in the room with him at night. "We've been married over 40 years," she replied. "I don't think I want to stay all night"

Somehow, the logic in her answer did not register with me.

Ephesians 4:1-3, "I urge you to live a life worthy of the calling you have received. Be completely humble and gentle; be patient, bearing with one another in love. Make every effort to keep the unity of the Spirit through the bond of peace."

Friday, January 18, 2002.

Mark will get his hair cut today and he is really looking forward to it. I find people to help me transfer him to a wheelchair and then take him downstairs on the elevator by myself. We use the freight elevator because his long legs stick out so far that we cannot get him on the regular elevator. Once off the elevator I have two sharp angles to maneuver around to arrive at the beauty shop." I feel awkward, and am concerned that we could bump Mark's foot, but we get to the shop with out mishap.

The stylist is very welcoming and gives Mark a good, thorough shampoo, sympathizing that it has been a long time between shampoos and begins to give him a haircut.

A delightful woman named Mrs. R. sits under a hair dryer next to the chair I sink into. She is 92 years old and, we are told by her personal nurse who sits across from me, she is hard of hearing and does not see well.

Mrs. R. looks at me to say, "I can relate to her. I had both my legs broken once."

The four of us in the room exchange amused glances; not because Mrs. R. had broken legs of course, but because she referred to Mark as "her."

"We never have young men in here," the hair stylist explains, "but look at the length of those legs sticking out!"

We all laugh.

I attempt to have a conversation with Mrs. R., but because of her hearing problem and the hair dryer surrounding her head, it is difficult. "That's a man," I say loudly, forming the words carefully so she can read my lips. "He is my son."

"She will be fine." Mrs. R. offers. "She'll get through this. She is young." And then she delivers the clincher. "She's very lovely...So are you. Are you related?"

I get the impression Mrs. R. is very lovely and very gracious. She has a gift of encouragement, but we are all struggling to keep from laughing out of respect for her.

I am prepared to give it one more try and start to say "I am <u>HIS</u> mother." Instead I lean in to her and say "I am <u>the</u> mother."

"She is lucky to have you. You are both very lovely."

We talk as best we can. Mrs. R. is extremely unhappy living in the nursing facility. Her nurse tells me she has needs that require a facility like this but that she could go to assisted living if her family would sign for it. In the short time we are here I get a pretty good picture of Mrs. R's family and I feel sad that they do not take time to see how miserable this precious woman is. How can they just leave her here when there are other options?

Before long, Mark's very short haircut is finished and he looks good. We manipulate his outstretched long legs and face the wheelchair toward the door in this tight space. Before leaving, I bend over to say goodbye to Mrs. R. I wish her well and tell her it was nice to meet her.

They stylist holds the door for us, and as I wheel Mark out of the room we hear Mrs. R. call out in her elegant southern accent, "She is lovely; just lovely."

Immediately outside the door, the stylist, Mark and I dissolve in laughter.

As Mark's wheelchair rolls off the freight elevator he observes, "It was good to laugh. Do you know it is almost impossible to smile when you are in a wheelchair?"

I bend over to see his face. Is he teasing?

"Really," he says, "you look down when you are in a wheelchair. Who wants to smile at the floor?"

We decide we need to be sensitive in the future to people in wheelchairs if they might seem to scowl and, on our walk down the hall, Mark encourages me to take time to write about his haircut experience. We anticipate that, someday, it will be one of our favorite stories to tell.

When we get back to the room, Brian is waiting. He watches as Mark eats some of his lunch, omitting the pureed fish. Fish through a straw or by spoon somehow is not too appealing and we have found the smell is awful. I take advantage of Brian's visit and leave to get a sandwich from The Grille and stop by TCBY for smoothies for all of us. I take time to return a movie a friend rented for us and arrive back in short order.

As soon as I am back, Brian and I help Mark on the commode. Nearly every friend who visits regularly has helped Mark onto the commode. I marvel at that. The friendships he has run so deep, and close, that there is no hesitation to help as needed.

Once Mark is back in bed, Brian and I go to the little eating area for residents and he has his smoothie while I eat my sandwich. The tables are sticky and so are the chairs.

On our way back to Mark's room we are met by a man who looks familiar.

"Are you Mark's mom?"

I recognize him as a representative for a recording company. Mark became acquainted with him when he worked for a Christian bookstore in St. Paul. The man is in Nashville for the day and I think it is great that he would take time to stop to see Mark on his way to the airport. Unfortunately, the timing was such that he went to Mark's room to find him on the commode. Mark asked him to go and get me.

I find a tech to alert him that Mark needs to be transferred and ask Brian to assist also. I explain to Mark's friend from Minnesota that Brian will let him know as soon as he can go in to see Mark. I hurry back to the room to spray it with an air freshener. One long trip down this hallway will reveal that most rooms in this place do not receive the same attention we give to ours.

Mark is very happy to see this man and they have a short but good visit. Mark's appreciation of the time taken for this visit is evident. After Mark's visitor leaves, Mark and Brian tell me about the tiny Dachshund that someone brought in earlier. When I walk Brian to the elevator I go in search of the Dachshund.

Could it be, Lord? Would you bring a Dachshund to this place too?

I find the tiny bundle of fur in the occupational therapy kitchen on a blanket. I can't wait to hold her and once I pick her up, I do not want to put her down. She is a little red shorthair and very cuddly. With permission, I take her back to Mark's room. It is the first time I have enjoyed a walk down the long and smelly hallway.

A tech calls to me from a room with an open door, "Mrs. Williams, Mrs. Williams! Can we see the puppy?"

I take the puppy into a room that houses a sweet, tiny lady and her guests. They exclaim over the puppy and then I go three doors further to Mark's room. I place the pup on his chest and he strokes her with his left hand. I take some pictures of them together and then Mark says. "I want to take a picture of you with the puppy."

I hand him the camera and he snaps a picture. We laugh at how it will come out because he cannot aim and shoot well with only one hand.

I can barely stand to return the warm, snuggly pup to its owner who promises to bring her for another visit soon.

Mark and I decide we definitely want a Dachshund when we get back to Minnesota. We know all the obstacles. We live on property that is home for deer, fox and raccoon. All of those animals are bigger than the puppy we desire to have but somehow we need to entertain the possibility.

Jason arrives at 3:30 p.m. to sit in on Mark's therapy and I drive to the rehabilitation hospital to get Mark's mail. Because he is blessed to get a lot of mail, they have been kind enough to hold it, knowing he may return there in a couple of weeks.

Our favorite time of day is when we open the mail. Today there is a great collection! One package is from an 8th grade class at a Christian school in Texas. The kids had made individual cards for Mark. Awesome!

Around suppertime, Chris and Carole knock on the door. We are amazed that they are able to give us so much time. They travel very often, but for "some reason" this is a season when they are available. How loving is our God!

Chris expressed a desire to spend time alone with Mark when he called earlier today, so Carole and I walk out into the hall to visit. We have a great conversation and soon Chris comes out to talk to us. He said they had a great "man-to-man" conversation. We all agree it's important for Mark to have a man that is older than himself and a Pastor as a bonus, to confide in or to ask questions if needed.

We are surprised when we get back to the room to see Mark's friend, Tosha, there. Somehow she passed us in the lobby.

Ann-Marie stops by about 6:30 p.m. and Chris and Carole leave around 7:00 p.m. Tosha stays till 8:30 p.m. and then leaves to drive to her home in Atlanta, which is about four hours away. She has asked Mark to sing at her wedding in July. *Lord, let it be possible!*

My Utmost for His Highest is incredible tonight. And we read from Isaiah 41:10 and 58:8 and 9 along with Exodus 14:14.

Scripture is the air we breathe!

Isaiah 41:10, "So do not fear, for I am with you; do not be dismayed, for I am your God. I will strengthen you and help you; I will uphold you with my righteous right hand."

Saturday, January 19, 2002

Ann-Marie brought us baked potatoes and chili from Wendy's. Mark's occupational therapist took time to smash the beans for him. It was a kind gesture and he enjoyed eating the warm concoction as he savored the frosted drink that was delivered with it.

We're blessed that visitors keep coming. Andrea is in town from Kentucky to see her "Pumpkin." I love to be around when Mark's college friends come by. They never fail to make me laugh even in tough circumstances. Andrea and Mark use their nicknames for each other instead of their given names almost with out exception and there is something really sweet about it. "Princess"Andrea is studying to be a medical doctor and she asks Mark many questions, absorbing all the information that is so pertinent to her study.

We were in the therapy room when the man I met at church came by again. This time he brought his son. They came into the therapy room to stand beside the elevated mat that Mark was on and they visited easily. It astounds and blesses us that people take time to get into their car and drive here to visit when they barely know us. This kind man expresses his joy that Mark looks so much better than the last time he saw him. And it is true, he does.

Back in the room, Mark's hip is causing him pain, so we try to prop a pillow under it. We are certain the pain is because the techs here like to muscle him and then toss him onto the commode like a sack of potatoes. They need to take more time and let him do some of the transfer by himself using his left arm. They do not understand his injuries and the challenge of working with them. The staff here is used to assisting the elderly, not trauma victims.

And while I am venting, I could get on a soapbox about insurance companies because I feel that they actually do more harm and hinder progress by forcing people to move from one place to another to wait out a situation like this. Mark would be way ahead if he could have just stayed at the rehabilitation hospital. Ah, that felt good.

Psalm 142: 1 and 2, "I cry aloud to the Lord; I lift up my voice to the Lord for mercy. I pour out my complaint before him; before him I tell my trouble."

Sunday, January 20, 2002

Last night was a long one. In our prayer time Mark confided a need to me and I found myself awake to pray long into the night. Then he awoke at 5:50 a.m. with pain in his hip. I went to get him some pain medication and when I returned we decided they are working his hip wrong in therapy. They lift it too high and it is aggravated. I reminded him how Becki had instructed that he has a right to refuse any treatment. He looked so relieved when I suggested that he skip therapy and rest today.

I can no longer deny that I have quite a bit of pain in my neck, shoulders and across my chest but what can I expect without one moment of true rest or relaxation for the last six to seven weeks and sleeping on chairs, cots and unforgiving hospital beds?

As Mark sleeps I decide that I need to go and get a massage. Back home I go on occasion to keep my neck and shoulders from muscle spasms. I convince myself that I can find time to leave Mark for one hour to get a massage. There is a place only a few blocks away that looks like a nice spa. I pick up the phone and make an appointment. The relief that follows that decision is delicious.

I go into the tiny bathroom to freshen up and to change my clothes. Every now and then I think of the person that I was before, in comparison to the person that I am now. I love hot showers with fragrant shower gels poured on nice fluffy sponges or buffs. I love to dry off and lather myself in rich lotion and then take time to style my hair and put on makeup. That is the Lana that was. This one is ready for at least one full day in less than ten minutes. I know that the first time I take a shower in my bathroom at home in Minneapolis I will cry. It's okay. I plan to. I look forward to it.

I struggle to turn around in the tight spot I am changing my clothing in when the phone rings. It is Andrea. It is 8:15 a.m. and she is glad we have not had breakfast yet. She is going to stop at Cracker Barrel on her way here. She can't know how excited we are about that. It is such a blessing that Mark can eat soft food and I am thrilled whenever I get a meal brought here!

When Andrea arrives with breakfast we fall totally silent as we devour the tasty food. When we finish eating, we look at each other and grin at our satisfaction and then have a great time visiting with "Princess."

The day proves fairly uneventful and Mark and I experience a rich time in The Word as we prepare for sleep! Scripture after scripture unfolds for us. We are in 1 Corinthians, Romans and John. As we read we sense that we are being directed toward a stronger unity. What we find especially exciting is that, as we begin our devotional time, I pray, "Lord, Mark and I are very tired at this point of the journey. We need encouragement, and endurance."

I immediately open Mark's Bible to Romans 15:5 which speaks of encouragement and endurance. It spurs us on, creating a sense of excitement in our spirits. The same thing happens over and over again. We become aware that we are having a conversation with God. We pray, He answers. He shows us scriptures on unity, one after another. It is very specific. I also open to two scriptures that I understand to be songs. "Listen to this, Mark. I think it is a song."

When I read it he says, "I was writing a song about that just before the crash!"

I turn to another page in his Bible and it has the notation "song" by the passage I planned to read. "It looks like the Lord is already answering our desire for unity."

We are awake now; this is an adventure we want to fully enjoy. Mark shares some ideas he has for new songs. He is anxious to be able to write the melody. That may take some time, but for now, the words are stored in his head and need to be put on paper. I offer to type for him if he wants and he decides to try to do some typing of his own soon.

For several days I have been struggling with a knee problem. About two years ago I had arthroscopic knee surgery and, in general, the knee functions very well, but it has been hurting the last few days. Perhaps from all the lifting that is necessary to move Mark from bed to commode or wheelchair. Tonight as we pray I include my knee because I need to be able to walk up and down the hallway, go home to wash clothes and generally get around without the problem of a painful knee. I have been limping the last few days.

As I stand beside Mark's bed in the near dark, he says, in a very sleepy voice, because his sleeping pill is kicking in, "Where is your knee?"

He reaches out his left hand and I lift my knee. He places his hand on my kneecap and begins to pray. Warmth emanates from his touch and his prayer is a sweet mix of gentleness and authority as he claims healing in the name of Jesus.

I slide under the covers of my bed smiling. This is Mark. When he does something for someone he does not hurry through as though it is a bother. He takes his time to do it right. He did not send up a bullet prayer but described to the Lord what the need was. He stayed in the moment, praying until he was satisfied with his holy communication.

We have shared such sweet moments in the midst of all of this because of our God who loves us so well. I am confident my knee is better and when I stretch out on my bed I feel ready for a good rest. We both sleep peacefully.

Romans 15:5, "May the God who gives endurance and encouragement give you a spirit of unity among yourselves as you follow Christ Jesus, so that with one heart and mouth you may glorify the God and Father of our Lord Jesus Christ."

Monday, January 21, 2002

We are having a parade of visitors today. It is Martin Luther King Day so both Ann-Marie and Becki have the day off from school and want to spend some time with Mark.

The Dachshund puppy came in to take a nap on Mark's left shoulder. How Mark loves the puppy's visit! She snuggles in the crook of his arm or cuddles by his shoulder. Today she shivered and he reached for a towel beside his bed to cover her. We are still amazed that we have a Dachshund to enjoy. *Lord, You are so good to us!*

Brian and April came to visit and brought little Courtney. I am teaching her to say "Minnesota" with an exaggerated accent. Brian and April have been reinforcing that and today she "performed" for Mark. He was highly amused by it. When Courtney gave me a big hug it was like good medicine.

I have been in contact with Mark's roommates. We need to continue to rent the house for another month. It is my hope that they will stay to help with the cost. I understand that his second roommate wants to leave, but Jason may stay one more month. He is hoping to buy a condo and staying in the house one more month will give him time to look.

If we cannot stay because of the cost of rent, I will need to find time to pack Mark's things and get them to a storage unit. April has assured me she will help. The dilemma then becomes…where will I stay if I cannot stay at the rehabilitation hospital when Mark transfers? No one who has room for me lives near the hospital. I would spend a lot of time commuting. Uncertainty rules a huge portion of our lives.

I have found out that the Robinsons are going to be out of town the same days that Chris and Carole will be gone on a business trip. I feel vulnerable. It means a lot to know I can pick up the phone if I need to talk with them. There really are plenty of wonderful people that I can call, it is only that they are more of a "parent" age as I am.

Among the decisions we deliberate today, we must consider if this is a good time for Dave's mom, Betty, to come to Nashville. We miss her greatly but do not think it is time yet. We could enjoy her so much more once we have moved to Mark's house.

> *Romans 5:1 and 2, "Therefore, since we have been justified through faith, we have peace with God through our Lord Jesus Christ, through whom we have gained access by faith into this grace in which we now stand. And we rejoice in the hope of the glory of God."*

Tuesday, January 22, 2002

With all the disjointed thoughts that run through my head as I awake, I take time to thank the Lord because I so appreciate the prayer Mark said for my knee last night. As the day progresses I am certain that the knee is better, but because I must constantly move and lift Mark's legs or body, it is continuously subjected to stress.

I will buy a knee brace at the drug store today and I have requested a chair to be placed in the hall outside of Mark's room. When I go out to wait for him to use the commode or have a bed-bath, it can be anywhere from 5-20 minutes and the continuous standing has not helped my sore knee. The chair will be great because I also keep a book by the door so I can readily take it with me as I hurry out the door to give Mark privacy. Both will work to make my "hall-time" more pleasant.

In spite of the changes I make to help us to feel at home here, I am struggling as this busy day progresses. I desperately want to cry and I cannot take the time to do it. Sometimes it weighs on me. *When can I cry, Lord? I need to cry!*

Help me! I pray as I sit in the hallway outside Mark's door. *Help me! I don't want to complain. Please, please help us both!*

In regard to my knee, things have gone downhill enough today that, at one point when Mark needs to get on the commode, I cannot move from my bed because of pain and the exhaustion that accompanies it. It is a definite low point for me to desperately want to help Mark, who is only a few feet away from me, and be absolutely unable to move. Mark buzzes for help but no one comes. We are beginning to wonder what will happen when a nurse opens the door to give Mark his medication.

"Can you get someone to help Mark on the commode please?" I ask from my prone position.

I expect her to go down the hall but instead she calls out in a loud voice, "Jim! Mr. Williams has to go to the bathroom again!"

"Who?" We hear the question travel the full length of the hallway.

"Mark!"

"Be there in a minute."

Mark and I begin to giggle and then to laugh so hard that I fear both of us will wet our beds!

When the tech comes in I ask him to pull the curtain that divides my bed from Mark's. I am usually out of the room when Mark uses the commode, but because I cannot get off the bed, this will have to do.

The tech pulls the curtain and leaves, but Mark and I are still struggling to stifle our laughter. I feel it begin to subside and am just beginning to breathe regularly again when I hear Mark say, "I guess everyone on this floor knows what I am doing right now."

We are lost to the throes of belly laughter again.

A little time passes and we find our laughter in control and the curtain pulled away again. I gingerly make my way to the little bathroom and pull my pajamas on and then we begin our prayer time. Tonight we are centered on the sufferings of Christ and on martyrdom and rejection. As we spend time in Timothy and Romans it does not escape us that we have been unwilling passengers on an emotional roller coaster once again today.

> *2 Timothy 4:18, "The Lord will rescue me from every evil attack and will bring me safely to his heavenly kingdom."*

Wednesday, January 23, 2002

It makes me sad to walk the halls of this place and realize that some residents have visitors only on weekends and then for a short time. There are people here who do not have visitors even on the weekends. We know we are blessed to have such good friends.

Jason and Ann-Marie have been here and Ann-Marie brought her friend who is a police officer. He has been keeping us up-to-date on Mark's case at the police department. Any information he has shared is a matter of public record, but we so appreciate his kindness to call now and then. He knows the officers who found Mark trapped in his car and I imagine he has heard first hand how awful it was. The young officer explains to us that the criminal part of this case is completely in the hands of the District Attorney. Somehow, the State of Tennessee is the victim. In a way I feel relieved that we do not have input as to how the drunk driver will be charged or sentenced. We do feel strongly that she should be charged with vehicular assault rather than driving under the influence, but even that is out of our hands.

Exodus 14:14, "The Lord will fight for you; you need only to be still."

Thursday, January 24, 2002

Neither Mark nor I are morning people and we love to sleep late here. Today it is nearly 8:30 a.m. before I get out of bed. I go to the tiny bathroom, which is crowded even more by the superfluous commode. Standing stationary in my tight spot in front on the sink, I sponge bathe; quickly smoothing Raspberry scented lotion on my skin in an effort to feel fresh. I put moisturizer on my face and brush my teeth. I pull my change of clothes from the little duffle bag I have perched on the commode and stand in place to climb in and out of my clothing. I quickly apply foundation, mascara and lipstick. I run the brush through my hair, fuss for a second, and spray. In a matter of a few minutes, I am ready for another twenty-four hours.

While I am in the bathroom Mark's tray arrives and as I open the door I see a man I have not seen before talking with Mark. He is the physical therapist d'jour. He informs Mark that he will be back to take him to therapy at 9:30 a.m. We need to hustle.

The tray holds grits again, so basically, no breakfast. But today I am prepared for that. I look at the three separate mounds of unidentifiable blended food on Mark's plate and put jelly on that which we have discovered, by process of elimination, to be bread. Then I go to the grocery bag beside my bed to pull out a banana and mash it with my contraband fork. I am rewarded with a huge smile when I pull a Krispy Kreme cinnamon roll out of my treat bag. I shred the roll as I probably did years ago when Mark was just beginning to eat finger food. It goes down very well. My breakfast is the same…only not mashed and smashed.

I call to let the nurse know Mark is ready for his morning medication because it is important that he takes it before therapy. The nurse arrives shortly to give his stomach shot and pain medication. Making use of every moment, I finish my job of the morning, which is clipping and cleaning Mark's fingernails. Then the aide comes in to help me transfer him to the commode. I place the call button where Mark can reach it. I have already moved the commode in place and pulled down the rail on the right side of the bed. We utilize a low window shelf for toilet paper and the television remote. I feel as though we are becoming very organized.

Once again the nurse appears, this time to draw blood ordered by the doctor after his visit yesterday. While she does that I put a topcoat of polish on my nails and pull out my journal. There is time to write before the physical therapist shows up for the 9:30 a.m. appointment… at 10:20 a.m.

While Mark is wheeled down the hall I take the elevator downstairs to send out our mail.

When the question is asked in therapy, Mark rates his leg pain, on a scale of one to ten, at a three. I think that is great, but then I remember he is taking some pretty strong pain pills.

We need to transfer Mark from the wheelchair to the elevated mat for therapy. The transfer is time consuming because the chair must be disassembled. I take one armrest off and that allows someone to help him scoot off the side of the chair onto another surface like the raised matt in therapy. I have to take the legs off the chair before he can get out and then put them on after he returns to the chair. It is like building a chair around him each time he must sit in or leave the chair.

The conversation between Mark and the therapist turns to Christian music. I sit quietly and observe as Mark leads the young man into deeper conversation about Christianity. I am blessed at the ease with which Mark talks about the Lord. He has always known Him, but a bold and obvious dimension has been added.

As the left knee is manipulated in this session it causes a great deal of pain. Mark allows himself to make some noises. A rather deep groan accompanies the manipulation and then he laughs lightly to himself in relief as the pain lessens when the leg is straight once again. I watch over the top of my book desperately wanting to protect him from this pain. It does not help that I have no confidence in the therapists in this place.

The therapist's job is to bend Mark's knee. When he has bent it as far as he possibly can he continues to push and push until it moves further. Once the pain reaches a point when Mark cannot tolerate it, the therapist holds it in that position long enough to measure it. It looks good on paper that he got the knee to that point, but the reality is Mark's knee cannot bend that far on its own. Yesterday they measured the bend to 85 degrees, today it went to 80 degrees. It depends on how much pain the therapist is ready to allow Mark to feel.

Every medical person we have met so far is very curious about Mark's feet. Though they are mostly covered by casts, the pins sticking out of his toes cannot be ignored. They evoke a wrench in the gut when people see them. It is the same with this therapist.

Today we are instructed to start to massage the scar tissue on Mark's knee. We sense it is a taste of what is to come with massaging all of the scars as they become exposed and need to heal. We are told that when scar tissue lays down it adheres to connected tissue beneath and it lessens motion. The therapist shows me how to massage the scar on Mark's knee.

I watch him carefully, but I hate to hear the "Aaah, uph, aaah" noises that escape from my son.

"Come on, this one counts." The therapist urges me on as I try to mimic his example.

Mark has graduated from "Aaah" to "Oh!" now. It is nearly impossible to make myself hurt him. The therapist tells us he is helping Mark build up his pain threshold. I wonder what the past weeks have done, if not that already.

It is good for me to look at Mark and see his smile has returned. He is very forgiving and tolerant. I can see why some people yell during their therapy sessions. It is a tough job for both therapist and patient. Mark has not had time to recover from the knee pain when a wooden slide board is placed under his left leg and he is instructed to slide his foot toward his hip and then back down the board in yet another effort to get the knee to bend.

The therapist pulls on Mark's foot as Mark pulls the foot toward himself while lying on his back. Suddenly the therapist pushes the foot too hard and too far. The knee that has been repaired with metal and immobilized for weeks resists. Mark is close to tears.

"I…can't." He has had his head lifted off the pillow slightly as if to watch and help. Now he collapses back, silent. For this moment he is defeated by pain.

I am sitting on the other side of the large elevated mat he lies on. My prayers truly never cease as my heart is wrenched once more. When I do look up I catch Mark's eye and he smiles at me. Amazingly, he is ready to try again. I swallow a lump in my throat and praise God for the blessing of my precious and very brave son.

We are both relieved to be done with this session as I wheel Mark back to his room. He has been instructed to stay in the wheelchair for awhile so we decide to play Scrabble; it will keep him busy so he does not dwell on the discomfort caused by sitting.

I have only played Scrabble a couple of times, and that was years ago, but I expect I will do quite well because I love words. That illusion lasts until Mark gets sixty-six points on one word early in the game. He loves competition and board games will be his outlet for awhile.

Our game is interrupted by a knock on the door. The case manager comes in to discuss transportation to our much-anticipated appointment with the orthopedic surgeons. A decision needs to be made because Mark cannot sit in a wheelchair for a long period of time and the appointment will take most of a morning. The three of us decide that it will be necessary for him to go by gurney even though it is difficult for the ambulance personnel to stay in one location so long. Once again, we realize how unique Mark's situation is even in this medical world.

When the blended lunch arrives we request coffee from one of our favorite techs. I have purchased a box of sugar cookies and we are going to dunk them in the hot beverage until they melt in our mouths. While we wait for the treat, I go downstairs to the beauty shop to see the owner. I want to buy the brand of shampoo she used because it left Mark's scalp with a bit of a tingle and made it feel really fresh. We cannot shampoo often, so we want to shampoo well.

She won't hear my offer to purchase it. She pulls a nice travel-size bottle out of her supply cabinet and gives it to me. "You tell Mark this is from me, and don't get any in his little eyes because it will burn." On the way back, in the elevator, I think that she is a perfect person to work in this place. She brings sunshine.

Because Mark has always enjoyed wearing nice clothing, we have begun to collect an assortment of boxer shorts and t-shirts that coordinate. It is progress to have him look good even if his attire consists of boxers and t-shirts.

After lunch we finish our Scrabble game, though the outcome was quite obvious from the beginning.

I get the wheelchair ready and then the occupational therapist takes Mark to the therapy room. I have decided to stay behind to use the computer. I also sneak a few potato chips out of a grocery bag I have beside my bed. I eat the chips and follow them with a candy bar. I would never eat those things in front of Mark, but I am very hungry and they are my lunch today.

I am just about to say goodbye to Dave on the phone when Mark is wheeled back in the room and instructed to sit in the wheelchair for one full hour. As Mark and I talk, our discussion turns to the organization, Mothers Against Drunk Driving. We agree that we will want to become involved at some point.

About the time we decide television will help distract him from the discomfort of the wheelchair, Becki calls. She will be coming over later and wants to play a new game she told us about. She is bringing food for me. Hooray!

Becki scoots into the room maneuvering her scooter into position so we can eat and play games on one of the mobile trays in the room. We have a really fun time laughing at the expression required of us by the game.

Ann-Marie joins us later and as she watches television with Mark I check our e-mail. How we love our laptop! Mark is excited when I read an e-mail from one of his vocal teachers at Belmont. She is going to come for a visit soon.

Back and forth, back and forth, back and forth. Our guests have left and we are alone. Around our room I move, back and forth, back and forth. Mark is not mobile so I must be. I go to the bathroom and get his bowl for him to spit in and gather his toothbrush and toothpaste and a washcloth from the chest near the bathroom door. I walk to his bed, hold the bowl for him to spit in, and go back to the bathroom to clean it. Then I get the articles needed to clean his stoma and then return them, next he works to stretch his jaw and I get the bands to put on his teeth.

I help the tech get him on the commode, and then go out to the hall to wait until I hear "Mom!" and then I go to find a tech to let them know I need help getting Mark back on his bed and then go into his room to help get him off the commode. I prop the pillows around Mark's body parts that hurt to be on a hard surface, even like a mattress. I turn off most of the lights and go into the bathroom to change into my nightclothes. When I am ready, I go into the hallway to tell the nurse that Mark is ready for his medication and then I reach for the Bible. First, as has become our habit, we read *My Utmost for His Highest* and then scripture. At that point, using all weapons of authority given to us by the blood of Jesus we launch our prayer attack. We do not want to leave one request unstated before our God who is able to do over and above anything we can ask or imagine.

It amazes me that I fall into bed exhausted but lie awake as scenes from each day flood my mind. Tonight the thought that assaults my desire for sleep is that this place is very sad. I need to "put on my armor" constantly and pray protection over Mark. Depression seems to lurk in the shadows.

Today I saw a medic leave a room with an empty gurney so I knew someone new had arrived. I heard him say as he left the room, "So you say you are hungry for chicken and dumplings?"

Oh, did that sound good, but I was immediately sad for the woman who had such a craving and would instead be eating the food served here.

When I made my return trip down the hall I glanced toward her room. Gray hair pulled back and held with an elastic band, she sat in a wheelchair staring ahead at the television set that was not turned on. Suitcases were piled on her bed. I wanted to go in and hug her, but I could not think fast enough to know if that would be a good or bad action and the terrible truth is, I did not have energy to do even that kind deed.

I want to dispel images of the woman on her first night in this place. I fluff my pillow, turn my face to the wall and think that a heart could break one hundred times a day in a place like this. I offer Ephesians 3:14-21 for our newest neighbor.

> *Ephesians 3:14-19, "For this reason I kneel before the Father, from whom his whole family in heaven and on earth derives its name. I pray that out of his glorious riches he may strengthen you with power through his Spirit in your inner being, so that Christ may dwell in your hearts through faith. And I pray that you, being rooted and established in love, may have power, together with the saints, to grasp how wide and long and high and deep is the love of Christ, and to know this love that surpasses knowledge—that you may be filled to the measure of all the fullness of God."*

Friday, January 25, 2002

My first thoughts this morning are of the e-mail we received from friends in Jerusalem last night. They referred us to 2 Chronicles 20:15 which exhorts us, "Do not be afraid or discouraged because of this vast army. For the battle is not yours, but God's." What a miracle to be able to hear from friends so far away and send off an immediate reply. The laptop has been a healing tool.

Also on my mind this morning is the prayer Mark prayed last night just before we went to sleep: "Lord, I say thank You for Mom; for her being here, for being strong, for being away from home. For doing what she felt the Spirit wanted her to do to stay and help me. I couldn't have done it without her."

I know Mark is grateful that I am here, but it touched my heart to hear him thank God for that. I silently added my own prayer. *As you hear this sweet prayer Lord, please continue to encourage and strengthen us both. Amen.*

Because Mark is still asleep, I quietly reach for my Bible and refresh myself on our readings from last night. We were in Psalm 37 for most of our scripture time and then turned to Malachi where we were told to walk upright. We know Mark can do that in the spirit though he is flat in bed.

As soon as Mark is awake we begin to deal with stress. There is no tech available again to help move Mark to his commode. The process is getting a little better as his left leg bends more but he needs two people. One to hold the legs and put pillows under the feet and one to put their arms under his armpits, being careful not to catch the pins extending out of his shoulder and to place him down gently because of the hip and pelvis injuries and without letting his feet bear any of his weight.

Out of desperation, we have devised a way to make the transfer with just the two of us. We move his right leg to the edge of the right side of the bed and then the left one in the same direction as close as possible. Moving one leg and then the other inches at a time, we get him to the edge of the bed where we put the legs over the edge, being careful not to bend the left one too drastically. Then I put my arms under his shoulders with my closed palms up, being careful of the pins that stick out. We count, "1-2-3" and he scoots using his good arm as I lift. It is not an easy effort. Mark is over 6'1" and I am about 5'3" tall; though he now weighs only about 112, that beats me by at least six pounds.

I am sure our self-devised procedure is not the best for his mending body, or for my back and knee, but we get the job done and manage to protect Mark's modesty at the same time by the use of towels. Immediately as he scoots over I move my arms from his armpits and reach to grab a "floor pillow" to put under his left foot. I keep a stack of pillows on the floor for this purpose. Then I move his call button as close as I can on the bed and place the television remote and toilet paper on the shelf next to the commode. I very quickly grab my book, which sits right beside the door, and leave as fast as I can.

I sit in my chair in the hallway by the door until I can hear him call my name or I see the red button above his door come on. If I can't get a tech we manage to get him back into bed by using a reverse system of the one we used before. I willingly do the work of the techs more than half the time because they are obviously short staffed, but I draw the line at emptying the commode.

Out of curiosity, today I decide not to turn off the call button just to see how long we will actually wait for a tech to respond to get Mark off the commode and back into bed. It has been eighteen minutes so far. That's a pretty long time to wait if you have to go to the bathroom or if you have been sitting on a portable commode with a broken hip and pelvis and need to get back to bed. Finally there is a response. A nurse pokes her head in the door to see if she should get a tech to help move Mark. I let her know that we got the job done.

"Good. Well, I am on my way to give the guy next door a super-duper enema because he has already had laxatives and suppositories and nothing is working."

She smiles and closes the door. Mark and I cringe and say a prayer for our next-door neighbor.

Bless the Lord, it has been a fairly quiet day. Our prayer time tonight is scripture enhanced; taking us on a journey from 2 Corinthians 1:3-5 to Philippians 1:6, and 3:10, to Hebrews 10:23 and back to 2 Corinthians 3:17-18. We thought we were nearly done when the Lord directed us to Psalms 71: 18-24 and 111:10. We are tired but happy when we finish with John 16:33.

What an awesome journey we are on. In the midst of this trial we are led by a God whose love for us overpowers the fear that would weigh us down. Though we would never choose to be where we are, we feel assured that God is closer than our breath. There is no way to express our gratitude and love for Him!

> *2 Corinthians 1:3-5, "Praise be to the God and Father of our Lord Jesus Christ, the Father of compassion and the God of all comfort, who comforts us in all our troubles, so that we can comfort those in any trouble with the comfort we ourselves have received from God. For just as the sufferings of Christ flow over into our lives, so also through Christ our comfort overflows."*

Saturday, January 26, 2002

I pass the same people in the hallway each day. I have come to realize that sometimes no response on my part is best because it seems to upset many of them. There is one very sweet petite lady that always looks clean. She fixes her hair, or has it done. She is in the hallway, at most any hour of the day, in her wheelchair. Her legs move to propel the chair around rather than using the wheels alone.

A couple of days ago I noticed a pile of things on the floor in front of her wheelchair and saw she was struggling to pick them up. She held a pillowcase in her hand. I bent to retrieve that which had spilled from that case. It was an assortment of envelopes, her bra, some tissues and a change of clothing.

As I reached up with the envelopes she instructed that they belonged on her lap under the tray that was attached to the arms on her chair. I tried, but they fell again because her knees sloped forward with her feet on the floor.

"They are for my church," she said. The envelopes were blank.

"Can I put them in here for you?" I asked motioning to the pillowcase.

"That's a better plan!" She said excitedly.

I put everything on the floor into her pillowcase and smiled at her.

"You're not running away are you?" I asked as a co-conspirator might.

She smiled back at me as though we shared a secret, "It is very last minute and you are an angel."

I didn't worry about her going any place she should not go and I thought it rather sweet, if not sad, that she would make such an attempt. But I have seen her since and she always has a purse or duffle bag with her. I am sorry that each day she holds out hope to herself that she will escape this place that I cannot wait to walk away from.

> Proverbs 13:12, "Hope deferred makes the heart sick, but a longing fulfilled is a tree of life."

Sunday, January 27, 2002

I cannot find my journal. This is interesting because we are in the middle of warfare, hot and heavy. Yesterday was fairly uneventful until evening.

Friends had come to visit and almost immediately after they left Mark became agitated. I could feel it too. He suddenly began to cry, something he does not do. It was pretty intense and I wanted to call a nurse because it frightened me, but I held back until he could talk.

"It is totally spiritual." he managed to say through strangled sobs.

I did not want to be alone with Mark. I called Dave and he said he had been given two words for us as he prayed that morning, "yield and rejoice." In the circumstances they seemed odd, but we accepted them and asked Dave to pray. When he finished praying over the phone, he suggested we call Chris or Mickey.

I had already thought to call Chris or Carole, but I knew their mailbox was full and they were out of town. Mickey is in Minneapolis and I needed someone who knew how to pray. I called one of Mark's friends from Mickey's church and got his answering machine.

Mark and I were praying even as I scrambled for support, but Mark was as I have never seen him before, absolutely distraught.

"Mark," I said. "I know that you need to hear the voice of someone whose spiritual authority you are under." He shook his head in agreement but could not quit sobbing.

I dialed the home phone of Pastor Jim in Minneapolis. The relief when he answered the phone nearly sent me to my knees. "Pastor, Mark is under attack, will you speak to him?" I handed the phone to Mark and he took the receiver.

As soon as Mark heard Pastor Jim's voice he began to sob anew. "I can't." He said and nearly dropped the receiver.

"Pastor," I spoke into the phone, "I am going to hold the receiver to Mark's ear."

After what seemed a long time I could see Mark begin to respond to the words Pastor was speaking to him. His breathing came easier. We were surprised and yet, not, when Mickey's voice came on the phone. He was in our pastor's home for the evening and he began to pray and instruct Mark.

Both Pastor Jim and Mickey prayed over Mark and, in time, he took the receiver from my hand and began to speak a few words back to them. He was spent when he handed me the receiver to hang it up.

We prayed to rebuke and chase from the room anything that had come in to discourage and depress! I actually went to the door and opened it instructing anything that was not of the Holy God of Heaven and Earth to leave in the name of Jesus. We began to feel peace return and the presence of the Holy Spirit wash over us.

The two of us talked late into the night about frustration and about God's leading. It was a pivotal time for Mark. Desperate and awful, yet he emerged with such determination telling me, "I want to leave everything before the crash behind. This is a brand new life. I don't want complacency in my life. I am so completely frustrated. It is not a bad frustration. I want to change. I don't want to fall back into the same boring place I was in before. I feel like I am not using this time properly but what can I do? I don't want to watch television but I can't see well enough to read or write until my eye heals more, and I need diversion."

Mark shared with me what had happened earlier when he had been in such despair.

Mark remembers:

"Something wanted me to be mute. It attacked me. I was thinking of the frustrations we just talked about and I kept thinking that a moment of joy was impossible; absolutely impossible. It felt so far away. And peace felt impossible too. It is hard to explain but I sense that it is how people who do not know the Lord feel. It was like a (Frank) Peretti thing. I got really dizzy and pictured claws going into my head.

I have a better understanding of what God wants me to do now and I feel inadequate to do it. I think I am not strong enough to do what God wants, but then I hear His voice say, 'Yes, you are!'"

Lana:

We realize that we need to step up our prayer time even more. We feel Mark has been "allowed" to feel the utter despair of those who do not know the Lord. There is a spiritual atmosphere in this place that we have been placed here to experience.

Oppression hangs like a weighty cloud in the hallway. It is as heavy as the unwelcome smells and sounds. Here in this room we keep the atmosphere cleaner after that first horrendous night when I battled into the dawn. But it is as if each time the door opens the dark oozes in and we begin at ground zero once again. *We are battle weary servants, Lord. Protect us and teach us Your ways!*

> *Ephesians 6:10-12, "Finally, be strong in the Lord and in his mighty power. Put on the full armor of God so that you can take your stand against the devil's schemes. For our struggle is not against flesh and blood, but against the rulers, against the authorities, against the powers of this dark world and against the spiritual forces of evil in the heavenly realm."*

Monday, January 28, 2002

Becki called this morning. She had been led to pray "deeply" for us during the night. Isn't God good?

Dave called with an entire list of scripture for us to write down and look up. He is going to come to Nashville in a few days with three of Mark's friends that have planned a trip to visit Mark. They are all women and welcomed his offer to drive with them.

We feel well covered in prayer as we begin this new day.

When Mark's voice teacher from Belmont comes to visit, I spend some time with them and then go for a walk in the hall so that they can have time alone to visit. He has been looking forward to seeing her.

In the hallway Mark's occupational therapist approaches me to say, "Mark needs to leave this place."

I am surprised at her comment but let her know I agree with her.

"This is no place for a young man. I can see it in him that it is hard here. I hope they say he is weight-bearing tomorrow." She tells me the light is gone from his beautiful eyes.

I thank her and tell her we appreciate her concern and prayer. If she can see the change in Mark and she has only known him a couple of weeks I guess there is a dramatic change in him.

Lord, it is time to move on. Please allow us to go back to the rehabilitation hospital!

The day progresses fairly well and soon we are in our prayer time. As we pray, Mark tells me the Lord has given him a vision.

Mark remembers:

"I saw me looking up at this Darth Maul (from Star Wars) type creature. I only came up to his knees he was so large. That is me in the natural, but in the spiritual I grew so big and I kept growing until that thing was something that could only reach out and grab my shoelaces. It was like an ant. I could squash him.

In the natural, Satan, or sin seems that big and overwhelming. If you stay in the natural he becomes so large that he can destroy you by making you feel smaller and smaller. What this says to me is Satan's power is nothing in the spiritual realm that we are supposed to live in."

Lana:

Our scripture time led us to Psalms 2 and 4. We prayed about the doctor's appointment tomorrow. If they can take off the casts and put on Bledsoe boots, Mark will be able to bear weight on at least one leg and we can move back to the rehabilitation hospital. Every fiber of our beings cries out to leave this place but we have learned that there is peace in surrender.

We agree in prayer that joy will bubble up in us and that we will be able to overcome the great oppression in our surroundings no matter what tomorrow brings.

As we drift off to sleep Mark's voice reaches across the room to assure me. "Wherever we are tomorrow is where we are supposed to be."

Psalm 4:8, "I will lie down and sleep in peace, for you alone, O Lord, make me dwell in safety."

Tuesday, January 29, 2002

We have referred to this day as our "Halleluiah Day" for weeks now. We have held it out in front of us praying for a good word from the surgeons that will examine Mark. The wonderful team in Minneapolis that signed up to pray for Mark at the New Years Eve benefit, have assured us that they are praying and fasting today. We are blessed that many friends in many places are walking beside us in prayer.

We travel to Vanderbilt Medical Center by ambulance and, because we will be here for so long a time, the paramedics leave and give us a number to call for our return trip.

Chris has been out of town with Carole, but he called to say that he wants to be with Mark today. It is an awesome comfort to Mark and me. I never would have thought to ask this much of him. Dave wanted to come down for this day but he cannot continue to take time from work. We know his prayers are with us and feel nothing but gratitude that he appreciates Chris being with Mark. I am grateful that, on this day that is filled with questions and unknown events, I will not be Mark's only tangible support.

They may remove Mark's casts, and they may pull the pins from his toes and shoulder. I have fought fear for quite some time in regard to the pins coming out. The pins that stick out of four of his toes go back into the foot, nearly to the heel. We are told there will be no anesthetic and I cannot imagine the pain.

The pins in the shoulder look huge to us. They are wide and long, extending from the bicep area into the shoulder and may be threaded. I truly am struggling to "get a grip" and hope that no one, especially Mark, knows how frightened I am.

In a naïve prayer, driven by desperation, we have prayed the pins will slide out without pain or difficulty. We are covered in prayer and as confident as we can possibly be.

Mark's greatest dread is the hard, cold x-ray table and having people move all the broken places, but we keep confessing that it will be better today than before. I made sure the nurse gave him a nice dose of pain reliever before we left the nursing facility. Before the x-rays can be taken the casts need to come off. We sit in the little room with curtains between the beds until we hear that, yes, Mark's casts are coming off.

Mark is at a sitting angle in the gurney when a man comes in with a saw and proceeds to take off the royal blue casts. I can see the vibration of the saw makes Mark's feet hurt but it is progress he has been waiting for.

Chris met us before all the activity began and now he and a hospital worker wheel Mark to x-ray and I follow behind the gurney. It takes five of them to move him on to the table. Once again the table is too short for his frame and his heels hit the edge causing him to wince in pain. Someone grabs a foam circle and places it under the painful heel. The team working to move Mark seems very aware and respectful of his condition. It is obvious they are trying to make things move smoothly. The technician is wonderfully sympathetic noting with amazement all the broken places she needs to x-ray.

Chris and I leave to wait in the lobby confident that Mark will be treated with care. Approximately a half hour passes before we are signaled to go in to see Mark. The technician smiles at me and says, "He is a trooper. The best patient we have had around here."

Mark's facial expression shows us that it has been an uncomfortable ordeal and he tells us that his right heel is in a lot of pain. Much care is taken by five of us to move Mark back to the gurney but there is a glitch…he has been put on to the gurney upside down and needs to have his head on the end that can be elevated. He has to be transferred back to the table, then they turn the gurney around and we all take our positions again and begin the count. 1..2..3, move Mark's body from table to gurney. To save time, Chris takes control of the gurney and we go down the hall to see the orthopedic surgeon.

The doctor, once again, blesses us by seeing Mark personally. He is absolutely pleased with what he sees. There is no sign of infection and he gives the okay to remove the pins and fit Mark with Bledsoe boots. This means he can begin to weight-bear.

"Halleluiah!" I cannot help but say it aloud as Mark and I grin at each other.

His nurse humors me when I barrage her with questions in the hall outside the cast-area where Mark waits in a curtained cubicle. "Try not to worry." She smiles at me because we have come to know each other through this ordeal. "I am more worried for you than for Mark."

The patient on the other side of Mark's curtain has been screaming and sobbing. They are taking pins out of her ankle. This could feed our apprehension but we begin finding and making excuses. She has a different type of devise and we convince ourselves that is why she is in such pain as they try to pull it out. We can hear the nurse and tech as they discuss giving her a shot for pain. Sounds like a plan to me.

In fact, not only were we were careful to get Mark his pain medication before we left the nursing facility, but I have a dose in my purse in case enough time has elapsed that he needs to take more. We know how long the pins in Mark's toes are and our interpretation of the x-rays we have seen is that they appear to cross over each other in the foot. The pins in the shoulder are thick and we do not know if they have threads on them or not.

For Mark, and even for Chris and for me, it is ready-or-not. The tech takes his position on a bench at Mark's feet and pulls out an instrument that looks like pliers. Mark cannot see it. I do not want to.

It is by instinct that Chris and I take our positions. I am at Mark's head on his left side. I lean in nearly sharing his pillow to begin to whisper in his ear. "Peace," I whisper, "The peace of Jesus." These words are meant for him but minister to me also.

Chris, who is even taller than Mark, stands at his left side also but by Mark's mid-section. He grips Mark's left hand, which is resting across a pillow they have placed on his stomach. Mark knows Chris can take it and he hangs on tight.

For the most part, we are all praying silently. We have prayed our way to this event and know it must take place for Mark to take the next steps in his rehabilitation. That does not exempt us from wishing it did not have to happen.

The man working on Mark's feet announces the first pin in the little toe is out. Mark takes a deep breath. "Not so bad," he says as though trying to convince himself.

Chris begins to narrate for Mark. "Next one…out."

I stay where I am, absolutely not interested in seeing the pins pulled from my son's flesh. I rest my hand on his head, sensing he would not want me to stroke it, and keep up my quiet prayer for peace.

The last toe-pin comes out and Mark has not made more than deep moaning noises. "That had to be the last one," he says now. "I couldn't do another one."

Wouldn't it be nice if we were done? The man whose title we do not know moves his stool to Mark's right side and looks at Mark. This man has not been spending any time on compassion, but now he tells Mark that he did a great job on the toes but that the shoulder may be a little tougher. Chris suggests to Mark that he not look at what is going on. He already saw the instrument about to be used and knows it will be best if Mark does not see it.

The man is pulling so hard that I feel Mark's body being tugged away from me as I stand on his left side. Pull and twist, pull and twist. Then it stops and I look up to see if he is done. No. He is sitting there shaking his hands to relieve them. This is hard work for him. He tries again and then gets up and walks across the room to a tool chest. It is identical to the red tool chest my husband has in the garage at home! We hear the rattling of metal on metal and then he returns.

Mark is sweating and I wipe his brow. The tech informs us that the pins are threaded and that he will need to use something like a reverse drill to draw them out.

Chris takes on his coaching role and soon anyone listening would think we were in a birthing room. "Okay, bro, hang on, he has it. It's coming. Take a deep breath. Breathe. Breathe. It's coming. I can see it. Hold tight bro."

I feel the upper part of Mark's arm move as he adjusts his grip on Chris's hand. I am still praying but no longer whispering in Mark's ear. He needs to listen to Chris.

"It's coming, Mark. Hang on, breathe. Take a deep breath, it's almost out, almost out…coming, coming. It's out, bro, you did it!"

Typical of Mark, he rests only a second before he quips, "Put my baby on the pillow for me to see it."

The tech shows Mark the pin. It is really nasty looking and more so because it is covered with blood and gunk. There is one more to go. After a repeat of the procedure, they clean and dress the wound and each one of us takes a deep breath.

The next step will be to fit Mark with Bledsoe boots. A young woman comes in to assemble the heavy black boots on Mark's feet and we are instructed that Band-Aids must remain on the toes for a certain amount of time and then are told how to care for the wounds when the Band-Aids come off.

We feel drained but ready to celebrate. It is over! The pins are out! Praise God!

Once again, it would be really nice to take a moment to reflect on this victory and rest, but we are already late for our appointment across the plaza to Maxillofacial Surgery.

Mark's facial surgeon comes into the room with a grin on his face. He so appreciates Mark's attitude and our words of appreciation to him. He is pleased with the way Mark's eye looks and tells Mark to keep massaging it. He then measures the distance Mark is able to open his mouth. Mark has been striving to stretch the jaw regularly but the device we were given to measure it showed he still had more range needed before they would allow him to chew.

We are a bit surprised, but more than happy when the doctor's assistant measures and says, "Looks good."

The metal bars attached to the gums have to be removed and that is a procedure that will need to be scheduled in about two weeks. We are told Mark will need a type of sedation for that procedure that will not put him out completely. He is also told to schedule dental work, as there is much to be done. He will likely have cavities and he definitely needs to have his teeth cleaned. At the very least, a lower front incisor has been fractured and the mouth, in general, needs evaluation. When the options are mentioned and braces may be one of them, we are not very happy to hear the news. Mark has already had braces that caused a lot of problems in his mouth. For now we try to put the information aside for another day.

We want some good news and the surgeon provides that when he says Mark may begin to chew soft food! I see the light in Mark's eyes!

Chris wheels Mark into the lobby and takes a couple of pictures of him on the gurney with the Bledsoe boots on with his ever-present digital camera.

I ask the receptionist to call for the ambulance and while we wait Chris decides to take a walk. When he returns he approaches from behind Mark's head resting on the pillow of the gurney. He rustles the bag in his hand and opens it to let the fragrance escape.

Mark grins. "McDonald's french fries!"

He carefully eats quite a few before the medics appear to take him back to the nursing facility.

This is what I call a long and eventful day and it is not yet noon.

Back at the nursing facility Mark rests and I go to his house to wash a load of clothes and make a quick stop at the grocery store for more breakfast supplies. I buy oatmeal that can be made in the microwave oven and we eat it nearly every morning.

I pull the containers off the grocery shelf and smile to myself as I think of this morning when I went to the nurse's kitchen to microwave the oatmeal. One of the techs came in and said, "Are you making oatmeal for Mark again? I never did see a young man like oatmeal so much as Mark does."

I had managed to smile and bite my tongue rather than to say, "He does not like oatmeal as much as he hates the grits that come on his breakfast tray every single day."

When I pull into the parking lot it is dusk and there are no spaces except at the far end. As I drive in I think I see a familiar form getting out of a car. When he stands still to wait for me I am certain. Greg Long!

What a bright spot in the long day! I give him a warm hug. Greg is one of those people who knows how to give a holy, welcome hug. He always makes me feel as though he is glad to see me and I will always be glad to see him. I know Mark will be pleased when we open the door and Greg walks in.

I keep busy with some organizing so that Mark and Greg can have time to talk on their own. We are even more blessed by Greg's visit when we hear how he had to track us down. He was out of town while we were at the rehabilitation hospital so this is the first visit since Trauma and we have moved twice. He tried to find Mark and finally went to The Grille to ask where he was. God is so good to allow us such wonderful friends. I sit back on my bed as though it were a sofa and watch Mark and Greg laugh and talk and encourage each other in the Lord.

Shortly after Greg's visit we are blessed by the news that we will move, as soon as possible, to the rehabilitation hospital. We were pretty certain the nurses there would find a place for us, because they promised they would when we left, but to be able to go so quickly is wonderful! This may be our last night here. We decide to prepare for sleep right away because we are ready to let the praises roll!

The Spirit is sweetly residing in this room when a tech comes in to empty wastebaskets. Mark and I do not even attempt to stop or slow down our prayers because we are in such a beautiful place. This particular tech has never mentioned his faith to us and yet as he leaves I say quietly, "Good night, God bless you."

"Bless you too," he says as he quietly closes the door behind him.

As soon as we decide it is time to sleep we realize that we are missing a very important piece of information. No one instructed us if the Bledsoe boots come off for bed, or stay on. We do not feel we can make the decision on our own. The general instruction was to never stand, even for one second, without them. How about sleep?

I go to the nurses' station and ask what the usual procedure is. No one has an answer. They think it might be best to sleep with them on until we can find an answer tomorrow morning.

Within an hour after we say good night, Mark is in pain. His feet are hurting and the boots are tight. I undo the Velcro, which is in four places, one across each foot and three up each leg. I loosen the boots as much as possible. It is effective for as long as five minutes and then he is moaning. We try one thing after another and then, in the middle of the night, I take them off and prop his feet on pillows. He is relieved and able to rest. I stay awake feeling fully responsible for my decision to remove the boots.

When Mark wakes in the middle of the night we put the boots back on. We know that, for now, we need to be accepting, if not content, with one or two hours of sleep. Tomorrow we will be at the rehabilitation hospital and they will know Bledsoe boots inside and out.

Proverbs 16:3, "Commit to the Lord whatever you do, and your plans will succeed."

PART V ✦ WEIGHTBEARING
January 30, 2002 – February 8, 2002

Lana:

True to our experience to date in this situation, our joy in leaving the nursing facility has been overshadowed by circumstances. Mark has a very upset stomach and I am literally handing him a paper cup of Mylanta as the paramedics wheel the gurney into the elevator.

They have barely transferred him to his bed at the rehabilitation hospital when he needs to use the commode. This is made more uncomfortable and complicated by the fact that he has a roommate. Mark obviously does not want to have to be assisted to a commode next to his bed and have to use it, possibly having diarrhea, in the same room shared by a person he has not even met, but he has no choice. As a nurse and I help him to the commode I note that his skin is clammy and he is sweating.

I have a flashback to my son at age six or seven, insisting that I take him to a specific restroom in a mall because it is more private than others. Aside from feeling very ill at this moment his modesty and dignity are being highly challenged. I say a prayer for him.

As soon as the commode ordeal is over, we transfer Mark back to bed, and someone comes in to take his blood pressure. This simple procedure has never been a problem but the sleeve malfunctions and continues to squeeze his arm tighter and tighter. He tries to say that he feels faint but only a whisper comes out. In desperation, Mark attempts to pull the sleeve loose but he cannot use his right hand.

I happen to look at him and see his expression and the way his body is torqued toward the wrap on his arm. When I realize what he is trying to do I reach for the sleeve at the same second the tech recognizes that Mark is about to faint. She pulls it off and rubs the area where the circulation had been cut off. There is a deep imprint. The tech hurries to the bathroom and returns with a cold washcloth which she presses against Mark's forehead. She is profuse in her apology.

Mark and I are ready to retire early after this long day. We look forward to the arrival of our Minnesota friends in the morning. It helps to know that we can take the Bledsoe boots off when Mark is in bed. That should make the night more comfortable. Thank God for the relationships we developed when we were here previously. Our friends on the nursing staff have managed to track down a cot for me. We have one half of the room and I push my cot up against our wall. Mark's hospital bed is close enough to my cot that I walk sideways between the two beds. We have a curtain separating our area from Mark's roommate.

We do not forgo our devotional or prayer time, but we do keep it short because we did not sleep well last night and have a full day ahead. When Mark's medication is offered about 9:00 p.m. he takes it and we say good night.

Isaiah 40:28 and 29, "Do you not know? Have you not heard? The Lord is the everlasting God, the Creator of the ends of the earth. He will not grow weary, and his understanding no one can fathom. He gives strength to the weary and increases the power of the weak."

Thursday, January 31, 2002

Okay. I need to make some sense of this. It is 6:45 a.m. and neither Mark nor I have slept yet, which is especially interesting because Mark took a sleeping pill. This is not acceptable.

Mark's roommate seemed nice enough when we first met. But bedtime showed otherwise. At 9:30 p.m. it was pretty much lights out as always in this facility. The roommate turned off the lights and Mark and I settled in. But a light in my eyes disturbed me so I looked up to see that the television set was on. As far as I know there is only one control for it and we do not have it. I silently debated if I should get up and quietly push the off-button, thinking the man had fallen into a deep sleep and did not know it was still on, but then he started using the remote to channel surf. Once he settled on a station the volume increased.

I reasoned with myself so I would not be upset. *It is still early and Mark should be able to sleep because of his medication. I will just lie here and pray for a little while.* But at 10:30 p.m. the television was still on, so I got up and pulled the curtain that divided the roommate's bed from ours the rest of the way around the foot of Mark's bed and my cot so we would not see the light of the television as brightly. To be honest, I wanted the roommate to know that we were not watching it and wanted to sleep.

Perhaps the television would not have been so awful if the phone had not rung so often. When the phone rang, and a conversation was conducted, for the third time after 11:00 p.m., I heard Mark sigh loudly.

The television was finally turned off at about 11:30 p.m. and my mind scrambled to get into relaxation mode quickly to sleep. That did not last long because the man then decided he needed ice water. Someone in the same room, pouring water from a pitcher with ice in it into a glass in the middle of the night can be heard. Distinctly.

The television was turned on again a little after 1:00 a.m. Light flooded the room and the volume was loud enough for me to hear every word. The television viewing and the phone conversations continued through the night.

And so here we are. Soon the breakfast tray will arrive and Mark will have his first therapy of this return visit and neither of us has slept the entire night. I hope to request a transfer today. Obviously I cannot reason with a person who would be so inconsiderate. I find it ironic; we desperately longed to escape the nursing facility, but we were able to sleep there. What did Paul say about being content in any and all circumstances?

Though we are tired, we are excited. At some point this morning we will have visitors from Minnesota. Three women from our church who have been good friends of Mark's for years are on their way here right now. They have driven through the night with Dave. I try not to think of the weather reports we heard that would have put them in the middle of some blizzard like conditions. I was certainly awake enough to pray for them through the night.

At 10:30 a.m. Dave calls to say that they are in town and at our favorite pancake place having breakfast. That means they are only minutes away.

It is a joy to see good friends and of course we are glad Dave is here once again! We are especially excited because Mark may be able to stand for the first time in therapy today. Dave, Suzy, Leah and Stephanie will be here to share the excitement!

The women will stay at Mickey and Barbara's home and will have a chance to visit with Becki who is a friend of theirs also.

Typical of our time with these friends, the chatter starts and is non-stop as Mark catches up on news from home. Once in awhile tears are wiped away but, just as we have done, they save the hard emotions for the hallway. It is difficult for them to see Mark this way. But we assure them he is much improved and looking forward to standing!

Someone from the Robinson household comes to get the women and they leave to shower and change clothes. They plan to return in a few hours and Dave leaves for Mark's house to take a nap. We remind him that the therapy session is around 4:00 p.m. and that he may want to be here for this big event.

Mark's evaluation goes very well. People are happy to see him back at this hospital and it seems someone from the staff is constantly poking their head in the door to say hello.

We had a very exciting moment when Mark's therapist helped him to stand beside his bed for the first time since the crash. The therapist confirmed that Mark will probably take a few steps at 4:00 p.m. today. They do not waste time here and we are so ready to move on.

I call Dave at Mark's house where he is resting and leave a message on the answering machine that he needs to try to get here to share the experience. I know how sound he will sleep after driving through the night in bad weather and we hope he wakes to get the message.

Chris and Carole call to say they are on their way over and I tell them the news. Carole's voice across the phone line is full of excitement.

"We'll be right there!"

I can picture Chris stepping on the accelerator.

Dave walks into the room only minutes before Mark is to take his first steps. The plan, we are told, is that he will stand with the walker, which will be customized tomorrow to accommodate his broken arm and shoulder. He will then step from the bed to a commode, which is about three or four steps. If he is able, he will then make a half-twist to be able to sit on the commode.

We all hold our breath as he stands. It is an awesome moment.

The therapist holds tightly to the wide gait belt they have fastened around Mark's waist and encourages Mark to take the two to three steps to the commode.

Mark remembers:

I remember taking my first steps with the Bledsoe Boots and the walker. We had tried a simple stand up and sit down a few hours prior just to see if I could handle that...and I could. So when the next therapy session came I was ready. Believe me, I was ready!

Oh, to walk to the bathroom and use a toilet again. To help myself to a snack! To bathe in a bathtub or to take a shower!

I never would have thought I would be thinking such thoughts in my lifetime. Seven weeks of "rest" had led me to that desire to stand and to walk again. I remember standing from the bed and taking two steps to the commode and then sitting down. It was hard. I was weak; but everyone was so proud of my effort and it was not enough to satisfy me. They gave me a short rest and then I tried again. My dad happened to be there with his video camera, as did Chris and Carole, so it all seemed well planned.

I stood up from the commode with a therapist holding tightly to my gait belt. Leaning hard on my walker, I took a few steps. My first thought was, *this sure is hard with these weird boots.* The boots are round on the bottom and it would be nearly impossible to walk in them without a walker even if one were completely healthy. My second thought was to encourage myself, *you can do this! Nothing is going to take away your ability to walk and to walk normally!*

I walked the distance that the therapist wanted me to walk and she asked me if I wanted to go further. I said yes! We went into the hall and I only stopped when my feet couldn't take any more, though my mind wanted my feet to go further still. I wasn't disappointed with my first attempt. It was wonderful to have so many supportive people there and to capture it on video. It was a huge achievement and it couldn't have come soon enough for me! I was happy but, in the back of my mind I knew, this was only the beginning. I had many more challenges ahead of me.

Lana:

I truly don't think the first steps Mark took just days before his first birthday were as exciting.

Once he stands in front of the commode and manages the little twist in direction, the therapist offers Mark an option. "Would you like to go back to bed or walk a few steps more?"

"Walk." There is no hesitation.

Carole and I hug each other's waists and hold back tears. When Mark walks a few feet from the commode to the wheelchair near the door we do not fight the tears any longer and we are smiling brightly. This is beyond the goal for the day, so everyone is amazed when Mark does not stop at the wheelchair, but walks into the hallway. Now Dave and Chris are also brushing away tears.

The therapist holds tightly to the belt around Mark's waist and has me follow Mark with the wheelchair immediately behind him. Dave and Chris each use both video and still cameras. Carole and I alternately snap shots also.

With so many cameras flashing, the therapist quips, "I didn't know there would be paparazzi, I should have done my makeup."

As Mark moves into the hallway we hear a great cheer from the nurses' station behind him. Nurses, techs and therapists stand clapping, crying and generally beaming with joy.

As soon as Mark rounds the corner to the hallway I literally run down the hall to find Mr. Hagewood. I saw him last night and learned that Cynthia is doing well. I am disappointed that he is not in Cynthia's room. It seems important to both Dave and me to share this accomplishment with him. As I hurry back to see Mark's progress I notice Dave grinning at me and pointing past Mark. Mr. Hagewood has walked off the elevator at the very time Mark is walking in his direction! He stands staring at Mark with a wide smile on his face and tears rimming his eyes. Awesome timing, Lord! There is a special connection between those of us who shared the first awful days in ICU. The blessing is even greater to share it with Mr. Hagewood.

Mark walks to the therapy room and then sits carefully into the wheelchair for the return trip. Nurses come down the hall to hug him, and therapists that have observed him in therapy these many weeks come out from behind the windows they have been watching him from with thumbs up. It is an event...a wonderful, blessed and happy event!

Back in the room, Mark is transferred to bed a very tired but happy man. Chris asks him how it felt to stand after such a long time, and what it was like to take steps for the first time since the crash.

"I felt so tall."

We all laugh, "Well, you are tall, Mark."

"I felt taller than ever before."

"Were you dizzy at all?"

"A little bit, yes, but it felt good to move like that."

Dave, Chris, Carole and I hug each other and grin. It is one of the best moments in a very long time.

When Suzy, Leah and Stephanie return Mickey is with them. They all rejoice in the exciting news that Mark has walked. We transfer Mark to his wheelchair and all of us take the elevator down to the courtyard to visit outside in the fresh air. The day is warm and beautiful, the fresh air a wonderful touch to our celebration.

Psalm 92:4, "For you make me glad by your deeds, O Lord; I sing for joy at the works of your hands."

Friday, February 1, 2002

Bless her heart, Leah stayed with Mark last night so I could go with Dave and get some sleep. She has said she will stay tonight also. When we arrive at the hospital today both Leah and Mark confirm that last night with the room-mate was as bad as the one before. I assure them I stopped to talk with the head of the nurses and she is working on getting us a private room.

Thanks to her effort, by midmorning we learn that we will move to third floor pediatrics! That means many good things. For one, it is a quiet floor. I take the elevator up to see the room, curious if I will have a place to sleep, and I am thrilled. It is the largest room we have had and I will have a bed to sleep in! We have been shown unprecedented favor once again and I hurry back with the good news.

The floor of the room is being cleaned by a man with a large machine and we are told it will be a couple of hours until it is dry and ready for us to move there. No matter; we are able to be patient for such a blessing.

Before we know it, we have moved the wheelchair and cart with Mark's belongings on it into our cheery new room. We have barely transferred him to bed before a therapist comes into the room to help Mark walk to the bathroom of this new room. The therapist holds tightly to Mark's belt and he leans on the walker on the slow walk across the floor. Then she helps him manipulate the walker so that he can back into the bathroom. She aids him to the commode, which has been placed over the toilet for height. She gives him some instruction and then leaves him there.

It is a bit unnerving to me. I can't help but feel concern that Mark could fall or faint or slip or, who knows what? But I apply the tongue biting that is a part of my role in this process and watch the therapist as she stands near the door in a responsible watch. She then shows me how to help Mark when he is ready to return to bed. It is a complicated process but in time Mark emerges from the bathroom pushing his walker, the therapist holding firmly to his belt. He wears a huge grin on his face.

"Did you hear that?" he smiles, "I flushed the toilet for the first time in eight weeks!"

Psalm 118:24, "This is the day the Lord has made; let us rejoice and be glad in it."

Saturday, February 2, 2002

Today Mark is allowed to sit in the shower. The nurse aids him as he uses the walker to get to the bathroom. Once in the nice sized room, she holds his belt as he backs up to the shower seat that sits high in the bathtub. The nurse and I have padded the seat with plenty of towels. Then the undressing process begins by removing the Bledsoe boots. Each part of the process is complicated because Mark is not allowed to stand for even one second without the boots on and fastened.

It is a painful process for Mark. Though we have the shower seat padded, it is not enough to protect the broken hip and pelvis from pain as he sits with his legs to the side of the tub, boot shod feet propped on a pillow on the floor.

When the Bledsoe boots come off the nurse checks the scars on his feet and discovers a stray stitch that had been missed. She reaches for a scissors and tweezers and removes it.

This bathroom is large and I am able to stand aside to observe and learn as she carefully positions Mark's feet in the tub and uses the hand held showerhead to wet him down before she begins to scrub him. He is given a good rinse and then she towels him off and helps him to put on his clothing. The boxers are slipped over his feet, which we notice are extremely swollen, and then she pulls the boxers to his knees. He has a towel on his lap the entire time for modesty. Before reaching for the boots we discuss what type of sock needs to go on underneath them. With the swelling, regular size socks will not work and his toes are very sore.

To give her a better idea of what she is dealing with, she pulls the Band-Aids off Mark's toes. That act reveals what looks like Sharpee pen dots on the tip of each toe that has had a pin removed from it.

We settle for a sock that looks, in texture and color, like an ace bandage. It is open at the toe so it is really more of a tube than a sock. This enables his toes to be exposed but protects the leg and upper foot from abrasion caused by the boot.

After the boots are on, Mark is able to stand with the aid of the nurse holding on to the wide and ever present belt. His boxers can be pulled to his waist by the nurse and he can drop the wet towel he has been holding onto. We put a dry towel over his shoulders and get him to bed and then we put his t-shirt on. He is more than ready to rest as he shivers from the new experience and our inability to get him completely dry.

The next obstacle, it seems, will be to get his feet healthy. They are shedding skin. Not as one would from sunburn, but more as a snake molts. Layers fall off and hang from the feet. I place a towel under his feet because they are leaving collections of skin at each movement. When we remove his socks, enough skin comes off with the sock to make you wonder how any can be left on the foot.

I devise a game plan. Ann-Marie is in the room when I decide what to do and she helps me. We wrap Mark's feet in wet, warm towels and then, after getting an okay from the nurse, I apply baby oil being careful to avoid the toes with open wounds. After the baby oil has been applied and allowed to sit for a few minutes, we start to wipe the feet with a towel, sloughing off the dead skin. The skin on Mark's feet is yellow and thick looking. As we gently work at the exfoliation, pinker skin is revealed and we are encouraged by the under layer of healthier skin. I find my previous experience of managing a spa has come in handy.

Soon our Minnesota friends will arrive for the day. I have been blessed with two nights of sleep next to my husband because Leah stayed with Mark. The women have convinced me that I should go to a favorite mall with them today. Becki, Barbara, Suzy, Leah, Stephanie and I will have a few hours out while Dave stays with Mark for some one-on-one time. I know it will be good for me to go shopping but it amazes me how difficult it is for me to leave Mark. I realize that though there will be a process of letting go again as he improves; it is all good.

It seems there is a continuous parlay of conscious and unconscious action on my part. At this moment, it is the fact that it is important for Dave to minister to Mark when he is here. I embrace that, and yet it is a dilemma because Mark and I have, out of necessity, devised our own way of accomplishing daily tasks. When Dave does something in a different way, I have to bite my tongue. This is happening now, so I go into the hallway for a short walk, which should quench my desire to instruct him to do it my way.

I see Leah in the hallway and it looks like she has been crying. It strikes me that I am so pleased with the improvement in the way that Mark looks that I have failed to realize his friends are seeing him in this condition for the first time and it is very sad for them.

The mall outing is a welcome escape, a sign that things are better than they were and a promise of good things to come. We have a great lunch accompanied by girl talk. Each friend is sensitive that I do not want to be away from the hospital for a long time, besides they each have their own plans for the rest of the day, so we do not plan as long of a trip as we might in other circumstances.

I really did not purchase much, in fact, only a couple of pairs of thick socks for Mark, and a facial moisturizer for myself, but it feels good to be on such an outing. It is a welcome glimpse of nearly forgotten "normal" moments with friends.

As we drive back to the hospital I am blessed by the love I have been shown.

Colossians 1:9-11: "For this reason, since the day we heard about you, we have not stopped praying for you and asking God to fill you with the knowledge of his will through all spiritual wisdom and understanding. And we pray this in order that you may live a life worthy of the Lord and may please him in every way; bearing fruit in every good work, growing in the knowledge of God, being strengthened with all power according to his glorious might so that you may have great endurance and patience, and joyfully giving thanks to the Father who has qualified you to share in the inheritance of the saints in the kingdom of light."

Sunday, February 3, 2002

It is Super Bowl Sunday, 2002! This is party time under normal circumstances, so we decide to stay with tradition. Ann-Marie is coming over and we are ordering pizza. *Thank You, Lord, for such a wonderful diversion!*

Dave is making quite the sacrifice today as he drives home with our friends and misses the Super Bowl. We feel sorry for him until we get a call halfway through his trip and hear that they are all tuned into the game and cheering on their teams. I am blessed that the car full of women would do that because I know Dave really wants to hear the game. *Bless them, Lord. Thank you that they came such a long way to cheer and encourage us. Help them to arrive home safely and to travel in good weather!*

I bask in the happy sound of Dave's voice after I hang up the phone. Blessings cannot be compared, each is unique and precious, but friendship has to be at the top of the ranking.

Mark is excited to eat pizza for the first time in many weeks. For some reason knives here are not serrated, so the pizza is nearly torn into bite size pieces as I try to cut it so he can taste it. Mark is unable to bite into food because of his fractured front tooth and the uneven bites I have prepared do not seem to matter as he places the small pieces in his mouth for his first taste of pizza in a very long time.

The Super Bowl game proves exciting to the last second and I am more than blessed by the light of excitement in my son's eyes.

Psalm 37:4, "Delight yourself in the Lord and he will give you the desires of your heart."

Monday, February 4, 2002

Today I am observing people as I sit on the raised mat in the therapy room. They watch, often with beaming faces, the progress of their loved one. It may be a first step or more steps than the day before. Perhaps it is a finger closing around a peg to place it in a round hole on a wooden board. I know the joy they feel, I share it with them though we have never met.

Mark is sharing this session with a man who is also in a wheelchair and, like Mark, learning to use a walker. Mark uses his walker to take steps from the wheelchair parked by the exercise mat to the entrance door of the therapy room, and then negotiates a turn to walk back to his wheelchair. It is then the other man's turn. He is young, not as young as Mark, but too young to be in a wheelchair and struggling to walk. The process is grueling for both men even though the other young man looks as though he was physically fit before his injury, as was Mark. Mark sinks into his chair when he returns but soon the young man is back

"Okay," the therapist nods at Mark, "walk again."

Mark looks at the young man and grins, "You can take longer next time."

The two laugh and banter in between their turns to walk. I smile, once again warmed by Mark's ability to put people at ease. Once the walking exercise is finished, Mark is told today will be his first time in "Circuit Group." He listens to the therapist's instructions but when she walks away he looks at me and sticks out his tongue to let me know he is not looking forward to it.

The therapist gives Mark a pair of gloves. They are similar to a glove worn for weight-lifting with a crocheted appearance on top and a leather palm. These will aid him in moving the wheels on his chair. I watch and try not to think about how long this process is and how many more steps will be needed before Mark can walk on his own. There is the occasional moment in life when one would like to wave a magic wand.

Mark is now wheeled to a Parabody machine, which will aid him in working on his left hand. As soon as the right hand can form a grip he will work on that also. They put the weights at the lowest level so he will not strain any muscles. Before the crash Mark lifted weights on a regular basis, now he sits before this ten pound weight and musters the courage to reach for the pulley. He lifts it for a few seconds and we all grin with the joy of another victory. He rests and then does it again.

They are going to work his shoulder today also. He sits in the wheelchair and is able to work his left arm with some ease. I am nearly weak with gratitude.

I sit in a chair and I continue my observation of the room. Mark and others are gently thrown huge beach balls. In Mark's case, he can bat it back as he sits on the edge of the elevated mat. He cannot catch it because of balance nor could he throw it at this point. Just batting it with outstretched arms seems to aid in gaining balance.

Other patients who are living in this place are putting small colorful blocks into round and square openings or sliding colored beads across a metal rod. Like a pre-school class, they tackle each new challenge and take pride in their accomplishment.

Mark is a determined man. He may smile at the elementary projects he is given to do, but he does not take them lightly. In fact, he cannot. These things are not so easy to do as they were before the crash. I can see him focus, accomplish, move on, focus, accomplish, move on, accepting each new task as another obstacle to be conquered.

I watch as the therapist holds Mark's right hand and gently moves it forward and then back, stretching the muscles and tendons that have been immobile for weeks. As they talk, we discover that Mark should not have been in the circuit group yet. It is too soon for a shoulder injury like his. Too late! He has already done everything he was instructed to do.

As much as I appreciate the wonder of therapy, I detest the lack of communication that seems inevitable in medical settings. Mark has been on the painful receiving end of that too many times. If we are seeing so much, when I am constantly monitoring, what happens elsewhere?

We know we must put our trust in this community of caregivers; we have no choice. We know they are of good quality. We expect this is common everywhere and that the frustration is compounded by our sense of helplessness.

I distract myself by more observation. I find the range of personality in this room more dramatic than the variety of injuries. Some patients appear focused, some smile as they concentrate, others are grouchy and unwilling to be pulled from complacency. I find myself wondering what my reaction would be to such gigantic obstacles.

Mark's age and weight definitely work in his favor; that and the fact that he was in excellent physical condition before the crash. His personality is also a factor; he is willing to be told what to do and taught if it means benefit. The qualities he possesses, along with a strong prayer covering will pull him through. I have never been more proud of the exceptional person I am blessed to mother.

Mark moves to a machine that is a UBE, or Upper Body Ergometer. This is like moving a bicycle wheel in front of you by peddling with your hands. He grins at me when he tries both hands. He is making progress with the grip on his right hand.

When we get ready to leave Mark is told to stay in the wheelchair rather than transfer to his walker. I look at the row of walkers against the wall and realize his is readily recognizable. There is a high right arm brace attached that towers over the other walkers. Tennis balls decorate the bottom of each leg, but the back legs are wider than the others in the row. It is definitely customized. I fold the walker into an easily portable shape and push the elevator button. Mark is able to propel himself onto the elevator. He looks over his shoulder to smile at me and I grin back. We are making progress. This is good. This is very good.

Back in the room, Mark is gaining more ground. He can now get to the bathroom using his walker and is able to go in by himself. It is a huge victory for him. He has also conquered use of the portable urinal. It was not a natural thing to have this little plastic container and use it to urinate while in bed. It took some getting used to, especially when he had so much trouble immediately after the Foley catheter was taken out, but he is pleased he has moved past whatever hindered him from using it before. It is a necessity because getting to the bathroom is still a time-consuming process. If he is in bed, we must put on his Bledsoe boots, move the walker, get him to a standing position and be sure he is belted. Then I grab the belt and we slowly move toward the bathroom. I am never comfortable if the door shuts tightly because he is weak and I want to hear if he calls. There is a call button, but he cannot reach it easily. I know that, in time, we both will be more confident about these daily routines that now seem such a concern.

We find the therapy this afternoon frustrating. It takes some effort to get Mark out of bed and into his boots and then transfer him to the wheelchair, grab the collapsed walker and head out the door to walk/wheel to the elevator and down to the therapy gym. We start at least fifteen minutes before we are due in therapy as we have been told it is our responsibility to get there and to be on time. Once there, at 2:30 p.m., his therapist talks to him for five minutes and then tells us she must get a phone call. We wait for her until 3:00 p.m. and then Mark asks to go back to the room because he is tired. I told another therapist to let his therapist know that Mark had to leave.

She comes to Mark's room shortly after we arrive back. I suspect she was told immediately that we had left. She tells him she will work on his arm in the room. It is a hard workout and as soon as she leaves I go to the nurses' station to request pain medication for Mark.

We move away from energy-zapping frustration by putting a DVD in our laptop and we watch snippets of the movie as interruptions take place, then we opt for a light supper as both of us have upset stomachs.

There is comfort and encouragement in the words we find in Timothy 4:8 before we go to sleep.

> I Timothy 4:8, "For physical training is of some value, but godliness has value for all things, holding promise for both the present life and the life to come."

Tuesday, February 5, 2002

My son's sense of humor has always been a delight to me. This morning I leave the room while Mark uses the urinal. Before I walk out the door, Mark mentions that he wants to go back to sleep but that is not possible because of his therapy appointments.

I stand outside his bedroom door until I hear him call my name, then I walk back into the room to say, "Okay, let's get you washed up."

I can see he has the covers pulled over his head and a falsetto voice comes from beneath them, "He's not here."

In the sweet way that he exercises his own style of stubbornness, he does not move from under his covering when I come to the bed with a basin of warm soapy water and washcloth.

I hold out the cloth, "Here, you go. Wash your underarms."

When he does not respond, I keep trying. "I have your boxers here, you need to wash up and change them."

When he remains silent, and I know he is smiling under the covers, I try a new approach. "Well, here is your nice warm soapy washcloth. You can use it now or wait until it is cold."

He pokes his head from under the covers, laughs a loud short laugh and grabs the cloth from my outstretched hand.

We manage to have fun nearly every day. We amuse ourselves with the circumstances that could overwhelm us. We are united, as we have prayed to be, and we work hard to make the best of this difficult situation.

When Mark was a teenager he had a sign on his bedroom door, "I don't do mornings." He never has. When he began kindergarten I requested afternoon sessions because I knew mornings would be a struggle and a less positive school experience than afternoons. So here we sit, at 7:45 a.m. breakfast eaten, bed bath finished and struggling to get Mark dressed.

He is sitting on the bed giggling because he has been trying to put a sock on his foot. I know he would rather cry than giggle because he is not able to accomplish the task. What people do not understand is that he has never been able to touch his toes from a sitting position without bending his knee. In elementary school he won awards for fitness but missed an overall award every year for one reason: He could not touch his toes without bending his knees because his legs were so long!

The therapist walks into the room. "Look at you! You are bending forward!"

Mark and I are both laughing at his attempts to hook his foot with the sock, but it is a laugh that covers the sharp edge of pain. We are frustrated and he is hurting. He absolutely cannot get the sock over the sore foot when the broken knee hurts to bend and his right arm cannot stretch. Add to all of that the problem he has always naturally had reaching his feet from a sitting position…I can barely watch.

"Take your time, there is no rush," the therapist says.

I want to say, "Unless you have to go to the bathroom!" But I bite my cheek and turn to sit on my bed.

"It has never been possible for me to reach my feet without bending my knee." Mark finally says with a deep sigh.

The therapist leaves for a minute and shortly after she returns a nurse comes in and, unbelievably, sits down to watch! It seems to me the nurse has been invited because Mark is not able to do this task and has very mildly protested the possibility of it.

Mark is now working to put on his Bledsoe boots. He is sitting on the edge of the side of the bed and trying to reach down to Velcro the foot part of the boot. It is not possible. He is in pain but he keeps trying. Though he does not say anything, he looks up to catch my eye and I see the frustration in his eyes. He is fighting tears, but he bends his body forward again, straining the hip to the point of pain and reaching his right arm as straight as it will possibly go. Before long he can use only the left arm as trying to force the right arm into a straight position is too painful. It is a struggle for me to sit still. I want to walk across the room because it looks as though he could lose balance and fall forward off the bed with the effort he is exuding.

The nurse, who should be busy with something else, impatiently chides Mark, "Come on didn't you tie your shoes before?"

I am amazed my cheek is not bleeding. I wonder if I will regret not saying to her, "He sure did and for many years. But that was before his hip and pelvis were broken, along with his knee and both feet…and don't forget that shoulder and wrist and hand that were also injured enough to require surgery!"

I absolutely cannot understand why this nurse feels it is her duty to make our difficult situation harder. She has been rude to us since we got here. I am also surprised that she has nothing else to do but to sit in on a patient's therapy session and berate him. When the therapist and nurse leave together, Mark lies back on the bed with tears in his eyes.

I am in a constant struggle to act and react in my son's best interest. I knew it was not my place to say one word while this was going on. I am not interested in being cast as a meddlesome mother, but I am interested in being supportive and compassionate to my son. I wait for his reaction.

"She needs to be reported," he says quietly.

"I know, but we won't be here long. Maybe she will be even worse if we report her."

His reply is quiet. "Let's wait. Let's hope she never is on duty again while I am here."

I swallow hard to keep from crying. It seems so pointless that a supposed caregiver would be so blatantly cruel.

"Well, it really is no big deal. I am here. I can help you with the boots whenever you need help. You are doing a great job in your therapy, everyone says so. No one can expect you to do something you could not do before the crash!"

His smile is sad, "It seems they do."

We decide to steer clear from this nurse with the nasty disposition. We will not ask for anything while she is on a shift unless it is an emergency. We remind ourselves that we have befriended every other nurse in this facility and that she is a sad exception. Mark also reminds me of an earlier observation he made, "She is not a nurse because she is called to it. She is here because it is a job. She does not have the gift of compassion necessary for her profession."

I appreciate the way he rationalizes and moves on. I need to work to get past the feeling of contempt I have toward this woman who has decided to exercise cruelty to someone who is struggling to overcome suffering. I open the Bible and read as Mark rests, trying to find a place in my heart to pray for the nurse I dislike so very much.

Psalm 125:1, "Those who trust in the Lord are like Mount Zion, which cannot be shaken but endures forever."

Wednesday, February 6, 2002

It is snowing, and for Nashville, quite a lot. I cannot get to Mark's house to start to prepare for our move there. I feel like a car whose engine is revved up and ready to go; with a flat tire.

Mark is crabby today. He certainly has a right and has had very few, if any, crabby moments. My own emotions are raw; I still feel they have been run through some kind of cheese grater to expose them as raw nerves. I am also struggling with physical pain from sleeping, or rather not sleeping, for two months in makeshift beds.

While Mark finishes his breakfast, I stand by the window to watch the snow fall, and blink away my tears. *Lord, help me. Strengthen me. Take my thoughts and make them Yours. I do not want to start to dwell on my needs when Mark has so many. Take away the pain in my body and my emotions. Take away my yearning for home and the life that was. Shield me from despair and make me a light in this darkness. Oh, God. It is in Your hands. I have no strength of my own. I claim 2 Corinthians 12:9. You know, Lord, it has been my personal verse for more than twenty years. I know that Your grace is sufficient for me. I know Your strength is made perfect in my weakness.*

Earlier, I took a quick walk to second floor while Mark ate breakfast and was pleased to see a woman I met when we were in the Quiet Room. We began to talk about how hungry we are for good breakfast. Wouldn't eggs and bacon be good this morning? Our conversation proceeded to fill each other in on the progress of our sons. Her son was shot in the head and though it is a hard road, he is moving along. It is surprisingly good to see familiar faces; kindred spirits in suffering and hope.

The conversation was like medicine and encouraged me to face the day renewed. I turn away from the window when the tech comes in to remove Mark's breakfast tray. The young man comments to me about the open shelves against the wall in Mark's room. Anyone can see they are stocked to the brim with a variety of food I have purchased at the grocery store.

I lightly reply, "Well, we are determined Mark will gain his weight back!"

As the tech leaves, he says he will return soon to get Mark into the shower. He smiles at me and I thank him brightly.

Mark snaps at me the second the door closes. "What are you so chipper about?"

He has no idea how I have worked to become "chipper" for his sake. I know that but still feel wounded. I decide to be honest. "I am trying to be up for you."

"Don't tell people I need to gain weight, it degrades me!"

We both are aware that anyone who sees Mark will know he needs to gain weight. He is over 6'1" tall and, at last weigh in was at 112 pounds. It is no secret, but it is a frustration for him. Though I have resolved to not be crabby in his presence, and in all our years as mother and child, we have never exchanged harsh words, I need to express myself. I need to establish some boundaries or I will fall apart.

"If we are going to lay down rules, then don't question me when I am in a good mood because I can get into a bad one really fast."

I understand his frustration and he knows that I was not divulging any secrets, yet we have managed to offend each other. God, in His great love for us, has protected us from times like this. Now we must realize it can happen easily while we live in intense stress with frustration as our constant companion.

Mark hits the remote and stares at the television set and I lay on my bed to "rest." I turn my back to him so he will not see the tears that I can no longer hold back. I want to cry...really cry. I want to sob and let my shoulders shake. I want the ache in my throat to find relief. I nuzzle under the covers to hide myself and cry. It is not the hard and desperate release I long for, but I let the tears overflow. I feel them wet the pillow and I take deep, slow breaths to control myself.

I am not crying just because I failed to be perfect today. I am never more than a breath away from despair at any moment. It happens I have given in to it today. The tears taunt me that it is all a façade. I am continuously playing a part that I am not equal to. For my audience I smile. I offer encouragement and express positive thoughts. Behind the curtain, under the covers, this is me. I am this person who shrinks in fear and is overcome with sorrow. This is me, this person who feels like a lost child in need of someone to bend down and pick me up and hold me.

When the tech comes in to take Mark to the shower I pretend I am asleep. I have not been able to get up to blow my nose and can barely breathe. Besides, I would be embarrassed for the tech to see me and I would embarrass Mark. I hear the tech help Mark to the shower and leave the room.

I get up and quickly blow my nose and begin to listen for Mark in case he needs help. I find myself wondering if he can reach to adjust the temperature or turn the water off if he wants to. So much has changed. I find concern in anything and everything.

I hear the shower water turn off.

"Need help?" I ask through the door between us.

"Yes."

In the bathroom I reach for the cord to ring for the nurse but Mark stops me. "No, don't."

The nurse on this shift is the cruel one that we now call "Yesterday Nurse" in our journal. She treated us both so poorly yesterday that neither of us is able to face her abuse again.

Mark is sitting on the towel soaked shower bench shaking from weakness and from cold. I dry his back quickly while he dries the rest except for his legs. As soon as his back is dry I help him put on a very large t-shirt. And then I reach into the tub and help him to pull his legs, one at a time, over the side of the tub. As I pat the legs and feet dry, skin falls everywhere. I work his boxers over his sore feet, being careful not to touch them. He struggles to lift them, keeping the towel on his lap. The effort is complicated further because he still cannot put any weight on his feet until the Bledsoe Boots are on.

I work as fast as I can, because he is cold and weak. I put a fresh towel across his shoulders to aid in warming him and pat his feet as dry as possible without rubbing them. Then we pull on the sleeves of fabric that serve as his stockings.

I am kneeling on the hard floor, something I do not do well, but it is the quickest way to get the boots on. Any place I touch causes pain for Mark so I am very cautious and I am sniffing constantly because of the residual of my cry.

"Quit sniffing," he says to me.

"Just a minute, sit still and I'll go blow my nose."

I do that and then we finish. As soon as the boots are secure, I put the belt around his waist and he fastens it. Then I help him stand, holding tight to the belt, and he pulls his boxers up the rest of the way, dropping his modesty towel. I kick the towels out of the way, my hand never leaving his belt and reach for the walker to pull it toward us. Mark clutches tight to the walker and begins the slow shuffle to his bed.

Before we get there, the door opens and someone comes in with a food tray. With my movements to help Mark into bed and pushing the tray cart to his side, I am back to denial and on with the day.

I decide not to be too hard on myself, though that is my inclination. I have been on call every minute of every day for two months. Anyone would be tired, I reason. Then again, I try not to allow myself to slip. I need to remain compassionate and in an attitude of serving because Mark needs me.

When the therapist comes to take Mark to therapy, I go downstairs with him carrying the walker and the therapist walks beside his wheelchair. But as soon as Mark is in the therapy room I return to his room to "check e-mail." I lie on the bed and cry. I turn my face to the wall and speak to it. "Just one minute," I say, "I will cry for just one minute."

When I know two or three minutes have passed I wipe my eyes and sit up. The tears refuse to stop just because I have decided to sit up so I stand and walk across the room, pull a handful of Kleenex from a container and blow hard. I am irresistibly drawn to the bed to lie down again.

When a tech comes in to get Mark's food tray I pretend I am asleep but then I realize she did not close the door behind her and so I get up to go and close it. My hand is on the door when I look up to see April with her mother, Sally, and sister, Angie. I love Sally and have not seen her for probably a year, but I am embarrassed that I am crying.

"You caught me." I say to April.

"I'm sorry. Is everything okay?"

I quickly assure her Mark is fine and she hugs me...no, she holds me. Of course her display of love and concern for me releases more tears.

"I'm okay," I manage to say. "Mark's great," I try to smile, "I'm just a bit homesick and overwhelmed."

"Maybe this will help." She laughs lightly and Sally holds up two containers from a favorite coffee place. She has brought a Mocha Decaf for Mark and a wonderful rich cocoa for me.

April is the sweetest friend to both Mark and to me and if anyone had to catch me with my guard down I am glad it was her. I have no doubt she understands. I hug Angie and Sally and we talk for a few minutes. I assure them I am fine though I feel embarrassed to have been caught "naked."

"Please don't tell Mark," I say to April.

She shakes her head. I know she will not say anything.

"We're going to therapy," she says. I know she is giving me an opportunity to pull myself together while they visit Mark.

I go to the sink and wash my face with cold water. I put foundation on to hide the red nose and blotchy face and throw on lipstick and mascara. I blink hard and will the tears to stop so the mascara will stay in place.

When the phone rings, I hurry across the room. It's Ann-Marie. This morning we were told that Mark will probably be released to go home on Saturday, and she wants to have cake and balloons at Mark's house when we arrive. It is a great idea and I give it my blessing.

I walk down the hall to the elevator to go to therapy but see April and Mark returning early. She is pushing his wheelchair and they are moving at a leisurely pace, enjoying conversation.

April does not stay because Sally and Angie have plans. I am very grateful for her visit as I sip the rich cocoa drink and think to myself that I have successfully banished my blues; or at least swept them into a corner where they cannot be seen.

We settle Mark into his bed and I concentrate on Galatians 6:9, "Let us not become weary in doing good, for at the proper time we will reap a harvest if we do not give up."

Mark has just tasted his coffee drink when a wonderful young nurse comes into the room.

"You look so good!" She beams at him. "I remember you from downstairs," meaning she remembers a few weeks ago before we left for the nursing facility.

"You have such a great family." She smiles at me. "That really helps."

She is pleasant and kind as is the tech that stops in with her. This is such a departure from the rude and actually cruel nurse we dealt with yesterday. We discuss the difference when the young nurse leaves.

Yesterday Nurse refused to help Mark back into bed when he needed to get from the wheelchair to the bed though he is not supposed to walk unassisted.

Today's Nurse did not have to be asked for help. She saw needs before they were mentioned and showed compassion and spoke words that could breathe life into our situation.

Yesterday Nurse looked at me with disgust and said to Mark, "Your mother SEEMS to think you have a doctor appointment."

I had to tell her to "please go and check your book because Mark does have a doctor's appointment and needs to have transportation arranged."

She found I was right and she would have been in a bind if she had not called to arrange transportation. She had treated me as though I were an unwelcome intruder, even though I had helped to keep her on her toes when she had failed to notice something important.

Today Nurse smiled at me and told Mark he had a great family enforcing what we have heard from doctors and nurses all along; people heal quicker and better when they have support.

Yesterday Nurse brought Mark his pills uncrushed. Even though the instructions she was left with must have noted they needed to be crushed, she sighed heavily as though he had asked her to drive to a pharmacy and get a prescription, fill it herself and then return and get it ready for Mark. In fact, all she had to do was walk out the door three feet to her station, stick the pills in a little device that crushes, throw them back into the little cup and bring them to Mark, per the instructions already written on his chart.

Today Nurse took a few minutes to let Mark know how thrilled she was to see his hard work show itself in the way he physically looks. She let him know he should keep it up, that he was doing great and that she was proud of his progress.

Which attitude motivates a patient? Which chases away the depression that can be part of being a victim of a violent crime?

From our patient point of view, when we saw that Yesterday Nurse was here today we were extremely disheartened. We decided to do as much by ourselves as possible. I expect that is why we had such a difficult day. Mark was not about to have her help him with his shower. We know we can learn from these personalities and last night we prayed for the unkind nurse and her family.

While Mark is back in therapy I decide to go home and wash some clothes and organize Mark's bedroom so it will be ready when he gets there on Saturday. I have only been home a short time when I get a call from Mark. He tells me that he had an upset stomach and barely made it back to the room after therapy before he needed to be on the commode. I did not ask how he got to the bathroom but he said that he rang for help when he was finished and still on the commode as this is what he has been instructed to do. The bathroom light is supposed to show up at the nurses' station as an emergency call from the bathroom but there was no response so he got himself back to bed. This is very dangerous. Someone is always supposed to hold the belt around his waist when Mark walks with his walker. He is still unstable on his feet and his legs are weak.

I hurry back to the hospital only to find I can barely get in the door of his room because his wheelchair is blocking it. I move the chair out of the entry area and hear the story about why it is blocking the door. When Mark had to find a way to get from the commode to bed by himself, he managed to get his walker around the wheelchair that was outside the bathroom door. He then used the walker to get back to bed by himself. He rang for the nurse and asked for Mylanta.

It was Yesterday Nurse who responded. She did bring his Mylanta but could not get into the room easily because of the wheelchair, which he had abandoned to get to the commode. And of course, there was no way for him to move it.

Even so, he had apologized. "I couldn't move the chair and I had an emergency."

"You want Mylanta?" She ignored his words entirely and extended her hand for him to take the paper cup of Mylanta.

She did not say one other word to him and left the room with the wheelchair still blocking the way.

It has been a long day as usual. In our prayer time we ask that tomorrow we will be given a nurse with compassion, at least with a pleasant disposition because it seems so important to us.

As we move on in our prayer, Mark sees a vision of a waterfall. Rainbow colors come off of it and wash over both of us. Each color represents something different God is giving us. Gifts we are receiving are Authority, Kindness, Love, Hope, Passion, Power, Peace, Gentleness and Compassion. He can see some colors as they represent a gift very clearly. Kindness is green, Love is red, Authority is purple, Passion is blue, Compassion is orange and Gentleness is yellow.

We recognize we are not born to be a singular color or to lack any color. With this in mind, we are led to read from Galatians 5 regarding fruits of the spirit. After a day lacking in peace, we go to sleep in peace, knowing that it is not by might nor by power but by the Spirit of the Lord that we will persevere.

Proverbs 25:11, "A word aptly spoken is like apples of gold in settings of silver."

Thursday, February 7, 2002

Our meeting with our attorney and Chris and Carole went well. We have each been given assignments by the attorney. Chris will write them out and e-mail them so we keep each other accountable and so we do not forget anything in the busy days ahead. Chris and Carole also have the name of an excellent dentist and we will try to get Mark's dental work done as soon as he is able to sit long enough.

Mark has an appointment with an ophthalmologist today. It will be his first time to be transferred by the rehabilitation hospital's van instead of ambulance. He will be okay in the wheelchair in back of the van as long as he can recline from time to time.

In the doctor's office Mark has to wait. They are very considerate to get him into the room, and to help get him into the examination chair, but once there we wait a very long time, long enough for Mark to become quite uncomfortable. Finally I go into the hallway and ask the kind young resident how long it will be. He comes in and talks to Mark for a minute. When he checks the chart to see that Mark has hip and pelvis injuries he is concerned about him sitting any longer and leaves to get help as soon as possible.

Mark tells me that it is not the hip that is the major problem. His feet are in pain. We try inventive ways to elevate them. I take the pillow I keep on Mark's wheelchair to cushion his hip and place it under his feet. When the doctor comes in she is immediately pleased by the look of Mark's eyes. Mark's left eye has to be probed with a metal instrument that looks fairly sharp, and it is very uncomfortable. The exam is thorough, including eye drops for dilation and the standard eye chart. It has been an uncomfortable experience for Mark but the news is good. His eyesight has not been harshly affected in spite of the severe injuries. The doctor decides that he should not change his prescription for eyeglasses. The change is slight enough that she feels another adjustment in his life is not necessary.

We praise God for another prayer answered. I cannot wait to tell Carole because she has felt led to pray for Mark's eyes since the early days when it caused fear to stir in our hearts when we looked at the beautiful eyes that had been so harshly traumatized. We are relieved by the good report and anxious to get back to the hospital so we can finish packing for the big move tomorrow.

I pack and Mark helps to direct, but we stop to spend some time in prayer with Becki when she stops by. We also welcome the break when Ann-Marie and Pat stop by, bringing shepherd's pie from a restaurant where it is a specialty. We enjoy our conversation and the food is absolutely wonderful!

Unfortunately, Mark cannot eat a lot of his dinner. He is experiencing slight nausea which becomes more intense as the evening progresses. A nurse comes in to give him a shot ordered by the doctor. Nausea has become part of his life, on and off, for the past few weeks. We suspect the high doses of pain medication cause or contribute to it. Despite his discomfort we are determined to stay awake to watch the opening ceremony of the Olympics.

When we turn off the television and enter in prayer Mark asks me to write down the vision he had of his battle with nausea.

Mark remembers:

"I had been nauseous for about two days this time. I sensed it was not a medical problem. It was difficult when, by the end of this second day, I still was not able to eat. I was relieved when everyone left the room so I could rest.

I closed my eyes to sleep and saw in the Spirit Realm. There was a creature whose hand was in my stomach twisting it to make me feel nauseous. Then I saw another creature with its claws pressed into my head causing a headache. I rebuked these demons and slowly felt the peace of the Lord fill in the places once agitated by evil.

I began to think, *this is really weird that I can see these creatures.* I really could see them, though I could not describe to anyone what they looked like. I was aware they enjoyed making me feel ill and robbing me of my joy.

Then I remembered that Lucifer had been a beautiful angel. When he became evil he became ugly; though he is still disguised as beautiful to those who are deceived. The vision reminded me of the movie, "Shallow Hal." Hal saw people who were beautiful inside as beautiful outside and people who were ugly inside as ugly outside even though they appeared differently to others.

I was seeing some creatures that were really horrific because of their nature and realizing that the Lord sees us on the inside. When I saw these creatures, I knew that they were evil through and through. I am becoming more aware of the spiritual realm."

Lana:

Tonight Mark is rejoicing because he was blessed with two new songs today. His excitement is contagious as God downloads songs into him. He grinned when he told me, "The melody of this one is really cool. I hear a black choir in the background praising the Lord!" It is a promise of things to come.

After prayer, we read from Romans 8 and turn out the lights nearly too tired to sleep. Tomorrow holds more of this overdose of the unknown. Tomorrow we go home where it will be just the two of us. No nurses, no techs, no adjustable hospital bed or call buttons. We are comforted that we have good friends and we are covered in prayer. I hold up my hand in the dark as though I expect Jesus to reach out and take it.

Here we are, Lord, on the brink of yet another adventure. We long to be on even ground with a clear pathway in sight, but it cannot be. Hold our hands, Lord. Guide us and put a hedge of protection around us. We know we can trust You and we pray, with confidence, in the name of Jesus.

Matthew 10:29-31, "Are not two sparrows sold for a penny? Yet not one of them will fall to the ground apart from the will of your Father. And even the very hairs of your head are all numbered. So don't be afraid; you are worth more than many sparrows."

Friday, February 8, 2002

Brian arrives early to help us move. He amazes me when he puts three times more on the cart than I ever would have imagined could fit. He smiles his explanation, "Bellman, Road Manager." Yes, he has worked in those positions.

Wow. I am even more impressed when I go down to drive my car over from the ramp and find that he has already fit everything into his car.

Mark will be transferred home in a van equipped with a wheelchair. Yesterday we practiced with the therapist, how Mark can back into and get out of a car. It is not easy and he needs a vehicle with fairly high seats. I have a little Nissan so we are once again wondering how things will come together.

Brian leaves for the house to unpack his car and Chris arrives to wait with us for the van. We move out of Mark's room so the man with the big machine can clean the floors just as he did the day we moved in here.

The floors are nearly cleaned and the van has still not appeared. I leave Chris and Mark in the little room we have been waiting in to go and check at the nurses' desk.

Yesterday Nurse is at the desk. I walk up to the desk to ask about the van and stand waiting for her to recognize that I am indeed waiting to speak. She does her best to ignore me as she continues conversation with a co-worker. Finally she says in a sarcastic tone, "What do you want?"

Even though she has been nothing but incredibly rude, I am surprised she would talk that way in front of two co-workers.

"Me?" I ask.

They all laugh. One of the women says, "Sure, she talks to patients and guests like that all the time."

Yesterday Nurse laughs like that would be absurd.

I immediately regret that I did not say, "Yes, I know."

I am informed that there has been a mix-up. They are not sure when the van will arrive. When I tell Chris and Mark, Chris asks Mark if he would be comfortable riding in his Suburban and Mark says, "yes," grateful to get going.

I walk back to the nurses' station to inform them that we are leaving. I fill out the necessary paperwork required for Mark to be discharged and then walk away and hurry down to second floor to say good-bye to the nurses who nurtured us here.

Before we leave, Chris offers a prayer for Mark and for me as we start our "newest transition." We also pray for the business trip Chris and Carole will take tomorrow and for Brian back at the house who has a job interview later today. Then we turn to leave this hospital.

As we wait for the elevator, Chris hugs me and says, "You get the 'Most Able To Change On Short Notice, Mother of The Year Award'." I appreciate the kind words and the knowledge that Chris is aware of the apprehension I feel about taking care of Mark on my own.

Chris pulls his Suburban up to the canopied entryway and we wheel Mark out and help him get into the vehicle that will finally take him back to his house. I hurry to the ramp to get my car and pull in behind Chris to follow them. We are on our way.

This is Mark's first passenger ride versus patient ride since the crash and I feel very blessed that he is with Chris and in a large vehicle. Once again, God has it all orchestrated. Even so, I am in constant prayer as I keep my eyes on the vehicle in front of me. I pull out my cell phone and call Brian to say we are on our way and tell him where the camera is. I ask if he will please take a picture of Mark arriving home.

2 Samuel, 20:29 and 30, "You are my lamp, O Lord; the Lord turns my darkness into light. With your help I can advance against a troop; with my God I can scale a wall."

PART VI ✦ OUTPATIENT
February 8, 2002 – March 28, 2002

Lana:

There is much excitement mingled with our apprehension to have Mark home. It is a victory and the cake on the table that says "Welcome Home Mark" along with balloons floating above the cake make that proclamation.

I could cry as I walk in the door, and not from joy. Brian and I must scramble to clear a wider path for Mark's walker because Mark's second roommate, who was supposed to be moved out by this date, has physically vacated his person but left all other belongings in a heap in the dining room which is the entry to the house. The mound of his belongings is high and spills over into the "safe area" where Mark needs to use his walker. Not only has he impeded the entry, but this room is the way from the bedrooms, living room and bathroom to the kitchen.

I am momentarily overwhelmed at the sight of this pile of belongings that covers about six feet by three feet of space and piled about four feet high! This is moving out? I know I cannot move the heavy boxes and clothing to the garage without hurting myself. I look away from the mess; to celebrate the moment. We are home and we must not allow our joy to be robbed.

Mark aims his walker in the direction of his bedroom. It is very emotional. The first time Dave and I came here to rest when Mark was in ICU, I knew his lease was up about this time of the year. I thought to myself he would never walk into his bedroom again. I had looked at the photos that he has on his walls and shelves of friends in happy times and I cried. Now I feel full of hope that he will have happy times with friends again and new photos with smiling faces will be taken.

We thank Chris and he leaves. Brian, Mark and I decide the first order of business is to get Mark to bed. He has not slept in his own bed for two months. While he is anxious to get into his own bed we see immediately that it will be a challenge for him because the bed does not have the adjustments he is used to.

Mark lays flat on his back and decides to rest and visit with Brian who has offered to stay long enough for me to run to the grocery store. I appreciate it greatly and head out the door with a promise to be back before he needs to leave for his appointment.

I buy the store out. I am not going to worry about the expenses because finances are already out of control. I want Mark to have food around that he can enjoy for the first time in months. I want to fill the house with fragrant cooking and see his face light up!

I stop at the pharmacy next to the grocery store and get all of Mark's prescriptions filled. The pharmacist takes time to talk with me. The drugs I am taking with me are very potent and he knows I am caretaker to someone who has suffered. As soon as I pull the car in the driveway, Brian leaves for his appointment. I carry the groceries into the kitchen and go to see how Mark is doing.

For a few minutes I sit on the foot of his bed and Mark and I stare into space and at each other. It is quiet but the thoughts we share make considerable noise in our heads…how will we do it? How will we get him showered and to the commode? Will I dispense all the medication correctly?

As if on cue, we look at each other and break into smiles.

"What's for supper?" My precious son grins at me.

As I put out ingredients for supper, I make a mental checklist of all we need to function. I ordered the commode and shower seat and a few other things the therapist said we would need a few days ago. I drove out to a medical supply house and picked them up. One item I brought back was a handheld shower hose.

Because God is our provider, yesterday a man came out to fix the dishwasher, which was leaking, and when we talked I mentioned the shower hose, which I thought one of Mark's friends could attach. The kind man went right into the bathroom and took care of it. I think we have our technical needs covered.

Mark continues to rest for awhile and I decide to unpack as much as possible. I look forward to putting my clothes in a closet for the first time in a couple of months. I have been using a little duffle bag to carry clothing back and forth since I got here, but when I open the closet door in what is now my bedroom my heart sinks. Mark's second roommate has not moved his clothes out!

As tired as I am, I start to pull his clothes from the closet thinking I will hang them in the hall closet, but when I open that door I find he has clothes in there also. I take the stack in my arms across the living room and into the dining room, placing them on top of the pile he has already created with the items he stacked in boxes and bags in that room. My arms cannot reach high enough to add to the top of the pile, so I clear a space in the laundry room and carefully place as many clothes as will fit from the two closets on the countertops as I fight tears of frustration.

I cannot get my clothes put away, because we need supper and estimate that we need to prepare for bed by 7:00 p.m. if we want to be ready for prayer time before 9:30 p.m.

We called that right. It is quite a process to get Mark ready, but we agree that each day we will get into more of a routine and I will become more organized to make everything work for us.

The floor plan on this home is ideal. Mark's bedroom is next to mine with a small laundry closet between. At his end of the hall is the bathroom, and at my end there is a closet and the door leading to the living room. Brian moved a large bookshelf full of books from the hallway to my bedroom so that Mark's walker will be able to move through the narrow hallway. I was amazed he moved it by himself…but Brian has amazed me much today.

Though the rooms are very close, Brian and April have lent us Courtney's Baby Monitor. I have it hooked up in case I fall into a sound sleep and Mark needs to call me. Now after good prayer time, I pull back the covers to the bed I have just put clean sheets on. I hear something and stand still, listening. I hear it again. It is a whisper.

"Can you hear me?"

I start to laugh. Mark is whispering into the baby monitor to see if I can hear him.

"Yes." I speak into the monitor. "Can you hear me?" The question proves I have never used a device like this before.

"Of course not!" I hear his laugh from the next room. "If I could hear you the baby would never get any sleep!"

Proverbs 15:30, "A cheerful look brings joy to the heart, and good news gives health to the bones."

Saturday, February 9, 2002

Mark and I were awake the entire night. When he first went to bed we thought it would be wonderful for him to be in his own bed after months away.

I propped pillows around him. One to cushion his hip, one to raise his lower right leg to protect the sore heel, one under his shoulder, and one between his legs to take pressure off the knee. But there was no way to adjust the bed and he had grown accustomed to the hospital bed.

He said, "Mom, I want to try to sleep on my stomach. I always slept on my stomach in this bed."

He inched himself over on his side little by little and kept moving until, after much effort, he was on his stomach. The second he did it he burst into laughter. "Help!" He called out trying not to laugh too hard. "I am like a beached whale."

"You are like a turtle on its back!"

We laughed hard but not for long because we were faced with the dilemma of getting him onto his back and that was not going to be an easy process! It probably took us at least five minutes to move him, inch by inch, using pillows to stop him from rolling back until we got him into a position where I could "flip" him without causing him pain. By then we were more than ready to sleep but it was not possible for him to be comfortable and I listened for every noise from the baby monitor as a new mother would her babe's first night home.

This first night has held so much expectation. We dreamed about it on long nights in the hospital when Mark wanted to go to sleep in his own bed. I am so disappointed for him that, when he is finally able to get into that bed, there is no comfort in it.

Matthew 6:34, "Therefore do not worry about tomorrow, for tomorrow will worry about itself. Each day has enough trouble of its own."

Sunday, February 10, 2002

The agony of a long night has mushroomed into disappointment and frustration for both of us. As I walk into Mark's room early this morning he looks at me and bursts into tears. I can do nothing but hold him. In his own home, for the first time in more than two months, he is free to let loose of some of the torment without wondering if someone will walk in on him. I hold my son as the sobs come hard and heavy.

I sit next to him on his bed with my arms around him and I stroke his hair. There are no words to speak. Truly there is nothing I can say. Our hearts share sorrow so deep that even pain cannot go there, but it is a place Mark must visit. This is an unavoidable stop in our journey.

Even as I hold my son and experience an agonizing, raw sorrow that mingles with his, I know this is a place where God can work to heal. We sit on the bed for a long time. There is no hurry and we do not want to visit this valley again. We both know that once Mark is able to quit crying we will simply move on.

When the sobs subside I hold him just a little closer for a few seconds and, still with no words, I go to the bathroom to get a washcloth and basin. We do not have energy to try the shower today.

When Mark is clean and refreshed, he asks for his notebook and pen and I leave him alone to write a song born of anguish. He needs time alone and so I work hard at getting the house in order, struggling to detach myself from the resentment I feel each time I have to work my way around, or come face to face with, the mountain of "stuff" that Mark's second roommate has left for me to deal with. I begin by cleaning the closet that is now mine as I am impatient to have a place to hang my clothing. I move what is left of the roommate's clothing onto his dining room "barricade" and then I tackle the thick dust that lines each baseboard in the room.

Having the bedroom clean makes a world of difference. I have just finished when Ann-Marie walks in to comment on how much better it looks.

Now I am on my way to Target to get a bed-seat so Mark can sit up to read in bed and a bed tray so I can bring him meals in bed as necessary. He can get up and walk around but it still involves the boots, belt and walker, so, at least in the morning, he will eat his breakfast in bed.

I am careening down the aisles when my stomach spasms and I cannot wait to get back home. As soon as I empty my shopping bags, I decide to rest for a half-hour before we enjoy a wonderful supper, brought by Sally and Angie. There are huge portions of meatloaf, macaroni and cheese and peas along with a wonderful cherry cobbler. As delicious as the food looks, I am not able to eat.

Mark enjoys the meal and relishes sitting on his sofa to watch television while he eats. We have taken a seat cushion from the loveseat and placed it on top of one of the sofa cushions so Mark can sit higher as he cannot bend his knee to sit down on the normal height of a chair or sofa. He finds that comfortable for a little more than an hour, then it is time to move back to bed.

We allow plenty of time to get ready for bed and plan ahead to spend part of our prayer time asking for a good night's sleep.

Isaiah 66:13, "As a mother comforts her child, so will I comfort you."

Wednesday, February 13, 2002

Mark is still asleep so I sit in my bed to write in my journal. I have not found time to write each day. Yesterday Mark spent a great deal of time in the word. He especially studied Jesus being forsaken. "I have suffered," Mark said, "But I was not forsaken. Jesus is my hero. He was alone in his suffering and, unselfishly, he did it by choice. I want to spend time researching the 'forsaken' element."

Our time together in the word last night led us to 2 Thessalonians, 3:5 and 1 Peter 5:10. We read Psalm 13 out of both the NIV version and from The Message.

This morning as I throw on my robe to head to the kitchen I think how strange it seems to be home. Physically, this is more of a challenge for me as there is no one to share in the tasks that must be done. Before we had nurses to bring the food that someone else prepared, and we had help with transferring Mark from bed to commode, bathing and the many other things he still cannot do on his own. I offer rather weak praise to God because I truly am grateful, but I truly am tired too, and He knows that.

Today is our first official "day off" since the crash! We are going to make it special. Three days a week we drive to the rehabilitation hospital for therapy. The first two days went better than we expected, and now we have a day with no appointment. To celebrate, we slept later than we have been able to for awhile. Before going to bed last night, we decided that, unless there was a physical need, we were going to sleep until we were ready to wake up.

It is 8:00 a.m. and before I go to the kitchen, I check to see if Mark is awake. He is sleepy but ready for his pain pills. I get the medications ready and put a bowl of cereal on the breakfast tray to take to Mark's room. The breakfast tray is a great tool. By using the bed seat to prop Mark into a sitting position, and then placing the tray over his legs, he is able to eat without having to get out of bed. Immediately after taking his medication, he decides to sleep some more.

I shower and by the time I am dressed and have eaten some cereal myself, Mark is ready to prepare for the day. We decide to get him in the shower. We have not had time to try it and have resorted to bed-baths the past few days. Now, we feel like we are on an adventure as I lift the shower seat into the bath-tub and pad it with several towels.

When I go back to my room after Mark's shower I sit on my bed with the comforter pulled up tight and decide to document the process we developed to allow my son to take a shower. I have never given much thought to the diffi-cult and lengthy process of rehabilitation after a car crash or to the role of the caregiver. I need to be able to share this with others like me.

The decision to take a shower is no longer simple for Mark. We begin with him sitting on the edge of his bed, carefully moving his feet over the side to rest on a pillow I have placed on the carpet. We put the Bledsoe boots on with great care because his feet are very sore in the morning. I kneel on the floor to Velcro the feet and ankles; at the same time, Mark bends forward to Velcro the top straps that go to his knees. Then I pull up his walker. He stands, holding on to the walker until he is steady. Then I place the wide gait belt around his waist and he fastens it. I grab the back of the belt, a little looser than the first few times we did this, and we walk slowly to the bathroom. As we walk out the doorway of his bedroom, the bathroom is immediately to the right. He must walk out the door and then turn around by moving the walker in a circle until he is facing his bedroom door. He then moves into the bathroom sideways to back up to the high-legged commode that covers his toilet.

I wait outside the door, gathering towels from the linen closet in the hallway. When I hear a flush, I knock. He uses the walker to turn himself around once again, so his back is to the tub and then he stands still, hands on the sink for balance, while I move the walker out of the small bathroom. I then have to lift the commode up and over the sink and place it in the hallway. This is a physical challenge for me.

While I hold the back of his belt, Mark lowers himself onto the towel padded shower seat. I help him take off his t-shirt, respectful of his limited shoulder movement. He removes his glasses. I open the Velcro on the boots and carefully remove each one, then help him to move his feet over the side and into the tub. Once he is in the tub, he pivots so his feet are in front of him as he sits on the bench facing the shower controls. At no time has he placed any pressure on his feet without the Bledsoe boots on. He then places a towel on his lap and slides off his boxers.

I make sure he has shampoo, washcloth and soap in easy reaching distance. I quickly pull the shower curtain closed and leave the door open a crack so I can hear him. While the water is running I straighten Mark's room, make his bed and lay out clean clothes, always listening to the running water!

Once the water stops running, I enter the bathroom with three towels in my hand. I dry his shoulders first so we can put a t-shirt on him. He is shaking from both cold and weakness. I try to work quickly in the small space. I use towel number two to dry his hair and we keep the towel on his head. The next step is to lift his feet and have him pivot to face his body out from the tub. I hold his feet until he does this and then help place them on a towel I have on the floor, being very careful they touch the floor gently. I dry his legs to the knees with another towel and gently pat the feet dry.

The boxers are the next step. I put them on over each foot, pulling them to his knees and then I hand him the elastic top. I turn my back while he finishes drying.

When I hear "okay," I put on the long tube type socks that expose his toes, but prevent the boots from irritating his skin. The only way for me to do this is to sit on the toilet seat and bend down. By the time we are done, my hips and lower back are screaming for mercy!

I help Mark stand and then I turn to the side, looking away, and he pulls the boxers up. We put the belt around his waist and he leans on the counter around the sink while I get his walker from the hallway and place it in front of him. I place a dry towel over his shoulder for warmth and grab his belt more firmly than necessary. He puts both hands on the walker and we begin the trip to the bedroom, which, under ordinary circumstances, is only steps away.

After manipulating the walker sideways between the two door openings, Mark backs up to his bed and sits. I help him lift his feet and he rests briefly before I hand him his comb and deodorant. I go to the bathroom to get the little bowl he spits in and I put toothpaste on his toothbrush and take these things to his room. We then take off the Bledsoe boots and pull on a pair of lounging pants. I look at him and smile. Good job.

While Mark rests I gather towels from the bathroom, realizing that we have used six towels to get him showered. I throw them into the washing machine right away; it will not take long to run out of towels at this rate.

The second I return Mark lets me know that he has worked up an appetite. That's a good thing, so I go to prepare lunch. I make him soft food; some macaroni and cheese, applesauce and a cupcake all at his request.

I finish chronicling the experience in my journal while he eats and then I go to the bathroom to comb my hair for the first time today and put on some makeup. I feel pressure to get some thank you notes out, though surprisingly, writing notes will take more energy than I have, so I put it off for another day.

Barbara Robinson calls to say she and Elizabeth want to come over to visit Mark and to free up my time to run errands. That is a blessing. While I would love to stay and talk with them, I am grateful to get to the grocery and drug stores.

When I get back I see that Barbara has made Mark something to eat. He grins when we tease him about all the women who serve him. I thank them for coming though I know they wanted to be here.

Shortly after they leave, the doorbell rings and I am delighted to see a man holding a very large gift basket. It is from a woman in Minneapolis who is a wonderful support to Mark by attending his concerts regularly. This generous basket and kind gesture touches our hearts.

We have so much fun looking through the basket, which is filled with a beautiful selection of fruit, candy, cookies and other snacks. It is topped by a soft stuffed dog. We are more than impressed with this gift and Mark does not put off writing a thank you note.

We stay up later than usual watching the Olympics on television and so we take steps toward getting ready for bed during commercials. It does not matter how late we stay up, we will not forfeit our precious prayer time. As soon as Mark is in bed, I reach for *My Utmost for His Highest* and we are immediately at the throne of God.

> 2 Thessalonians 3:5, "May the Lord direct your hearts into God's love and Christ's perseverance."

Thursday, February 14, 2002 Valentines' Day

When I wake at the exact moment I had hoped to awaken, I smile. *Thank you, Lord, you are always here for me.*

I am reminded of the words I spoke to Mark last night as we turned off the lights. "I'm right here if you need me."

Those words bring such comfort when they are full of sincerity and followed by action. We certainly have heard them spoken by well-meaning people whom we have not seen again during this ordeal. I find myself repenting of times when I spoke the words, "Call me if you need me," when I should have just called before I was needed.

I take a few minutes before my day begins to thank God that He has allowed me to be here with Mark. For all the turmoil and heartache, it has been a strangely sweet experience. Mark and I have been on a spiritual adventure together that would have never happened otherwise. I would not have chosen this path, and most certainly Mark would not have, but we are confident God will bring good from it.

When I go to Mark's room to get his day started, he protests. He wants to sleep longer (something he is very accomplished at, I think with a smile). I have my own agenda for the busy day ahead and so I tell him, "I will be your nurse today. You can choose which nurse I should be, Yesterday Nurse," I stretch out my arms, palms up, as though I am weighing his choices, "or our favorite on second floor." I repeat myself, "Yesterday Nurse or Second Floor Nurse."

He laughs loud and tells me not to ever mention Yesterday Nurse's name again.

"Let's get you cleaned up and fed," I say with a plan in mind, "And then you can do whatever you want. You can just crash for awhile if you decide to!"

He looks at me with the grin that melts my heart. "Mom, I can't crash. It takes me five minutes to get my boots off!"

We start laughing about all of the funny things that have happened to us in this experience and put off our morning routine.

"Remember when they told you that if I soaked my feet in vinegar that it would help me get rid of all the dead skin?" Mark wrinkles his nose.

"Of course, it wasn't so long ago."

But we both break into more laughter as we remember. I had heard that I should "Mix vinegar and water one to two cups." So I had prepared a large basin and poured in one cup of vinegar to two cups of water. The house reeked!

Mark had lowered his foot into the water and started to laugh at the smell. "Something's not right. How much did you put in here?"

"One cup vinegar to two cups water."

He pulled his foot out and lay back on the bed laughing hard. "No wonder it stinks! It should be one to two cups of vinegar in the entire basin full of water!"

We are constantly amazed at how much fun we can find in the weird circumstances we have been given to walk through.

After Mark is finally ready for the day, I shower and dress before we make our way into the living room. Our conversation turns introspective as we talk. We want to know how we can find the path to love God more.

"Your thing is filling time." Mark observes. "You're too busy. You'll find it when you don't do so many things." He is not talking about the unique situation we are in now, but my lifestyle in general.

"True." I agree. "I don't get over one obstacle before I focus on another. Sometimes I'm strategizing about the next problem before I thank God for solving the one I have just moved away from."

"We both are continually working at something."

"I wonder if most people are."

"I am good at dropping things to find time for enjoyment." Mark notes.

"You are. I've always admired that. I simply do not allow that for myself. Maybe it is being a mom, a wife, a woman. But I think many women do find time to relax. I will try to be better when we get home."

"We need something to look forward to," Mark states.

"Carrots. Good idea. Let's dangle some carrots in front of ourselves. What?"

"Well, I'd love to think of getting a Dachshund when we get home."

In the back of my mind the questions surface...will Mark stay in Minnesota or will he return to Nashville as soon as he is able to be on his own again? There are no answers, so for now, we will proceed as though he is going to be living in Minnesota. "So would I, but we need to be realistic about our location. I don't know if it would be good for a small dog with all the wildlife around."

"Let's think about it. And I want to go to the resort this summer."

"The resort" he refers to is a place we have gone to as a family a few times. It is a golf resort in Minnesota and we love to go and be away from busyness to enjoy each other as a family.

"Done," I say. "I'll look up their website and write for information on availability. We'll try to go around your birthday in June," I hesitate, "what if you can't golf by that time?"

I think it would be a horrible frustration if we went to a place where all we do is eat, golf, read and play board games and he could not swing a club. At this moment it seems a very remote possibility that he could stand and swing at the same time.

"I'll be able to. I'll work toward it."

"Then I'll make reservations," I smile.

"Okay, what do you want to do most right now?"

"I want to sit in a Jacuzzi and read a good book, then sleep for about a day and a half."

"Me too," Mark grins.

We each decide on a nap and when I wake to check on Mark he is sitting in bed with his notebook in front of him. "I've decided to write a song called "Morphine." He flashes a mischievous grin and begins to read the lyrics, "'you've got your morphine, you got your Vioxx, your Lortab and Ambien, man'...that's as far as I've gotten."

I give him a look that says he should not waste his time finishing it.

Ann-Marie is coming for supper tonight so I go to the closet shelf in my bedroom and pull down the Valentine's gifts I have stashed away for her and Mark and then go to the kitchen to start a supper fit for a holiday.

Luke 12:34, "For where your treasure is, there your heart will be also."

Friday, February 15, 2002

I am greatly encouraged and feel my load is lighter. The unsightly pile of boxes, clothing and household goods that covered the dining room area and blocked Mark from walking further than the living room has been removed.

Andy came over at 11:30 a.m. this morning and made countless trips to the garage with boxes I would not have wanted to lift. I took large garbage bags and wrapped all of the loose clothing, bedding and assorted pillows in them so they would stay clean.

I was actually relieved that Andy was annoyed at the mess. It validated my feelings. He walked from the dining room, making the u-turn to the kitchen where I waited to hold open the door. His face was hidden behind a huge pile of bedding. "I am happy to help you," he said as he turned sideways to fit out the door and carefully maneuver down the steps to the driveway, "but I wouldn't do this to a roommate that was in *good* health!"

Andy is a busy guy and he is a good friend to take time to do this for us. I called him for help knowing I could do that. Words cannot express the relief there is in knowing someone like Andy will come when you have reached the end of your rope.

Andy has done a great job! What a relief. Now Mark can get to the kitchen with his walker without the danger of things falling on him or into his pathway.

While Andy arranged things in the garage I helped Mark get ready for the day and took time to apply some makeup because the three of us are going to meet Brian, April and Courtney at The Green Hills Grille for lunch. Before we leave, Andy slices tennis balls to fit on the "feet" of Mark's walker so it will be safer. We are excited because it is Mark's first social event since before the crash last December.

At the restaurant Brian and April show us a picture of Courtney, recently published in the newspaper under the heading, "Cute Kids." I request a copy for my office at home. The manager at The Grille, comes to our table as do many of Mark's former co-workers. Everyone is so pleased to see him up and about. We order whatever sounds good to each of us and have a great time.

One thing we forgot was a pillow for Mark to sit on. I guess, in time, we will remember all that is needed to keep him comfortable. It was a concern but one of his friends was our server and she went and got Mark a pack of linens wrapped in plastic. He was able to sit on them.

Conversation became a bit tense when one of Mark's closest friends came to the table. Mark has been very hurt by him. Before the crash they spoke nearly every day and, initially this man was there for Mark and for us, but he has not come to visit nor has he even telephoned to inquire about Mark for many weeks. Mark has left messages on his home phone but he has not returned them. Of course, in the tight knit group around this table, everyone knows what has happened and we try to give grace knowing each person deals with tragedy differently, but the situation feels awkward.

A balloon is brought for Courtney and we all order dessert even if we are full. This is an all-out celebration. When the bill comes, and it is a healthy one with all five of us celebrating, we are informed the manger has said, "No charge!" How wonderful!

Mark is extremely tired. This first outing has been a drain on him and he is ready to go home to bed. Brian and Andy help Mark stand until he is stable and then get his walker unfolded and in place and then they each walk beside him to "guard" him as he slowly walks to the car, parked in a handicap zone outside the entrance. They show him so much love and respect, it touches my heart.

I watch as Mark's other friend looks on. I cannot read his mind, but I like to think he is sorry he abandoned his friend at such a time and that he will make an effort after today to spend time with Mark very soon.

It is simply wonderful to look forward to a weekend! No therapy and no commitments on our time. We are excited, but in the midst of positive things we need to deal with insurance and bills. They could be overwhelming aspects of this drama we are living, but we try to be responsible without taking on more than we need to. In truth, we will not know for a long time how much we are responsible for and how much the drunk-driver will help pay. It is stress each time a bill comes in with the daily mail.

Today, when I bring Mark the mail, he looks at a hospital bill and quips to me, "How do we know where the comma goes?" The dollar amounts are staggering.

He decides to take a quick nap because we are blessed that Brenda and Roger will come to the house this afternoon. Roger has an appointment at Vanderbilt and they called a couple of days ago to let us know that friends would be driving them here and that they would like to visit.

Mark is in bed resting when they ring the door bell and we hug and greet each other and I show them to the living room. Roger is sitting on the sofa, facing the doorway to the hall of Mark's bedroom when Mark comes through that door with his walker. Roger begins to sob. He is so blessed to see Mark upright.

We comment that Roger looks good and I think that Brenda is so sweet when she calls me her angel. I know what it is like to have friends who are as angels and I am honored she thinks of me that way.

We have a good but fairly short visit before they have to leave to return to Kentucky. At the door Roger begins to cry again as he hugs Mark.

"Be strong," I say to Roger as he walks out the door. "You look so good."

"He makes me strong." Roger points to Mark. Roger knows his strength comes from the Lord, but we all know he is saying Mark has been an encouragement and inspiration to him. He tells us Mark's music in his life spurs him on.

God is so unbelievably awesome to have allowed me to be drawn to Brenda that first day she entered the Quiet Room. At that time I could never have dreamed the joy I would receive in her friendship.

At the end of another long day, we notice that getting ready for bed seems to go smoother now than it did a week ago. Praise God! There is much to do. Aside from changing clothes and brushing teeth and sometimes soaking Mark's feet, we have faithfully been massaging all his scars with lotion that contains vitamin E and have noticed a visible difference.

Our early evening routine now involves watching the Olympics and we enjoy that so much! The stories of athletes that have overcome great physical challenges to come to a point of victory in their lives have inspired Mark.

> Matthew 7:7, "Ask and it will be given to you; seek and you will find; knock and the door will be opened to you. For everyone who asks receives; he who seeks finds; and to him who knocks, the door will be opened."

Sunday, February 17, 2002

Mickey is speaking at a church about a half an hour from here and Mark wants to go to hear him. When the alarm goes off at 7:00 a.m., I go into the shower and get myself ready for church. At 7:50 a.m., I go in Mark's room to help him. He is disappointed to report that not only is he tired, but also nauseated. We pray against the nausea and I prepare a bowl of cereal to see if that can settle his stomach, in case the nausea is caused by the irritation of his harsh medication.

I finish getting dressed in case we are able to go, and Mark rests a little longer. Mark lets me know that he is determined to go and we take it slow as we get him ready. In the past Mark would have had to have a nice long shower and put on just the right clothing to go someplace. Today he is content to feel clean with a bed bath and put on whatever clothing he can get into. He has lost a lot of weight, aside from the fact that it is difficult to pull clothing over all the sore places on his body that have little flexibility, so his clothing choices are limited.

With much help, Mark puts on a pair of jeans for the first time since the crash; this pair was chosen carefully as the leg opening must fit over the bulky Bledsoe boots. A t-shirt is next and then a shirt that I bought Mark for Christmas weeks before the accident. It has a suede feel and the loden green color looks great on him. It buttons up the front, which works quite well. We use his "fleecy," which we bought for getting back and forth to doctor appointments in the hospital, for a jacket. It is a simple grey fleece jacket but it is an extra large size and gets the job done because it fits over other clothing easily and he does not have to stretch his arms to get into it.

We have mastered getting into the car with our trips to therapy. I walk beside him holding onto the belt in the back and he uses his walker. I have parked the car halfway back in the driveway so he can walk the short sidewalk in front of the house and then back into the front seat. The seat is pushed as far back as it will go. Once Mark is seated sideways in the car, I take the walker and fold it into the backseat. We both work to lift his legs into the car carefully and I go back into the house to close the front door. Then I walk to the back so I can lock up the house. Mark has always used the back door of this house so that is the door his key will lock. For now the front door must be used as his exit and entrance door because there is only one step to go up or down, while the back has three.

We take back roads to the church to avoid traffic. At the church, we use the handicap-parking sticker we obtained last Monday. Becki comes into the church at almost the same time we do as we have planned to meet here. A couple of other people who know Mark come over to greet him. Mickey and Barbara are either not here yet or in a prayer room.

It is obvious that Mickey is happy to see Mark. He has a right to feel proud of Mark because he has been a coach in the effort that brought Mark this far. He mentions Mark as he opens the service.

"Did any of you have trouble getting here today?" He tosses the question and then asks Mark to stand. It is not easy for Mark to stand, but he does and smiles at his good friend, Mickey.

Mickey may be one of the very few who understands how hard it was for Mark to get to church. He has been there. There is no reason to deny or make light of it. It was work, but it is good to be in the house of the Lord.

We had hoped to go out to lunch with Becki, as in the good old days, but Mark is too tired. I invite her to come over and offer to make brunch. She accepts our invitation and we all enjoy brunch and fun conversation. Shortly after eating, Becki leaves because she recognizes how tired Mark is. He sleeps most of the rest of the day.

Jeremiah 29:13, "You will seek me and find me when you seek me with all your heart."

Monday, February 18, 2002

Mark's shoulder is creating quite a bit of interest in therapy today. Several therapists have been called over to look at it and give their opinion about how it has been put back into place. It does not want to move and that is not acceptable. Tonight we will concentrate on praying for this important part of Mark's healing.

It is good to be able to send requests via cyberspace to our prayer team. Once again, one of Mark's injuries is a mystery to the medical community, but all things are known to God.

After lunch we take time to read the beautiful devotional that Mary Beth sent us. Then Mark spends a good part of the afternoon writing the last two lines to a song he had nearly finished days ago. It is funny how that works. So often the main body of a song comes easily and then a couple of lines take a good deal of work, time and creative strain. It's a great song titled *Stronger Than Before*.

There are many details to attend to this day. Jason will move out on Thursday. We are excited for him that he has purchased a condo. I will need to find a bed to sleep on; in fact, we will need two beds because Dave's mom, Betty, is coming to stay with us for about a week. Both Mark and I look forward to seeing her. It will be a quick and tiring trip for Dave as he will bring Betty and have to turn right around to go back to Minnesota. He is willing to do that; in fact it was his idea. He is so unselfish with his time and energy because he knows it will be good for all of us to have Betty here.

Any block of time I find open in a day is spent getting Mark's things packed so that Dave can load the car with boxes to take back to Minnesota. It will take the crunch off our trip home.

> *I John 5: 14 and 15, "This is the confidence we have in approaching God: that if we ask anything according to his will, he hears us. And if we know that he hears us—whatever we ask—we know that we have what we asked of him."*

Sunday, February 24, 2002

Nearly a week has passed since I opened my journal! I think it is a good sign that we are busy with life once again. I decided my short time with Dave would not have any interruptions, even by my journal.

Betty is here and Dave has made his U-turn. He left at 5:45 a.m. this morning to return home. Mark and I had hoped to go to church with Chris and Carole today. I have not met their Priest yet, though he visited Mark in the hospital twice; but our good intentions were cast aside because I was awake all night with a headache and Mark did not sleep well either. We have found we cannot push our physical endurance beyond a certain point. We are learning our boundaries.

The moving date for both roommates has been changed several times. Most recently it went from Thursday to today but last night we gave Jason a call to find out what time they would be here today and found out it has changed again to tomorrow. I am trying to go with the flow.

Mark had a wonderful treat today. Chris and Carole called; spur of the moment, to say they were going to a rehearsal for a group that is recording a new CD. Chris is coaching them. Mark knows most of the guys in the group as he spent time with them in San Francisco when they auditioned. That was a great experience for Mark and the guys became friends. Mark is a couple years older than the others in the "Boy Band."

Chris called and talked to me to ask if I would consider letting Mark go to see them. This was very respectful. Chris and Carole know how hard each step is and that, even though Mark has made his own decisions for years, the dynamics have temporarily changed. I told them I would trust Mark with them above anyone else and handed the phone to Mark.

He was really excited when they came by to get him for this major outing. Chris certainly knows Mark's restrictions and needs and so I am more excited than anxious about them going for awhile. In fact, Betty and I have decided to go to the mall. I have two gift certificates from Christmas I can spend and it will be a good way for us to have "girl" time.

This trip to the mall is short, but like medicine. I find a black belt for Mark to replace the one that had been cut off in the ambulance after the crash. He is starting to wear regular pants on occasion now and will need it.

Chris has told us what time they expect to return Mark and so we do not tarry. I purchase a spring sweater set with one of my gift certificates and decide to save the second certificate for another day.

We arrive home about twenty minutes before Chris and Carole bring Mark to the door. Mark had a wonderful time. I prayed through some concern because I knew he had performed dance routines with this same group in an audition setting and that he would be watching them move and dance across stage as well as sing. I wondered if he would despair that he cannot even walk on his own, much less dance. Not Mark. He says it has motivated him. He is animated as he tells us how the guys called out to him from the stage when he first walked into the auditorium and how they spent their break time talking to him. He seems wonderfully energized.

What a blessing that Betty is preparing supper for us tonight. We all enjoy the leisurely meal and conversation and then Betty decides to go to sleep early.

Mark and I go through our routine of readying him for bed and then I am treated to a blessing as Mark reads to me from our devotional and from scripture. I take deep breaths of gratitude as I savor the sound of his rich voice as he ministers to me.

Proverbs 16:9, "In his heart a man plans his course, but the Lord determines his steps."

Monday, February 25, 2002

What a full day!

Chris and Carole brought over a day bed with a trundle yesterday. We separated the two pieces and I have a bed in my room and we have put Betty's bed in the back part of the large living room. As soon as Jason moves from his bedroom, today or tomorrow, we will move Betty's bed in there and she will have a bedroom and bathroom to herself! We invite her to come with us today but she opts to stay behind as I take Mark to therapy and then to the dentist.

Today is Mark's first time in hydrotherapy. It is cold this morning and Mark is not certain he wants to get into a pool, but we both have an excitement about the mobility the water will give him. At the hospital, I have to accompany him to the small dressing area and help him change, and then we put the boots back on and he walks out to the pool area, using his walker. He is told to back up to, and sit on, a white plastic chair and then take off his Bledsoe boots. The chair is attached to a metal arm that the therapist "cranks" to move the chair out over the water. Then Mark is slowly lowered into the warm pool. He is thrilled to realize that he is actually able to stand in the water. It is exciting to watch and I blink back the tears that well in my eyes.

The warm water is inviting and the freedom of mobility is more than he has experienced in months. The grin on his face as he looks my way tells me that hydrotherapy is a hit with Mark.

The therapist that is in the pool with him and always beside him, holding his belt, is continuously questioning Mark in regard to pain as he stands in the water.

"It doesn't really hurt," he assures her, "it is just a very weird feeling."

She instructs him to "describe weird."

He tells her the right foot feels very tight or drawn beneath his toes but he wants to continue. Moving forward is what the therapist wants, but she asks questions continuously to be sure he is not stressing his feet in a negative way.

With both hands on the safety bars that edge the pool, and facing the tiled area surrounding the pool, Mark begins to walk sideways along the edge. It is a slow process. Eventually they move to the deeper water. There he is instructed to hold onto the safety bar with his arms behind his back to perform a scissor movement with his legs. He tries to reach behind for the bar, but his shoulder will not allow it, so they work with him holding on in front.

I am amazed and thrilled to watch my son move more freely than he has in months. "Mark, that has got to feel good!" I say to him as I sit on the tiled apron of the pool.

He smiles up at me and I snap a picture with our ever-present camera.

The therapist looks at him, "Did you just smile at her?"

She seems so surprised; perhaps because they are in the middle of a movement that is causing quite a bit of discomfort for Mark or perhaps because people do not smile often in the middle of this therapy.

He grins at her and shrugs, "We have so many pictures of me when I could not smile. At Christmas my dad brought a Santa hat to the hospital and put it on my head, but I just couldn't smile!"

So many things pull at my heart. It is poignant to realize that Mark wanted to smile as much as I ached to see him smile those long weeks.

The therapist directs Mark back on the plastic chair and raises it up. Then before she swings it around, she literally hoses him down. She tells him that the chlorine is hard on his skin and this will help because he cannot get into the shower.

We have to put his boots on though he is dripping wet, and get him to the dressing room and then we take the boots back off again, dry him and struggle to get the socks on his feet and the rest of his clothes back on. We find we do not have the knack to keep all the clothing, or the chair he must sit on, dry, and he ends up leaving a bit damp in some places.

Mark is always famished after therapy and today is no exception. What is fun for me today is that Betty makes sandwiches for both of us. Then Mark brushes his teeth and changes into dry clothing and we drive out to Brentwood to visit Chris and Carole's dentist. As we maneuver the walker through the entrance, the receptionist welcomes us as though we are friends.

In fact we are grandfathered-in friends because, as happens so often, God has this visit planned. "By chance" Carole has the appointment before us to have her teeth cleaned. Chris greets us in the waiting area and we stand talking when we hear a voice call out from the other room, "Hi, family!" Carole's bright greeting confirms what I feel in my heart. We have become family.

We appreciate the dentist immediately. I think that he is the first dentist I have ever met that makes me feel like I actually want to have him work on my mouth. He has a wonderful personality and is extremely professional in all ways. I am blessed at this provision for Mark.

The hard but expected news is that Mark is going to have to go through some long and grueling appointments. But this dentist, in the process of the unwelcome evaluation, has planted some excitement in Mark that his mouth will look good once again. The dentist's excitement and passion for his work creates an atmosphere of hope and anticipation.

One option explained is for Mark to endure braces for eighteen months. Not! His first experience with braces was awful and caused all kinds of problems resulting in miserable surgery. We discuss other ways to repair the fractured tooth and bridge in the front of his mouth. The teeth have been jarred but the doctor discusses good options and we can tell Mark is greatly encouraged. He will also help to whiten the teeth that have turned dark from the medicated mouthwash Mark had to use while his jaws were wired shut. This man really cares! He can see what Mark has had to endure and he has an excitement about helping him. We are so blessed.

When we get home we find that Betty has worked to organize the kitchen while we were gone and it is great. I feel like I can function here for however long we must stay. Betty assures us she slept well in her corner of the living room. That is good news because we are not certain when we will be able to move her into Jason's room.

I am personally excited because this afternoon I go to get my hair colored for the first time since November. Betty can stay with Mark while I visit April's hairstylist.

I have great directions and find the building easily though it is an area of the city I have never visited. I enjoy the company of the engaging young woman who encourages me to try a different color than ever before. She has heard our story from April and now she suggests I need a lift and should do something fun. I follow her lead and leave feeling very different; very good. I love the color and am glad she directed me to a new look.

Mark likes my hair and can't wait until he can sit long enough and walk far enough to go to get his done.

When I talk to Barbara we learn that Mickey has pinched a nerve or some painful thing in his back and that their son, Michael is in the hospital. No one is free from heartache and pain in life. We spend time lifting them in prayer.

It is late afternoon, Mark has had an encouraging visit to a wonderful dentist, I have a new hair color, we can smell Grandma's excellent chili brewing in the kitchen and the scrabble board is set up on the card table. Mark rests on the loveseat and I sit in the chair across from him. We simply look at each other and smile as we savor this emotion we have missed so desperately. We are happy.

The chili tastes wonderful and is barely cleared away before we move the scrabble board in place. The three of us laugh at the assortment of furniture left in this house. We have a small love seat with extra seat cushions piled high so Mark can sit on it, two folding chairs and a folding table where Betty and I eat our supper. Mark's supper is served on a television tray. When we play board games, we pull the table and chairs to the loveseat. Chris brought us an office chair on casters, which is quite comfortable and affords us an extra seat. The coffee table has been converted to a kitchen counter most of the time and serves the dual purpose of a dining table for guests. It is not House Beautiful, but it is home and we are enjoying being here more now that we have organized a few things.

I push aside thoughts of tomorrow when I need to visit the Government Building. I don't know where it is exactly and dread going to see if Mark is eligible for assistance. Dave and I have paid partial rent for these months and now it is our responsibility alone. It seems overwhelming financially and yet there is a ridiculous pride in me that does not want to go and apply for help with his rent.

The good news is Dave's sister, Debbie, will drive down with him this weekend when he comes to get Betty. It is a great relief that Dave will not drive alone and it will be fun to see Debbie and get more news from home. They may drive her SUV so we can send some boxes home.

I am beginning to formulate plans in my mind to celebrate our anniversary. It is not until March 18, but when Dave arrives next weekend we will have Debbie and Betty here to stay with Mark and it would be wonderful to go to a nice hotel for one night. Mark encourages me to make plans.

> *I Kings 8:22, "O Lord, God of Israel, there is no God like you in heaven above or on earth below-you who keep your covenant of love with your servants who continue wholeheartedly in your way."*

Tuesday, February 26, 2002

I did not go to the Government offices this morning because it snowed. I called them and they understood, saying "I would not have gone out today if I did not have to."

The weather is pretty nasty. We will be fine inside, plenty of groceries and entertainment. I am relieved at the reprieve and grateful to spend a quiet day with Mark and Betty. I will go tomorrow.

Psalm 29:11, "The Lord gives strength to his people; the Lord blesses his people with peace."

Wednesday, February 27, 2002

I got lost on the way to the Government offices today. It was not a panic type of lost, but certainly frustrating. I was concerned about driving into an area I have never been in the first place. I realized some directions must not have been clear when I saw a familiar street. Because I knew the street, and how to get home from it, I took it back towards the house. I parked in a church parking lot and used the cell phone that I could not live without to call the office. It was readily straightened out and they said it was okay to come even though I would be about fifteen minutes later than planned.

After all that experience, and a meeting that joggled my pride a bit because of the personal information I had to give out, I am told we could "possibly" receive a one time award of $350.00. I am sure that sounds generous to someone who is unemployed and in need, but somehow I had hoped for more. We will be happy to get it, but rent will be $1,200.00 and there is no income for either Mark or me right now.

I selfishly move forward each day without dwelling on where the money is coming from that was not in our budget before. Dave must really be scrambling to cover everything.

On the drive home I push aside the ever present need to cry. I manage to hold it all back until Dave calls me and when I hear his voice I cry. Poor man. He is like my safety net. I hang on this trapeze that I swing from by my fingertips and when I hear his voice I allow myself to drop for just a short time. We both know I will be on the ladder to the trapeze again before he hangs up the phone.

Thank God we have been married so many years. I can let go for a few minutes and know that he understands. Dave has told me that he is nearly as concerned for me as for Mark. He tells me others "back home" are also worried about me. Most people who have known us for any length of time know how close Mark and I are. In their hearts they know I am devastated by all that has happened. I am blessed when Dave says people are encouraged by my strength. *MY strength Lord! I have none. YOUR strength is made perfect in my weakness. You equip me to deal with all we face on an hourly basis. My hope is in YOU!*

Dave tells me that he cannot come to Nashville this weekend. There is snow falling as we speak and blizzard conditions are predicted. He apologizes and then apologizes more. I assure him he does not have to explain to me. I know Minnesota winter. This is no surprise and not even a great disappointment because we have so enjoyed having Betty with us.

I go into the living room to tell her that she will need to stay another week. I am a bit sheepish about it, because we have been hinting broadly that we want her to stay longer. She would prefer to return home where she has a life to live, but she goes with the flow as she is prone to do. She is no stranger to Minnesota winters either.

While Betty and Mark watch a game show on TV I take a nap but I do not sleep. I stare at the ceiling and release my lament to the Lord. *I have never felt so alone, Lord! Thank you for all you have done and are doing. Please help me to get over this feeling of loneliness. It is not because Dave is not here. Sadly, he fits into the category of anyone besides Mark and me. No one can understand. I can be in a room full of people, receiving a hug and still feel ready to explode! No one knows how desperately I desire to run to a quiet place, soak in a hot bathtub, have a massage, read a book and have everything in life be okay. Really and truly okay, and not the pretend existence I fabricate each day. I am such a fake. The face and demeanor I put on like clothing. Inside I am defeated but for You, Lord. Take this from me! Make me strong! Make me capable! God, you are so merciful. Mark seems to be faring better, emotionally, than I am. I cannot know because though we have spent much time in prayer and brutal honesty, he may be hiding from me the very feelings I hide from him! Be with us both! We will persevere because You are Lord of our lives!*

I can smell dinner cooking. Betty is making hamburgers. My vent with the Lord has been a wonderful remedy. I can cope once again. *Thank you, for being my cheerleader, Lord. I mean it with all the respect I can give it. You are my everything!*

I go to the kitchen to toss a salad and share an evening with two of my favorite people in this world.

> Proverbs 8:34 and 35, "Blessed is the man who listens to me, watching daily at my doors, waiting at my doorway. For whoever finds me finds life and receives favor from the Lord."

Sunday, March 3, 2002

Though I am writing less in my journal, the week went well. We are so busy all day and I take time in the evening to enjoy Mark and Betty. We are making our adjustments. It seems easier getting to therapy the last few times as we have a routine. We are also getting the hang of showering Mark so he is able to have a shower nearly every day now. A great deal of this is because Betty is here to take care of the meals and household needs and because both Mark and I enjoy her company. It is an amazing relief.

We went to church with Chris and Carole today. It was a good service with the priest mentioning Mark's visit and that he was the young man they had been praying for that had been in a car crash. After church we went to a Mexican restaurant for lunch, and then came home to rest.

Betty is enjoying herself and I am glad for that. I was concerned another week here would get her down.

After our nap, Brian and April arrive, bringing Courtney to brighten my day. They also treat us by bringing Buffalo wings. I toss a large salad and we eat chocolate cake for dessert. Food seems so important to us these days. Ann-Marie also joined us for the evening as we watched a video and visited. How wonderful to be able to write that it was a fun day.

Tonight after our prayer time, Mark reaches up his arms for a hug. He squeezes me really tight and we both bask in the blessing of the strength that is returning to him. I have missed his hugs more than I can express and, evidently he has missed them too.

I turn off his light and walk the couple feet to my room quietly so I do not disturb Betty. I pull back the covers and get into bed with a smile, so very grateful to our Lord for the healing that is taking place in my son!

Psalm 72:18, "Praise be to the Lord God, the God of Israel, who alone does marvelous deeds."

Monday, March 4, 2002

We are up early today because it is another day packed with activity. Mark has a dental appointment and we need to leave by 8:45 a.m. The plan is for Mark and me to go to the dentist and then return home to get Betty before we leave for Chris and Carole's studio for Mark's voice lesson.

I am nearly ready and Mark is in the shower when the phone rings at 8:15 a.m. It is Dave's aunt Grace. She is dear to me and when she asks to talk to Betty without any other conversation, I know something is wrong. I am especially concerned because her husband, Bob, has been having health problems.

"Are you okay?" I ask Grace as I walk to Jason's former bedroom where we have moved Betty's bed.

"No."

I do not ask more but sit on the bed beside Betty and speak her name softly. She sits up to answer the phone when I say, "It is Grace."

I stay near, hoping my intuition is not correct, but from Betty's quiet reply and the tears that immediately follow; I know that her brother, Bob, has passed away. When she hangs up the phone we hug and then start discussing plans that need to be made.

"Grace won't know when the funeral is until later today."

"Well, we need to get you home. She will need you there."

There is no argument. Betty and Grace are as close as sister-in-laws can possibly be.

In typical fashion of the mother-in-law I love like my own mother, Betty wipes her eyes and tells me, "You go to the dentist appointment. We won't know more till you are back anyway."

"But I don't want to leave you alone."

She makes a face at me. "I'll be fine. Go."

We know she is right. We are on a tight schedule to get as much dental work as possible finished before we can return to Minnesota.

The visit is difficult. We may appreciate the dentist, but the procedures are hard and Mark has to sit for long periods of time. The dentist and his assistant are more than accommodating for him and even show movie videos. Mark has been invited to bring any movie he might want to watch to his next appointment. If they only knew the full collection he has!

It is as though the air is heavy in this day. We all love Bob so dearly. He was one of those great teddy bear guys; big, warm and friendly. He and Grace welcomed me into their family long before I actually became a member and I have loved them for years. I remember Bob holding newborn Michael in the palm of one of his large hands and how he always greeted me with a warm hug and called me "honey." How we will miss him! We are also sad because there is no way Mark or I can be there for the funeral.

We also know that it is not possible for Dave to come to Nashville for the weekend. Selfishly, that is a disappointment for me. Our wedding anniversary is now two weeks away and Dave and I had planned to stay at the Opryland Hotel for one night. We have wanted to spend one night there for years now. I shake my head as though it may never happen and then chastise myself for my selfish attitude.

After the dental appointment, we drive to the house to get Betty and then drive the long distance to Chris and Carole's house for Mark's voice lesson. The drive is on rural roads that are narrow, hilly and that wind in every direction. I am very aware of Mark's silence and I can hear the deep breathing exercises he is performing in the seat beside me. This is his longest car trip to date since the crash and we seem to be climbing one hill after another.

Mark has been blunt to state that he does not want to be in a car on hilly roads, nor does he wish to drive in a car after dark, and if it is raining he does not care where we need to go, he will not get into a car. We all hope this is not a permanent fear, but for now it certainly is understandable. We are all aware of this and there is not much conversation in the car. I am intent on driving, Mark is struggling to stay in control of the fear that is trying to overtake him, and Betty is dealing with the new grief of losing her brother.

When we get to the house, Mark confesses that the trip brought him as near to a panic attack as he has ever come. It all seems okay once he sees Chris though. They banter easily and go into the studio to work on Mark's voice. Today they will analyze to see if he still has pitch. His hearing is different with the metal in his face and because of a fracture under his left ear. That is a concern as is the breath support that Mark is known for when he sings. This will be a strategy session for them.

Last night I asked Mark how we would pay for the coaching even though I knew we would do it no matter what the cost. True to the person Chris is in Christ, he had already discussed this with Mark and is not going to charge him. Praise God!

Betty and I go upstairs and have fun discussing some decorating questions Carole has. We do a little strategizing of our own and have an interior design plan for their living room by the time Chris comes up the stairs. Obviously, Mark cannot come up the stairs, so we go downstairs to see the CD Chris has given him on breathing and to hear the good news that Mark's pitch is right on.

It was good for Betty to go with us today, but the minute we get into the door of Mark's house we begin to work on getting her home to Minnesota. Airfare can be very expensive between Nashville and Minneapolis and this is short notice. My first call offers a rate over $1000.00 so I call Dave to ask what I should do. He offers to leave immediately and drive down to get her and turn around to go back without staying to rest. No way.

"I'll think of something," I tell him, "In fact, I have an idea! I'll call you back in an hour or so."

I quickly check on two more ways to reduce fare. It seems there is no bereavement fare and, though Betty is a Senior Citizen, the airfare is still beyond our means and so I decide to put in a call to a Music Minister in Minneapolis who owns a travel agency. Mark had been scheduled to be a soloist at the Christmas program at his church and so he knows our story. I quickly explain the circumstances and he tells me he will get to work on it.

Dave calls to say his sister and brother will contribute to the cost of the airfare, so do what needs to be done. As soon as our friend in Minneapolis calls with good news of a decent price and great flight time, I call Brian. Is there any way he can take Betty to the airport tomorrow? I do not want to drive there and park with all the security regulations that are so new to us since September 11th. No problem, he assures me he can do it.

Mark says he can be alone for the hour or so that it will take to get his grandma to the airport. I can go with Betty, stay until she is checked in and Brian will get me back home in short order.

When Grace calls I tell her, "I am sending your buddy home."

I love the tenderness in her voice when she replies, "I knew I could count on you."

There are many people and situations to consider in our evening prayer time and we are touched by tenderness from the Holy Spirit as the news of our loss begins to absorb into our consciousness.

John 14:1-3, "Do not let your hearts be troubled. Trust in God, trust also in me. In my Father's house are many rooms; if it were not so, I would have told you. And if I go and prepare a place for you, I will come back and take you to be with me that you also may be where I am. You know the way to the place where I am going."

Tuesday, March 5, 2002

I help Mark out of the shower and back to his bed, making sure he has a phone, water, snacks, and the television remote on the bed beside him so he will not have to try to walk anyplace by himself. I hand him the plastic urinal we had put away some time ago. He grins at my overzealous attempt to think of anything and everything he could need.

While Mark was in the shower I found a pretty note card and penned words to Grace. I wrote that we know each other too well and have loved each other too dearly for me to try to apologize for not being able to be there for her. I am confident that she knows that if it were at all possible, both Mark and I would be there. I also told her how I thought she and Bob were an example of the verse in the Bible that says, "The two shall become one." And I told her I love her. Now I hand the envelope to Betty to carry to Grace.

Brian arrives right on time and drives Betty and me to the entrance at the airport. We get in line. I am determined to stay with her as long as possible. Would you not know it! They randomly pick Betty to check her suitcase. A nice looking lady in her mid-seventies and they are going through her underwear!

We laugh at it and she says she is more than happy to allow them to do it, knowing it is for a good reason.

I stand behind the rope that is my boundary and watch her go through security with her bags and then wave and walk to the curb to wait for Brian. It is an emotional good-bye for me. I will miss Betty, I am grateful that she was able to be with us and to bring some relief to our situation, but I am sad she is going home to sorrow.

Brian returns me to the house in one hour, which is especially good because he has plenty of time to get to work and Mark needs to eat lunch before his therapy appointment.He was told to bring a pair of tennis shoes.

Mark was told to bring a pair of tennis shoes to this appointment. It is challenging for the therapist to help get those tennis shoes on as his feet are still swollen and so very tender. The two of them work together and, before long, Mark stands beside the raised therapy mat, for the first time since the crash, in "real shoes." Mark is not able to keep the shoes on very long, but it is long enough for us to experience pure joy in this monumental moment. Mother and son stand beaming at each other over another victory.

And there is still more! I sit and praise God as I watch Mark ride a stationary bike. Halleluiah! Mark's knee is bending enough to allow him to make a few full circles on the bike. There is no question it is not a simple feat nor is it pain free, but when we think back to a time, not so long ago when the knee would not even bend…wow!

It was an incredible therapy session, full of encouragement and we leave the hospital with light hearts…and empty stomachs. I did not take time to eat between the airport and therapy and Mark always leaves therapy ravenous so he suggests that we stop at Sonic. I eat my first sonic burger ever and it tastes great.

We have no choice but to rest a short while after we get home. Then we begin the process of packing. We want a head start so we do not feel so stressed whenever we get the green light to go to Minnesota. We have had enough last-minute moves for a lifetime.

After this busy day we are blessed by a quiet evening and happy to accept Ann-Marie's offer to bring pizza. We try to watch a movie, but by 10:00 p.m. Mark is very tired. He did not sleep well last night and it was my fault. I have been concerned because he takes a sleeping pill every night. The doctor told him he should wean himself off the narcotic he takes for pain and he has been doing a great job at that by taking a lesser dose or skipping on occasion, but the sleeping pills have become a great comfort to Mark. Being over concerned is part of my makeup, so I told him that sometime I would leave the sleeping pill off of his mix of bedtime medications. I did that last night and listened often during the night to hear if he was restless. When he mentioned in the morning that he had not slept well I had to confess.

Now, as I make the trip to the kitchen to get his meds, he calls out, "Don't forget my Ambien." Then, because he can't resist teasing me and fueling my concern, he says in an exaggerated tone, "Ambien is my friend."

We have an awesome prayer time during which Mark receives a vision. "There was an angel beside my bed and he held a large golden sword that became bright as liquid gold or molten lava. The bright liquid was poured into all parts of my body for healing."

We are excited about this promise of healing. Mark told me he saw an angel beside me too. I am glad because I miss Betty being here and I am lonesome for Dave.

We spend time praying in the spirit as we have been instructed in the scripture Mark felt led to read, and then go to sleep anticipating the healing we will notice in Mark's body when he wakes tomorrow!

Tonight, as I climb into my bed, I spend time dwelling on a mystery; a small one perhaps, but significant. I am not a premier memorizer of scripture. Whether I am lazy or not gifted can be discussed. I just do not do well with exact word-for-word memorization. Yet, for weeks before the crash the Lord had me reading Habakkuk, 3:19. "The sovereign Lord is my strength. He makes my feet like the feet of a deer and enables me to go on the heights."

I did ask, "Why this scripture, Lord?" He did not answer. Still it was impressed upon me to read it over and over until it was committed to memory.

Now, I pray that verse every night as we intercede for Mark's feet to heal. We pray for literal healing as well as for future ministry. And slowly it sinks in, this was for me too as the Lord truly is strength for each of us in this unwelcome journey, and He has enabled us to walk in a place we never would have imagined we could.

The scripture Mark was given tonight was Jude 20-23. He just suddenly looked at me and said to read those verses, not sure what they were. I turned the pages in Mark's Bible in expectation and we were not disappointed in what the Lord wanted to share with us.

> Jude 1:20-23, "But you, dear friends, build yourselves up in your most holy faith and pray in the Holy Spirit. Keep yourselves in God's love as you wait for the mercy of our Lord Jesus Christ to bring you to eternal life. Be merciful to those who doubt; snatch others from the fire and save them; to others show mercy, mixed with fear-hating even the clothing stained by corrupted flesh."

Wednesday, March 6, 2002

Chris called fairly early to remind us that their church offers Eucharist at noon. We have been focused on our dental appointment at 2:15 p.m. and so needed the reminder. Mark is not certain that he has energy for both church and the dental appointment and so I continue with my morning activities. But, at 11:00 a.m. as I am talking on the phone to Mary Beth, Mark looks at me and mouths the word "church."

I manage to dress and put on makeup while speaking with Mary Beth. Our friendship has often hosted calls where one or the other of us is getting ready to go someplace while we talk. We laugh that it is happening once again.

Mark and I arrive at the church a little before noon and are the only ones except for a kind man who greets us. Chris and Carole arrive almost immediately as do many others. It is a beautiful service and we are blessed to share it with our good friends.

The service is short and we hurry home to have time for me to make Mark a grilled cheese sandwich before we leave for the dentist. The dentist plans to do "as tolerated" sessions with Mark. There is a lot to accomplish before the broken tooth and bridge can be fixed. There is a lot of decay from not being able to clean the teeth for the length of time the jaw was wired shut. Mark hands me the movie, *Sister Act* as we leave the house.

It is rather fun that, as we prepare to leave the dentist's office today, his assistant hands us a list of movies they have available in the office. I am more impressed at their kindness and professionalism each time we visit.

Today Mark managed to lie in the dentist's chair for two hours! They were careful to adjust it so his hip was comfortable. It is wonderful to get so much work done. We find it interesting that the majority of cavities are on the left side of Mark's mouth. That is the side he put the syringe in when his jaws were wired shut because the right side was too sore.

Mark can eat soft food tonight and he came home really hungry so I make his favorite casserole dish. As much as he enjoys the food, he is as tired as he is hungry and so am I. We decide to get ready for bed as soon as I clear away the dishes and clean up the kitchen.

I take care of e-mail while Mark washes for bed. Even with our early start, it is 10:00 p.m. before we know it.

We have each started individual reading every night after prayer time and just before bed, so we are back in the habit of going to sleep later. Reading is something we both love to do and I find I sleep better when I do not keep busy up to the moment I put my head on the pillow.

I finished, *Desecration* tonight and Mark finished *The Lion, The Witch and*

The Wardrobe. We talk back and forth through the wall dividing our rooms to discuss the books. We have each read the other book before so it is an interesting discussion.

Mark's response in our discussion grows increasingly slower. He is falling asleep despite the fact that, by his own decision, his night medication has been cut in half. We are happy it is working for him because it is progress toward getting off the heavy medication.

> *Proverbs 2:6, "For the Lord gives wisdom, and from his mouth come knowledge and understanding."*

Thursday, March 7, 2002

This will be a day of contrasts. It is my sister-in-laws birthday and at 10:00 a.m. Dave's family will gather for Uncle Bob's funeral. I look at the clock and it reads 9:45 a.m.; I send prayer in their direction.

I keep thinking how strange it is that you can be so connected to people and have such contrasting scenes play in your lives at the same moment. I will carry the family in my heart as we go through this day just as they have carried us the past few months.

In more news from home, Mark's friend, Stephanie, who was here just a short time ago, became engaged on Valentine's Day. Once again, the contrast in connected lives is evident. Last night Stephanie called to ask Mark to sing at her wedding this summer. It is good to think ahead to a joyful date.

Mary Beth called to say that the people promoting the concert she and Mark are performing to benefit Joni Eareckson Tada's organization, *Joni and Friends*, would like to do a promo concert on April 12th. That is so soon! Mark has barely started to sing again, and he is still walking with the walker. *Well, certainly*, I reason in silent conversation with myself, *that is not an obstacle.* Everyone at the concert will know what happened to Mark and be happy to see how he has progressed. Mark is not concerned about being ready to sing, he is excited!

Strange, we have been dreaming of going home for so long and now I feel a bit fearful of it. Are we ready? Will people understand anything about what we have gone through and who we have become? We are two very different people in so many ways. I especially feel fearful of expectations that people will have for and of me. Will I be expected to pick up where I left off with my responsibilities at home, work and church? I am fully aware of how depleted I am. If demands are made on me I feel I will crumble. *I guess I will have to trust you for this next step also, Lord!*

I cancel our room reservation at the Opryland Hotel and try to convince myself that it is okay that Dave and I will not be together on our anniversary for the first time in more than thirty years. "It is okay," I say aloud. And then I realize that it really is okay. We are so blessed that Mark is healing and we will soon go home.

It seems most days I have a topic I dwell on. I think about it while I write in the journal, wash clothes, clean Mark's room, etc. Today I find myself dwelling on personalities; more specifically, on how various personalities deal with tragedy. Mark has many friends and we have watched each one cope with this tragedy in their own way. Chris and Carole have been perfection, absolute role models for friends of those suffering. They have supported us spiritually, mentally and physically. They seem to anticipate our every need. They are a gift from God.

Brian and April could not be better friends, nor could Ann-Marie or Becki. They have been here for the most awful parts of this. They have loved, supported and nurtured us. Others who know us less well have been here in unexpected ways, by visiting, sending cards, letters and e-mails. I think of ways people have used their gifting to bless us, like Jonathon giving of his time and talent with his violin music.

My heart warms to think that those who were close to us before the crash are now closer still: the Robinsons, Ann-Marie's mom Pat, Mark's friends at The Grille and friends from college. However, we are discovering not all people perform well in tragedy. Mark has been deeply wounded by the friend we saw at the restaurant. There was such sadness in Mark's eyes when he told me that he no longer waited for that friend to call. We must extend grace. Pain and suffering are not easy to witness and we are so very grateful for those who have shown us kindness and compassion.

And then there is Mark's second roommate. After he left us with the incredible mess of his belongings piled in our dining room, he finally came to haul things from the garage...he did not take them all away, but instead he hauled most of them to the curb. I voiced my concern that the garbage men would probably require extra money from us for the additional pick up. I know that, at home, we would have to call ahead to inform the garbage collection company and that we would expect an additional charge for that kind of monumental pick up, but Mark's other roommate assured me it was not a problem and continued to create a barrier on the curb of open boxes stuffed full of miscellaneous items.

Well, I made the mistake a few minutes ago, of going out to get the mail. I stood at the mailbox and froze when I heard a man yell loudly from about a block away, "Lady, Lady!" He was waving at me as he called in an angry manner. I was so embarrassed when he began to verbally correct me from a good distance away. "Lady, we don't take that much garbage at one time. What do you think?"

I wanted to run in the house. As he got closer he told me, "if you want us to take away that much "stuff" (he used another word), you need to slip us a little something, understand?"

It is the kind of scene that could attach itself to my day, but I put aside my frustration because I am taking Mark to get his hair cut and highlighted today. He is excited and we will concentrate on that and I will call the other roommate when we get back.

We have to park across a busy street to get to the hairstylist. We watch traffic for awhile and then find our opportunity. Mark can only walk so fast with the walker. Once inside, he does well in the chair and his hair looks great. As happy as he is to have some style back in his life, he immediately goes to bed for a nap when we get home.

I call the other roommate to tell him about my encounter with the garbage man and he brushes it off as I expected he would. The other day he came over to get something, and he stood at the door to the living room and looked at Mark who was sitting on his special pillow on the sofa, walker beside him, Bledsoe boots planted firmly on the ground and he said, "How are you?"

I do not know what Mark would have answered because this man did not wait for a reply. "Better than me, I'm sure. I'm so busy." And he launched a lament over his busy schedule.

I had to walk away. I went to the bedroom and turned my emotions over to the Lord and then was able to return to the living room with more peace in my heart.

I am dealing with these emotions anew today because of the garbage episode so I go before the Lord to ask His help. I realize that, in this intense setting, our emotions are vulnerable. My feelings are hurt and I have found that hurt can be another name for anger and anger is draining. I have no reserve to spend on it and I need to repent.

Acts 3:19, "Repent, then, and turn to God, so that your sins may be wiped out, that times of refreshing may come from the Lord, and that he may send the Christ, who has been appointed for you— even Jesus."

Friday, March 8, 2002

Mark has decided it's time to go and see a movie. We both love to go to movies and we have missed the wide screen and smell of corn popping. We check the newspaper to find which movie will fit our stringent criteria. It is not the genre as much as that it must be available on an early afternoon to avoid crowds. We also prefer it would not attract small children. Mark suddenly sees little children as a threat with their abrupt movements and unexpected change in direction. And he should until his balance is better.

The theater needs to be nearby and have handicap parking on the floor of the main entrance so an escalator is not necessary. We plan to take a pillow for Mark to sit on, but even with that, he can't sit for a very long period of time, so it can't be a long movie. We also need to eliminate stairs to stadium seating.

It is quite a bit to consider but we are determined to go. We finally decide on a film called *In the Bedroom.* Perhaps not our first choice for viewing but it fits the criteria and we like the actors.

In the theater we find we need to take an elevator and even this simple task seems daunting with the walker, but we manage. We find plenty of seating at this time of day and choose seats where we can leave without bothering other viewers if Mark needs to exit.

About halfway through the film I am acutely aware that it is moving horrendously slow. I wonder if Mark is thinking the same and I sneak a look at him. It happens he is echoing my thoughts and movements and when we lock eyes we explode into laughter at an inopportune moment of angst on screen. We quickly turn away from each other and struggle to reach decorum but we are lost.

Somehow we manage to stay to the end of the movie and, still laughing, we make our way to the car. As I wipe my eyes with my popcorn napkin Mark comments, "Why are we such dweebs that we cry when we laugh?"

I can't answer him; I am laughing…and crying, too hard.

> *I Peter 5:10 and 11, "And the God of all grace, who called you to his eternal glory in Christ, after you have suffered a little while, will himself restore you and make you strong, firm and steadfast. To him be the power for ever and ever. Amen."*

Monday, March 11, 2002

Once again, a few days have passed with no journal entry. I have been thinking of my role as mother. I am pretty overwhelmed by the honor that God has trusted me to be Mark's mother. I have often felt that way about both of my sons. They are precious men that I would admire even if I barely knew them.

I have allowed my mind to wander today. I wonder about the drunk driver; if she thinks of Mark whenever she gets into a car. I wonder if she thinks of him at all. It is peculiar how much it would mean to me to hear her say she is sorry, to hear her say that she prays for him. I want to hear her say she has changed and will never drink and drive again but I am aware that I live in a fantasy world from time to time. I must be content with the consensus: She either has been told not to contact us or she is a person who does not know any better. I have been led to pray for her more than once.

In the middle of all of my preponderance, I am touched by a most precious thing and I am still in awe of what happened while Mark was in therapy today. I went to second floor to talk to one of the nurses and could not believe my eyes when I saw Marilyn Lyle walk around the corner.

We saw each other about the same time and hurried for a hug.

"Is Scott here?" I asked about her son.

"Yes, he's in therapy. Oh, you have to meet him. He's doing so well. Is Mark here?"

"He's downstairs in outpatient."

We hurry like two schoolgirls to find Scott. I cannot resist giving the young man with the bright smile, who sits in a wheelchair, a big hug.

"We prayed for you so many times. I am so blessed to meet you!" I tell him.

He looks good and his memory is good. I am in such an attitude of praise I can barely contain myself. Marilyn, Scott and I take the elevator to see Mark who is just finishing his session.

"Mark," I say nearly breathless from joy. "This is Marilyn Lyle from the Quiet Room!"

Mark has heard us speak of her and takes a step toward her, with his walker, to shake her hand, but she moves to embrace him. Both Marilyn and I are crying.

I call Dave at his office, once again grateful for my cell phone, and say, "You can't guess who I am here with! Marilyn!"

I hand the phone to her and they talk for a few minutes, and when she hands the phone back, Dave's voice is laden with emotion. I am so grateful he could share in the moment. I know how hard it is for him to only hear about things that happen here.

I am more filled with joy than I have been for a very long time. I cannot quit smiling. God is so good to answer the prayers of this sweet couple. It is as though someone has risen from the dead. He could not respond to his parents and now he can. I know things are not the same for them as before Scott's accident; they are so different for us too. But we are two moms who rejoice in our sons and trust in our God!

Back home after therapy, we decide to put lotion on Mark's scars as he rests in bed.

"Mark," I say as I apply the lotion, "have you thought about the CD cover prophesy?"

"A little."

A woman from our church had called a couple of months before the crash and had described a CD cover that she saw in her mind as she prayed for Mark. Immediately we understood that it was more prophetic than actual, but we had no clear understanding of it.

"The cover was black and white, divided in the middle by a thin stripe," She related, "the right and left sides were also divided, but diagonally. There were five pearls on the cover. Two were nearly obscured in the darkness that covered them. It looked as if a veil were over them. Then there were white pearls covered by a thinner, lighter colored veil. In the center was a golden pearl, solid gold and shining brightly. It was more than 24 carat and shone like the sun. It was 'the pearl of great price' that Jesus gave up all he had for. In a diagonal from upper left to lower right on either side of the pearls were the words, 'Not quite there yet'. The golden pearl was split in two by that blank line that came down the center from top to bottom."

At the time she was not sure if it meant Mark would be used to mend splits in the church or if there was a part of his ministry not yet revealed that would be as a pearl of great price. We remember this now and wonder if the lines had to do with a different kind of brokenness and the pearls of wisdom that will come from such an experience.

Sometimes it is a very good thing that we do not understand prophesy clearly at the time it is received.

We pray for more revelation.

> *James 1:5, "If any of you lacks wisdom, he should ask God, who gives generously to all without finding fault, and it will be given to him."*

Tuesday, March 12, 2002

The therapist took Mark to the gym today. She had him stand on the basketball court and she gave him a ball.

He looked at her with a question on his face.

"Just try to make a basket, I don't expect you to move your feet."

"Good," he said grinning at me.

He threw the ball, missed and tried again until he made the basket. "My feet are glued to the floor!" he moaned.

Mark is a pretty good basketball player, a good athlete in general. I can't help but wonder how it feels to be on the court, shoot a basket and not be able to move his feet. He answers that for me when he calls across the court, "That was strange! But I did it!"

Once again he demonstrates the importance of dwelling on that which can be accomplished and celebrating each step of progress as a victory.

Another wonderful step in this progress is that Mark is greatly enjoying the freedom of using a cane rather than a wheelchair or walker. I feel protective but keep my thoughts to myself. His balance is still not great. If someone were to bump into him, he would most likely fall. He is willing to take that small risk to escape the walker he hates so desperately.

Added to his enjoyment is the fact that he has a "cool" cane. Mark had a vocal appointment with Chris today and when Chris saw that he had graduated to a cane, he loaned him a walking cane that has a really contemporary look. Mark took to it right away and is doing very well.

I love the conversations we have. As we contemplate the blessing of this new progress, Mark asks, "Why do many Christians have a hard time being bold about their faith?"

"Well," I muse, prepared to give my opinion, but he already has an answer.

"I think it is because they do not know The Word and how to use it to win a conversation or debate. They are afraid they will appear ignorant. It is probably more fear than not wanting to stand up for their belief. I think if most people could quote scripture and feel intelligent about God's word, they would naturally become bolder."

My mind spins to the times I have failed to be bold when I had opportunity. "I think you are right about that."

Since our conversation has taken this path, I find myself asking questions of my own as I write in my journal.

Why do unbelievers say Christianity is a crutch? And when they do, why are we so offended?

When Mark could not walk on his own strength, he was thrilled to use a walker because it provided for his need and inspired hope of things to come. And now he has a cane, a crutch I suppose.

I see it this way: A crutch is not something you use when you are at full strength, but it is very welcome and even brings joy when it is available as your knees buckle. What life on this earth has escaped such times? People who make a statement about our belief being a crutch have not realized, or are unwilling to admit, that they are not capable on their own. Pride blinds them. At some point they will have a terrible wake up call and cry out for such help as we have readily available to us in Christ Jesus. I do not see a crutch as a sign of weakness, but as a sometimes-necessary symbol of hope.

We are blessed Mark can now walk with a cane. We are blessed he has a "cool" cane instead of an "old man" cane. *In fact, we are just plain blessed to be called by your name, Lord!*

> *Isaiah 40:31, "But those who hope in the Lord will renew their strength. They will soar on wings like eagles; they will run and not grow weary, they will walk and not be faint."*

Wednesday, March 13, 2002

Mark has an appointment today with the Maxillofacial Surgeon. They will remove the bars that allowed the jaw to be wired shut. He will need to have a type of sedation that allows him to go home immediately after the procedure.

Getting to the appointment presents new problems. Mark was transported to the clinic by ambulance and van in the past and it is not possible to simply drive up to the clinic entrance and let him out at the door. Handicap parking is also not an option as the complex is large and Mark could not possibly walk that far. Jason comes to our rescue. He drives us to the entrance where collapsible wheelchairs are available to patients of the clinic.

The plan is to call Jason at his workplace when we are ready to leave and we will meet him at this entrance. It is awkward getting Mark out of the car and the wheelchair is not exactly state of the art but we figure out how it opens from its collapsible state and I push Mark to the Maxillofacial area.

The appointment goes well and the surgeon is pleased with Mark's progress. We are instructed that Mark needs to take additional pain medication today and tomorrow and to eat only soft foods. Jason picks us up at the entrance and takes us home where Mark briefly rests and then we leave for physical and occupational therapy sessions.

> *Psalm 7:10, "My shield is God Most High, who saves the upright in heart."*

Thursday, March 14, 2002

I cannot say I have arrived with Paul who confidently states, "I am content in all circumstances." But today as I read *Traveling Light* by Max Lucado and observe Mark in the hydropool, I realize that I have been delivered of some excess baggage. I truly do not equate who I am with what I own. I do not equate my worth with how I look. I am not living in "want."

I have recently asked myself to fill in the blanks to the question, "I'll be happy when...?" Sometimes I think it will be when Mark and I can go home. But I know better. There will be challenges and adjustments there too. Will I be happy when we can pay the overwhelming medical bills or clear the credit card debt we are accruing during this time? No doubt that will feel good, but I cannot base my concept of happiness on any thing or any circumstance. I have been on this journey to free myself of baggage for some time. Even before the crash.

One thing I am not free of...I desire control in my life. I have discovered in a very dramatic way, what it feels like to have no control. I am reduced to faith. Or am I promoted? Enough of my soul searching, therapy is over and my son is hungry.

Tonight we will begin to massage Mark's toes a bit more aggressively because the therapist evaluated them today and told us it is necessary. We have been lightly massaging them but they remain stiff and unyielding and therefore his balance is challenged.

With supper and another challenging day behind us, we prepare for bed and I begin to massage the scars on his feet and then gently start to touch his toes. Mark quips, "Don't forget Great Toe."

Some weeks ago, the surgeon cautioned him that the "great toe" on his right foot could cause future problems because of the extensive repair required and the tendon placement. Mark has called his big toe "Great" ever since and has come up with names for the other injured toes. Each toe has such an unusual look that they almost personify a personality.

"How does Stubby look tonight?"

"Pretty good, how does it feel?" The toe we are talking about appears as though it has been divided in half horizontally and caved in at the middle. The one next to it is "loose" and appears to have no bone structure at all. Mark inquires of it, "How is ET?"

I let him know ET is not cooperative in movement. And the little toe, well, we think the surgeon was tired of lining everything in Mark's foot up and just put the pin in quickly. It now faces outward and below it is a strange protrusion, like a bunion, which appears to be a stray bone.

We feel confident the toes will look more normal as they heal, but for now, to cope with the change in his body, Mark has decided to deal with it as he does with so many things, by using his sense of humor. He laughs as I massage each toe. It is a mask of sorts, the laughter. I can tell it hurts to have his toes touched.

"Guess I won't be wearing sandals any time soon."

"Well, you never know," I say honestly as I look at the patchwork quilt pattern of scars on my precious son's feet. "The stitches look so much better than a week ago, and the toes are beginning to separate."

My comment sends us into laugher again. The toes did not separate for some time and Mark had joked that he was "webbed." In fact, all five toes moved as one. I have worked to pull them apart gently using my fingers and Q-tips, and by massaging them individually; willing each one to regain individual identity.

"Beautiful on the mountains are the feet of him who brings good news," I remind him.

"Get me to a mountain," he says with a twinkle in his eye.

Tonight as I lie in bed and meditate, I think of Corrie Ten Boom and her rich testimony. She is my heroine. I can almost hear her rich accent as she says, "There is no pit so deep that God's love is not deeper still."

In the darkness of this night I lift my hand to touch my face. I cannot see it. But it is surely there. "I love you Lord," I whisper, certain He is surely here.

Isaiah 52:7, "How beautiful on the mountains are the feet of those who bring good news, who proclaim peace, who bring good tidings, who proclaim salvation, who say to Zion, Your God reigns!"

Friday, March 15, 2002

Mark and I have become the people infomercials were created for. We watch television more than we usually would and are vulnerable, in pain and in need of a "fix." We are absolutely aware of it and have decided to give in to it knowing it is temporary. In fact, we are enjoying it in a strange way.

Today I return from the mailbox and call to Mark with excitement in my voice. "It's here! The video is here!"

I hurry to get the sofa pillows propped correctly and Mark comes into the living room, tapping his cane on the wood floor as he moves past the walker we have parked against the wall for several days now. We get settled and I slide the video in the machine. We grin at each other and then stare at the screen in anticipation.

The music swells, the scenic background rolls and then...there it is! A hot tub! We both moan as we think of how good it would feel on aches, pains and weary psyches to sit, soak and heal. We dream of getting one when we return home. We nearly convince ourselves it will happen.

It's the carrot again. Like the Dachshund, we place it before us to keep us going a little longer, to motivate us for more progress.

We watch the video and for a few moments the mountain of medical bills is forgotten. The credit card debt is set aside in our weary minds. We know the very things causing our stress are the same that will keep us from getting the hot tub, no matter how therapeutic it would be, but we allow ourselves to enter a dream world. We relax and watch beautiful people sitting in warm water with jets directed at their sore shoulders and we sigh. We will play the infomercial game a little while longer.

Lunch follows the video and then we have the opportunity to meet with a representative from MADD. She rings the doorbell and enters the house with a warm smile and a lot of valuable information. We are too weary right now to do more than receive that information. In my heart I ask God to please let me be of some use to this organization in the future.

One of the wonderful things she does is to put us in touch with the Victim Advocate Representative from the District Attorney's office. She assures us she will call and give our phone number to that office and they will be in touch with us. She also takes time to express her sympathy for the tragedy and turmoil that has been part of our lives since a woman decided, and was allowed, to drink herself past the point of reason and get into a car, drive in the oncoming lane and crush Mark in his car. She opens our eyes to the horror of this situation in our society by telling us that the number of people affected by drunk driving each year in this nation is the equivalent of three jetliners going down every single week of the year!

What are we doing about it as a responsible society?

Before she leaves she gives us reading material that will help us to understand the emotional stages we will most likely encounter as we move forward. "She knows," we whisper to each other as we close the door behind her. "Someone knows."

The Victim Advocate from the District Attorney's office calls before the close of the business day! Not only does she express her sympathy and revulsion at what happened, but she makes a promise that she will come to the house with the District Attorney to meet us sometime before we leave for Minnesota. I immediately like this woman. She is easy to talk to and we look forward to meeting her in person.

I called the representative from MADD back to let her know that we found out the blood alcohol content of the woman who hit Mark was .22. I know nothing about what that means but both of these women assure me it is shocking. That is more than double the legal limit and even worse because she was underage and because the results were obtained at the hospital, so time had lapsed since the accident. This information makes it obvious that she was not a novice at drinking. We are told that no one could drink that much without some experience and that it would be difficult to get into a car, much less try to drive.

The woman from MADD, whom I also feel I would love to get to know, was so kind. She said she has been playing Mark's *REALITY* CD that we gave her earlier and found it very meaningful. She has written him a note and we should receive it soon. We look forward to that.

When I answer the doorbell again today it is to greet a flower-laden delivery man. Dave has sent me an incredible bouquet. My favorite flower is the Calla Lily. This large and exceptionally beautiful arrangement is Calla Lilies and red Roses. I feel very loved.

Tonight Ann-Marie will come over for awhile. We plan to watch *America's Funniest Videos* together and then I will leave them to their board games while I concentrate on packing a few more boxes.

We are in constant prayer as we gear up for the big doctor's appointment on Tuesday the 19th. At that time we will get an okay to return to Minnesota...or not. Chris and Carole will be with us for that appointment. We were at their home for a voice appointment yesterday when Carole asked me, "Can I go to the appointment with you on Tuesday?"

"Of course, we would love that."

"It's her birthday on Tuesday," Chris informed us.

"Your birthday?" I asked Carole. "Are you sure you want to spend it in a hospital waiting room?"

"Yes."

God is so good. He knows I am trying to put things into perspective and not feel sad that Dave and I will not spend our anniversary weekend together. Having good friends near who love us is a wonderful gift and a great comfort.

Matthew 18:20, "For where two or three come together in my name, there am I with them."

Sunday, March 17, 2002

Dave and I had a nice phone conversation last night. Mike has moved into our home for a few months and his companionship has been a blessing to Dave. Both Dave and I are aware that our anniversary is tomorrow and we feel concern for each other because we have never been apart for an anniversary before. In our conversation he assured me that he will spend a nice evening with Mike tomorrow and that we will plan to have a fun evening out together when I get back home. That sounds good to me.

It has been a pleasant Sunday and I am getting supper ready in the kitchen when there is a knock on the door. I look out the window to see my husband standing there.

Impossible! I just talked to him last night and that would mean he had to leave in the middle of the night to get here!

"Hi," he says as though he has just driven across town.

"I just talked to you last night and you said nothing."

"I decided at the last minute to come. I couldn't stay away from you on our anniversary, could I?"

Dave has to return on Tuesday so it will be a short stay. He wants to be with us for Mark's appointments with his surgeons on Tuesday morning. He has no expectations for us to go out and celebrate. He just wants us to be together. I could not ask for more.

> Ephesians 5:25, "Husbands love your wives just as Christ loved the church and gave himself up for her to make her holy, cleansing her by the washing with water through the word and to present her to himself as a radiant church, without stain or wrinkle or any other blemish, but holy and blameless. In this same way husbands ought to love their wives as their own bodies. He who loves his wife loves himself."

Tuesday, March 19, 2002

Very early today we made the decision that Dave should not wait for the doctor appointment because he will lose precious daylight traveling hours. It is our experience that the appointments can be very lengthy. A morning appointment often extends into the afternoon; especially when so many x-rays are involved.

I had been awake, in bed, for some time before we came to this decision. We had pushed the two trundle units together in "my" bedroom and I lie staring at my husband in the near darkness, his face only inches from mine. I allowed myself the tormenting thought that I could not stand to have him drive those long hours back to Minnesota all alone…again! Those endless hours would take him further and further away from us and he would experience increasing loneliness with each mile. I worry and dwell on missing him and do not welcome those feelings. I remained quiet so I would not wake him, and brushed tears away from my eyes.

When Dave woke, he reached to hold my hand and realized I was crying. He moved to hold me. It was then we decided he should leave soon. It was the wisest way to do it and would hurt no less for him to leave in one hour then four to five hours from now.

We busied ourselves. That always seems to work. We carried box after box and bag after bag to the car. We loaded the car good and full and felt some satisfaction that part of the move was being completed.

We had time to pray together and then Dave left at 9:00 a.m. and Mark and I finished getting ready to go to his appointment.

We are relieved that we can drive to this appointment and park in a ramp, using Mark's handicap sticker. We allow time to arrive at the hospital early so I can go to get Carole a small gift. We have not found any time to shop and I know there is a gift store with some lovely things not too far away. I am delighted to find a small carved figurine of an angel holding a dog. How could it be more appropriate?

I hurry back to find Carole sitting in the waiting room. I look around and assume the guys have gone into x-ray. As I slide into the seat next to Carole, I hear a bird call. Carole and I smile at each other. I doubt there are too many birds in the x-ray area of the hospital, Chris is letting me know he is with Mark.

The x-rays take a long time as usual. Each time he has x-rays we hope they will be easier for him and take less time, but the reality is that there are so many places to x-ray and so many necessary angles and those angles are not easy to get at with Mark's broken body. Once the x -rays are complete we wait to be called for our 10:45 a.m. appointment. At 1:00 p.m., the doctor's assistant motions us in.

We feel bad because it is Carole's birthday and we had planned to go for lunch, but as we wait, we exercise our habit of trying to find some good in the current situation and decide to switch our lunch location choice and go someplace that will be fun in the middle of the afternoon. We are certain that we will be bringing hearty appetites.

The assistant is very apologetic and explains that the doctor's schedule is exceptionally full, as he had to be out of town a few days prior.

A resident comes in first to evaluate Mark and he asks him, "So how are you?"

"Pretty good." Mark smiles.

"Really?" the young man replies surprised. "Really?" he asks again "I have just been reading your charts."

Mark grins back. "Well," he says, "if you ask how I am doing compared to before the crash, not very well. But if you ask how I am since…I am doing pretty good."

The surgeon enters the room and is noticeably amazed at how good the scars look. We feel some satisfaction that our diligent application of lotion and massage are paying off. The doctor is also pleased with the progress of Mark's flexibility, though it seems nearly nonexistent to us.

He sits on the desk opposite the examining table and smiles at Mark. "Impressive," he remarks.

We all smile at each other because he is grinning like a proud papa.

"I wish all my patients did as well as you. I just used your x-rays in a presentation I did in Canada. You are an interesting case."

He has the young resident get a camera. "In fact, Mark, I am going to take a few pictures for myself! You have a long way to go, but you have a lot in your favor," the surgeon smiles, "you are young, you were in good physical shape at the time of the crash, you are not overweight and you have a lot of support."

He smiles at the small group that has once again crowded itself into the room to be wherever Mark is.

The doctor tells Mark that his shoulder will continue to be the slowest to respond and that he needs to continue in therapy for quite some time. He asks if we have a therapist in the cities and we tell him we have made contact with someone who can use hydrotherapy.

He is pleased with that information and tells us to e-mail him with any needs.

We mention the hot tub, perhaps hoping he would prescribe that. He simply says, "Yes, everyone should have one of those…I should have one of those!"

The doctor writes new prescriptions including one that will explain that Mark has a lot of metal in his body if he has trouble getting through security at an airport. Then he gives us the name of an associate in the Minneapolis area in case we have a need. We set up an appointment to see him again in October and he sends us off with well wishes.

On our way to the restaurant Mark comments, "It is good to see him so happy with the work he did."

"Well," I reply, "remember how he said you were a challenge to him."

We meet Chris and Carole and are in the middle of a great lunch and a great mood when my cell phone rings.

"I just pulled into a rest area," Dave tells me, "I had to stop to clean my glasses."

I knew the three people at the table with me were listening so I was discreet. "Why?"

"Because I'm crying."

"I thought so. Dave, we just got out of the appointment a little while ago. It went well, but it lasted this long, and you would not have been able to drive in much daylight if you had waited."

"It is not that; I'm not sad about that. I'm just so glad I am finally going to be able to bring you home."

We are too close a group at this table. Everyone knows Dave is having a hard time. Carole reaches across the table for the phone.

"Someone wants to say 'Hi'," I say lightly though I could easily cry.

As she talks with him I whisper, "He is crying."

Mark looks down and Chris nods, "Ah, I thought so. This is hard for him."

Dave assures me he will be fine and I have no choice but to believe him as we say goodbye.

We thank Chris and Carole for being beside us once again and hurry home because, to top off our long day, we have a very special evening planned. We are dressing for our big evening out when Greg Long calls.

"He's doing great." I answer when Greg inquires about Mark. The last time Greg saw Mark, we were at the nursing facility and Mark was not upright yet.

"In fact, we're being very brave and going to TPAC to see "Mama Mia" tonight."

"You're kidding…are you kidding?" I hear him talk to his wife. "They're going to Mama Mia!"

I can hear her happy amazement in the background of our conversation. Greg laughs and tells me, "Janna says Mark is Superman."

It is absolute joy for me to share progress with those who have held Mark in their prayers and more so if they have seen Mark, as Greg did, in the horrific circumstances of ICU.

What I do not share with Greg, or even with Mark, is the apprehension I have of taking Mark to a crowded place. His balance is still not good and I know he will insist on using the cane rather than the walker. Since he graduated to the cane, the walker is something he avoids.

Ann-Marie arrives at the house dressed for a nice evening out and the three of us leave to have a great time at the theatre. I carry a pillow for Mark to sit on and hope no one in security will question it, and they do not. We use intermission time for Mark to stretch in an area near our seats. By using the valet parking and leaving before the rest of the audience is ready to leave, we manage quite well.

True, it is a different experience from our other trips to theatre productions, and we do not have the energy needed to go to eat before or after as is our custom, but it is wonderful to enjoy being in public again. We have had a very enjoyable evening and it is another victory to celebrate.

We rejoice much in our prayer and praise time before going to bed with a new measure of satisfaction and assurance that our prayers will be answered for Dave to arrive home safely.

Deuteronomy 33:12, "Let the beloved of the Lord rest secure in him, for he shields him all day long and the one the Lord loves rests between his shoulders."

Wednesday, March 20, 2002

I find little time to record this day, but I want to write so we remember how busy and stressful this recuperation time is. We are up early to arrive at Mark's dental appointment by 8:00 a.m. It is a long appointment; nearly four hours. We barely have time to get Mark a milkshake and then to therapy at 1:00 p.m. and at 1:45 p.m. We drive home for a light lunch and are back in the car for the drive to Chris and Carole's house for a vocal lesson at 5:00 p.m. I have supper ready by 7:00 p.m. We eat and then pack a few boxes and prepare for bed and prayer time by 9:30 p.m. Recovery is a full time job.

Joel 2:25 and 26, "I will repay you for the years the locusts have eaten-the great locust and the young locust, the other locusts and the locust swarm-my great army that I sent among you. You will have plenty to eat, until you are full, and you will praise the name of the Lord your God, who has worked wonders for you..."

Thursday, March 21, 2002

Today is Betty's birthday. I remember a year ago when we held a surprise party for her 75th birthday in our home. I had printed up little mystery gift cards from nieces and nephews families along with our more immediate family. As she opened them, each one disclosed a little more information until the last card instructed us to turn on the VCR. We played a video of Disney World where Dave and I planned to take her as a gift from the entire family. What a great evening that was and what a wonderful trip we had!

I had been so impressed of the Lord to organize that trip while Betty's health was good and she could enjoy it. Now I wonder if it had been for us also. A gift of time away in a place we love, before life would change so drastically. Certainly today is different from one year ago. I cannot seem to stop crying.

I am moving Mark from one home to another and there are decisions to be made. If I am truthful, I fear going home. It is almost as though the very thing that has been my dream for months is now something to be feared. I wonder if I have the mental strength for it. It will be a new set of dynamics after I have struggled so long to adjust to the ones I am in. I am so very different, have I lost the person that I was or will I feel like myself some magic day?

Will everyone realize that Mark is not completely healed even though we are making this physical move? Will Mark and I find time to study The Word and pray together, or will it be ushered out of our lives by the routine of a busy lifestyle?

Can anyone possibly know how tired I am? I passed exhaustion months ago. I am fragile, vulnerable and feeling inadequate for change. While stress is and has been prevalent for months now, a new kind of stress could be insurmountable. I fear crumbling. I fear having to get in touch with the raw emotions that I have kept at bay because of the intensity of each day. I fear coming face to face with the realization of exactly how physically depleted my body and mind have become.

Will friends expect me to pick up relationships where we left off? All the wonderful social aspects of friendship seem difficult to me right now. How will it be for Dave and me? We have been apart for months. I have become, through a baptism of desperation, incredibly independent. I sleep alone now. I make decisions without consulting anyone.

Mark will still need me to cook, to be the "gopher." He will need to get to therapy and he will need to have his scars massaged and all the things that we do now. And that takes all of my day, but now I will add caring for others and errands and a job and a social life and a house to tend, and the dynamics of blending with others into the equation. Perhaps in weeks or months to come I will look at this journal entry and think how silly I was. How could anyone be so concerned about the normal things that comprise life as we know it? But somehow, I think I will remember the feeling of depletion and the fear that I have no more to give no matter how much I want to, or how much will be expected of me. The fear is that I am a rubber band stretched to its maximum stress point, frayed and ready to break.

I find myself preoccupied with our financial situation. Dave has been shouldering it. I took care of the bills before this happened and I do not know the situation now. Will we owe tax dollars in April? How bad have things gotten without my income, with the additional expenses and with Mark out of work for an undetermined amount of time?

And the most poignant thought: how will Mark adapt to being home when his situation is so different from when he was there before?

Lord, please take these questions that churl and swirl through my mind until I feel dizzy from the spin. Take the feeling in my stomach that I am inadequate and remind me that your grace is sufficient for me. You have so evidently been by our side. Please allow me the strength it takes to exercise my faith to believe you will continue to hold us up. You will provide, you will sustain. You are God Almighty! Thank you, Lord. Thank you so much for loving us so well. Amen.

Psalm 121:8, "The Lord will watch over your coming and going both now and forevermore."

Saturday, March 23, 2002

Yesterday the McGregor family came to Nashville. Roger had a doctor's appointment and they called ahead to see if we could meet for lunch. Mark and I managed to squeeze in an income tax appointment before we met them at The Grille to enjoy a wonderful lunch. Roger and Brenda's son, Zachary, was with them and it was good to meet him. Ann-Marie joined us and she drove Mark home because I had an appointment to get my hair cut.

We all expressed our pride in Roger because he was able to drive to Nashville yesterday. We may not see them again for a very long time, but we are certain they will always be in our lives.

Today we look forward to a wonderful opportunity. We will go to the Passion Play at Brian and April's church. We have chosen the afternoon performance to avoid driving at night, but when we pull into the large but overflowing parking lot we find that all the handicap spaces are occupied. Mark is not dismayed that he has to walk a little further on this beautiful day. He smiles at me and says, "You know us handicapped folks, we like to come out in the daytime."

The play is beautiful and wonderfully presented.

We have been blessed to share Eucharist with Chris and Carole on Wednesdays and that along with this wonderful play have worked to prepare our hearts for Easter, but somehow it still does not seem like that holy day is one week away.

> Psalm 62:1, "My soul finds rest in God alone; my salvation comes from him. He alone is my rock and my salvation; he is my fortress, I will never be shaken."

Sunday, March 24, 2002

Sharing the Palm Sunday Service with Chris and Carole today is poignant. It will be a long time before we sit together in church again.

The day holds a promise of excitement though, because the Academy Awards are on TV tonight and I am more than happy to see Mark swing into action because this is, traditionally, a big night for us. Over the years it has evolved into quite a production with friends gathering at Mark's house to enjoy a party. There is plenty of food and conversation. But Mark takes all of that a step further. Each person is given their own "voting sheet." This has usually been put together on the computer and lists each category with nominees. We are instructed to vote before the televised program begins.

A most interesting and fun part of this celebration is the large poster that he places somewhere near the television set. For this poster he uses photos from entertainment type magazines. He places the "head shot" of each star in a major category on the poster. As the results of the evening are revealed, he moves each "head" into its winners circle. Mark is quite competitive and that is contagious. We all try our best to choose winners and there actually is a small trophy placed on top of the television set and given to the winner. The trophy tends to stay in Mark's possession.

A fun part that I have always enjoyed is the national aspect. Mark receives calls from around the country from friends who have spent an "Oscar Evening" with Mark in the past. The calls are spurred on by events in the program or during the red carpet segment. At a time in the program when someone walks out in weird attire or if there is an upset in the voting, we may hear the phone ring and see via caller ID it is from another state.

"What was that?" may well be the extent of the conversation, but it brings laughter and camaraderie.

Tonight Mark, Ann-Marie and I comprise the party and I know we will have fun. I am making a supper that I feel certain they will enjoy and the two of them are in the living room putting together the poster and readying the voting sheets. Mark has a way of making ordinary things fun and I am more than blessed that he is not passing up this chance to do that just because he is not feeling 100%.

When I walk into the living room, I am handed my voting sheet. I quickly realize that I do not know many people on it. We have definitely missed out on key movies this year; however, I know it will do no good to make excuses. I need to cast my votes and see how well I do. The pressure is on and I am very happy.

As we prepare for bed after an evening in front of the television, I pull our devotional book off the shelf in Mark's room. It is sitting next to the mini Oscar-trophy that has, once again, been awarded to the winner.

> John 12:13, "Hosanna! Blessed is he who comes in the name of the Lord! Blessed is the King of Israel!"

Monday, March 25, 2002

We are on a countdown to moving day. The first order of the day is to drive Mark to Vanderbilt to see an ear, nose and throat doctor. He has some trouble hearing out of his left ear. He has been told there were fractures under his ear that could affect his hearing and that is an added concern because that will, obviously, affect the way he hears music when performing.

I have been in the examination room with Mark for most of his appointments, so today I need to remind myself that I do not have to go in the room with him. When his name is called, he stands, leaning heavily on his cane. He walks slowly across the waiting room and follows the nurse. Letting go; it seems I have been here before in a different way. Letting go is a process; at least I know that this time out. I will work at it. I will swallow hard, bite my tongue and say my prayers and I will rejoice in each step my son takes toward the independence we both desire for him.

I spend my waiting time observing as I always do. Today it is a painful observation. I see a world of imperfect bodies here. Standing very near is a child with headphones on. He moves as any child would and he is communicating with the person I imagine is his mother. But there is something quite obviously different. His face is misshapen. It reminds me of a movie I did not see except for the promotional trailers. I believe Cher was the star and it was titled *Mask*. This child breaks my heart. What is he here for? Can he be helped?

A young, lovely woman in blue jeans stands from her seat and reveals, by her walk across the room, that she has a prosthetic leg.

I hear a man across the room speak with a voice that has been cut away and I see a woman with gauze dressing over one half of her face. I am surrounded by people moving with walkers, wheelchairs and canes.

I cannot help but think of last night as we watched the Academy Awards. People wore expensive clothes that revealed bodies that had been highly invested in. What kind of world do they live in? I am led to think it is as fabricated as the movies they make. Surely they do not know about this place. I close my eyes and sigh. I cannot judge. I did not know about this place either, until we were forced to be here.

With my eyes still closed I hear the little boy with the large face say, "I wish I could play baseball. The doctor says I can't."

Sometimes people are trapped in their bodies. I do not mean that as a stupid remark because it is obvious. I guess what has been such a new revelation for me is how *many* people suffer that way. We have a church friend who has cerebral palsy and cannot communicate except by writing in a painstaking method. She has always amazed me and I have been aware that she would love to physically soar. In this environment I am aware of the many forms of prison the body can become.

For most people, life is far short of perfection. I become introspective as I ask myself what idolism has set the standards for my life? Why have I not been more aware that I live in a world of intense suffering? Do I blame it on ignorance, denial or apathy?

My life takes place in a wonderful world where each spring I wonder if my legs will look okay in a swimsuit; in this world people move without legs. I fret that I am too thin, or too fat, when I have seen people being weighed by having their body lifted in a hammock-like apparatus, or wheeled onto a platform in a chair because they cannot use any limbs. I want to go to work or to a social event with my makeup on, but there are people in this world who have gauze dressings on their faces, deformity, or scars that may never heal.

Help me, Father! Deliver me from the superficial prison of my vanity and ego! Replace my ignorance with wisdom and my apathy with compassion! Bring to my remembrance each day the joy of counting my blessings!

I open my eyes to see Mark approaching. He knows more about this world than I ever want to know. He looks so very tired but he smiles at me and I know the news he received today has not been bad. The appointment has been timely in comparison to most and the news is indeed as good as we could expect. The doctor told Mark there is a very slight hearing loss and he may even regain it. It is another aspect of healing to entrust to the Ultimate Healer. We praise God for good news!

In the car our thoughts turn immediately to the therapy sessions this afternoon. Mark will go to both physical and occupational therapy here in

Nashville two more days after today, but the last day will be centered on evaluation.

At the afternoon session, the physical therapist assures us they will write detailed instructions on how to continue therapy in Minnesota. They are very excited for Mark that he is able to go home. They are aware of the long road he has traveled. While none of us pretend this is the end of his healing and hard work, we know it is a positive step.

Proverbs 9:10, "The fear of the Lord is the beginning of wisdom, the knowledge of the Holy One is understanding."

Wednesday, March 27, 2002

What a day! Early in the morning we drive out to Chris and Carole's house to have a vocal lesson. This is as close to saying goodbye to them as we will come. Not one of us can say the words and not one of us can express the emotion. For Mark and for me, there is a slight frustration that we will never be able to tell these precious people how much their gifts of time, love and encouragement have meant to us. They have been the Angels By Our Side.

The four of us exchange hugs and say, "See you soon," though we know the next time we are together it will be for the purpose of saying goodbye for quite a while. Emotions are deep but this friendship is deeper and we know we will work at keeping it strong.

When we get home I make a quick lunch because we are expecting guests at 1:00 p.m. An Assistant District Attorney is coming over along with the woman we have been talking to, the Victim Witness Advocate. We already like her immensely but wonder what it will be like to meet a District Attorney!

We need not have fretted. Both of the people who come to our home are kind and considerate and we feel blessed they would take the time to meet us before we leave for Minneapolis. It is good they can see how Mark is struggling. He has made wonderful progress but it is quite evident his life has been devastated. They seem genuinely concerned and want to do whatever is just in this case. We are told to direct any questions to the Victim Witness Advocate. We give each of them a CD so they will know Mark better and thank them for their time. The drunk driver who took so much from Mark is in their hands. We have little to say about her future.

They have barely pulled out of the driveway when we leave ourselves. We are off to Brentwood for another dental appointment. These appointments are very hard on Mark, as he sits for long hours with his mouth open.

The jaw is mostly healed but the fractured area is sensitive and his hip and pelvis ache when he sits too long. Thank the Lord we have a Christian dentist, a man of compassion with passion for his work. How often I marvel at God's mercy to us!

We arrive home tired and Mark lies down to nap. I try to lie down for a few minutes but I am getting excited and developing nervous energy. Dave and our friend, Bill, will be arriving sometime tonight. The minute they walk in the door I will believe we are going home at last!

Bill's generosity in coming with Dave is not lost on us. He has been in Israel with his wife for several months and he is just settling into a new job in Minnesota, and yet he is taking three days from work to help get us home. He is a strong, capable and kind man and we will feel very comfortable having him drive Mark home in a van while Dave and I drive back the Nissan.

Friends from church have loaned us their new van for the trip. I hear they have included walkie-talkies so we can communicate car-to-van. They will use our car in place of their van and we will trade back in church on Sunday. We should have room in the van for all of Mark's belongings that we plan to take to Minnesota. Mark has a storage unit reserved and Dave and Bill will move Mark's furniture and larger items into that unit. We will make a trip to Nashville in the future to empty the unit, or Mark will return to live here. So much is unknown.

I am so excited for Dave and Bill to arrive that I decide to call Dave on his cell phone to see how far away they are.

"Not far," Bill says in his cheery voice.

"Are you hungry? I am thinking of ordering pizza."

"Good!"

"What time will you be here?"

I hear the men discussing an arrival time.

"5:57 p.m." Bill tells me, "We will be pulling into the driveway at 5:57 p.m."

This is typical of my husband so I go with it. "Okay, I will see you at exactly 5:57 p.m."

It is nearly 5:00 p.m. now, so I wait a few minutes and then order a variety of pizzas. I decide I have time to make Dave his favorite banana cream pie if I use a prepared crust so I set about doing that to keep busy as I wait for them.

I am just pouring the filling into the crust when I hear a car door. It is a juggling act for me to hold the large pot over the crust and spoon out the filling and still walk the few feet to the door, so I decide to take the extra few seconds to finish what I am doing rather than run to the door.

When I hear the footsteps on the stairs, I call over my shoulder in an exaggerated, friendly, sing-song voice, "Who is it? Who is there? Hello! I'm glad you are here! Welcome! I'll be right there!"

I know they can hear me and are probably grinning at my silliness as they climb the stairs. I put the pot down just as I hear their knock on the door. I grab a kitchen towel to wipe my hands and reach for the door handle. I throw it open with a big welcoming grin on my face that says I have been waiting for this moment!

"I am so glad you're......here."

The last word falls flat as I look at the horrified face of the pizza deliveryman.

The guys have a good laugh about it when they arrive five minutes later. "Well, the pizza did arrive exactly at 5:57 p.m." I tell them.

Romans 8:28, "And we know that in all things God works for the good of those who love him, who have been called according to his purpose."

Thursday, March 28, 2002

I am sure Bill was not entirely comfortable on the twin bed but at least we had a private bedroom to offer him. The beds will be moved out on Friday morning right before we leave. Mark says he slept fairly well on the other half of the twin bed in "my" bedroom and Dave and I shared Mark's queen size bed. Soon we will all be in our own beds!

Bill rides along with us to the rehabilitation hospital for Mark's therapy session and after that we take him to Pancake Pantry for lunch. We are glad the schedule allows him to visit one of our favorite places. Tonight we will all dine at The Grille.

Dave and Bill begin to work as soon as we arrive back home. The van is nearly packed to the hilt! With a good deal of strategy, they manage to get Becki's old scooter in there so she will have one to use when she gets back to Minneapolis to visit her parents.

Chris and Carole stop by for one more visit before our trip home and it is fun for Bill to meet them because the man he worked for in Jerusalem is a friend of Chris and Carole's. The world becomes small when we have Jesus in our lives.

We don't say goodbye to Chris and Carole because it is not possible. We cannot and they cannot. For many years now Chris has admonished Mark each time they see each other to walk upright. That is in stature, which is important for his vocal abilities, and in the Lord. Chris has been a beloved mentor for years but now this precious couple means more to us than we can express.

Mark assures Chris he will stand tall and Chris tells Mark, "I've already told myself I'll cry when you are gone."

It is almost unfair to them. They have given so much to bless us so wonderfully and now we are walking away. When Chris tells me they love Mark like a son I know it is true. We are taking their son quite a distance away. For me, it is another bittersweet moment. I love them deeply. They have been a tangible piece of heaven. Carole and I are bonafide girl friends. I have confided easily to her and her to me. Chris has shared moments with Mark that only someone who holds the deepest place of respect in a heart can share. If any two people on this earth know the pain we have been through as a family, it is Chris and Carole because they walked through it with us. We say goodbye as though we will see them next week. It is the only way.

Brian and April come by to visit and to help load things in the van and Courtney runs, full-speed, up the sidewalk and into my arms before they leave. I hug her tight knowing I will miss her. Over the years I have often thought that April is like a daughter to me and I love the friendship she and Brian have with Mark. It is a proven and tight bond that I cherish greatly. They have given of their time and love with abandonment. April has blessed me in sweet ways, seeing my needs, not only as a mom in tragedy, but as a woman in pain. She has shown me such tender care and concern. Mark is their beloved friend but I have reaped the benefits of that friendship. I know that when Mark is in Minnesota and says he misses Nashville it is often Brian and April that he thinks of.

Ann-Marie will meet us at The Grille for supper and will be over in the morning for the last minute moving and cleaning. I am aware that we will want an early start and will not leave the house as perfect as if we had a full day to clean, but I am determined to leave it in good order after experiencing the frustration we went through when Mark's second roommate left us with such a mess.

Jason will come over when he gets back in town to move a few things left behind that belong to him and he will close out the house. We want it as easy as possible for him. He has been a good friend for many years.

Brenda called to wish us well and remind us that as soon as he is able, Mark should visit them in Kentucky to do a concert at their church. God ordained our meeting and we have walked together in deep sorrow that has formed a tight knot of friendship.

Our dinner at The Grille is twofold in purpose. Mark is able to say goodbye to friends at The Grille and Bill can taste their food, which he finds impressive. We have a wonderful time eating and visiting.

We are not home a long time before we turn out the lights; everyone is ready for sleep.

1 John 4:11-12, "Dear friends, since God so loved us, we also ought to love one another. No one has ever seen God; but if we love one another, God lives in us and his love is made complete in us."

PART VII ✦ GOING HOME
March 29, 2002 – March 31, 2002

Lana:

Moving day.

We are up early and content to have a breakfast of Krispy Kremes that Dave and Bill bring back from their trip to the storage unit. I have several bags of food and staples that I offer to Ann-Marie. The things she will not be able to use are hauled to the curb. Any frozen items that are fresh I leave in the freezer for Jason.

Ann-Marie scrubs both bathrooms as I finish in the kitchen and we wipe up the hardwood floors as they become clear of boxes. It is nearly departure time.

When the house looks sufficiently empty, I hug Ann-Marie and thank her. It is, once again, a hard thing to do. She is the one who called us to say Mark had been in a car crash. She has been there for us, as has her mother, Pat. Scenarios float through my mind. I am thankful for all the food she brought us in the hospital when we would have gone to bed hungry. I am thankful for her moral support and for the physical support as she helped me to lift and move Mark so many times. She never ran away from the reality of the situation, she never turned her back on difficult tasks and I so appreciate her.

This goodbye between Ann-Marie and Mark deserves the privacy they have not had for so long. They had only been dating a couple of months before the crash jolted their lives. They were only beginning to explore a new aspect of their friendship. I am reminded once again, that drunk drivers not only devastate the lives of their victims but the repercussion is endless. For now, they must say goodbye to each other and to their questions about a future together. They are all too aware that Mark's world has been turned upside down and absolutely everything in his life is on hold.

I walk into the house as Ann-Marie and Mark walk out. The front lawn will have to be their place to say goodbye.

I shake my head and blink away the tears; desperately wishing for a moment of relief in the painful theme of this new and unexpectedly altered life and then I take the last load of my lightweight cargo to the car and watch Ann-Marie drive away.

I have two bags in my hand containing snacks and pop cans for the trip. I can barely fit a bag between the seats that Mark and Bill will sit on. The same is true when I open the door of the Nissan.

As I walk back to the house I see two women on a leisurely walk. They are pushing baby strollers and are dressed in shorts. I grab the camera and snap a shot of them. When Mark looks at me as if to question why I would take a picture of two strangers on a walk, I explain, "It's not going to be this warm at home."

Finally we pull out of the driveway and turn toward Minneapolis. It has been nearly four months since I have been home but my thoughts are with Mark. What emotion is he feeling as he pulls out of this driveway and this city? We are praying for him.

We all share concern that the ride will be too stressful physically for Mark. He is sitting on the special pillow I purchased from a medical supply house and we are prepared to stop as often as he finds necessary to stretch his legs or hip. I am confident he will be honest with Bill who is patient and understanding.

We are only two hours away when Mark uses the walkie-talkie to say he needs to stop. My heart flipflops. We have fifteen hours of driving time ahead of us and we really want to be home tomorrow night so we can be in church for Easter Sunday. Dave and I discuss it and decide if it takes us three days, then that is what it takes.

Mark stretches and we all fill up on McDonald's food. He states that he is positively good to go and we get back into our vehicles. One more hour into the trip my cell phone rings.

"This is Mark's other parents calling," the familiar voice says, "How is it going?"

I fill Chris in, telling him we have stopped once already and, knowing he loves any type of toy, I tell him about the walkie-talkies and let him know Mark is doing fine.

"We had such fun today when the doorbell rang. Thanks for the basket."

Mark and I had called to order a basket sent to them. We called the same place that had sent a basket to Mark around Valentines Day. We were so delighted with it that it seemed the best choice to send to Chris and Carole. I spent time on the phone with the salesperson, requesting a special dog for the top of the basket.

"It has to be soft and floppy with a cute face," I told her, not caring if she thought me a bit odd.

She put me on hold for awhile and came back sounding quite happy. "I have one that looks like that!"

Now Chris says to me, "we especially like the dog. He fits right in with the gang." He is referring to their collection of floppy dogs, "we'll call you when we name him"

Later in the day I smile when the phone rings and Chris announces, "Tell Mark we have named him 'Williams'."

We stop fairly early to have supper and check into a hotel. We are tired even though we have stopped often. Our accommodations are excellent and Bill is right down the hall. We plan to meet for continental breakfast in the lobby at 7:00 a.m. We have managed to cover quite a few miles and feel confident that we will be home about this time tomorrow night.

Ecclesiates 3:1, "There is a time for everything, and a season for every activity under heaven."

Saturday, March 30, 2002

We enjoy a continental breakfast at the hotel and climb into our vehicles for the second and last leg of our journey home. Our stops become less frequent as the trip progresses. Everyone wants to get home as soon as possible.

I have wondered how it will feel to be home but we are too relieved and tired to touch most of our emotions when we walk in the door.

I hug Mike tightly and express my gratitude for how nice the house looks. I quickly inspect, with delight, my kitchen that was remodeled four months ago. It is new to me.

Mark cannot go down the stairs so the daybed in my office will be his bed. I am blessed that Dave, or Mike, has placed fresh linens on the beds. I prop pillows around Mark and touch his forehead as I whisper the words, "Welcome home, Son."

I pull our devotional from the overnight bag and sit on the chair beside his bed to read. He is asleep before I finish.

Psalm 101:1 and 2, "I will sing of your love and justice; to you O Lord, I will sing praise. I will be careful to lead a blameless life-when will you come to me? I will walk in my house with a blame-less heart."

Sunday, March 31, 2002 Easter Morning

I open my eyes without a thought in my head. I am not surprised to see the beautiful pine dresser topped by a sculpted metal mirror. I know that if I turn my head I will see the window that looks out on the river and the island beyond. After nearly four months, I am in my own bed.

Sunlight threads its way between the slats on the blinds to form a cross on the ceiling. I had forgotten how I love to watch that cross appear in the early morning.

I thank Jesus for his resurrection. and The Father for giving His son for it is by His wounds we are healed. I move my arm to place it across Dave's chest and he turns to me and smiles.

"Finally," he whispers.

In his soft blue eyes I can see how hard it has been for him to wake each day alone and lonely. I can sense the strength it took to get out of bed, go to work and to drive home each day knowing I was not going to be there to spend time with him. His heart has been separated from his body for too long a time.

My eyes rest on the book on my bedside table; the marker left where it had been placed months ago. I smile at the book's title, which refers to "Finding Time in Your Life."

I hear geese honk on the island and though I do not want to see it, Dave tells me that snow is falling. I was content to miss winter, and do not want to see snow, but I know Mark will be quite happy to see snowflakes.

I pull myself out of bed to get ready for church early so I can help Mark on his first day back. When I get out of the shower I lift the portable shower seat into the tub and place towels on it for padding. New surroundings, same routine.

I dry my hair and put on my makeup and then place the portable commode over the toilet seat and go to wake my son. My knock is light on the door, which opens to Mark's temporary bedroom. I know that he would prefer to be in the bedroom downstairs. He desires the privacy and independence that will be his when he can go down stairs to an area with his own bedroom, bathroom and living area. For now he must be content on this narrow bed in my office.

"Good morning, Son, happy Easter."

He moans and I smile to see he slept with the eye mask he became accustomed to in the hospital.

Unspoken between us are the words, "what is next?" We have already expressed to each other our concern that no one can possibly understand where we have been and where, or even who, we are now.

He puts on his slippers, takes his cane and walks to the bathroom down the familiar hallway. Everything looks the same; everything is different.

Grandma Betty rings the doorbell and enters armed with the two baskets of goodies I have asked her to purchase. Mike and Mark will not "hunt" for them this year, but they will not be without chocolate bunnies.

My two handsome sons stand beside Dave and me in front of the fireplace in our hearth room and Betty takes our picture. Four smiling faces are testimony to the miracle working power of our timeless God.

We gather in the foyer, putting on our coats. Mark will not be able to get to the car through the garage because of the steps and I know the sidewalk could be slippery. I want to say "Watch Mark on the sidewalk!", but it is not necessary. Dave and Mike walk, one on each side of Mark, who firmly plants his cane with each step. No one in this family is going to make light of this journey and there is no room for pride in Mark; he has worked too hard and become too wise.

I close the door behind me to join them. My heart is full of gratitude and I am fighting tears. I am no stranger to reality; this is not a happy ending; it is challenging beginning, but there is no need to fear because I am also well acquainted with my faithful Savior and I can almost feel his hand in mine.

Too many traditions have been interrupted and I long to grasp hold of the ones that remain, so as we walk to the car in a winter wonderland of fluffy snowflakes, I proclaim rather loudly, "He is risen!"

Mark stops to look over his shoulder and send a smile to his mom as he replies, "He is risen indeed!"

Ephesians 3:20 and 21, "Now to him who is able to do more than all we ask or imagine, according to his power that is at work within us, to him be glory in the church and in Jesus Christ throughout all generations, for ever and ever! Amen."

Amen.

Decisions

Dear Reader,

Life is full of decisions. One rainy night in December of 2001 a young woman, not legally old enough to drink alcoholic beverages, decided to consume alcohol until her blood level reached nearly three times the legal limit. She then made the decision, and was allowed, to get behind the driver's seat of a vehicle and alter a young and healthy life forever, devastating a family.

The victim in such a situation has no decision to make. In the case of Mark's crash, by the time he saw the headlights come over the rise in the road there was no opportunity for a decision.

We have been told that each year the number of lives devastated by drunk drivers equals the number of people in two jet liners crashing every single week without interruption!

Will you please read the last paragraph again?

While these incidents are often referred to as "accidents" there is certainly nothing accidental about them. They are the result of a conscious and very selfish decision. These life-altering, devastating crashes are 100% preventable.

We have been asked many times, "Do you wonder, why? Why Mark?" It is natural for people to expect that we have asked "Why, God?" While we have not been without our questions, frustrations and tears, we have not asked, "Why, God?"

God will provide our comfort and He will work to bring good out of this situation. If we allow Him to, He will even bring blessings that will glorify His Name. But God did not cause this to happen and God is not to be asked the question, "Why?" One person has the answer to that question and that is the woman who decided she could drive a two-ton vehicle into an unsuspecting approaching car. Others who may have answers would be those who provided and served the alcohol and those who allowed her to drive when she was so desperately drunk. As is so often the case, drunk driving can be a joint effort.

In our case, we will be allowed to continue on, never as it was before, but at least we can move toward the future. Many victims of drunk driving are not given that chance. Too many families will never hold their loved one again.

Mark will live with the results of the decision made by another person for his entire life. His family has experienced emotional upheaval, financial stress, physical depletion and many other devastating results of the drunk driver's decision. One thing saved us from falling into a pit of depression and hopelessness; the presence of the risen savior, Jesus Christ, in our lives. We serve a God of hope and we found strength in the faith that we had nurtured and invested in.

As Dave and I drove to the hospital that fateful night, I said to him, "This is what it is all about. Either we have the strength, by the power of God to do this, or we have been living a lie."

God proved His promises are true and that He is sufficient. If you have read this story you know we did not breeze through it. We suffered and as I write, we still face challenges. Life has changed in a way we would have never wished it to, but life will always change. There is only one unchanging facet of life; our God who changes not. His mercies are new every morning. His grace is sufficient, for His strength is made perfect in our weakness. 2 Corinthians 12:9. These words are not simply quotes or clichés, they were our daily bread in the midst of circumstances too harsh to confront on our own.

Jesus does not tell us that we will not have trials in this life. We were serving Him quite actively when the crash happened. He does promise He will never leave or forsake us. As He has been beside us, He longs to be beside you. In every trial of life He will hold you up; in every victory, He will rejoice beside you. All you have to do is ask.

Do you know Him? Have you met the Savior of your soul? The one who gave His life for you that you might have life abundant and eternal? He is so wonderful! He is the friend you dream of, the lover you long for. He is Jesus.

In this letter I have talked about a wrong decision, and now I want to talk about the right decision. It will be the best you ever make. No regrets with this one. If you have not already, will you meet Him today? Would you accept into your life the One and Only God? You will be met by peace and assurance that you will never walk alone.

Mark and I have already prayed over the decision you are making, and agree with you in spirit as you pray this prayer:

Dear Heavenly Father,

I want to have the reality of Jesus in my life. I understand that you sent your only son to die that my sins may be forgiven. He was resurrected and sits beside you in Heaven and that victory assures me of eternal life with you.

I want to know you. I want to serve you and I want to walk with you beside me in all that happens in my life.

Today I accept you, Jesus, into my life as my Lord and personal savior. I thank you for forgiving me of my sins. I will not look back. I will walk away from that which has been wrong in my life. I will make good decisions based on prayer.

Thank you, precious Father, for the gift in my life of Jesus Christ. Come Holy Spirit and fill me until there is nothing left of the old me. Make me new, cleanse me and heal me of hurt that would slow me down in my walk with you. I want to make a difference in this world. I want to live for you.

Welcome to the family of Christ! Do you know that the Bible says in heaven angels are rejoicing because of the decision you just made? It is true!

It is important to tell someone of your decision. You must share the joy. If you do not have a friend or loved one you can talk to, please write us a note and send it to our P.O. Box, or send us a note through our website. We will rejoice with you. And please, find a good church that teaches the word of God and become an active member.

Finally, if you or someone you know has been impacted by the decision of a drunk driver and you need help dealing with the nightmare of that choice, please contact your nearest chapter of MADD. They will be of immense help to you.

If you have been a drunk driver and someone has suffered because of your decision, know that there is forgiveness in Christ Jesus. He loves you beyond your mistakes. It is only important that your heart is right and you desire to walk away from that lifestyle. May I suggest to you that you also contact your local chapter of MADD. You can show your repentance by speaking with a victim impact panel. Your testimony to others who have been convicted of drinking and driving could dramatically change lives.

Wherever you are in your walk with Him, we pray that God will bless you in this unpredictable, ever changing journey of life.

Lana Williams

We took dozens of photos...
it was hard to choose only a few to share.

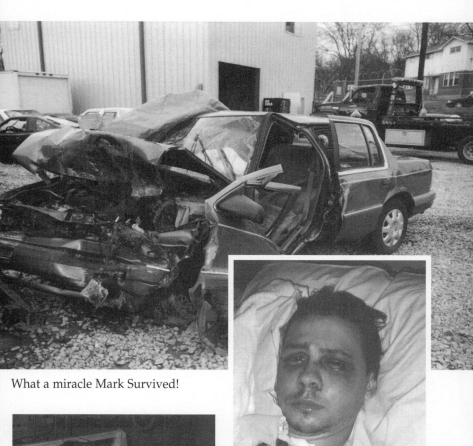

What a miracle Mark Survived!

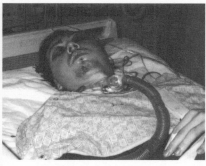

We did not recognize our son.

We honestly told Mark, 'You look good', by the time this picture was taken.

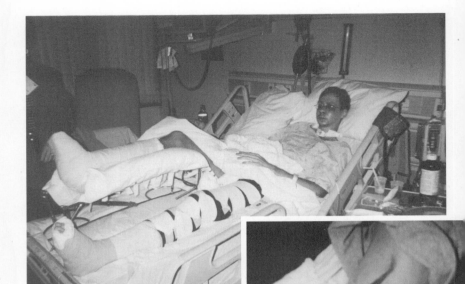

With five trips to the O.R. behind him, Mark's only usable limb was his left arm.

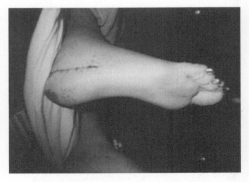

These pins went into Mark's shoulder and were pulled out without benefit of anesthetic.

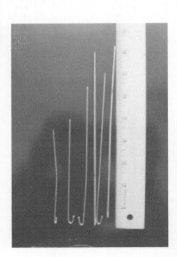

The day they removed the pins we placed them beside a ruler.

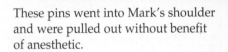

The toe pins were gut-wrenching.

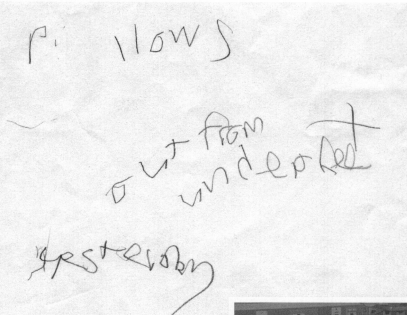

The first words Mark wrote were, 'Give me hope!' We saved later communication. Here he requests we move pillows from under his feet.

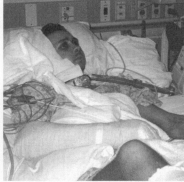

Mark was hooked up to an assortment of machines.

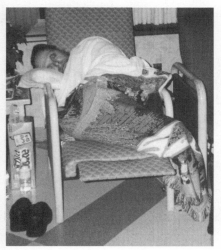

Dave asleep in his torchercliner.

Sitting for just a few minutes at a time was the start of therapy.

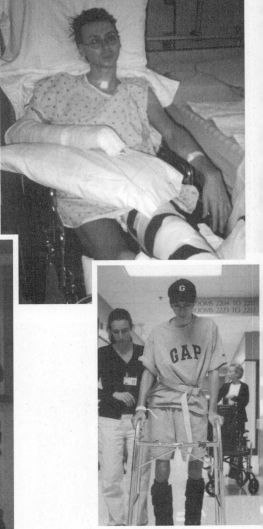

It was a long road to arrive at this day! Chris & Carole Beatty, our 'Angels By Our Side' were with us the day Mark took his first steps.

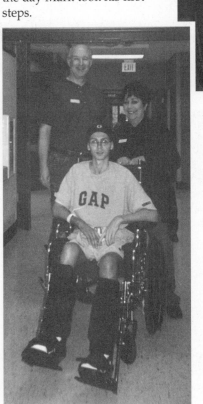

Mark's first steps were an emotional time for everyone.

There was a rule, two visitors at a time. We stretched that as Mark improved.
Clockwise from bottom left: Jonathan, Suzy, Lana, Stephanie, April, Charles,
Tosha, Ann-Marie, Brian, Andrea, Barbara, Mark and Mickey.

Easter Sunday, 2002. Together again and home at last. A very
blessed family: Mike, Lana, Dave & Mark.

Bless the Day

MARK DAVID WILLIAMS

Mark's CD, *Bless The Day*, was released in September of 2003. It is comprised of songs born of suffering that offer hope.

Since the last journal entry
of this book:

- The "REALITY" CDs that were in the backseat of Mark's car at the time of the crash, and hit him in the back of the head, were saved. At his "Victory" concert, Mark presented the CDs to representatives from churches that had supported him before the crash and that had stayed by his side during the time written about in the book. Mark taped the CD cases together and told the people he gave them to, "The cases are broken and put back together, but the music still plays."

- The CD, *Bless the Day*, Mark's testimony in song, was released in September of 2003. It is a CD that brings much healing as people listen to Mark's witness of God's faithfulness. Mark's friend, Matt Garinger, wrote or co-wrote several songs on the CD.

- Gabriel Quentin Williams, a precious Sable Dachshund, became part of our family on December 23, 2002. He is an absolute joy in our lives.

- We did get to the golf resort for Mark's birthday the summer after the crash. Mark used a golf cart, as he probably always will from now on, but he golfed! And he golfed well!

- Each Christmas Eve Dave and Lana prepare twelve gift bags containing things they appreciated having in the Quiet Room. They deliver them to a local trauma center waiting room with a note enclosed to assure recipients that they are being prayed for.

- We still keep in touch with the Watts family, Jim and Cynthia Hagewood, Mr. and Mrs. Lyle, and the McGregor family.

- Mark, Dave and Lana visited the McGregor family in Kentucky and Mark sang at their church, just as Brenda requested in the hospital.

- Remember the three friends who visited from Minnesota on the day Mark took his first steps in the Rehabilitation Hospital? One of them was Leah Pagel. Mark changed her name to Leah Williams when they married on November 28, 2003.

- In February 2004, Mark was named "Minnesota Idol" in a statewide contest sponsored by a record company and a popular local news station.

- Mark continues to perform concerts and is a popular speaker/singer at churches and other venues in Minnesota; he also works as a Vocal Coach.

- Lana stays busy working as Mark's manager and agent, working part-time, writing, sharing her story at speaking engagements and enjoying the blessing of her family.